The Life of the Right Honourable Horatio Lord Viscount Nelson, Vol. II (of 2)

James Harrison

Contents

THE LIFE OF
LORD NELSON, DUKE OF BRONTE, &c. 7

THE LIFE OF THE RIGHT HONOURABLE HORATIO LORD VISCOUNT NELSON, VOL. II (OF 2)

by

James Harrison

THE LIFE OF
THE RIGHT HONOURABLE
HORATIO LORD VISCOUNT NELSON:

Baron Nelson of the Nile,
and of Burnham-Thorpe and Hilborough in the County of
Norfolk; Knight of the Most Honourable Military Order
 of the Bath Doctor of Laws in the University of Oxford;
Vice-Admiral of the White Squadron of His Majesty's Fleet;
Duke of Bronte, in Farther Sicily;
Grand Cross of the Order of St. Ferdinand and of Merit;
Knight of the Imperial Order of the Ottoman Crescent;
Knight Grand Commander of the Equestrian, Secular,
 and Capitular,
Order of St. Joachim of Westerburg;
 and Honorary Grandee of Spain

Lord Viscount Nelson's transcendent and heroic services will, I am persuaded, exist for ever in the recollection of my people; and, while they tend to stimulate those who come after him, they will prove a lasting source of strength, security, and glory, to my dominions.

The King's Answer to the City of London's Address
on the Battle of Trafalgar.

THE LIFE OF
LORD NELSON, DUKE OF BRONTE, &c.

IN tracing the history of a hero so active as Lord Nelson, the mind can scarcely be allowed a moment's pause. His multifarious transactions, indeed, frequently arise in such rapid successions, that they become far too much involved with each other to admit of any precise chronological arrangement. Operations are commenced, which cannot always be soon brought to a conclusion: and, while these are transacting, an attention to other occurrences, of more or less magnitude, becomes perpetually requisite; which are, in their turn, subjected to similar procrastinating delays and necessarily diverted attentions.

The cares of Lord Nelson can hardly be said to have one minute ceased, even when he landed, in safety, at Palermo, the royal and illustrious characters, and their immense treasure, which he had successfully conveyed thither, amidst such alarming difficulties and dangers. His anxious bosom, it is true, was now relieved from the apprehensions which it had suffered during the storm; and felt, no doubt, as it ought, a sympathetic sense of the grateful felicitations of beloved friends, on the event of their happy arrival at a place of secure refuge. He could not, indeed, fail to rejoice in their joy: but it was, with all of them, a joy mingled with melancholy; and, with him, it was particularly so.

An intellectual tempest, at this apparently enviable period of our hero's glory, was violently agitating the secret recesses of his too susceptible heart. Justly jealous of honour, his soul ever kindled with alarm at the most remote idea of aught that could, by any possibility of implication, be considered as having the smallest tendency to sully or impair a single particle of that celestial inheritance which he felt conscious of having a legitimate right to possess in undiminished lustre, If it should be thought, by the more calmly philosophical mind, that he might sometimes too soon take the alarm; let it, at least, not fail to be remembered, that the true votary of honour must never be, even once, a single moment too late.

The reader who has attentively perused the preceding part of Lord Nelson's history, will long since have discovered, that one grand trait of character, in this exalted man, was a determined resolution of accomplishing, to it's fullest possible extent, the business, whatever it might be, which was once committed to his charge; and that, in every expedition, it formed his chief pride, to effect even more than could have been expected, by those who had, from the greatest possible confidence in his skill and ability, selected him for the enterprise. It was this invariable principle that, by prompting him to serve on shore, at the batteries before Calvi, cost him the vision of an eye; and it was to this same cause, that he owed the loss of his arm at Teneriffe. Conformably to this grand characteristic, having so honourably received the Earl of St. Vincent's orders to seek and to destroy the French armament, which he had at length gloriously encountered at the mouth of the Nile; he still internally regretted, that the wound on that occasion received in his forehead, by rendering him almost wholly blind, had proved the sole cause of a single French ship's escape. Not that this undoubted conviction in his own bosom, that he should certainly have captured or destroyed the whole fleet, conveys the smallest reflection on any other officer for not having effected the same purpose: for, most assuredly, though many captains in this noble squadron might boast of equal bravery with himself, and of much skill too, Lord Nelson greatly surpassed them all, and perhaps every other naval commander, in that promptitude of vigorously winged imagination which instantaneously rises to the exigency. The moment Captain Berry had, on first beholding the position of the French fleet at anchor, fully comprehended the entire scope of his adored admiral's design for the attack, he exclaimed, in an extacy—"If we succeed, what will the world say?"—"There is no if in the case," coolly replied the admiral: "that we shall succeed, is certain; who may live to tell the story, is a very different question!" So positive was this great man of success, even before the battle commenced.

Though Lord Nelson had hitherto failed in taking the fugitive ships from Egypt, and the transports were not yet destroyed at Alexandria; he never relinquished the idea, that some of his "band of brothers," the heroic captains of the Nile, might finally fall in with, and either take or destroy, the two line of battle ships, and two frigates, which had alone escaped, and thus complete the destruction of all the ships of war. Nor had the comprehensive mind of our hero limited it's hope to these alone: he trusted that some of his brave band would at least assist in effecting the destruction of the transports; as well as in preventing every remaining Frenchman, who had been landed in Egypt, from ever returning to France. For this purpose, he had not only left Captain Hood on the coast; but solicited, both at home, and of our allies, the requisite bomb-vessels, &c. by repeated most urgent epistles.

At length, the necessary preparations had been made, and dispatched from England, under the command of Sir William Sidney Smith, brother of the English minister, Mr. Spencer Smith, at the Ottoman court. The high character of Sir Sidney Smith—as he is usually called—for intrepid gallantry, as well as for incomparable dexterity and address in that species of naval exploit which may be denominated incendiary warfare, seemed to justify sufficiently the judgment of the Admiralty in selecting a character so respectably enterprising for this service, and the measure was certainly extremely popular at home. Every thing, indeed, was expected from Sir Sidney Smith's ability: and truth requires the acknowledgment, that neither government, nor the people, were finally disappointed; as the history of the siege of Acre, where he commanded on shore, and fairly defeated Bonaparte, will for ever afford a most satisfactory and substantial proof.

A very obvious consequence, however, attended this appointment; which, strange as it may seem, undoubtedly escaped the attention of the Admiralty, as well as of the country at large: the former of whom, it is certain, would not have adopted, nor the latter have applauded, any act which they had foreseen could be liable to hurt the feelings of their chief favourite, the gallant hero of the Nile.

Not only did this measure introduce a new British hero to assist in the full accomplishment of the business originally committed, by the Earl of St. Vincent, to Admiral Nelson; appearing, to his lordship's exquisite feelings, an implied defectiveness in his noble band of brothers for the completion of the enterprise: but, by the circumstance of Sir Sidney Smith's authorization to take under his command Captain Hood, and the ships left with him in Egypt, Lord Nelson felt himself deprived of a part of his squadron, in favour of a junior officer, who would consequently be placed above his brave friends.

The day after leaving Naples, his lordship had received dispatches from Sir Sidney Smith, then off Malta, in his way to Egypt, apprizing him of these intentions; and, on the 27th, at Palermo, others from the Earl of St. Vincent, who does not appear to have been previously consulted, respecting the appointment of Sir Sidney Smith. It is probable, therefore, that the noble earl might participate with his gallant friend in the unpleasant feelings thus excited. Unfortunately, too, Sir Sidney had written, about this period, to our hero's friend, Sir William Hamilton; in terms, as it should seem, of insufficient caution; originating, perhaps, merely in the ebullitions of an honest overflowing heart, alive to it's own importance. Be this as it may, that of Lord Nelson was fired with an indignation, which he thus vehemently expresses to his commander in chief.

"Palermo, 31st Dec. 1798.

"MY DEAR LORD

"I do feel, for I am man, that it is impossible for me to serve in those seas, with a squadron under a junior officer. Could I have thought it; and, from Earl Spencer? Never, never was I so astonished, as your letter made me. As soon as I can get hold of Troubridge, I shall send him to Egypt, to endeavour to destroy the ships in Alexandria. If it can be done, Troubridge will do it. The Swedish knight writes Sir William Hamilton, that he shall go to Egypt, and take Captain Hood, and his squadron, under his command. The knight forgets the respect due to his superior officer. He has no orders from you, to take my ships away from my command: but, it is all of a piece. Is it to be borne? Pray, grant me your permission to retire; and, I hope, the Vanguard will be allowed to convey me, and my friends Sir William and Lady Hamilton, to England. God bless you, my dear lord! and believe me, your affectionate friend,

"Nelson."
"Earl of St. Vincent."

His lordship now, certainly, had it in contemplation to retire, as expressed in the above letter. He even went so far, as to request the Earl of St. Vincent's permission, that he might leave the command to his gallant and most excellent second, Captain Troubridge, or some other of his brave friends who so gloriously fought at the battle of the Nile—if his health and uneasiness of mind should not be mended. In the mean time, he resolved to send Captain Troubridge to Egypt, as he had before intended, that he might endeavour to destroy the transports in Alexandria; after which, he was now to deliver up the Levant Seas to the care of Sir Sidney Smith.

Piqued as Lord Nelson evidently was, on this occasion, by what he felt as the obtrusion of Sir Sidney Smith, to the exclusion of his favourite band of brothers, he nevertheless wished him all possible success, and readily yielded him every requisite assistance in his power. At the same time, with abundant address, his lordship selected, from the dispatches which had been transmitted to him, an extract from Lord Grenville's instructions, which he transcribed into the following letter to Sir Sidney Smith, as a gentle hint that this officer's authority was not wholly without restriction.

"Palermo, Dec. 31, 1798.

"SIR,

"I have been honoured with your letter from off Malta, with it's several inclosures: viz. An extract of a letter from Lord Grenville to John Spencer Smith, Esq. &c.--"And his majesty has been graciously pleased to direct, that your brother, Sir Sidney Smith, shall proceed to Constantinople with the eighty-gun ship Le Tigre. His instructions will enable him to take the command of such of his majesty's ships as he may find in those seas--unless, by any unforeseen accident, it should happen that there should be, among them, any of his majesty's officers of superior rank; and he will be directed to act with such force, in conjunction with the Russian and Ottoman squadrons, for the defence of the Ottoman empire, and for the annoyance of the enemy in that quarter:"--Also, an extract of another letter, from Lord Grenville to yourself and brother--And the Earl of St. Vincent having sent me an extract of a letter from Earl Spencer to him; saying that, for certain circumstances, you should be the officer selected for the command of a small squadron in the Levant Seas: and, his lordship having also informed me, that Captain Miller was the officer of your choice; and directing me to give you a frigate, or a sloop of war, till Captain Miller's arrival--You may rest assured, that I shall most strictly comply with the instructions sent by Lord Grenville to your brother; also, those of Earl Spencer, and the Earl of St. Vincent. For this purpose, I must desire that you will lose no time in proceeding to Alexandria, to take upon you the command of the blockade, &c. which I shall direct to be delivered up to you; and, from my heart, I wish you every success. The united squadrons of the Turks and Russians, and of two sail of the line under your command, must be sufficient for the two ships *armee en flute*, and three frigates; which, thank God! are all the enemy have left in those seas.

"I have the honour to be, Sir, your most obedient servant,

"Nelson."

It is by no means improbable, that Lord Nelson, while coolly transcribing the above passage from Lord Grenville's judiciously guarded instructions, to convince Sir Sidney Smith, that he was not restrained, had in some measure convinced himself that those instructions could not possibly be intended to give him, or his gallant friends, the smallest just cause of offence.

On this same day, the last of the glorious year 1798, his lordship also wrote the following answer to a letter from John Julius Angerstein, Esq. Chairman of the Committee at Lloyd's, which he had just received.

"Vanguard, Palermo,
31st Dec. 1798.

"SIR,

"I have had the honour of receiving your's of the 10th October, inclosing a circular letter addressed to the commanders in the squadron under my command, requesting them to favour the committee with the lists of the killed and wounded on board their respective ships at the battle of the Nile: and I beg leave to acquaint you, that I have given the necessary directions to the captains of the ships at present under my command to furnish the committee with lists, agreeable to their wishes; and will write to the captains of those ships which are gone down the Mediterranean with the prizes, to do the same as soon as possible, in order to forward their charitable intentions.

"I have the honour to be, with the greatest respect, your most obedient and humble servant,

"Nelson."

However, neither this nor any other pleasing employ, amidst his lordship's numerous indispensible avocations, could hastily reconcile him to the unpleasant circumstance of not being left to finish the business which he had so nobly commenced, and so nearly closed. Even the soothings of his amiable and illustrious friends were ineffectual; and, on the next day, the first of the year 1799, he wrote to Earl Spencer for permission to return to England. This fact will appear in the following letter; though, happily, by the timely and judicious interference of the Earl of St. Vincent, added to the earnest and united requests of the King and Queen of Naples, and Sir William and Lady Hamilton, he was induced finally to continue a command which the royal sufferers felt so necessary for their protection.

"Palermo,
1st Jan. 1799.

"MY DEAR LORD,

"I have transmitted to Mr. Nepean, by way of Vienna, a duplicate of my letter to the commander in chief: which, of course, will likewise be sent you from him; and it will inform you of all which has passed, from the determination of leaving Naples to our arrival at Palermo.

"The day after I left Naples, I received a letter from Sir Sidney Smith, with several inclosures. I send you my answer. Every thing which the extracts sent me by Sir Sidney Smith point out to him, has been fully talked over, and fully explained, by Kelim Effendi; a person holding the office similar to our under-secretary of state, who had been sent with my Order of Merit: for, by the form of the investiture, that seems to me the properest name to call it.

"And now, my lord, having left the command of the two sail of the line in the Levant Seas to Sir Sidney Smith--than whom, I dare say, no one could be so proper--Commodore Duckworth will ably, I am sure, watch Toulon; for I shall very soon, I hope, be able to send him one or two sail of the line: and, Captain Troubridge, or some other of my brave and excellent commanders, being left to guard the One Sicily, and the coast of Italy; I trust, I shall not be thought hasty, in asking permission to return to England for a few months, to gather a little of that ease and quiet I have so long been a stranger to.

"Captain Troubridge goes directly to Egypt, to deliver up to Sir Sidney Smith the blockade of Alexandria, and the defence of the

Ottoman empire by sea; for, I should hope, that Sir Sidney Smith will not take any ship from under my command, without my orders; although Sir Sidney, rather hastily, in my opinion, writes Sir William Hamilton, that Captain Hood naturally falls under his orders. I am, probably, considered as having a great force; but I always desire it to be understood, that I count the Portuguese as nothing but trouble. Ever believe, my dear lord, your most obliged

"Nelson."

"January 2d. General Acton has just wrote me, that the French are within thirty miles of Naples, on the 30th. Marquis De Niza is prepared to burn the ships when the French get a little nearer. Mack is at Capua, with a strong force, numbers not mentioned. Dreadful weather! The great queen very ill: I fear for her.

"N."

Two causes, in a short time, particularly contributed, as it should seem, to tranquillize the mind of our hero, with regard to what he could not but consider as Sir Sidney Smith's too great assumption of authority: one of these was, the hope that his friend Captain Troubridge might effect the destruction of the transports at Alexandria before Sir Sidney's arrival; and the other, immediate information from the Earl of St. Vincent, that he was as little satisfied as Lord Nelson himself, with the business which had so deeply affected his feelings, and had therefore exerted his own power to prevent any such future occurrence. "Sir Sidney Smith," says his lordship, writing this month to Captain Ball, "from a letter he wrote the Earl of St. Vincent off Malta, has given great offence; having said, that he presumed, all the ships in the Levant being junior to him, he had a right to take them under his command. His lordship has, in consequence, given him a broad hint, and taken him handsomely down; and, to prevent any thing of the kind happening in future, he has ordered Sir Sidney to put himself *immediately* under my command." These great men, however, though they felt jealous of their own command, had minds superior to the retention of any continued animosity; and, when they fully understood each other, became very sincere friends. They were all equally anxious for the good of the country; for the honour of the profession; and, for their own individual reputation. Their differences consisted more in the manner than in the form and substance of the thing; and, perhaps, on the whole, Lord Nelson's excess of feeling may be regarded as having, for a time, punished both himself and Sir Sidney with far more severity than the necessity of the case, when coolly considered, could by any means render requisite.

One of the first public measures taken by his Sicilian majesty, after arriving at Palermo, was that of sending away, from the whole island of Sicily, every Frenchman it contained, of whatever description. A resolution which, if it did not originate with our hero, was too consonant with his lordship's known inveterate Antigallicanism, not to have received his hearty approbation.

The following notice, dated on board the Vanguard, 6th January 1799, was accordingly issued by Lord Nelson.

> "His Sicilian Majesty having directed, that all French, of whatever description, should leave the Island of Sicily--A ship of six hundred tons, an English transport, will be ready, by to-morrow morning, to receive French emigrants; say, two hundred. She will have put on board her biscuit, salt provisions, peas, oatmeal, and the common wine of the country. As this will be an additional gratuity, on the part of the King of Great Britain, the *emigrees* will, if they chuse it, lay in such stock of fresh provisions, and other comforts, as they please.
>
> "All those pensioned by Great Britain, will be received by a note from the British agent; and all those pensioned by his Sicilian Majesty, by a note from the Neapolitan agent.
>
> "A Neapolitan corvette to be attached to this ship, to convey her to Trieste, and back again, and to receive on board such *emigrees* as the court shall direct. The transports and corvette out to sail

as soon as possible. Their time of departure will depend on the king's order."

On occasions of this sort, no doubt, there will always be some cases of peculiar hardship; but the difficulty of discriminating between the treacherous and the sincere, among a people so excessively insidious, and the danger to be dreaded from deceit, by those who were so severely suffering it's effects, maybe considered as sufficiently justifying the measure.

Captain Troubridge, having arrived on the 5th, sailed on the 7th, with the Culloden, Theseus, Bulldog, and victuallers, for Syracuse; with orders to collect the bombs, and proceed with them and the Theseus to Alexandria, for the purpose of making a vigorous attack on the shipping in that harbour. In writing, on this subject, to the Earl of St. Vincent, Lord Nelson says—"If the thing can be done, Troubridge will do it."

Captain Louis, of the Minotaur, the present celebrated Admiral Louis, ever one of his lordship's most deservedly favourite friends, had been now ordered to command on the coast of Italy towards Leghorn: and Commodore Mitchell, of the Portuguese squadron, was directed by Lord Nelson, if he could not, by the rules of the Portuguese service—a subject which, his lordship remarked, this was not the time to enter on—put himself under that very old and respectable officer, Captain Louis; at least, to co-operate with him in the service on which he was ordered, and to remain on that service till farther orders from his lordship, or Captain Louis's consent for leaving it. In a letter of this day, to the Earl of St. Vincent, his lordship says—"Minotaur is gone to Leghorn, to endeavour to do good; and Louis will act, I am sure, for the best, as circumstances arise." This very letter, sent by Captain Hope, he thus concludes—"I must refer you, my dear lord, to Hope, who is very zealous and active." So warmly affectionate was the heart of this great and good man to all his worthy officers; and, indeed, to every deserving person under his authority.

On this day, Lord Nelson wrote no less than five public letters: that already noticed, to the Earl of St. Vincent; another, to Earl Spencer; two to Constantinople, one of them for Spencer Smith, Esq. and the other for Francis Wherry, Esq. a fourth to Commodore Duckworth; and the fifth, to the Honourable Lieutenant-General Stuart.

Besides what has been extracted from the letter to the Earl of St. Vincent, it contains the following intelligence relative to the then state of Naples—"On the 4th, the French were not at Naples; but were only sixteen miles distant, negociating with the *nobles* of Naples, for the exclusion of the king. The French long to give them the fraternal squeeze. Another party is for making the Duke of Parma's son, married to the king of Spain's daughter, now at Madrid, king under French protection. The lower class are the only loyal people; and they, we know, may any moment take a wrong turn. Mack is at Capua; but, it was determined, should retreat towards Salerno. On the 3d, at night, the French attempted to force the lines of Capua. They did not succeed. What occasioned their retreat, is difficult to guess; although the Neapolitan army is twenty-five thousand, and the French not eight thousand. Is not this a dream! Can it be real?"

The letter to Earl Spencer is as follows.

"Palermo, Jan. 7, 1799.

"MY DEAR LORD

"Our news from Naples has been daily from bad to worse. On the 4th, the enemy was not at Naples. There are parties, in the capital, for a republic; and another for making the Duke of Parma, who is at Madrid, king: but, I believe, the fighting party is very small. The events which have taken place in the kingdom of Naples have been so rapid and extraordinary, that it appears a dream. The king, God bless him, is a philosopher; but the great queen feels sensibly all that has happened. She begs me not to quit Palermo; for that Sir William and Lady Hamilton, and myself, are her only comforts. I shall, as is my duty, do every thing in the best manner I am able, for the honour of our country. General Stuart, from Minorca, calls for me; Mr. Windham, from Florence, does the same; and the affairs of Egypt and Malta are endeavouring to be brought to an issue. Captain Ball has done wonders; and, I trust, will soon succeed. The bombs, from Malta, go to Egypt, and are to make a vigorous attack on the shipping at Alexandria. These two points successful, will set us quite at our ease on the sea. With every sentiment of respect, believe me, your lordship's most faithful servant,

"Nelson."

The letters to Spencer Smith, and Francis Wherry, Esqrs. contain little more than a reference to Sir Sidney Smith, as the new defender, by sea, of the Ottoman empire, and a polite termination of his lordship's public correspondence with these gentlemen.

What his lordship wrote to Commodore now Admiral Duckworth, contains so many interesting particulars, that it must necessarily be presented entire.

"Palermo, 7th Jan. 1799.

"MY DEAR SIR,

"You will have heard, by Captain Richardson, who left Naples on the 22d of December, of what had happened, to the astonishment of all Europe. It is incredible; but, such things are! I have received the notification of the force expected from Brest; and, if they do get into the Mediterranean, I am confident, they will first go to Toulon: which, when you are apprized of, I submit to your consideration, in concert with his Excellency General Stuart, the propriety of uniting our forces, at what point will be best; but, I shall be truly happy in coinciding with the general and yourself. I am well aware of the small force of the general and yourself, should an invasion of Minorca take place: but, I have a most detestable opinion of the Spanish officers and troops, and the very highest, from experience, of General Stuart; who, by his abilities, would make a bad army a good one. From the situation of affairs here, and having now got bomb-ships, I have determined to bring our matters to issue, both at Alexandria and Malta, as expeditiously as possible; for which purpose, Troubridge goes this day for Egypt, with my orders to make a vigorous attack on the ships in Alexandria. Captain Ball has, at this moment, I hope, finished with Malta. He was using the bombs, by the last account; and intended, about this time, storming the Bormola, the left side of the harbour: by which all the shipping must fall, and the French be close kept up in the town of La Vilette. I wish to send you two sail of the line, and to request your look-out upon Toulon: I am sure, it cannot be in better hands. But, our situation respecting Italy every day alters from bad to worse, so that I cannot answer for my present intentions. I have, under my command, four Portuguese ships of the line; you are most heartily welcome to them all, if you think they will be useful. I own, I consider them as nothing; except trouble in writing orders, which are intolerably executed. However, you may be assured of my ardent desire to do every thing which can render your command pleasant; and, for the security of the valuable acquisition of Minorca.

"Ever believe me, dear Sir, your faithful and obliged.

"Nelson."

In the letter to General Stuart is a recapitulation of the affairs of Naples; with the observation that such things are, if he is not dreaming! "The conduct of the Emperor," he writes, "is to me extraordinary; the loss, at least, of his new Italian dominions, will be the natural consequence. Tuscany must drop from his family; and, whether a month sooner or later, is of little importance. You have seen the movements of Austrian armies, so have I; and found, unhappily, all their generals traders, making the most of their command, by oppressing the poor soldiers. I feel, very much, my dear general, for your situation, in the invaluable possession which your excellent judgment placed under the dominion of his majesty; and, believe me, I shall have the greatest pleasure in doing every thing you can wish me." After observing that his force is merely nominal, and repeating his intentions, as expressed to Commodore Duckworth, his lordship concludes—"The Vanguard is at Palermo, their Sicilian Majesties desiring me not to leave them; but, the moment you want me, I fly to your assistance."

The fact is, that Lord Nelson did not entertain apprehensions of any serious attack on Minorca; and, therefore, without weakening more essential service, prudently kept merely an eye to the remote possibility of such an event; nor did his lordship's judgment, on this occasion, prove to be less judicious than usual.

On the 8th, our hero received a most flattering encomium, indeed, from England; which, certainly, could not fail fully to compensate for every temporary mortification which he might have experienced. This was nothing less than an elegant complimentary and congratulatory epistle, written to his lordship by Earl Howe, expressive of that noble and illustrious veteran's high admiration of the glorious victory off the Nile. What his lordship may be supposed to have felt at the perusal of this most acceptable testimonial to his transcendent merits, cannot be more effectually impressed than by reading the following admirable answer, which he appears to have instantly written, while his heart was overflowing with gratitude.

"Palermo, 8th Jan. 1799.

"MY LORD,

"It was only this moment, that I had the invaluable approbation of the great, the immortal, Earl Howe; an honour the most flattering a sea-officer could receive, as it comes from the first and greatest sea-officer the world has ever produced. I had the happiness to command a band of brothers; therefore, night was to my advantage. Each knew his duty; and, I was sure, each would feel for a French ship. By attacking the enemy's van and centre, the wind blowing directly along their line, I was enabled to throw what force I pleased on a few ships. This plan my friends readily conceived, by the signals--for which we are principally, if not entirely, indebted to your lordship--and we always keep a superior force to the enemy. At twenty-eight minutes past six, the sun in the horizon, the firing commenced. At five minutes past ten, when L'Orient blew up, having burnt seventy minutes, the six van ships had surrendered. I then pressed forward, towards the rear; and, had it pleased God, that I had not been wounded, and stone-blind, there cannot be a doubt but that every ship would how have been in our possession. But, here, let it not be supposed, that any officer is to blame. No; on my honour, I am satisfied each did his very best! I have never, before, my lord, detailed the action to any one; but I should have thought it wrong, to have kept it from one who is our great master in naval tactics and bravery. May I presume to present my very best respects to Lady Howe, and to Lady Mary; and to beg that your lordship will believe me, ever, your most obliged

"Nelson."

This was a rich repayment to the venerable and illustrious earl, of the exalted praise which he had so liberally transmitted our hero: praise which, however excessive, could scarcely be, on either side, too much.

On the following day, the 9th, an opportunity occurs to exhibit our incomparable hero in a new and most amiable light; the irresistible Christian advocate of humanity, pleading for the emancipation of Mahometan captives from slavery.

The ambassador, and his suite, from the Grand Signior, who had arrived at Naples, and were now at Palermo, were about to take their departure; having long since fulfilled, as was formerly described, the object of their mission, by investing our hero with the Ottoman dignities. Their return appears to have been delayed by the affairs of Naples, which would not sooner admit of a ship's being spared for their conveyance to Constantinople. The Bonne Citoyenne, however, commanded by Captain Nisbet, his lordship's son-in-law, had now the honour of that service. Accordingly, as Kelim Effendi, the Turkish ambassador, was passing, in a boat, to go on board the Bonne Citoyenne, near the Portuguese man of war, the Principe Real, then laying in the mole, several Moors and Turks called to him, from that ship, where they were confined as slaves. The ambassador immediately sent to Lord Nelson, requesting his interference in procuring their liberty; and his lordship, with all that amiable humanity which so highly distinguished his character, immediately wrote as follows to the Marquis De Niza.

"Palermo, Jan. 9th, 1799.

"MY DEAR MARQUIS,

"You have some Turkish slaves on board. I beg, as a friend--as an English admiral--as a favour to me, as a favour to my country--that you will give me the slaves. In doing this, you will oblige your faithful friend,

"Nelson."

The marquis very handsomely gave up, instantly, all the Moors and Turks he had oh board, twenty-five in number; and they were sent, by his lordship, to the Turkish ambassador, Secretary Kelim, who took them with him to Constantinople, blessing their noble benefactor.

On the 11th, intelligence was received at Palermo, that Commodore Campbell had prematurely burned all the Neapolitan ships of war; though the French were not then at Naples, or near it: "for," says his lordship, "while an army was covering Naples, the enemy could not be considered as near taking it." Of this conduct, Lord Nelson expressed his entire disapprobation; and his Sicilian majesty was, as he had just reason to be, greatly displeased on the occasion. The commodore, however, who had evidently acted too precipitately, yet with the best intentions, being under a Portuguese commander, happily escaped the enquiry of a court-martial; to which he would undoubtedly have been subjected, had he served in the British fleet. The King and Queen of Naples, indeed, satisfied of Commodore Campbell's upright, though unadvised conduct, graciously condescended to intercede in his behalf; and Lord Nelson, shortly afterwards, though he had at first been exceedingly angry, convinced the worthy commodore that he retained not the smallest animosity, by employing him on a confidential expedition to the Bey of Tripoli.

The fate of Naples was, in truth, at this time fast approaching. The Prince

General Pignatelli had signed an armistice with the French, in which the name of the King of Naples was omitted to be mentioned, who could not but entirely disapprove of such a proceeding; and the French, who were in possession of Capua, now visited Naples as a friendly place. In this situation of affairs, his lordship, though very unwell, offered to go to the Bay of Naples; but both the king and queen so earnestly pressed him not to move, that he was unable to withstand their intreaties: they were, they freely acknowledged, full of apprehensions, and had confidence in him only for their safety.

What the abilities of a Nelson might have effected, had it been possible for him to have headed, at land, the loyal Lazzaroni of Naples, is incapable of being ascertained; but no skill or valour could alone have long preserved a nation so corrupt and pusillanimous from the destruction which, by their meanness, the generality of the upper and middling classes were inviting. There wanted, only, what their subtle invaders well knew was never far distant, some plausible artifice suddenly to prevail over the simplicity of the honest but credulous vulgar, which could not fail to divert that powerful torrent, into whatever channel should most rapidly lead them to the gulph of perdition.

Without entering into the history of this war, which is neither practicable, nor requisite, on the present occasion, it may be briefly remarked—that Championet, the French general, is well known to have informed the Directory at Paris that, by means of a correspondence with the disaffected party, he should be master of Naples by the time they received the news of the capitulation of Capua—that this treachery soon becoming suspected by the Lazzaroni, who were in the royal interest, they seized all the arms; parading the streets, and vociferating the names of the king and their tutelary St. Januarius—that General Mack was regarded as a traitor; and the remains of the army which he had commanded were considered as jacobins whom French gold had corrupted—that Mack, not very unfavourably to the suspicions of the Lazzaroni, fled from them to Championet, who gave him a passport and escort to Milan; where, however, with true French protection, he was seized as a prisoner of war, by order of the Directory—that the Neapolitan army, equally terrified with their general at the menaces of the numerous Lazzaroni, deserted, to that of the French, and was in two days quite disorganized and annihilated—that the Lazzaroni, urged to fury by the escape of their prey, attacked and drove in the advanced posts of the French, and penetrated even to the line—that Prince Molliterno, who had been chosen their general, did not escape their menaces, when they found that he was entering into a negociation with Championet—that they now every where plundered and massacred the objects of their suspicions, however well or ill founded—that Prince Molliterno, and his friends, seizing on the forts, called the French to their assistance—and that, after numerous severe struggles, in which vast numbers of the French, as well as of the Lazzaroni, were slain, the latter were only finally subdued by stratagem.

In the momentary cessations from mutual slaughter, Championet offered his protection to several of the terrified inhabitants. He professed a most profound veneration for St. Januarius; and gravely invoked the all-powerful saint, for the preservation of human lives, and the restoration of peace, in the suffering city of Naples. A French guard of honour was stationed at the church of the tutelary apostle: and "Respect for Januarius," adopted as the consign of their army. The report of such sincere devotion to their favourite saint, flew with the celerity of lightning along the ranks of the Lazzaroni. "Vivent les Francais!—Vive la republique!"—"Long live the French!—Long live the republic!"—soon followed, in thundering applauses, through the lines. In short, without pursuing the various scenes of the wretched farce by which these miserable devotees of superstition were betrayed into an opinion that Championet possessed nearly as much sanctity as St. Januarius himself, and was scarcely less entitled to the adoration which many of the simple souls were now weak enough to pay him; the shouts of admiration, and of joy, universally succeeded to the shrieks of anguish, and the fearful cries of desperation; the contest was immediately brought to a close, and peace everywhere loudly proclaimed. Wonders were not wanting on the occasion—The blood of St. Januarius miraculously flowed this very evening, at the intercession of the venerable archbishop, and his pious clergy; whose devotion to the saint, appears to have far surpassed their loyalty to their sovereign: and, though a fiery eruption of Mount Vesuvius, which had been tranquil for the preceding five years, was actually seen to burst forth on the very day, the 24th of January 1799, even that ancient proof of the anger of the saint was, in the madness of the moment, considered as an additional token of his holiness's approbation! Such is the inconsistency of untutored folly, and the fate of misinstructed superstition; the power of superior cunning, and the effect of unprincipled deceit.

The concern of the good King and Queen of Naples, at the calamitous effects of these successful stratagems on the deluded people, could not fail to be excessive; and that of our indignant hero, and his estimable friends, were little inferior. The despicable frauds, by which the miserable vulgar had been ensnared, were to them abundantly manifest; but they well knew that, had they even been present, and assured the credulous creatures, that the liquification of St. Januarius's blood, and even the blaze of Mount Vesuvius—which was unaccompanied by any natural overflow of the lava—were both easily effected by a simple chemical process, and a few kindled faggots and barrels of gunpowder thrown into the crater, they would most probably have been instantly massacred for what the priests must have necessarily pronounced, for their own safety, the most blasphemous of all possible impieties.

In writing, on the 28th of January, to the Honourable Mr. Windham, at Leghorn, Lord Nelson thus foretells the fate of Tuscany, and of all the Emperor of Germany's Italian dominions. "Alas!" says his lordship, "the fancied neutrality of Tuscany will be it's downfall. You see it, and it cannot fail soon to happen. Tuscany does not, or cannot, support it's neutrality for us or Naples; only to protect the French, is this name prostituted. Seratti, who is a man of sound sense, must see it. When the emperor loses Tuscany and Naples—which, I am bold to say, the conduct of his ministry conduces to do more than the arms of the French—his newly-acquired dominions will not keep to him. Active, not passive; actions, are the only weapons to meet these scoundrels with. We can, as your excellency knows, have no desire to distress the Grand Duke by our conduct; on the contrary, it is our duty to support his royal highness against the tyranny of the French. Your excellency will be so good as to say, for me, to his royal highness, that an English ship of war shall, as long as he pleases, remain at Leghorn, ready to receive his person and family; for, unless the emperor acts speedily, the British flag will be his only security. Tuscany has the choice, to act like men, and take the chance of war; or, in a few weeks, to become another conquest of the French, and to form a new republic." Speaking of Naples, he, says—"We have heard nothing since the 19th; and, from those accounts, it is difficult to say, what turn the mob will take; at that time, they were certainly loyal. The nobility, to a man, Jacobins. Mack has disappeared, and no one knows the route he has taken." Such, it appears, was the uncertainty of the royal family of Naples, with regard to it's fate, on the 28th, at Palermo; though, in reality, it had then been already determined.

In fact, on the 25th, the following curious advertisement, for a grand Te Deum, in consequence of this desirable event, was actually published at Naples; and the archbishop, with the rest of the clergy, solemnly assured the people, that great faith, and extraordinary prayers, had induced their saint to testify his entire approbation of the measure.

> "All the faithful citizens of Naples are invited to be present this day, (Friday, the 25th of January 1799,) at two in the afternoon, at the celebration of Te Deum; which the archbishop, accompanied by the chapter, the clergy, the general in chief and staff of the army of Naples, will sing in the cathedral church, to thank the Most High for the glorious entry of the French troops into this city; and who, protected in a peculiar manner by Providence, have regenerated this people, and are come to establish and consolidate our happiness. St. Januarius, our protector, rejoices in their arrival. His blood miraculously liquified on the very evening of the entry of the republican troops."

Lord Nelson, in the letter last mentioned, thus speaks of the state of Sicily—"As to this island, I cannot take upon me to say much: that they all hate the French, is certain; but, still, they feel themselves an oppressed people. On the 20th, at Augusta, a French vessel, with a hundred and forty officers and soldiers, arrived from Egypt. The boat people, and those of the town, attacked them. Eighty-seven were killed; the remainder escaped on board a Neapolitan frigate, who protected them. Sir William and Lady Hamilton, and I may add myself, are all unwell. The great queen is far from well. The king is the best of the party. As the queen is very anxious to hear of the fate of Tuscany, I shall direct Captain Louis—who, I was sure, your excellency would like—to send either Terpsichore, or this brig, back to Palermo."

In a letter of the same date to Captain now Admiral Louis, his lordship says, observing that all in the house had been ill, and were still far from well—"The air of Palermo is very bad, in my opinion." His confidence in Captain Louis, as well as in Mr. Windham, is thus strongly expressed—"You will, I am sure, my dear Sir, act in that way, which will always meet my wishes and do credit to our country. Whenever Mr. Windham tells you, that his Royal Highness the Grand Duke his no occasion for his majesty's ships, I shall be very glad to see you here; but consult with Mr. Windham, and you cannot err."

On the last day of January, Lord Nelson received, from England, official communications of the votes which had been passed by the House of Peers, the House of Commons, and the Irish House of Commons, conveying their thanks, by their respective speakers, to his lordship, his officers, and men, who fought in the battle off the Nile; which he instantly acknowledged, by most respectful answers to Lord Loughborough, the Right Honourable Henry Addington, and the Honourable John Foster.

On the same day, he also received letters from the Lord Mayor of London, the Clerk of the Drapers Company, and the Mayor of Liverpool; to which he immediately wrote, respectively, the following answers.

"Vanguard, Palermo, 31st Jan. 1799.

"SIR,

"I have only this day received the honour of your letter (when Lord Mayor) of the 16th October; and I beg that you will convey to the Court of Common Council my sincere gratitude for all their goodness to me; and assure them, it shall be the business of my life, to act in the manner most conducive to the prosperity of the city of London, on which depends that of our country.

"I am truly sensible of your politeness, in desiring me to say what particular devices I should wish on the sword which is to be presented to me by the city of London; but, I beg to leave that to the better judgment of my fellow-citizens. Believe me, when I assure you, that I feel myself your most faithful and obliged servant,"
Nelson.

"Sir William Anderson, Bart late Lord-Mayor of London.

"Vanguard, Palermo,
31st Jan. 1799.

"SIR,

"I have this day received your letter, conveying to me the great honour conferred upon me by the worshipful Company of Drapers of London, by presenting me with the freedom of their company. I beg you will, Sir, have the goodness to convey to the worshipful Company, how much I feel honoured by their kind notice of my services; and assure them, that it shall be the study of my life, to preserve their good opinion. Allow me, also, to thank you, for the very flattering manner in which you have executed the orders of the company. Believe me, Sir, with great respect, your much obliged and most obedient servant,"

"Nelson."

Henry Smith, Esq. Clerk of the Drapers Company.

"Vanguard, Palermo,
31st Jan. 1799.

"SIR,

"I am this day favoured with your letter, conveying to me the unanimous resolution of the Common Council of Liverpool, to honour me with their thanks, and also the freedom of their town. I beg you will assure those whom, from this moment, I am to call my brother freemen, that my future exertions shall never be wanting, to approve myself worthy of the high honour conferred upon me by the representative body of the second sea-port in the kingdom; and believe me, with the highest respect, your much obliged and obedient servant,

"Nelson."

"Thomas Leyland, Esq. Mayor of Liverpool."

The transactions of this busy day were of a nature which could not fail highly to gratify the feelings of our hero. He also received, either on this day or the following, a most kind, friendly, and highly satisfactory epistle, from the Earl of St. Vincent; the purport of which is sufficiently obvious from this answer, dated on board the Bellerophon, to which he had now shifted his flag.

"Bellerophon, Palermo, 1st Feb. 1799.

"MY LORD,

"I have to acknowledge the receipt of your letter of the 16th of January, inclosing a copy of one from Sir Sidney Smith, off Malta, with your answer; as, also, your lordship's order to take him under my command. I consider myself highly honoured by your lordship's letter, and flattered by your attention; and will order Sir Sidney Smith to put himself under my command the very first opportunity. I am, with the highest respect, my lord, your most obedient and faithful servant,

"Nelson."

The Vanguard, and La Minerve, had just been sent to Malta; and the Bellerophon wanting a little repair, his lordship had now shifted his flag on board that ship till the Vanguard's return. He was not without hope, that Malta would soon fall; and chose rather to let Captain Ball have the credit of driving the French out, after having, as he observed, gone through "all the hard fag," than permit the Portuguese squadron, now at Messina, to participate the glory, who had been unwilling to encounter the fatigue, which his lordship had originally wished them to partake. In mentioning the Portuguese officers to the Earl of St. Vincent, he says—"As for the great commodores, their rank is as much a plague to them as it is to me. Niza is a good-tempered man. We are, apparently, the very best friends; nor have I, nor will I do an unkind thing by him." But, he had torn himself away from Malta, at the commencement, and his lordship was determined not to send him at the close.

Three letters were this day written by Lord Nelson to the Earl of St. Vincent; one of them has a conclusion so forcibly interesting, on several accounts, that it must on no account be omitted. What a picture it affords, of a contrariety of contending passions, struggling, at the same moment, in the bosom of this wonderful man; ever, as it should seem, feeling with too much energy, for the stability of it's own prolonged peace!

> "All in this house have been ill, and are still. Our great queen, who truly admires you; our dear, invaluable Lady Hamilton; our good Sir William; and give me leave to add myself, to this excellent groupe; have but one opinion about you: viz. that you are every thing which is great and good. Let me say so, about Sir Sidney Smith! I thank you, most truly. My health is indeed, very indifferent; but, whilst I live, if the queen desire it, I remain for her security. No consideration of my own health shall make me abandon my honourable post, in which you have placed me. A parliament is called here: the queen has her doubts about their temper; and I have promised, under my hand, not to leave her; unless by her desire. Let me thank you, for your goodness to Captain Nisbet. I *wish* he may deserve it; the thought half kills me! My dear lord, there is no true happiness in this life; and, in my present state, I could quit it with a smile. May God Almighty bless you with health, happiness, and long life! is the fervent prayer of your affectionate friend,
>
> "Nelson."

To the intelligent reader, here is ample scope for reflection, in a very short compass. Felt gratitude, warmly expressed, to the Earl of St. Vincent, for his kind and generous attentions; lofty eulogiums of his lordship's royal and illustrious friends on the conduct of the noble earl; severe mention of his friend Sir Sidney; complaint of ill health; firm attachment to the royal family at Palermo; fearful apprehensions for a beloved son-in-law, whom he had brought tenderly up with all the anticipatory hopes of the fondest paternal affection, and for whose future conduct he seems, by some untoward circumstances, to have been now filled with all a feeling father's anxieties and alarms; and, lastly, as the consequence of defeated expectations, a desponding willingness to relinquish even life, from an experienced conviction that it affords no permanent or perfect felicity.

On the 3d, his lordship received, through the Earl of St Vincent, the thanks of the House of Peers of Ireland, to himself, and the captains, officers, seamen, and marines, of the detached squadron under his command at the battle off the Nile, and immediately returned a respectful answer by the same channel. He also wrote the following true sailor's letter to the earl, respecting Malta.

"Palermo, Feb. 3, 1799.
"MY DEAR LORD,
"The Incendiary is just come from Ball, off Malta; and has brought me information, that the attempt to storm the city of Valette had failed, from—(I am afraid, I must call it)—cowardice. They were over the first ditch, and retired, *damn them*! But, I trust, the zeal, judgment, and bravery, of my friend Ball, and his gallant party, will overcome all difficulty. The cutter just going off prevents my being more particular. Ever your most faithful,

"Nelson."

"Naples is declared a republic, and the French flag flying. We are low in spirits, but all in this house love you."

His lordship should have considered, before he pronounced the above naval anathema against the Maltese, for pusillanimity, the wretched starving state of the poor fellows carcases; of this he could not be ignorant, since he had, this very day, written to Sir John Acton in their behalf. "If," says he, "six thousand salms of corn are not sent directly to Malta, the inhabitants are in that state of want, that the worst consequences for the interest of his Sicilian Majesty may be apprehended. All these poor people want is, that the king should give them six months credit; when they could make their payments, in money or cotton. The case is important, and demands instant compliance.

"The inhabitants have not seven days bread." He wrote, the day following, to his friend Captain Ball, and inclosed him a satisfactory answer just received from General Acton on the subject: adding—"This evening I saw the king; and he is exceedingly angry, to think that his faithful Maltese subjects should want for any comforts or necessaries which it is in his power to bestow." He addressed, at the same time, a seasonable letter to the deputies of the Maltese people; containing, also, a copy of General Acton's letter, with assurances of Captain Ball's protection, and his own determination to afford them every assistance in his power. In short, though his lordship execrated all appearances of cowardice, he compassionated every species of distress.

Lord Nelson, in a letter, dated the beginning of this month, addressed to Admiral then Commodore Duckworth, thus regrets the difficulty which he experiences, in consequence of having lost his right arm, with regard to writing—"I thank you, most truly, for your several very interesting letters, and beg that I may be favoured with your correspondence whenever opportunity offers. You will, I am sure, make allowance for a left-handed man; but, my inclination to write longer letters is great. I can get but slowly over the paper." This, added to the numerous avocations necessarily arising from so widely extended a command as that in which he was now engaged, will sufficiently account for any seeming neglect of continued correspondence with old friends; whom, however, he was not the man ever to forget. The truth of this observation more particularly manifests itself in the following letter written to that esteemed veteran, Captain Locker; who had sensibly felt the effect of this difficulty, though not the last to congratulate his honoured pupil on the success of his most splendid victory. This excellent letter has been repeatedly published, but it well merits to be again printed.

"Palermo, 9th Feb. 1799.

"MY DEAR FRIEND,

"I well know, your own goodness of heart will make all due allowances for my present situation; in which, truly, I have not the time, or power, to answer all the letters I receive, at the moment. But you, my old friend, after twenty-seven years acquaintance, know that nothing can alter my attachment and gratitude to you. I have been your scholar. It was you who taught me to board a Frenchman, by your conduct when in the Experiment. It is you who always hold--"Lay a Frenchman close, and you will beat him!" And my only merit in my profession is, being a good scholar. Our friendship will never end, but with my life: but, you have always been too partial to me.

"Pray tell Kingsmill, that it was impossible I could attend to his recommendation. Indeed, I had, not being a commander in chief, no power to name an agent. Remember me kindly to him.

"The Vesuvian republic being fixed, I have now to look out for Sicily: but revolutionary principles are so prevalent in the world, that no monarchical government is safe, or sure of lasting ten years.

"I beg you will make my kindest remembrances to Miss Locker, and all your good sons; and believe me, ever, your faithful and affectionate friend,

"Nelson."

"Lieutenant-Governor Locker,
Royal Hospital, Greenwich."

As the Vesuvian republic had been now formed on the ruins of the Neapolitan monarchy, under the protection of the French, and was consequently at war with Great Britain, Lord Nelson gave directions for the property of all persons who had not left this new state to be seized as lawful prize. Application was again made to the emperor; a survey taken of the island, for the purpose of ascertaining it's strength and security; and every endeavour used to obtain, during the war, a truce with Tunis and Tripoli. The opinion of Lord Nelson, with regard to the safety of Sicily, is conveyed in the following letter to Sir John Acton, Bart, expressly on that subject.

"Palermo, Feb. 11, 1799.

"MY DEAR SIR,

"I have to thank your excellency for the honour of your letter; and for sending, for my perusal, the report of various officers on the situation of this island, and of it's means of defence. Respecting an invasion of the French, *in propria persona*, I own, I have no alarms; for, if this island is true to itself, no harm can happen: but, I own my fears, that revolutionary principles may be sown here; and, the seasons being propitious to the growth, will produce fruit. If the emperor will not move, and save--(himself, for his throne must fall if the late measures of his councils are persisted in)--the good King, Queen, and Family of Naples, in the possession of their kingdoms; we may lament, but what must follow is certain. Having thus openly declared my general opinion, it is perfectly proper, no doubt, to be prepared for defence; and, if Calabria is occupied by the French, the first object is the preservation of Messina and the Torre del Faro. As to the other ports of the island, if the inhabitants are loyal, the French may be defied; they will not venture their carcases. But, indeed, my dear Sir, it is on the fidelity of the islanders we must depend for it's defence. When Captain Troubridge returns from Egypt, I shall have the power of having more ships on the east coast: as to Palermo, it shall never be without a proper defence in shipping from all attacks by sea; that is, from what the French have at present in the Mediterranean. In all other things, I beg that your excellency will have the goodness to assure his Sicilian Majesty, that nothing shall be wanting, on my part, for the defence of his kingdoms, and whatever can administer to his comforts; and I beg your excellency will believe with what great respect I am your most faithful and obedient servant,

"Nelson."

The safety of Messina appearing to be the first object for the preservation of Sicily from the French, five hundred troops were immediately ordered thither by the Portuguese ships; and his lordship also urged his Excellency, the Vice-Admiral Theodore Uschakoff, who commanded the Russian fleet then before Corfu, to send as many ships and troops as possible to Messina, for the promotion of the common cause, and the good of his Sicilian Majesty in particular.

On the same day, February 15, his lordship wrote also to his Excellency Abdul Cadir Bek, Vice-Admiral of the Turkish fleet, likewise at Corfu, with a similar request for ships and troops. "Your excellency, without doubt," writes his lordship, "has heard of the melancholy news from Naples. The French, not content with having, by perfidy, declared Naples a republic, have forced a great part of Calabria to erect a Tree of *Terror*, which these unbelievers call of *Liberty*; and their emissaries are sowing the seeds of anarchy into this island, particularly at Messina." His lordship adds, that as he has several ships in Egypt, for the Grand Signior, he earnestly requests such Turkish ships and troops as can be spared, to prevent Messina's falling into the hands of the French.

On the 24th of February, Lord Nelson had the satisfaction to distribute the following sums of money, given by his Sicilian Majesty, among the several persons who assisted in conveying the Royal Family from Naples: one thousand ounces of silver to the officers, seamen, and marines, of his Britannic Majesty's ship the Vanguard, as a mark of the king's approbation of their conduct during the time he was on board; one hundred ounces to each of the two barges crews who brought off the royal family from the palace; one hundred ounces to the admiral's servants; and one hundred ounces to the barge's crew of the Alcmene. The thousand ounces for the several persons on board the Vanguard were thus apportioned, by his lordship's directions—The wardroom, one hundred ounces; twenty-seven gentlemen of the quarter-deck, and warrant-officers, four ounces each; five hundred and seventy-nine seamen and marines, one and one-third of an ounce each; twenty-six boys, half an ounce each; and a surplus of seven ounces, to be expended for general use.

While Lord Nelson was busily exerting himself for the security of Messina, as the key to the island of Sicily, the masters of English merchant vessels at Palermo were impatient for convoy, that they might convey their cargoes to Leghorn. On the hazard of visiting a place so critically situated, he felt it his duty strongly to remonstrate; and, aware how often danger is disregarded, where the loss is to fall on underwriters, he even suggested the impropriety of thus incurring risks which could not possibly be in the contemplation of the parties at the time of effecting the insurances, before he gave his reluctant consent for their departure.

This great man was indifferent to nothing by which either national or individual honour might be affected. A just sense of Lord Nelson's services, in this respect, has probably contributed, in no slight degree, to the extreme popularity of that most laudable institution for the relief of suffering seamen and marines, and their distressed families, so happily commenced and continued by the Committee at Lloyd's. Nor is, perhaps, the idea very chimerical, when we reflect on the magnitude of the contributions, which looks forward to a possible permanent establishment, at no distant day, on this very basis; in which the voluntary subscriptions of benevolent and opulent individuals shall almost vie, in the extent of it's charity to this meritorious class of society, whose services can alone preserve the united kingdom and it's extended commerce in full security, with the grand and munificent public endowment which so nobly adorns our country at Greenwich: to which, also, some national augmentation might, with much propriety, be at the same time made; not only to keep pace with the increase of our navy, but to afford an equally needful asylum for those deserving and greatly exposed auxiliaries, the unfortunate and super-annuated Royal Marines. A sight of such noble institutions, with suitable pictures and statues of naval heroes and their glorious atchievements, in which Lord Nelson and his transcendent actions must for ever stand pre-eminently conspicuous, would far surpass, in genuine grandeur, perhaps, and certainly in rational and philosophical contemplation, the loftiest and most stupendous pillar or pyramid ever raised by human art and industry, for little other purpose than to attract the gaze of profitless admiration, with the vain attempt of mocking the powers of tempests and of time, by which the proudest of these trophied monuments must necessarily be bowed to subjection, and finally crumbled into dust. The solitary hermitage, which shelters a single hoary head, is more interesting to the feeling heart than the proudest display of barren pomp that neither rises over the tomb of departed worth nor affords any living mortal a comfortable habitation. The grand naval pillar, to commemorate the battle off the Nile, for which a large sum was some years since subscribed, without any previously decided plan, and which is said to be still undisposed of, if employed in erecting a respectable edifice for the residence of those brave veterans by whom that battle was fought, and such of their successors, for ever, as should live to find such a residence desirable, might be so constructed and endowed, with the money contributed, as to afford a higher satisfaction to the subscribers; a superior, and perpetually renewable, memorial of the event; and a far more gratifying object of contemplation, even for such of the brave heroes who may never need such a sanctuary; than the loftiest and most embellished obelisk that human ingenuity can ever devise, or human industry execute. This is a subject on which the author could with pleasure dilate; and the promotion of which he would gladly assist, in every way, with all his slender abilities: but, at present, it is an agreeable reverie, in which he feels that he must no longer indulge.

He will, however, transcribe one of Lord Nelson's letters written on the subject which led to this digression, as a satisfactory proof of his lordship's attention to the mercantile interests of his country in that respect, and at this particular period.

"Palermo, 25th Feb. 1799.

"GENTLEMEN,

"I have received your letter of the 23d. I can assure you, I have always the greatest pleasure in paying attention to the representations of the masters of merchant ships; who, at this distance, act for their owners in Great Britain. I can have no difficulty in granting you a convoy to Leghorn; but it is my duty to again point out to you the expressions of Mr. Windham's several letters, and the request of the English factory at Leghorn to Captain Louis: and, at the same time, you must be sensible that an English man of war cannot always lay in the neutral port; and I expect, that the Minotaur is now on her passage to join me. If, under all these circumstances, you still persist in going to Leghorn, I will grant a convoy to that port as soon as possible. You cannot, of course, expect that, when all the knowledge you have, here, of the situation of Tuscany, is known in London, that the underwriters, or myself, can in the smallest degree be answerable for what may happen to your ships or cargoes. I can only again assure you of my readiness to afford you all the protection possible, compatible with the other important duties entrusted to me; and that I am, with great respect, your most obedient servant,

"Nelson."

"To the Masters of the English Ships in the Port of Palermo."

To this it may be sufficient to add that, on their persisting in a desire to sail, he granted them the convoy; repeating, in another letter, "but still with the reservation for the underwriters and myself, as I think the case requires." He also wrote to Mr. Windham, informing that gentleman of the necessity which he had felt himself under to comply with their desire; and requesting him to acquaint Captain Derby, whom he sent on that service, in the Bellerophon, whether he might with safety leave them at Leghorn. If not, his lordship observed, the signal should be made for convoy; and those who chose to quit a place of danger might be brought back, with the comfort of having lost the present convoy for England. However, he adds, it is his duty, and it is his inclination too, to do every thing for the protection of our commerce consistently with the other important duties required of him. Captain

Derby was directed, should circumstances require, to wait a reasonable time for such of the merchant ships as might have perishable cargoes on board, to enable them to dispose of them.

In the letter to Mr. Windham above quoted, his lordship says, alluding to the cruelties of the French, who were then over-running Italy—"Your excellency's account of the treatment of his Royal Highness the Grand Duke, of the King of Sardinia, and of the poor old Pope, makes my heart bleed; and I curse, in the bitterness of my grief, all those who might have prevented such cruelties!"

It will be recollected, that the venerable Pope Pius VI, who had been seized and carried off by the French, and whose fate Lord Nelson thus feelingly commiserates, as if anticipatory of the event, was at the period of being thus forced from Rome in his eighty-second year; and that his holiness expired, at Valence, on the 19th of August following, after a captivity of six months: his body being consumed, by unslacked lime thrown into the grave, to prevent it's receiving, at any future period, the honours which might be esteemed due to a modern martyr; who, perhaps, possessed equal piety and resignation, with many holy sufferers of ancient times, for a like rigid adherence to the Christian religion, who have been canonized by the Roman Catholic church.

On the last day of February, the 28th, Lord Nelson sent instructions to his friend Captain Ball, at Malta, to preside over the meetings of the Maltese people: their deputies having represented to Sir William Hamilton and his lordship, that he had, by his address, frequently united the jarring interests of the different chiefs, at their distracted councils, and that they were therefore desirous of his future assistance; which was, also, the wish of his Sicilian Majesty. Captain Ball, therefore, was vested with full power to leave his ship in charge of the first-lieutenant, directing him how to proceed, and to be on shore whenever he should deem it necessary, either to attend such meetings, or assist the Maltese army; his lordship observing that, though neither Sir William Hamilton nor himself had power to grant any salary for the extraordinary expences he must thus necessarily incur, it would be proper to keep an account of them, that it might be represented to his majesty's ministers in England, and the amount allowed him.

At the beginning of March, Lord Nelson was made a citizen of Palermo; which the court thought might have a good effect, by shewing the attachment of the

English hero to the royal family. This, with other information, is more particularly mentioned in the following letter to Earl Spencer, which appears to have been written immediately on Captain Nisbet's return from Constantinople with La Bonne Citoyenne, bringing several important dispatches.

"Vanguard, Palermo,
6th March 1799.

"MY DEAR LORD,

"I send you a copy of the Turkish admiral's letter to me, from Corfu; also, one from the Emperor of Russia: and one from Sir Sidney Smith, those parts of which, that are ministerial, are--I doubt not--very proper; but, indeed, my dear lord, those parts of Sir Sidney's letter which, as a captain of a man of war to an admiral commanding the squadron in the Levant, are not so respectful as the rules of our service demands from the different ranks in it. No man admires Sir Sidney's gallantry and zeal more than myself; but he should recollect, how I must feel, on seeing him placed in the situation which I thought naturally would fall to me. You may be assured, that I shall take care and arrange proper plans with the Porte for the service of Egypt, and shall support Sir Sidney to the utmost of my power. It is matter of regret, that no squadron of Turks and Russians are yet gone to Egypt; for, I want all our ships for Malta, Sicily, Naples, and Leghorn: and my only wish is, that the Turks and Russians would take care of all the French to the east of Malta. Our situation here is quiet; but who can say, if the French get into our neighbourhood, that we shall remain so? In Calabria, the people have cut down the Tree of Liberty; but I shall never consider any part of the kingdom of Naples safe, or even Sicily, till I hear of the emperor's entering Italy: when all my ships shall go into the Bay of Naples, and I think we can make a revolution against the French; at least, my endeavours shall not be wanting. I hope to go on the service myself, but I have my doubts if the King and Queen will consent to my leaving them for a moment. A few days past, I was presented, in due form, with the freedom of the city of Palermo in a gold box, and brought upon a silver salver. I have endeavoured so to conduct myself, as to meet the approbation of all classes in this country, and I hope to be equally fortunate in meeting your lordship's. A ship is in sight, from Malta. I shall keep this letter open till her arrival; but I do not expect any thing particularly good. The blockade must continue, to the end of the chapter; for neither Maltese, nor Italians, will fight by themselves. Ever your lordship's faithful, and obedient,

"Nelson.

"P.S. I send your lordship copies of Captain Ball's letters from Malta. It is not for me to judge the propriety of Captain Ball's plans; but, I can assure you, he is a man of great judgment and abilities, and ought to have a recompence for all his expence and trouble."

The letters of Captain Ball principally related to taking men into British pay; those of the Turkish and Russian admirals, from Corfu, were highly satisfactory, giving assurances of all possible assistance; and that from the Emperor Paul of Russia, congratulatory of the glorious victory of the Nile, was in the highest degree flattering, and accompanied by the emperor's picture, in a box magnificently set with diamonds. His lordship, however, learned that Corfu, though daily expected to fall, had not yet surrendered; and that Le Genereux unfortunately escaped the vigilance of the blockading squadrons, on the 5th of February. From Constantinople, he received the agreeable information that the Grand Signior had ordered ten thousand Albanese troops to Sicily; but Sir Sidney Smith's letters, luckily blending his naval and ministerial characters, so outraged Lord Nelson's nice sense of propriety, that it renewed all those keen sensations of inquietude which had been so recently tranquilized in our hero's breast.

This circumstance produced the following letter to Sir Sidney Smith; which serves to shew that his lordship, though displeased on the occasion, was not altogether unjust in requiring better future discrimination.

> "Vanguard, Palermo,
> 8th March 1799.
>
> "SIR,
>
> "I have received your letters of January the 23d, February 6th, 10th, and 23d. Your situation as Joint-Minister at the Porte, makes it absolutely necessary that I should know who writes to me: therefore, I must direct you, whenever you have ministerial affairs to communicate, that it is done jointly with your respectable brother, and not mix naval business with the other; for, what may be very proper language for a representative of majesty, may be very subversive of that dicipline of respect from the different ranks in our service. A representative may dictate to an admiral, a captain of a man of war would be censured for the same thing: therefore, you will see the propriety of my steering close between the two situations. I have sent you my orders, which your abilities as a sea-officer will lead you to punctually execute. Not a ship more than the service requires shall be kept on any particular station; and that number must be left to my judgment, as an admiral commanding the squadron detached by the commander in chief to the extent of the Black Sea. I shall, of course, keep up a proper communication with the Turkish and Russian admirals, which net captain of a man of war under my orders must, interfere in. I am, Sir, your very humble servant,
>
> "Nelson."

"Sir William Sidney Smith."

The above epistle, which was accompanied by a regular order, dated the preceding day, for Sir William Sidney Smith, captain of his majesty's ship Le Tigre, to put himself under Lord Nelson's command may certainly be considered as sufficiently severe; and, it is probable, his lordship was of that opinion: but he judged it necessary, for his own comfort thus plainly to deliver his sentiments, however painful the task, that he might escape any repetitions of what must continue to excite unpleasant feelings.

On this day, too, Lord Nelson wrote to Captain Ball, from whom he had received letters which gave hopes of a speedy termination to his long and arduous labours. The deputies lately arrived from Malta had solicited supplies of arms, ammunition, and money, from his Sicilian Majesty; and their application, it will appear, had not proved in vain. Money, cloathing, &c. Lord Nelson informs Captain Ball, are difficult to be got; however, some will be sent. "You will," he adds, "receive seven thousand ounces, which the king confides in you to dispose of to the best advantage. Whenever the French are driven out, you are certainly fitted for the station of chief, and I should suppose his Sicilian Majesty could have no objection to give you the proper appointments. You are sure, I shall do every thing that is in my power, for your honour and benefit. Having said this, I will finish, for I am tired to death with writing." His lordship, however, does not conclude without observing that he trusts to nothing but his blockade for the reduction of Malta; that there is yet no news of the emperor's movements, but move he must; that all the lower order of the kingdom of Naples are ready to take arms against the French; that ten thousand Albanese are near Messina; and that ten thousand Russians are on that side Constantinople, for the same destination, besides the Russian army passing the Tyrol. "Apropos," he at length concludes, "the Emperor of Russia has sent me his picture, in a magnificent box; but, this shall not prevent my keeping a sharp look out on his movements against the good Turk."

Part of the money mentioned in this letter, as well as of the arms, ammunition, &c. requested by the deputies, and three of the deputies themselves, were conveyed, in La Bonne Citoyenne, by Captain Nisbet, to Malta, in his return to Constantinople; who was charged with dispatches for Sir Sidney Smith, Spencer Smith, Esq. his brother, and his Excellency Constantine Upsilanti, at the Ottoman court. The remainder of the arms, ammunition, stores, and money, with the other three deputies, were sent to Malta by Captain Gage in the Terpsichore: who was afterwards to deliver a letter from Lord Nelson to his Sardinian Majesty, at Cagliari in Sardinia; to call at Minorca, for any dispatches which Commodore Duckworth might have for the Earl of St. Vincent; and, finally, to join the commander in chief at Gibraltar, or wherever else the earl might happen to be.

On the 10th of March, General Sir Charles Stuart arrived at Palermo, with the thirtieth and eighty-ninth regiments; who immediately departed for Messina. This, his lordship observes, in a letter to Mr. Windham, a few days afterwards, would not only save that important place from all danger, but had already acted like an electrical shock over the whole island, and must extend it's influence to Naples.

With abundant address, at this period, Lord Nelson offered himself as a mediator between the Bey of Tunis and Bashaw of Tripoli, and his Sicilian Majesty and the Queen of Portugal: for which purpose, he wrote to Perkin Magra, Esq. the British consul at Tunis, as well as to the bey himself; and to the Bashaw of Tripoli, as well as to Simon Lucas, Esq. Consul-General at that court Mrs. Magra, and her family, it appears, were then residing in the hospitable mansion of Sir William Hamilton, as well as his lordship; for he says, writing to the consul, and mentioning his lady and family, "they will give you all the chit-chat of the place. Lady Hamilton is so good to them, that they in truth require nothing from me; but, whenever they think it right to go to Tunis, a ship of war shall carry them."

On the 17th, Captain Troubridge and Captain Hood arrived with the squadron from Egypt, where every endeavour to destroy the transports at Alexandria proved quite ineffectual. The French had, after the departure of Lord Nelson, very strongly fortified all the points of the harbour; and the transports could not be destroyed by shells, as all the mortars burst, and six fireships were lost in a gale of wind. This was a mortifying circumstance to our hero, and it did not come unaccompanied. Captain Troubridge was the bearer of Sir Sidney Smith's dispatches; which, with their usual fatality, again offended his lordship in one of the nicest points. The cause, and the effect, will at once be seen in the following most peremptory epistle.

"Vanguard, Palermo,
18th March 1799.

"SIR,

Captain Troubridge arrived here last evening: and, as he has delivered to me all the papers he received from you, amongst which I see a form of a passport; and Captain Troubridge tells me, that it was your intention to send into Alexandria, that all French ships might pass to France--now, as this is *in direct opposition to my opinion*; which is, *never to suffer any one individual Frenchman to quit Egypt*; I must, therefore, *strictly charge and command you*, never to give any French ship, or man, leave to quit Egypt. And I must also desire, that you will oppose, by every means in your power, any permission which may be attempted to be given by any foreigner, admiral, general, or other person; and you will acquaint those persons, that I shall not pay the smallest attention to any such passport after your notification: and you are to put my orders in force, not on any pretence to permit a single Frenchman to leave Egypt. Of course, you will give these orders to all the ships under your command. As I am very, anxious for the return of the Emma polacre, I have to request that you will not detain her more than two hours. As I shall hope to have a constant communication with you, through the means of the Turkish or Russian admirals, all letters for your squadron, I shall direct to be left in the Vanguard.

"I am, Sir, your very humble servant,

"Nelson."

"Sir William Sidney Smith,
Captain of his Majesty's ship Le Tigre."

Not even the judicious plan which his lordship was now busily engaged in arranging for the recovery of Naples, with all the other objects of his incessant care, could divert his attention from that grand object, the entire destruction of the French armament sent to Egypt. He had just received information of the, surrender of Corfu; and, about this time, a very elegant and flattering letter had been written to his lordship by the King of Sardinia, full of gratitude for the protection of the British flag in conveying him from Leghorn. In writing to the Earl of St. Vincent, after mentioning these subjects, with the return of Captain Troubridge's squadron from Egypt, he observes that it is his intention to send a small squadron, under that commander, into the Bay of Naples, "I wish, first," says his lordship, "to take the Island of Procida, which will secure a tolerable anchorage, and effectually blockade Naples. It must, also, have the effect of preventing the French from detaching any troops from Naples to to the provinces, who are all loyal. The court tells me, that twelve thousand Russians, and fifteen thousand Turks, are ready to cross the Adriatic, to land in the kingdom of Naples. If so, our squadron will create a powerful diversion." Having stated the reasons which have been seen for Captain Troubridge's failure at Alexandria, he adverts to Sir Sidney, who has now the blockade of that place. "I send you," says his lordship, "copies of my letters to him; for the victory of the Nile would, in my opinion, be useless, if any ship, or Frenchman, is suffered to return to Europe. I hope you will approve of my conduct; for, as a captain to an admiral, either Sir Sidney Smith, or myself, must give way. Bonaparte is at Cairo, not more than sixteen thousand strong. He must and will fall, sooner or later, if Sir Sidney Smith does not allow him to retreat by sea. As to myself, I am, at times, ill at my ease: but, it is my duty to submit; and, you may be sure, I shall not quit my post, without absolute necessity. If the emperor moves, I hope yet to return the royal family to Naples. At present, I cannot move; would the court but let me, I should be better: for, here, I am writing from morn to eve; therefore, you must excuse this jumble of a letter."

Neither of these letters, however, mention the very important circumstance of Captain Troubridge's having intercepted Bonaparte's dispatches, on his way to Constantinople; which is contained in the following communication to his Excellency the Honourable William Windham, for the purpose of having that satisfactory intelligence transmitted to England. This letter, as well as other dispatches of the 21st, to Mr. Windham, was written on board the Culloden; into which ship Lord Nelson had shifted his flag, having that day sent Captain Hardy to Tripoli with the Vanguard.

"Culloden, Palermo,
22d March 1799.

"MY DEAR SIR,

The ambassador of Bonaparte being intercepted by my friend Troubridge, on his way to Constantinople, among other articles of his instructions, is a very important one; viz. an offer to enter on terms for his quitting Egypt, with his army. This offer is what I have long expected the glorious battle of the Nile would produce; but it was my determination, from that moment, never, if I could help it, to permit a single Frenchman to quit Egypt. Captain Sir William Sidney Smith, who has the present command of the squadron off Alexandria, I have reason to believe, thinks differently from me, and will grant passports for that part of the French army which God Almighty permits to remain. I have, therefore, thought it highly proper to send Captain Sir Sidney Smith the order of which I transmit a copy; for, I consider it nothing short of madness, to permit that band of thieves to return to Europe. No! to Egypt they went, with their own consent: and there they shall remain, whilst Nelson commands this detached squadron; for never, never, will he consent to the return of one ship or Frenchman.

"I beg your excellency will take the earliest opportunity of sending this important information, and a copy of my letter to Captain Sir Sidney Smith, to England; and ever believe me, with the greatest respect, your obliged and faithful servant,

"Nelson."

On the 25th of March, Lord Nelson says, in a letter to Captain Ball, dated at Palermo—"Now, my dear friend, Captain Nisbet is appointed to the Thalia, a very fine frigate, and I wish he may do credit to himself, and in her. Will you do me the favour of keeping her, and sending me La Minerve; for I want Cockburne, for service of *head*. As soon as Captain Barker's surveys, &c. are over, make one of the small craft bring him here. I have sent Vanguard to Tripoli, to scold the bashaw. Tunis behaves well. As Corfu has surrendered, I hope Malta will follow the example very soon. I am not well; but keep rubbing on, from day to day. God bless you; finish the business as soon as you can."

Captain Dunn, in the Thalia, for Captain Nisbet, was the bearer of the above letter with other dispatches to Captain Ball; and Captain Maling took his passage in the Thalia, to supercede Captain Nisbet in La Bonne Citoyenne. Captain Dunn went to supercede Captain Barker in the Incendiary; on his appointment to the Barfleur; and he was required to join Lord Nelson by the very first opportunity, being wanted to go down the Mediterranean.

This day, too, his lordship wrote congratulatory letters to the Russian and Turkish admirals, on the surrender of Corfu; and invited them, respectively, to co-operate with him in placing the good King and Queen of Naples again on their throne in the capital of that kingdom. To Speridion Foresti, Esq. the consul at Corfu, Lord Nelson wrote, also, the following very flattering encomiums, in a letter which contains some additional reasons for his lordship's complaint with regard to Sir Sidney Smith.

"Palermo, 26th March 1799.

"SIR,

"I feel myself very much obliged by your interesting and important letters, which I have sent to the Earl of St. Vincent. Give me leave to say that, throughout my command in the Levant seas, you have done yourself the highest honour; and rendered, as far as was possible, the greatest services to your country. This public testimony, from a stranger to every thing except your good conduct, will, I trust, be not unacceptable. I observe what you tell me of Lord Grenville's orders to obey Sir William Sidney Smith. You will, of course, follow Lord Grenville's orders, as Sir William Sidney Smith is considered as a minister at Constantinople. I, also, know him in that capacity, jointly with his worthy brother; but, Captain of the Tigre, and in all matters relative to naval operations, he is under my orders: and this I would have you perfectly understand; and explain, when it may be necessary. For an idea seems gone abroad, very injurious to my credit in the world; that, although I was entrusted with the command of the detached squadron, even into the Black Sea, should the French have got there--that, although I had the happiness of commanding the squadron who obtained the glorious victory off the Nile--Captain Sir William Sidney Smith was sent out to command somewhere, in prejudice to me, and four or five captains now serving with me, in the Levant. Having stated this fully to you, you will be equal to every explanation. Whenever you favour me with your very interesting correspondence, I shall receive it with pleasure. As Sir William Hamilton writes you, I shall not repeat, &c. &c.

"Nelson."

Speridion Foresti, Esq.

Every exertion was at this time making, by Lord Nelson, and Captain Troubridge, in concert with their Sicilian Majesties, for the recovery of Naples from the domination of the French. Cardinal Ruffo, who united, in himself, the three important characters of statesman, prelate, and general, had raised a large army of loyalists in the provinces, by the powerful operation of the Catholic cause, and headed in person what was denominated the Christian Army. The French, with their usual insatiable thirst of plunder, officers as well as men, had attended to little else than their own individual gratifications, since they entered Naples; and this did not fail to produce it's customary concomitant, a speedy spirit of insubordination. The fiery population of Naples, in the mean time, like the volcano in it's vicinity, though at present apparently tranquil, might be expected suddenly to burst forth, and overwhelm every obstacle to the progress of it's destructive torrent. In this state of things, it was judiciously resolved that Captain Troubridge should proceed to the Bay of Naples; for which purpose, Lord Nelson—who had, by the general promotion of admirals, on the 14th of February, been made Rear-Admiral of the Red—furnished that brave officer with the following instructions.

By Horatio Lord Nelson,
K.B. Rear-Admiral of the Red, &c.

"Whereas it is of the utmost importance, that the city and towns in the Bay of Naples should be immediately blockaded, to prevent the French forces in those places from getting any supplies of corn or other articles by sea; and it being expedient that an officer of your distinguished merit and abilities should command the blockade, in order to render it the more effectual--

"You are hereby required and directed to take under your command, the ships named in the margin--[Minotaur, Zealous, Swiftsure, Seahorse, Perseus bomb, and El Corso sloop]--embarking on board them the Governor of Procida, and two hundred troops, as also such officers as are ordered by his Sicilian Majesty to embark with them, and proceed to the Bay of Naples. And it being necessary that the squadron employed on this service should have some safe anchorage, the more effectually to carry on the said blockade, and the Island of Procida affording the anchorage desired, you will do your endeavours to seize and get possession of the said Island of Procida, if possible, and reinstate the governor in the command thereof, and using every means in your power to conciliate the affections of the loyal part of the inhabitants; and, also, of those of the islands of Ischia and Capri; and, if possible, bring them to their former allegiance: and, also, to communicate with the loyal inhabitants of Naples, as much as in your power, and by every opportunity; but, by no means, to fire upon the city, without farther orders from me, or circumstances render it necessary to fire on some parts of it, in case of the loyal taking arms against the French. And you will use every effort to prevent all supplies of corn, or other articles, from entering the city and ports in the Bay of Naples; and also of Gaietta and it's vicinity, and along the Roman coast to Civita Vecchia: and, as it is said, the Ponzo Islands continue in their allegiance to his Sicilian Majesty, you will direct that all protection and assistance may be given to them, should they stand in need. And you will consider that every means is to be used, not only by yourself, but by all those under your command, to communicate with the inhabitants on all the northern coast of the kingdom of Naples, and the islands before mentioned; and, as much as in your power, to cultivate a good understanding with them, and conciliate their affections, in order to induce them to return to their allegiance to his Sicilian Majesty, and to take arms to liberate their country from French tyranny and oppressive contributions.

Palermo, 28th March 1799.

To Captain Troubridge,
his Majesty's ship Culloden.

Captain Troubridge, who was also armed with additional powers by his Sicilian Majesty, sailed on the 31st of March to the Bay of Naples, for the purpose of carrying into effect these important orders. It is a singular fact that, even at this very period, when Lord Nelson was thus engaged in securing Sicily from the French, as well as labouring to obtain the restoration of Naples, attempts were making, by the Governor of Messina, then actually protected by British troops, to prevent the condemnation of a French prize which had been taken near the entrance of that port, as if it were still in a state of neutrality. It is difficult to decide, whether this strange conduct originated in a pusillanimous dread of French resentment, or a traitorous disaffection to his Sicilian Majesty. Lord Nelson, however, soon satisfied the prize agents, Messrs. Birch and Broadbent, at Messina, that such shameful conduct would not be submitted to by a British admiral. He wrote, accordingly, the following spirited letter to those gentlemen, which immediately produced it's desired effect.

"Palermo, 2nd April 1799.

"GENTLEMEN,

I have received your letter of the 26th of March, and am exceedingly surprised that the Governor of Messina should presume to interfere in the captures made by a British ship of war. Captain Foley is justifiable in taking the French tartan, although she was going into the port, or even in the port. You will, therefore, claim from him the materials of which the vessel has been plundered; and, at the same time, demand from him what he has done with the French prisoners of war taken in the vessel, as it is highly presumptuous in him to interfere with British prisoners of war. As to demands made against the vessel, it is my desire that they are not paid, nor has he any right to make them; on the contrary, the captors have a right to demand, from him, satisfaction, for the employment of the vessel on the coast of Calabria. I am, gentlemen, your very humble servant,

Nelson.

The Vanguard this day arrived from Tripoli; and Captain Hardy brought, with other pacific promises, from the bashaw, the most positive assurances that no provisions should be sent to Malta by any of his subjects: but, his lordship observed, interest is, we know, their main spring, and they are not to be greatly depended on. The bashaw of Tripoli had, in fact, made a treaty with Bonaparte on the 24th of February, when he received a present of a diamond; the pernicious effects of which, to Great Britain and her allies, his lordship was thus determined totally to counteract.

On the 5th of April, in a letter to his Excellency Sir Charles Whitworth, the British minister at Petersburgh, Lord Nelson thus writes respecting Malta—We certainly have, at an expence of fifteen thousand pounds a month, so closely blockaded the port of La Valette, that the appearance of the Russian troops on the island must insure it's fall in a week, if famine does not force it's surrender before their arrival. The garrison are mutinous, and in dreadful want of provisions. The scurvy cannot be checked. His lordship then observes, that his anxiety to get possession of Le Guillaume Tell, and two frigates, which escaped after the battle of the Nile, will not be doubted; and that these ships, but for our close blockade, would probably have long ago been in France: all which, he begs, may be submitted to his Imperial Majesty, the Emperor of Russia. He has, he adds, given directions to Captain Ball to co-operate in the most cordial manner with the Russian troops; who so ably conducted himself, not only as a sea-officer, but as conciliating the affections of the Maltese, that he was, unanimously, by the islanders, and with the approbation of his Sicilian Majesty, elected their general and chief. His lordship trusts that, should the order be restored, Captain Ball would be a knight of it; "for a more gallant, able officer, does not grace this world. I feel," continues he, "I have said a great deal; but, with my honour, I pledge myself for the truth of it." Then, with the most consummate address, Lord Nelson proceeds to remark—"His imperial majesty will know, that the poor islanders have often, in their distress, and as a mark of their gratitude, offered—as far as they could—themselves for subjects of our king, and made their request to his Sicilian Majesty; but both Sir William Hamilton and myself, knowing that no views of individual aggrandizement actuate the breast of our gracious sovereign, have invariably refused every offer of that nature: but, in the present situation of his Sicilian Majesty, and by his desire, his colours and the British flag fly together, to mark that Great Britain protects the flag of his Sicilian Majesty. It is proper in this place to mention, as the heart of the emperor overflows with justice, that in many instances the islanders have been grievously oppressed by the order; probably, more by their consummate pride, than by a wish to oppress. I know, it is only necessary to mention this matter, for the consideration of the present illustrious Grand Master, to have it remedied; by which, a brave and industrious people will be rendered happy." His lordship concludes this exquisite proof of diplomatic dexterity, with observing, that he impatiently waits the arrival of the Russian troops; by nine or ten thousand of whom Naples would be recovered in a week, and his imperial majesty have the glory of replacing a good monarch and an amiable queen, again on their throne.

Captain Troubridge, in the mean time, was executing, with all possible activity and success, the very important duties which he had been sent to perform. The islands of Procida, Ischia, and Capri, immediately surrendered; and the inhabitants in general, who had been greatly oppressed by the usurpers, manifested such a spirit of loyalty, that they gladly delivered up all the municipal officers for the disposal of their lawful sovereign, and the principals were received, as prisoners, on board the British squadron. The information of these auspicious commencements diffused universal joy at Palermo; and greatly revived the drooping spirits of their Sicilian Majesties, who readily sent the distressed islanders all the relief which it was in their power to bestow, both in provisions and money. The consideration of those distresses, however, while they excited the compassion of their majesties for the oppressed, necessarily called forth their indignation against the oppressors: and, with the relief sent under convoy of La Minerve, for the most distressed of the former; a judge was sent out by his Sicilian Majesty, on board that vessel, charged with a special commission for the trial and execution of the most criminal among the latter.

In writing, on the 12th of April, to the Earl of St. Vincent, respecting these events, his lordship says—"Captain Troubridge is in complete possession of Procida, Ischia, and Capri; the inhabitants of which islands have joyfully hoisted his Sicilian Majesty's colours, cut down the Tree of Liberty, and delivered up all the municipality and the detested Jacobins; all of whom are confined on board ship, and in the chateau of Ischia. The French in Naples are not more than two thousand, the civic guards about twenty thousand; but, as these last will not remain fighting for the French if there is any risk, I am warranted in saying that ten thousand troops would place the king again on his throne." The health of his lordship appears to have been, at this period, very indifferent. Indeed, the air of Sicily seems by no means to have ever agreed with him. He says, in this letter, speaking of Sir William and Lady Hamilton—"We, of this house, are all anxious to get home; yet, in the present moment, cannot move. Indeed, we have been the main-spring, joined with you, that have kept, and are keeping, this so much out of repair machine from breaking to pieces." The difficulties, indeed, of supporting a government every way so feeble in what constitutes the true strength of a state, perplexed our hero in no small degree. He saw, every where, that inactivity and indecision which so little accorded with his own prompt and active mind; and he languished for the busy scenes of action, from which he was detained by the alarms of their Sicilian Majesties, and the constant claims on the wisdom of his councils, which they could not always find the means, or even the firmness, completely to carry into execution.

Captain Ball had transmitted a painful picture of the wretched state of the inhabitants of Malta, but their Sicilian Majesties were incapable of affording them relief; Captain Troubridge had been obliged to part with all his flour, to preserve the recovered islands from starving. "I have," says his lordship, in another letter to the Earl of St. Vincent, dated the 17th of April, "eternally been pressing for supplies; and represented that a hundred thousand pounds, given away in provisions, just now, might purchase a kingdom. In short, my dear lord, my desire to serve, as is my duty, faithfully their Sicilian Majesties, has been such, that I am almost blind, and worn out; and cannot, in my present state, hold out much longer. I would, indeed, lay down my life for such good and gracious monarchs; but I am useless, when I am unable to do what, God knows, my heart leads me to."

Happily, this sombre state was a little relieved a few days after, by the arrival of a cutter from England; which brought considerable supplies, both of consolation and money, for his Sicilian Majesty. On the 21st of April, his lordship now writes to Captain Ball, that his efforts to obtain a small sum of money for the unhappy Maltese had been useless, till the arrival of this vessel from England; "which," says he, "brought the court such accounts of goodness, that Sir William and myself again touched the point about Malta, when the queen gave up seven thousand ounces; for, although the island has granted two millions of money, yet not one sixpence is collected; therefore, they are in distress enough. If any person can keep the Maltese in good humour, it is, my dear friend, you and you only; therefore, for all our sakes, try hard till the arrival of the Russians, who cannot now be long before they make their appearance." Then, adverting to Naples, his lordship adds—"All goes on as it should, on the other side. The lower order only want a little support from the regular troops, and the business is over."

Captain Troubridge, indeed, was proceeding with great vigour; but the Sicilian judge, it appears, did not accord with our naval heroes in his notions of criminal justice. Cardinal Ruffo, too, seems to have entertained what they considered as erroneous ideas of lenity. If the judge and the cardinal really meant to be merciful; whatever might be the effect of such good intentions, the motive is not possible to be condemned: they might be weak, but they would not be criminal. On the other hand, the possessors of that wisdom which perceives when it is necessary to make examples of the incorrigibly guilty, for the preservation of the menaced innocent, as well as of those who are yet unconfirmed in crimes; and of that firmness and fortitude which then induce them to risk all the obloquy of contrary appearance, for the sake of producing true lenity in it's fullest extent; are not to be considered as by any means less inclined to mercy than those who, without loving it more, do not conduce so much to it's genuine interests. Often, however, the really merciful, for the openly avowed and honest discharge of a severe duty, are condemned, by the inconsiderate zeal of weak and vulgar minds; while those who are induced artfully to draw dispositions of a malignant, treacherous, or sanguinary nature, in the semblance of merciful habits, for the mere purpose of acquiring the popularity of that applause to which this divine attribute must ever entitle it's amiable possessors, are idolized by the unreflecting crowd, as the sincerest friends of the very virtue to which they are, in truth, the severest enemies.

The following letter to Captain Troubridge, who had communicated his sentiments on this subject to Lord Nelson, fully demonstrates his lordship's disdain of any improper interference with the criminal jurisdiction of his Sicilian Majesty's government, however it might fail to meet with his approbation. It speaks, his free sentiments both of the judge and cardinal; but hastens to other topics, of better aspect, and comprehends several points of interesting elucidation.

"Palermo, April 25, 1799.

"MY DEAR TROUBRIDGE,

"I thank you, again and again, for your letters, and for the ability and exertion you shew on all occasions. As to Mr. judge, he must hang, or let it alone, as he pleases. It has been that miserable system, which has caused much of the present misery in Naples. In respect to the cardinal, he is a swelled up priest. If his letter had been directed to you, his answer would, I am sure, been proper. Such impertinence, in treating of the assistance of England, deserves reprobation. He makes his army great or small, as it suits his convenience. He is now frightened at a thousand men going against him: which, at one time, is thirty thousand; at another, not three thousand. In short, my dear friend, without foreign troops, the stream will sometimes run different ways. Some Russian ships are said to be at Otranto; but, we know less than you. If the Austrian armies are beaten, Naples will be lost; if victorious, our exertions, with the constant loyalty of the lower order, will hasten the king's return. What are your ideas of the king's going into the Bay of Naples, without foreign troops? If it should cause an insurrection in Naples, which did not succeed, would it not be worse? The king, if a rising of loyal people took place, ought to be amongst them; and, that he will never consent to. Alphonso is going to Tripoli; the bashaw has taken another twist. Lord Spencer disavows the conduct of Sir William Sidney Smith, as being in any manner independent of me. What will his lordship say, when he reads the passports? Your wants and wishes shall, as far as I am able, be complied with. Your bill for extra expences, if the court will not pay, I will answer for. With kind remembrances, &c.

"Nelson."

The mode adopted by Lord Nelson, with regard to the Bashaw of Tripoli, on this occasion, was a master-stroke of policy. In order not to commit the country, with too much precipitation, though resolved to act with all requisite energy at the moment, his lordship employed a Portuguese ship in the business, and selected that of Commodore Campbell for this confidential service. His knowledge of mankind taught him, that this officer would not fail to feel gratified by the honour of such a mission; consequently, be induced to execute it with his best ability. Simon Lucas, Esq. his Britannic Majesty's consul at Tripoli, had found it expedient to quit that court for Palermo: but he consented to return with Commodore Campbell, in order to assist the negociation; and, should it appear advisable, to resume there his ministerial functions. The letter which Lord Nelson sent by Commodore Campbell is much too curious to be omitted. It is, indeed, highly characteristic of it's able author.

"Palermo, 28th April 1799.

"SIR,

"When I received your highness's letter, by Captain Hardy of the Vanguard, I was rejoiced to find that you had renounced the treaty you had so imprudently entered into with some emissaries of General Bonaparte; that man of blood, that despoiler of the weak, that enemy of all good Mussulmen: for, like Satan, he only flatters that he may the more easily destroy; and it is true that, since the year 1789, all Frenchmen are exactly of the same disposition. I had sent your letter to the Great King, my master; I had done the same to the Grand Signior: for I never believed, that your highness would say a word that was not strictly true. A lye is impossible for a true Mussulman to tell; at least, I had always believed so. What, then, must have been my astonishment, to have heard, from his Britannic Majesty's consul, Mr. Lucas, that the moment the Vanguard sailed, the French consul, and all the French, were liberated; and, also, the French vessels in the port allowed to fit for sea: and one, to my knowledge, had sailed for Malta! Why will your highness be thus led astray by evil counsellors; who can have no other object in view, but your ruin? Your highness knows that, although a powerful squadron of Portuguese ships has been since last August under my command, by every means in my power they have been prevented from cruizing against the ships of your highness, or from approaching your coast. It is now my duty to speak out, and not to be misunderstood. That Nelson, who has hitherto kept your powerful enemies from destroying you, can and will let them loose upon you, unless the following terms are in two hours complied with; viz. that the French consul at Tripoli, vice-consul, and every Frenchman, are delivered on board her most faithful majesty's ship Alphonso, to Commodore Campbell, in two hours from Mr. Lucas's setting his foot on shore; that hostages are also sent on board, to remain till every Frenchman in the state of Tripoli shall be sent off, which shall not exceed four days. N.B. There shall be no reservation, or trick, about the French consul, &c. at Tripoli; he shall be on board in two hours after the demand's being made. All French vessels, or vessels pretended to be taken from the French, shall be destroyed in two hours. These terms complied with, Commodore Campbell will, as he has done upon the passage, refrain from taking your vessels, till his arrival at Palermo. If, then, proper terms are not complied with, I can no longer prevent the ships of her most faithful majesty from acting with vigour against your highness.

"Your highness will, without difficulty, write me a letter, the substance of which will be dictated by Mr. Lucas: you will also, as a convincing proof of your detestation of the evil councils which have been given to you by Hamet Reis, your captain of the port, either cause him to be delivered to Commodore Campbell, that I may send him to Constantinople, or dispose of him in such a manner that he may for ever be incapable of giving your highness any advice; for his heart is so black, that I am informed he can give you no good.

"Your highness will, I am confident, approve of the open and unreserved manner of this letter; and consider it as a proof of the honest and upright intentions of the great monarch who I have the honour of serving, and that it comes from your highness's most obedient and faithful servant,

"Nelson."

"His Highness the Bashaw of Tripoli."

Mr. Lucas was furnished with a copy of this letter; and instructed, if possible, to bring the bashaw to a proper way of thinking, by forcibly representing the numerous evils which bad counsellors would be sure to bring on him, should he persist in his present disloyal conduct. The dismissal of the captain of the port, though a very desirable thing, was not to be persisted in, so as to occasion the hostilities of Commodore Campbell against his highness; for, Lord Nelson observed, "every master has a right to chuse his own servants." The other articles were not in any manner to be given up. It was, however, directed to be carefully pressed on the bashaw, that his Britannic Majesty was not at war with him; and that his lordship would be happy still to interest himself in preventing depredations on his highness's coast, provided he should immediately return to a proper way of thinking and acting.

On the 30th, Lord Nelson writes to the Earl of St. Vincent, that his friends are doing wonders on the continent: Hood had taken Salerno, twenty-eight miles from Naples, and garrisoned the small castle with his marines and loyalists; and had caused Sorento, &c. to Castello a Mare to rise and massacre the Jacobins. The Swiftsure was anchored at the latter place, which is opposite Naples, though twelve miles distant by the round of the bay. These events, so near the capital, with the successes of the Austrian army both on the Rhine and in Italy, had induced the French to call in all their out-posts, leave five hundred men in the castle of St. Elmo, and retire from Naples to Capua; taking with them all their sick, as well as every description of plunder. The Jacobins, too, with the traitor Carraccioli among them, were retired to the castle of St. Elmo. Lord Nelson was preparing to send eight hundred troops, with three hundred cavalry, but, his lordship observes, the court being poor, and having no revenue, made things slower than they would otherwise be: "however," he adds, "we make the best of the slender means we possess.

I own, my dear lord, myself much fitter for the actor than the counsellor, of proper measures to be pursued in this very critical situation of public affairs; but, at least, their Sicilian Majesties are satisfied that my poor opinion is an honest one. Their majesties are ready to cross the water, whenever Naples is entirely cleansed; when that happy event arrives, and not till then, a desire will be expressed for the British troops to be removed from Messina into Naples, to guard the persons of their majesties. Whenever your name is mentioned, I can assure you, their expressions are the very handsomest that tongue can utter; and, as is my duty, both as my commander in chief, and my friend, I do not fail ever to speak of you in the only way, if truth is spoken, that you can be represented, as the very ablest sea-officer his majesty has, and as the best and truest friend that can be in this world. My dear Lady Hamilton is always my faithful interpreter, on all occasions; and, never with so much pleasure. My dear lord, you will forgive my short sketches of what is going on here; for neither my head, nor my hand, is equal to what is absolutely necessary for me to write: therefore, all private correspondence is given up; for, I cannot answer a letter. Three of Sir William Sidney Smith's ships, with sick Frenchmen, are stopped by Troubridge; the poor devils are sent to Corsica. I am very much displeased with this Levant commodore with a broad pendant. I send one of his passports. We are not forced to understand French! Malta is as usual, the moment a land force arrives it will fall. God bless you, my dear lord."

In a letter written the preceding day to Earl Spencer, Lord Nelson says, speaking of the affairs of Naples—"I think it very probable that, in ten days, their Sicilian Majesties will be again in Naples. These happy prospects have been brought about, first, by the war of the emperor; secondly, by the wonderful loyalty of the lower order of the people; and, lastly, I flatter myself, I may say, by the conduct of the English. Captain Troubridge has given a portion of that spirit he possesses to all who communicate with him. On the 25th, Macdonald left the town, for Capua; with all the troops, except five hundred in the Castle of St. Elmo. Orders have been given, by the Jacobin government, for the batteries not to fire on the English ships. In short, the communication with Naples is so open, that a general took a boat from the city, and came on board Troubridge, to consult about surprising St. Elmo. The civic guards have individually declared, that they assembled to keep peace in the city, and not to fight. Many of the principal Jacobins have fled, and Carraccioli has resigned his situation as head of the marine. This man was fool enough to quit his master, when he thought his case desperate; yet, in his heart, I believe, he is no Jacobin. The fishermen, a few days ago, told him, publicly—"We believe you are loyal, and sent by the king; but, much as we love you, if we find you disloyal, you shall be among the first to fall. I am not, in person, in these busy scenes; more calculated for me, than remaining here, giving advice. But their majesties think the advice of my incompetent judgment valuable, at this moment; therefore, I submit: and can only say, that I give it as an honest man, one without hopes or fears; therefore, they get at the truth, which their majesties have seldom heard."

The French, in evacuating Naples, in their retreat to Caserta and Capua, robbed all the shops as they passed along: the Neapolitan republic, however, continued organizing their troops, as yet disinclined to give in; and the royalists remained inactive, probably waiting for the departure of the French out of the kingdom before they ventured to commence their operations. The band of brothers, in the mean time, who had so nobly fought off the Nile, were fast gathering fresh laurels on the Neapolitan coast; and inspiring, by their example, other naval heroes of merited celebrity. To these brave men, Lord Nelson paid the just and honoured tribute of applause which their conduct merited, in the following very flattering epistle to Captain Troubridge.

> Vanguard, Palermo,
> 8th May 1799.
>
> "MY DEAR TROUBRIDGE,
>
> I desire you will express, to Captain Hood, the true sense I have of his conduct, not only at Salerno, but on all other occasions; and, that I never expect any but the most useful services, where he commands: and I beg you will say the same for me, to Captains Louis, Hallowell, Foote, and Oswald; not forgetting Captain Harward, and Commodore Mitchell, as far as they have been concerned. As to yourself, your conduct is so all of a piece, that I can only say, what is true, that the last services seem to

eclipse the former ones. You have an arduous task in your present command; and no officer in his majesty's service could, I am convinced, perform it with more judgment and advantage for his majesty's service, than yourself: and I beg that you will ever believe me, your faithful, affectionate, and obliged friend,

"Nelson."

This day, the Neapolitan ship Lion, Captain Dixon, arrived from Egypt; and brought information that three or four French frigates, and as many corvettes, had escaped from Alexandria. Sir Sidney Smith left that place on the 7th of March, and these ships got away between the 5th and 18th of April. Captain Dixon finding these ships gone, came away; without hearing more of Sir Sidney, than that he had arrived at St. Jean D'Acre.

At this momentous period, when the king's restoration to his Neapolitan dominions was daily to be expected; when the fall of Malta was judged scarcely possible to be long delayed; and Lord Nelson was anxiously looking forward to a temporary cessation of his toils, and a speedy return to his native country; intelligence suddenly arrived, that the French fleet from Brest, having escaped Lord Keith's vigilance, had been seen off Oporto, and was expected to effect a junction with that of Spain at Cadiz. On the 12th of May, at six o'clock in the evening, this information was brought to Palermo, by L'Espoir brig; which, at midnight, such was his lordship's dispatch, sailed for Procida, Minorca, and Gibraltar, with letters for Captain Troubridge, Captain Ball, Admiral Duckworth, and the Earl of St. Vincent. To Captain Troubridge his lordship writes, that he must immediately send the Minotaur, Swiftsure, and St. Sebastian, with either the Culloden or Zealous; and either himself, or Captain Hood, remain with the Seahorse, La Minerve, &c. at Procida, and get the Lion from Leghorn, in exchange for one of the small craft—To Admiral Duckworth, that he is sending him eight, nine, or ten, sail of the line, with all expedition, that they may be ready to form a junction with their great and excellent commander in chief; for which purpose his lordship ventures to offer an opinion, that it will be better for the ships to remain under sail off Port Mahon, than in the harbour: and adds best wishes for success, as he is not permitted to come—And, to the earl of St. Vincent, that these several ships will be ready to obey the earl's orders off Mahon; and that, hoping the Russians are off Malta, he has requested some of that admiral's ships may be sent to Minorca.

> "In short," his lordship concludes this last letter, "you may depend on my exertions, and I am only sorry that I cannot move to your help; but, this island appears to hang on my stay. Nothing could console the queen, this night, but my promise not to leave them, unless the battle was to be fought off Sardinia. May God Almighty bless and prosper you, is the fervent prayer of your obliged and affectionate
>
> "Nelson."

His lordship also wrote to Captain Ball, desiring him, if the Russian squadron were before Malta, to proceed with all the line of battle ships, and the Thalia frigate, off Port Mahon, under the orders of Admiral Duckworth; laying his lordship's letter before Vice-Admiral Uschakoff, as well as the Ottoman admiral, should he be there, and procuring such ships as they could both spare for Minorca: but, if they were not with him, to send the Audacious and Goliath to Mahon.

At nine o'clock in the evening of the 13th, the lieutenant of the Petterel arrived, by land, at Palermo. The sloop not being able to get up, owing to strong east winds, Captain Austin very properly sent the lieutenant on shore. He brought intelligence, that the French fleet had actually passed the Straits Mouth: and this news induced his lordship to alter his intended plan of sending such ships as he could collect off Mahon; instead of which, he now resolved to rendezvous with the whole of them off the Island of Maritimo. Of this change he instantly sent to apprize the commander in chief, as well as Admiral Duckworth; trusting that the latter would send his squadron there, which might enable him to look the enemy in the face. He hoped, indeed, that if the Russians and Turks were off Malta, he should get a force, of different nations, equal to the enemy; when it was his determination, that not a moment should be lost in bringing them to battle.

Though the French fleet consisted of nineteen sail of the line, and that of the

Spaniards with which it was about to form a junction no less than twenty-five, his lordship determined to sail, with all possible expedition, for Maritimo.

On the 17th, the Culloden, Minotaur, Swiftsure, and St. Sebastian, arrived off Palermo; but it blew so hard, from the east south-east, that the ships were obliged to strike yards and top-masts. This gale continued till the 20th, when his lordship put to sea; and, on the 24th, in the morning, arrived off Maritimo.

In a letter of this day's date, to the Earl of St. Vincent, his lordship observes that, not having been yet joined by Captain Ball or Admiral Duckworth, he has only to remain on the north side of Maritimo, to keep covering Palermo, which shall be protected to the last, and to wait the earl's orders for regulating his future proceedings. "Your lordship," he adds, "may depend, that the squadron under my command shall never fall into the hands of the enemy; and, before one is destroyed, I have little doubt but the enemy will have their wings so completely clipped, that they may be easily overtaken." Yet, at this period, it is to be observed, his lordship had only five British ships of the line, with three Portuguese, La Minerve Neapolitan frigate, L'Entreprennante cutter, and the Incendiary fireship. In a postscript, his lordship concludes—"No doubt, by this time, the Austrians are at Leghorn; and, if this event had not happened, we should have been in Naples."

Lord Nelson remained at sea till the latter end of May; when, having on the 28th been informed, off Trappano, by the Earl of St. Vincent, that he might, from the then state of the French and Spanish fleets, act as he thought best, in the situation of affairs; his lordship determined on returning to Palermo, for the purpose of completing the provisions of his squadron to six months, with as much wine as they could stow, that they might be in momentary readiness to act as circumstances should require. In the mean time, by continuing on the coast of Sicily, to cover the blockade of Naples, he was certain of preserving the former from any attack; to which it would not only be more exposed, were the ships withdrawn, but the spirits of the people receive such a damp that they would make little or no resistance.

On the 30th, Lord Nelson arrived at Palermo; and, having learned that the Bey of Tunis had stopped several vessels with his lordship's passports, he immediately wrote a very spirited letter to Mr. Magra, the consul, and another to the bey, which he dispatched in the Earl of St. Vincent cutter on the 4th of June. In these letters, however, he again offers his services, as the mediator of a truce, or peace, with his

Sicilian Majesty, as well as with the Portuguese; and observes, that the Marquis De Niza is ready to send a ship for this latter purpose. His lordship assures the Bey of Tunis, that he has granted no passports to any vessel which his highness, and every good man, will not highly approve of; and, that those who would, or dare, counsel his highness to prevent food from being given to those who are fighting in the cause of God against those vile infidels the French, are no better than Frenchmen. "I will," says his lordship to the consul, "have my passports respected, given only to serve the cause in which his highness ought to be as much interested as I am. This you will state clearly and forcibly to the bey—that, as I will do no wrong; so, I will suffer none: this is the firm determination of a British admiral."

In a letter written to the Earl of St. Vincent on the following day, June 5, his lordship says, after noticing the conduct of the Bey of Tunis, "I hope to bring this gentleman to reason." He adds—"My time has been so taken up, that I have not been able to pay that attention to the Barbary States I could have wished, but I know these people must be talked to with honesty and firmness."

His lordship had, indeed, just received, from Tripoli, a tolerable good proof of the efficacy of his mode of dealing with the Barbary States, in the success of Commodore Campbell, of which his lordship thus writes to the earl—"We are better friends with the Bashaw of Tripoli than ever. Commodore Campbell, whom I selected for that purpose, in the first place, because he was fit for the business; and, secondly, to mark that, although I could *censure* when wrong, yet that I have no resentment for the past; having done, on that occasion, what I thought right. The commodore has, on this occasion, conducted himself with proper spirit and judgment; and he has, by it, made a very advantageous peace for Portugal."

So completely did Commodore Campbell act up to the spirit of Lord Nelson's orders, that the bashaw actually delivered to him all the French who were at Tripoli, nearly forty in number. These, his lordship sent in the Susannah cartel, carrying French prisoners to Genoa, which sailed on the 6th of June; honourably stating, that they were not to be considered as prisoners of war, having been sent from Tripoli, in Barbary, for political reasons.

On the 7th of June, in consequence of his lordship's recent information of being promoted to be Rear-Admiral of the Red, he quitted the Vanguard; and, on the 8th, hoisted it on board the Foudroyant.

While Lord Nelson was engaged in provisioning his squadron, without losing sight of the blockade of Naples; and anxiously expecting to hear that the Earl of St. Vincent had fallen in with the French fleet, and obtained another brilliant victory; he had the mortification to be again suddenly impeded in the prosecution of his plan for replacing their Sicilian Majesties on the throne of their Neapolitan dominions, by a letter from Lord Keith, dated the 6th of June, who appears to have been alarmed for the supposed fate of Minorca.

At the receipt of this letter, the 13th of June, Lord Nelson was actually on his way to Naples, with troops, &c. in order to finish matters in that kingdom: but, considering the force of the French fleet on the coast of Italy, then said to be twenty-two sail of the line, four of them first-rates; and that, probably, the ships at Toulon would have joined them by the time he was reading the letter; the force with his lordship being only sixteen sail of the line, not one of which was of three decks; three being Portuguese, and one of the English a sixty-four very short of men; his lordship considered himself as having had no choice left, but to return to Palermo, and land the troops, ammunition, &c. which he accordingly did. He then proceeded off Maritimo, hoping to be joined by such reinforcements from Captain Ball, &c, as might enable him to seek the enemy's fleet; when, his lordship said, there should not be a moment lost in bringing them to battle:

> "for," concludes he, in his answer to Lord Keith, dated the 16th of June, on board the Foudroyant, at sea, "I consider the best defence for his Sicilian Majesty's dominions is, to place myself alongside the French. That I may be very soon enabled to have that honour, is the fervent prayer of your lordship's most obedient servant,
>
> Nelson."

Though Lord Nelson felt that he had no force fit to face the enemy, and was resolved never to get out of their way—"I cannot think myself justified," said his lordship, writing to the Earl of St. Vincent, this same day, "in exposing the world—I may almost say—to be plundered by these miscreants. I trust, your lordship will not think me wrong, in the painful determination I conceived myself forced to make; for agonized, indeed, was the mind of your lordship's faithful and affectionate servant."

The fact seems to be, that Lord Nelson had not the smallest apprehensions of any serious designs on Minorca; and greatly feared that, if he should entirely quit the protection of Sicily and Naples, they would both soon be irrecoverably lost. It was, therefore, with extreme reluctance, that he proceeded on the present business; and having, next day, the 17th, been joined off Malta by the Alexander and Goliath, his force was now fifteen sail of two-decked English ships, and three Portuguese, with a fireship and cutter.

On the 20th, the Swallow Portuguese corvette brought dispatches of the 17th, from the Earl of St. Vincent; acquainting Lord Nelson of the near approach of the squadron under Sir Alan Gardiner, and that Lord Keith was going in search of the French fleet. Having now, therefore, no hope of any sufficient reinforcement to enable him to do the same, his lordship determined once more to offer himself for the service of Naples, which he seems to have imagined the French intended to visit; and, indeed, information to that effect had repeatedly arrived, by different ships, as well British as foreign. Accordingly, having parted for Palermo, he arrived off that port on the 21st; but, the ship being becalmed, he was under the necessity of proceeding some leagues in his barge. Having reached Palermo early in the morning of this day, he waited on Sir William Hamilton; and requested that, the instant they had breakfasted, the carriage might be ready to take himself, with Sir William and Lady Hamilton, to the king and queen. Nothing could possibly have been more opportune than this unpremeditated visit; for his lordship now learned, that General Acton had actually written to him, by the desire of their majesties, though he had not yet received the letter most earnestly intreating his return, for the purpose of going into the Bay of Naples, and there completing the business which had been so auspiciously commenced under his judicious arrangements. Such, indeed, was the then critical state of affairs at Naples, that it required both the ablest heads, and the best hearts, to seize the favourable moment, already beginning to flit away, for effectually restoring loyalty and order in that devoted country. During the absence of Lord Nelson and Captain Troubridge, from Sicily and Naples, Cardinal Ruffo, with his army of twenty thousand Calabrese and other loyalists, aided by some hundred Russian troops, had defeated the Neapolitan republicans, after the evacuation of

Naples by the French under General Macdonald, who succeeded to Championet; and, in consequence, was actually in possession of all the capital, except the castles of St. Elmo, Ovo, and Nuovo, the two latter of which were momentarily expected to fall. In this state of things, with many doubts respecting the firmness rather than the fidelity of the cardinal, and much apprehension with regard to the pernicious effects of the imposing plausibility of several chiefs of the numerous parties into which the distracted country was unhappily divided, every precaution was considered necessary to be adopted that human sagacity could contrive, and all the fortitude judged requisite to be preserved that the most magnanimous bosom could exercise. Their Sicilian Majesties well knew, that they had now before them a man, devoted to their just interests, who possessed, in the supremest degree, these rare and most estimable qualities. They intreated him, therefore, to undertake the arduous task, which could not be securely committed to any other hands than his own. His lordship was sensible of the importance of the charge, and overwhelmed with generous sentiments for the noble confidence expressed by the royal sufferers in his abilities to render them those essential services which their peculiar situation demanded. Difficulty could never deter the mind of Lord Nelson from any attempt; for, where there is no difficulty, heroism is without an object. His lordship had, therefore, not a moment to pause, with respect to his ready acquiescence in the will of their majesties; but, from his very imperfect knowledge of the Italian language, he expressed his apprehensions that he might be subject to fatal deceptions, if he should trust to the fidelity of any interpreter among a people so generally corruptible. He did not, however, state the objection, without proposing a remedy. If, his lordship said, Sir William and Lady Hamilton would accompany him into the Bay of Naples, that he might have the assistance of their able heads, and excellent hearts, to consult, correspond, and interpret, on all occasions, he should not have the smallest doubt of complete success in the business. Sir William, and his lady, were accordingly requested, by the king and queen, to afford their requisite aid on the occasion: to which they agreed, without a moment's hesitation; and, in less than three hours from the time of his first landing, such was the dispatch thought necessary, that her ladyship, having packed up a few articles of the first necessity, proceeded in the barge, with Sir William and his lordship, on board the Foudroyant, which instantly sailed for the Bay of Naples.

Lord Nelson, it may be supposed, had received very full powers from their Sicilian Majesties; with the advice of their equally brave, wise, and skilful privy-counsellor, General Sir John Acton: but, such was the delicacy of his lordship in the exercise of his almost limitless authority, that no single instance can be with truth adduced, where he ever interfered with the criminal jurisprudence of the country; except, indeed, on the side of mercy, to which his excellent heart, it is well known, constantly inclined.

On the 24th, they arrived in the Bay of Naples; where Lord Nelson saw a flag of truce flying on board the Seahorse, Captain Foote, and also on the Castles of Ovo and Nuovo. Having, on the passage, received information, that an infamous armistice was entered into with the rebels of those castles, to which Captain Foote had put his name, his lordship instantly made the signal to annul the truce; being determined, as he said, never to give his approbation to any terms, with rebels, but unconditional submission. The fleet was now anchored in close line of battle, north-west by north, and south-east by south, from the mole head, one mile and a half distant; flanked by twenty-two gun and mortar boats, which he had recalled from Procida.

His lordship sent, instantly, Captains Troubridge and Ball to the Cardinal Vicar-General Ruffo; to represent to his eminence, the opinion which he entertained of the infamous truce entered into with the rebels. They were also charged with two papers to his eminence, expressive of these sentiments; one of which was intended for their perusal, previously to the agreed surrender. The cardinal, however, declared that he would send no papers; and that, if his lordship pleased, he might break the armistice, for he was himself tired of his situation. Captain Troubridge then asked this plain question—"If Lord Nelson breaks the armistice, will your eminence assist him in the attack of the castles?" His answer was decisive—"I will neither assist him with men nor guns."

After much talking, to very little purpose, his eminence expressed a wish to see his lordship on board, that he might converse with him respecting this situation of affairs; and they, accordingly, accompanied him thither. Sir William Hamilton interpreted between Lord Nelson and Cardinal Ruffo, till he was almost exhausted with fatigue. The dispute lasted about two hours, and frequently ran very high; the cardinal, however, proved more than a match for Sir William and his lordship together in volubility, though far from equal to either in true eloquence. The venerable Sir William, at length, vexed and wearied, calmly seated himself; and requested his lady, though less loquacious than the generality of her sex, to assist their honourable friend, who continued pacing the cabin with the most determined perseverance, in conducting this war of words. The pleasingly persuasive voice of her ladyship, delivering the manly sentiments of his lordship, made no impression on the cardinal. He would not submit to reason, nor his lordship to any thing else: so that the lady was in a fair way of becoming soon as desirous to desist as Sir William had been before her, and for the same reason too, if Lord Nelson had not suddenly put an end to the argument, by observing that, since he found an admiral was no match for a cardinal in talking, he would try the effect of writing. He wrote, therefore, the following opinion, which he immediately delivered to Cardinal Ruffo—

> "Rear-Admiral Lord Nelson, who arrived in the Bay of Naples on the 24th of June, with the British fleet, found a treaty entered into with the rebels; which, he is of opinion, ought not to be carried into execution, without the approbation of his Sicilian Majesty--the Earl of St. Vincent--Lord Keith."

Thus terminated the interview: the cardinal retired in disgust; and the rebels, after having notice of his lordship's resolve, persisted in coming out of the castles, which were immediately occupied by the marines of the squadron.

Much has been said, by weak persons, respecting the justice of thus annulling a truce which had been actually signed before his lordship's arrival. They know little of this great and honourable man, the glory of human nature, as well as of his country, who can for a moment conceive that any part of Lord Nelson's character, public or private, need shrink from the severest scrutiny to which the actions of terrestrial beings may with justice be subjected. He was, it is maintained, among the best, as well as the bravest, among the most just, as well as the most judicious, of mankind. With regard to the right which his lordship possessed of putting an end to the armistice, notwithstanding the capitulation had been signed, while the castles remained unsurrendered, a few plain words will be allowed sufficient, by the sober part of mankind, for whom they can, indeed, scarcely be necessary, to set the question at rest for ever. Had the French fleet arrived, instead of the British, would the capitulation have been at all regarded by those who had agreed to surrender these castles? Would they have delivered them up to the then overpowered besiegers? On the contrary, would they not have instantly directed the guns of these very fortresses against the persons to whom they had just signed their submission? These questions are so obvious, that they scarcely need any reply, since there cannot possibly be two opinions on the subject. If there exists, in such derogations, any departure from strictly moral justice, which admits of much doubt, it must be ascribed to the rigorous necessities inseparable from a state of war, and not to any want of rectitude in the breasts of those honourable men on whom devolves the severe task of dictating the operations of that dreadful but unavoidable chastiser of the human race. The besieged, by the laws of war, would have had a right to avail themselves, as is suggested, in the case of such an arrival of the French fleet; and, unquestionably, that of the British, which actually occurred, was alike entitled to alter the effect of the unexecuted capitulation.

It appears, however, that Lord Nelson, though he would not sanction an armistice which he considered as dishonouring the sovereign for whom he was acting, had not the smallest desire to interfere with the disposal of the rebels whom he was so anxious to secure. It was not for their punishment, but for the security of those whom he feared they might contaminate by their principles, that he resolved to keep them in safe custody till the farther pleasure of his Sicilian Majesty should be known; and, in this, even Cardinal Ruffo, it seems, at length, reluctantly acquiesced.

On the morning of the 27th, having embarked all the principal rebels in the several ships of the British squadron, and the rest in polacres anchored under their care, his lordship ordered Captain Troubridge to land with a detachment of troops, for the purpose of cutting down "the infamous Tree of Anarchy," which was immediately burnt before the king's palace. His Sicilian Majesty's flag was now every where flying in Naples, except on the Castle of St. Elmo. This fortress still remaining in the hands of the French, Captains Troubridge and Ball, who had now, in some degree, conciliated the cardinal, taking with them thirteen hundred men from the ships, five hundred Russian troops, and a considerable body of royalists, proceeded to invest it.

As there could be little doubt that this place, though exceedingly strong, must in a few days yield to the vigorous operations of the brave and skilful officers by whom it was besieged, which would complete the repossession of the Neapolitan capital, Lord Nelson wrote to General Acton; requesting that his Sicilian Majesty would come into the Bay of Naples, as well as the general, to sanction and direct, by his royal presence, and their united councils, the requisite measures for completing the important business now in so fair a train for being happily concluded.

At the surrender of the castles, Carraccioli had effected his escape; but he was soon apprehended by the royalists, who were clamorous for his execution; and, on the 29th, after a fair trial, by a board of naval officers of his Sicilian Majesty, for rebellion against his lawful sovereign, and firing at his Sicilian Majesty's frigate La Minerve, he was hanged at the fore-yard-arm of that ship.

Lord Nelson greatly lamented the fate of this unhappy man, though he could not deny the justice of his sentence; and he would, undoubtedly, have recommended him as an object of mercy to his Sicilian Majesty, had he not well known that such an interference, in the then temper of the people, must have rendered himself an object of their suspicion; and thus have operated against the king's interest, without finally preserving the culprit from the worst effects of their fury. When it is considered that, a very few months before, Carraccioli had received, at Palermo, the supreme command of the small remains of his Sicilian Majesty's fleet; that, on his departure for Messina, he had been earnestely and most pathetically conjured by the queen, while taking leave of her majesty, to do every thing in his power for the promotion of the welfare of her little family; that he had, soon after, under pretence of assisting the royalists in Calabria, abandoned his sovereign, and actually joined the republicans with the force committed to his charge; he cannot be well regarded as an object entitled to any very extraordinary degree of commiseration.

On the 3d of July, Lord Nelson had the high gratification of receiving official notice of the liberal grant of ten thousand pounds, which had been unanimously voted to his lordship by the Honourable East India Company, for his services at the battle off the Nile; and his considerate regard to their interests, demonstrated by his judicious conduct immediately after that glorious event. To the letter from Sir Stephen Lushington, Bart. Chairman of the Court of Directors, which conveyed this agreeable information, his lordship instantly wrote the following answer.

"Foudroyant, Naples Bay,
3rd July 1799.

"SIR,

"I was this day honoured with your letter of May 1st, conveying to me the resolutions of the Honourable East India Company. It is true, Sir, that I am incapable of finding words to convey my feelings, for the unprecedented honour done me by the Company. Having, in my younger days, served in the East Indies, I am no stranger to the munificence of the Honourable Company; but this generous act of their's to me so much surpasses all calculation of gratitude, that I have only the power of saying that I receive it with all respect. Give me leave, Sir, to thank you for your very elegant and flattering letter, and to add, that I am, with the greatest respect, your most obliged and obedient servant,

"Nelson."

Nor did this generous man, for whose just praise language must ever be at a loss, rise from the table at which he had penned the above letter of thanks, till his liberal soul, invited every dear relative in the first degree to a kind participation of the bounty which he had just received; by making out drafts, of five hundred pounds each, for his venerable father—his elder brother, Maurice Nelson, Esq. of the Navy Office—the Reverend Dr. Nelson, the present Earl—and his two most amiable sisters, Mrs. Bolton and Mrs. Matcham: thus nobly disposing of a fourth part of what he had so honourably acquired, in a way which must ever reflect unfading glory on his memory, and no inconsiderable lustre on the characters of those who were thought thus uniformly entitled to the tender regards of such an exalted as well as kindred mind. It will scarcely be supposed possible, that any human being could convert this generous token of his lordship's affection and esteem for his family, into a cause of violent complaint. There was one person, however, who did complain on the occasion; and that with such piteous lamentations, as absolutely induced his lordship's father, in whose house she was at the same time residing, to decline accepting his portion of his son's most honourable gift. The mention of this undoubted fact, has no other object, than to demonstrate how very distant from a unity of sentiment, in some important respects, Lady Nelson and her illustrious husband, must necessarily have been; the unfortunate want of which, is ever likely to occasion a proportionable degree of connubial infelicity, and to account for all it's disagreeable consequences, without resorting to grosser motives.

On the 6th of July, Captain Ball, who had been commanding at St. Elmo with Captain Troubridge, was ordered by Lord Nelson to resume his situation at Malta; for which place he accordingly sailed in the Alexander, with the Portuguese ship Alfonso de Albequerque, and Captain Peard in the Success.

During the siege of St. Elmo, many of the Neapolitans came out, every day, in boats, to the British squadron; and the leaders of different parties, with various views, but all affecting the strictest zeal and most loyal attachment to their sovereign, paid congratulatory visits to Lord Nelson and Sir William and Lady Hamilton: it was not, perhaps, always possible to discover the insincere; but this illustrious triumvirate, as they merit to be denominated, by their extreme circumspection and address, made all of them conduce, whatever might have been their original design, to the promotion of the royal cause. Her ladyship, on these occasions, was eminently successful in conciliating those who had entertained unjust prejudices against the queen; and, by the well timed distribution of necklaces, ear-rings, and other trinkets, among the most active of the female partisans, said to be the gracious gifts of her majesty, who had not any present means of more profusely showering her bounty on her beloved people, in which assertion there was but little departure from truth, such an astonishing progress was made in the attachments of them and their numerous admirers, as would appear scarcely credible to those who are unacquainted with the wonderful influence of the Neapolitan women.

On the 10th of July, his Sicilian Majesty, with his principal ministers, arrived in the Bay of Naples; and went on board the Foudroyant, when his royal standard was instantly hoisted. At the first notice of this event, the Neapolitan royalists came out in prodigious numbers; and, rowing round the ship, called, in the most affectionate manner, for a sight of their beloved sovereign, under the denomination of their dear father. "The effusions of loyalty," says Lord Nelson, in writing to Lord Keith of this event, "from the lower order of the people to their *father*, for by no other name do they address the king, is truly moving!" It was, indeed, very affecting to hear them; and their transports of joy, on beholding him, are not to be described. Every day, which their king remained on board, did these loyal people continue to flock out; crying—"Father! father! let us only see your face, and we will be satisfied." It was truly pathetic to hear the generous creatures; and to behold the amiable condescension of their worthy sovereign, who never refused to indulge them with a sight of his person. From half past twelve, however, the constant time of dining, till four in the afternoon, when the king usually slept, the most profound silence was preserved by the many anxious and impatient people with whom the surrounding boats were crouded. If the smallest noise occurred, silence was immediately insisted on—"Do you not know," they would softly, but fiercely, say, "that our father is asleep? Would you dare to disturb him?" Then, as the time of his awaking drew near, they generally asked for their good mistress, the name by which they addressed Lady Hamilton; requesting that she would kindly let them know when their father was ready to see them. This, her ladyship never failed to do; and they immediately resumed the eager and affecting cry of—"Father! father!" &c. when the king instantly presented himself to their view, and often spoke to them with the most consoling affability. The effect of Lady Hamilton's continual presents and kind remembrances from her majesty, soon occasioned them to make similar enquiries after their good mother, the queen; and their dear children, the royal offspring—"When shall we again behold our good mother? When shall we once more see our dear children?" In such simple expressions of affectionate regard, did all the humble classes of Neapolitans pour forth their effusions of loyal attachment to their beloved sovereign; while the generality of those who possessed titles of honour, seemed wholly destitute of it's principles. "The conduct of the nobles," Lord Nelson remarked, in the letter above noticed, "has been infamous; and it delights me, to see that his majesty marks the difference in the most proper manner. It has been, and is, my study, to treat his majesty with all the respect due to so great a personage; and I have the pleasure to believe, that my humble endeavours have met with the royal approbation."

The painful anxiety of the king, as he viewed the hostile flag on the distant

Castle of St. Elmo, feeling both for the besiegers and the besieged, was excessive; but, when on the third day after his arrival, it was visibly lowered, as he stood on the deck, with Lord Nelson and Sir William and Lady Hamilton, he threw his arms round them in an extacy of gratitude, and hailed those generous friends by the appellation of his preservers and restorers.

In fact, the castle surrendered, on the 12th, by capitulation, after a close siege of eight days, with open batteries; in which, the bravery of Captain Troubridge, and the other British officers serving under him, with a most heterogeneous army of British marines, and Russian, Portuguese, Albanese, Calabrese, and Swiss troops, was eminently conspicuous. The particulars of this siege, as well as it's success, will appear in the following letter sent by Captain Troubridge to Lord Nelson.

"Antignano, near St. Elmo,
July 13, 1799.

"MY LORD,

Agreeable to your lordship's orders, I landed with the English and Portuguese marines of the fleet, on the 27th of June: and, after embarking the garrisons of the castles of Ovo and Nuovo, composed of French and rebels, I put a garrison in each; and, on the 29th, took post against Fort St. Elmo, which I summoned to surrender. But, the commandant being determined to stand a siege, we opened a battery of three thirty-six pounders and four mortars, on the 3d inst. within seven hundred yards of the fort; and, on the 5th, another, of two thirty-six pounders. The Russians, under Captain Buillie, opened another battery of four thirty-six pounders and four mortars, against the opposite angle; intending to storm it, in different places, as soon as we could make two practicable breaches in the work. On the 6th, I added four more mortars: and, on the 11th, by incessant labour, we opened another battery of six thirty-six pounders, within a hundred and eighty yards of the wall of the garrison; and had another, of one eighteen pounder, and two howitzers, at the same distance, nearly completed. After a few hours cannonading from the last battery, the enemy displayed a flag of truce, when our firing ceased; and, their guns being mostly dismounted, and their works nearly destroyed, the inclosed terms of capitulation were agreed to and signed.

"In performing this service, I feel much satisfaction in informing your lordship, that I received every possible assistance from Captain Ball, for the first seven days: when your lordship ordered him on other service, and did me the honour to place Captain Hallowell under my orders in his room; whose exertions and abilities your lordship is acquainted with, and merit every attention.

"Lieutenant-Colonel Strickland, Major Cresswell, and all the officers of marines, and men, merit every praise I can bestow: as does Antonio Saldineo de Gama, and the officers and men belonging to her most faithful majesty the Queen of Portugal; their readiness, on all occasions, does them great honour. The very commanding situation of St. Elmo, rendered our approaches difficult; or, I trust, it would have been reduced much sooner. The ready acquiescence to all our demands, and the assistance received from the Duc di Salandra, I beg, may be made known, by your lordship, to his Sicilian Majesty.

"I feel myself also much indebted to Colonel Tschudy, for his great zeal and exertions on all occasions.

I have the honour to be, &c. T. Troubridge,

The Right Honourable Lord Nelson, K.B."

Articles of Capitulation agreed upon between the Garrison of Fort St. Elmo and the Troops of his Sicilian Majesty and his Allies.

I.

The French Garrison of Fort St. Elmo shall surrender themselves prisoners of war to his Neapolitan Majesty and his allies; and shall not serve against any of the powers actually at war with the French republic, until regularly exchanged.

II.

The English grenadiers shall take possession of the gate of the fort in the course of the day.

III.

The French garrison shall march out of the fort to-morrow, with their arms, and drums beating. The troops shall lay down their arms on the outside of the gate of the fort; and a detachment of English, Russian, Portuguese, and Neapolitan, troops, shall take possession of the castle.

IV.

The officers shall keep their arms.

V.

The garrison shall be embarked on board the English squadron, until the necessary shipping are provided to convey them to France.

VI.

When the English grenadiers take possession of the gate, all the subjects of his Sicilian Majesty shall be delivered up to the allies.

VII.

A guard of French soldiers shall be placed round the French colours, to prevent their being destroyed: that guard shall remain until all the garrison be marched out, and it is relieved by an English officer and guard; to whom orders shall be given to strike the French flag and hoist that of his Sicilian Majesty.

VIII.

All private property shall be reserved for those to whom the same appertains; and all public property shall be given up with the fort, as well as the effects pillaged.

IX.

The sick, not in a state to be removed, shall remain at Naples, with French surgeons, and shall be taken care of at the expence of the republic. They shall be sent back to France as soon as possible after their recovery.

Done at Fort St. Elmo, the 22d Messidor, in the seventh year of the French republic, or 12th July 1799.

Signed,
Il Duca di Salandra, Captain-General of the Forces of his Majesty the King of the Two Sicilies.

Thomas Troubridge, of his Britannic Majesty's ship Culloden, and Commander of the British and Portuguese troops at the attack of St. Elmo.

Chevalier Belle, Captain-Lieutenant, commanding the troops of his Imperial Russian Majesty at the attack of St. Elmo.

Jh. Mejau, commanding Fort St. Elmo.

Return of Killed and Wounded at the Siege of the Castle of St. Elmo.

Marine forces landed from the squadron--John Hickman, private, of the Vanguard, killed; Daniel Elliott, Christopher Calonie, privates of ditto, wounded. Serjeant Morgan, of the Foudroyant, Thomas Jones, and Benjamin Cole, privates of ditto, wounded.

Royal Artillery--Lieutenant Millbank killed.

T. Strickland, Lieutenant-Colonel of the Marine Forces.

Swiss Regiment--Two officers, seven privates, killed; nine privates wounded.

Albanese Volunteers--Four privates wounded.

Russians--One officer, three rank and file, killed; one officer, three rank and file, wounded.

Calabrese Regiment--One officer, twenty-one rank and file, killed; four officers, sixty-four rank and file, wounded.

Total--Five officers, thirty-two rank and file, killed; five officers, seventy-nine rank and file, wounded.

Foudroyant, Naples Bay, 13th July 1799.

The Castle of St. Elmo, at the time of it's surrender, had no want of ammunition or provisions: of the former, besides abundance of shot, shells, grenades, cartridges, &c. they had twenty-five thousand pounds of powder; and, of the latter, with eighteen oxen, upwards of three hundred barrels of salt beef and pork, nearly three thousand quintals of wheat, a hundred and fifty-eight of biscuit, two thousand one hundred and sixty-seven of flour, and numerous other articles of food in proportion, they had fifty thousand pints of wine, and six thousand of brandy.

Lord Nelson, immediately on receiving these dispatches from Captain Troubridge, wrote the following official letter to Lord Keith.

"Foudroyant, Naples Bay,
13th July 1799.

"MY LORD,

"I have the pleasure to inform you of the surrender of Fort St. Elmo, on the terms of the inclosed capitulation, after open batteries of eight days; during which time, one heavy battery was advanced within a hundred and eighty yards of the ditch. The very great strength of St. Elmo, and it's more formidable position, will mark with what fortitude, perseverance, and ability, the combined forces must have acted. Captain Troubridge was the officer selected for the command of all the forces landed from the squadron. Captain Ball assisted him for seven days, till his services were wanted at Malta, when his place was ably supplied by Captain Hallowell, an officer of the most distinguished merit, and to whom Captain Troubridge expresses the highest obligation.

Captain Hood, with a garrison for the castle of Nuovo, and to keep good order in the capital--an arduous task, at that time--was also landed from the squadron; and I have the pleasure to tell you, that no capital is more quiet than Naples. I transmit you Captain Troubridge's letter to me, with a return of killed and wounded.

"I have now to state to your lordship, that although the ability and resources of my brave friend Troubridge are well known to all the world; yet he had difficulties to struggle with, in every way, which the state of the capital will easily bring to your idea, that has raised his great character even higher than it was before: and it is my earnest request, that your lordship will mention him, in that way, to the board of Admiralty, that his majesty may be graciously pleased to bestow some mark of his royal favour on Captain Troubridge; which will give real happiness to your lordship's most obedient and faithful servant,

"Nelson."

"Right Honourable Lord Keith."

Besides the above letter, Lord Nelson this day wrote three other letters to Lord Keith, and one to Earl Spencer; so indefatigable was his lordship in the performance of every branch of his duty. Yet, at this very moment, he was hazarding the imputation of too little regarding it, by those who have not his ability to discern in what it truly consists, or the magnanimity to hazard the consequences of a nominal and apparent breach, for the sake of securely seizing the spirit and substance of it's unquestionably intended effect. A truly great man, must sometimes even venture to expose his character, as well as his person, in perilous situations; though he will seldom be so presumptuous or rash as wantonly to commit either, on trivial occasions.

The fact is, that his lordship had, at this very critical juncture, been ordered, by Lord Keith, to detach a considerable part of his squadron for the reinforcement of his lordship, then at Minorca; with this order, however, having already parted with two ships for Malta, it was not possible to comply, without again putting the safety of Naples to a most imminent hazard. He ventured, therefore to remonstrate against the measure, in the following apology to Lord Keith; describing his precise situation, of which the commander in chief could not have any possible knowledge at the time of sending such orders.

"Foudroyant, Naples Bay,
13th July, 1799.

"MY LORD,

"I have to acknowledge the receipt of your lordship's orders of 27th June; and, as soon as the safety of his Sicilian Majesty's kingdoms is secured, I shall not lose one moment in making the detachment you are pleased to order. At present, under God's providence, the safety of his Sicilian Majesty, and his speedy restoration to his kingdoms, depends on this fleet; and the confidence inspired, even by the appearance of our ships before the city, is beyond all belief: and I have no scruple in declaring my opinion that, should any event draw us from the kingdom, if the French remain in any part of it, disturbances will again arise: for, all order having been completely overturned, it must take a thorough cleansing, and some little time, to restore tranquillity. I have the honour to be, with great respect, your lordship's obedient servant,

"Nelson."

"Right Honourable Lord Keith."

With these accounts of the operations at Naples, copies of which were transmitted by Lord Nelson, to England, for public information, his lordship wrote the following private letter to Earl Spencer; in which, among other interesting particulars, descriptive of his then state, he alludes to the impropriety of hastily detaching any ships for Minorca.

"Foudroyant, Naples Bay,
13th July 1799.

"MY DEAR LORD,

"I have much to say; but am unable to write, or speak, half so much as my duty would make it right: therefore, I must be brief. On my fortunate arrival here, I found a most infamous treaty entered into with the rebels, in direct disobedience of his Sicilian Majesty's orders. I had the happiness of saving his majesty's honour; rejecting, with disdain, any terms but unconditional submission to rebels. Your lordship will observe my note and opinion to the cardinal. The rebels came out of the castle with this knowledge, without any honours; and the principal rebels were seized, and conducted on board the ships of the squadron. The others, embarked in fourteen polacres, were anchored under the care of our ships. His majesty has entirely approved of my conduct in this matter. I presume to recommend Captain Troubridge for some mark of his majesty's favour: it would be supposing you, my dear lord, were ignorant of his merits, was I to say more than that he is a first-rate general. The king holds his levees on the quarter-deck of the Foudroyant, at the same hour as he did when in his palace. His Majesty's health is perfect, and he is in the highest spirits and good humour. May I offer my kindest respects to Lady Spencer; and, believe me, I am sensible of her goodness. Lieutenant Parkinson will, I am sure, meet with your kind protection; he is an officer of great merit. Lord Keith writes me, if certain events take place, it may be necessary to draw down this squadron for the protection of Minorca. Should such an order come, at this moment, it would be a cause for some consideration, whether Minorca is to be risked, or the two kingdoms of Naples and Sicily. I rather think, my decision would be, to risk the former. I am told, the alteration of the government is began in this capital, by the abolition of the feudal system, and that it is meant to be continued through the country. Sir John Acton is with his majesty: I need not say more, than that he has the wisest and most honest head in this kingdom. Sir William and Lady Hamilton are, to my great comfort, with me; for, without them, it would have been impossible I could have rendered half the service to his majesty which I have now done: their heads, and their hearts, are equally great and good. With every sentiment of respect and attachment, believe me, my dear lord, your obliged and faithful

"Nelson."

"Earl Spencer."

In the public letter to Evan Nepean, Esq. which inclosed the several dispatches, Lord Nelson also recommends Lieutenant Parkinson, who is the bearer, to the notice of the Lords of the Admiralty; observing, that this officer is sent, by desire of his Sicilian Majesty, to mark that monarch's approbation of his lordship's conduct. Then, apologising for the brevity of his letter, when he has so much to communicate, his lordship adds, that he is writing in a fever, and finds it barely possible to keep out of bed; but, to the last, begs he will assure the board, that every exertion shall be made for the honour of his king and country.

By the surrender of St Elmo, the King of Naples had once more the satisfaction to behold his own flag waving over the capital, and all the forts by which it was defended. The only places now remaining in the hands of the French and his Neapolitan Majesty's rebellious subjects, were Capua and Gaieta. Against the former of these, on the 14th, Captains Troubridge and Hallowell began to make preparations, by landing a thousand men from the squadron; which, uniting with four thousand other troops, of various denominations, marched in a few days to effect it's reduction.

On the 17th, Lord Nelson, by the desire of his Sicilian Majesty, sent a letter to Captain Troubridge, directing him, when he sent in a summons to the commander of the French troops in Capua, to state that, on condition of immediately giving up Capua and Gaieta, both being under his command, the French garrisons, after laying down their arms, should be permitted to go to France without any restrictions; but, if this were not complied with, they should be considered as prisoners of war, with as degrading terms as it was in his power to give them: in short, the allies must dictate the terms. To this letter, there was a remarkable postscript; which serves to shew, with what marked contempt his lordship regarded those whom he had reason to consider as traitors—"There is a person," says his lordship, "who has been a *notorious rebel;* but, now, *pretends* to serve his king faithfully. If he should attempt to come even into your presence, I earnestly request, that you will never voluntarily admit him to your sight, much less speak to him; for honour and loyalty, which you possess, never ought to be contaminated with infamy and rebellion. His name is said to be *Roccaromara*." There can be no doubt, that Lord Nelson had good reasons for this positive caution: the want of which might, perhaps, have been prejudicial to the expedition; if not fatal to this his lordship's favourite commander, for whose honour and welfare he was to the full as solicitous as for his own.

Just as every thing was arranged, ready to march against Capua, the event which his lordship had anticipated in his letter to Earl Spencer actually occurred. A peremptory order arrived, on the 19th, from Lord Keith, directing him to detach, immediately, from the Island of Sicily, the whole of his squadron—or such part, at least, as might not be necessary in that island—for the protection of Minorca. Lord Nelson, however, well knowing, that Lord Keith, at the time of sending this order, could not be informed of the change of affairs in the kingdom of Naples, where all the marines, and a considerable body of seamen, were now landed, in order to drive the French scoundrels out of the kingdom—which was likely, he said, with God's blessing, to be very soon effected, when a part of the squadron should be instantly sent—he thought it right, till the French were all driven from Capua, not to obey his lordship's order for sending down any part of the squadron under his command. After stating these reasons, as his apology for thus acting, his lordship thus concludes—"I am perfectly aware of the consequences of disobeying the orders of the commander in chief; but, as I believe the safety of the kingdom of Naples depends, at the present moment, on my detaining the squadron, I have no scruple in deciding, that it is better to save the kingdom of Naples, and risk Minorca, than to risk the kingdom of Naples, and save Minorca. Your lordship will, I hope, approve of my decision."

Though Lord Nelson's heroic bosom could by no means fail to be violently agitated on this very alarming occasion, his resolution was not to be shaken by any consideration of personal suffering: had the refusal been attended with the certain loss of life, he would not have consented to part with a single ship; such was the inflexible firmness of this invincible man, when his determination was once fixed. He did not, however, set danger at defiance; though he so little regarded it's weight, when placed in the scale which opposed his own conscious sense of duty. Desirous to be duly understood, and to obtain the indemnity of which he could not but consider himself as worthy of receiving, he had ventured to hope for Lord Keith's approbation of his conduct. He judged it right, however, to be prepared against the worst that could happen, by immediately addressing Earl Spencer, also, in a private letter on the subject; as well as the Admiralty in general, through their secretary, Mr. Nepean. These valuable documents, at once self-criminating and exculpatory, are finely characteristic of his lordship's firmness, sensibility, and honour.

"Foudroyant, Naples Bay,
19th July 1799.

"MY DEAR LORD,

"You will easily conceive my feelings, at the order this day received here from Lord Keith; but my mind, your lordship will know, by my letter sent by Mr. Lieutenant Parkinson and Mr. Silvester, was perfectly prepared for this order: and, more than ever, is my mind made up. At this moment, I will not part with a single ship; as I cannot do that, without drawing a hundred and twenty men from each ship now at the siege of Capua, where an army is gone this day. I am fully aware of the act I have committed; but, sensible of my loyal intentions, I am prepared for any fate which may await my disobedience. Capua and Gaieta will soon fall; and, the moment the scoundrels of French are out of this kingdom, I shall send eight or nine ships of the line to Minorca. I have done what I thought right: others may think differently; but it will be my consolation, that I have gained a kingdom, seated a faithful ally of his majesty firmly on his throne, and restored happiness to millions. Do not think, my dear lord, that my opinion is formed from the arrangements of any one. *No*; be it good, or be it bad, it is all my own. It is natural I should wish the decision of the Admiralty, and my commander in chief, as speedily as possible. To obtain the former, I beg your lordship's interest with the board; and, in all events, I shall consider myself your lordship's, &c. &c.

"Nelson."

"Earl Spencer."

The letter for the Lords of the Admiralty, addressed to Evan Nepean, Esq. their Secretary, was as follows.

"Foudroyant, Naples Bay,
19th July 1799.

"SIR,

"I send you a copy of Lord Keith's orders to me, my answer, and a copy of a letter written since my letter to Lord Keith. My decision was taken, and I feel the importance of it in every way; and know, I must be subject to trial for my conduct: but I am so confident of the uprightness of my intentions for his majesty's service; and for that of his Sicilian Majesty, which I consider as the same; that I, with all submission, give myself to the judgement of my superiors.

I have the honour to be, with great respect, your, &c.

"Nelson."

By this open and dignified manner of appealing to the honourable Board of Admiralty, as well as to his commander in chief, Lord Nelson not only escaped any public censure, but even obtained great private applause, very much to the honour of all parties. It was, they well knew, no light departure from duty, originating in presumption or ignorance; but a necessary deviation, dictated by the most profound wisdom, and justified by the truest discernment.

Lord Nelson appears to have been of opinion, about this time, that the French fleet, which had effected a junction with the Spanish, making together forty-three sail of the line, and were reported to have sailed from Carthagena on the 29th of June, had hostile designs against the kingdom of Portugal. This he mentions to Sir Sidney Smith, in a congratulatory epistle on the first successes of that able officer in Egypt. "Yesterday," his lordship says, writing on the 24th of July, "brought me letters from your worthy brother; and we had the great pleasure of hearing that your truly meritorious and wonderful exertions were in a fair train for the extirpation of that horde of thieves, who went to Egypt with that arch-thief Bonaparte. I beg you will express, to Captain Miller, and to all the brave officers and men who have fought so nobly under your orders, the sense I entertain of your and their great merit." To Sir Sidney's brother, his lordship writes with still stronger praise of that spirited and enterprising officer—"I thank you, truly," says his lordship, "for your letter of June 9th, containing an extract of one from your brother, who has done so much at Acre. It is like his former conduct; and, I can assure you, no one admires his gallantry and judgment more than myself. But, if I know myself, as I never have encroached on the command of others, so I will not suffer even my friend Sir Sidney to encroach upon mine. I dare say, he thought he was to have a separate command in the Levant; I find, upon enquiry, it never was intended to have any one in the Levant separate from me." This candid explanation may be considered as a manly acknowledgment of his lordship's, that he had pushed his severity against his friend Sir Sidney sufficiently far.

Lord Nelson also received, from Constantinople, among other dispatches, the approbation of the Grand Signior for his conduct at Tripoli and Tunis: to whom he had constantly sent copies of his correspondence with the bashaw and the bey; and now, in a letter to his Excellency the Grand Vizir, observed that he had no other object in view, than to fulfil the orders of the great king, his master, by proving him a most faithful ally.

On the 28th, the garrison of Capua surrendered to Captain Troubridge, and the commanders of the other allied troops; of which event he informed Lord Nelson, next day, in the following public letter.

"Culloden, Naples Bay,
29th July 1799.

"MY LORD,

"Agreeable to your lordship's orders, I marched on the 20th inst. with the English and Portuguese troops from Naples, and arrived at Caserta the following morning. After resting the people, we marched and encamped near Capua. The Swiss, under Colonel Tschudy, the cavalry under General Acton, and the different corps of infantry under General Boucard and Colonel Gams, took up their appointed situations: the former, to the left of the camp; and the latter, to the right of the river.

"On the 22d, a bridge of pontoons was thrown over the river, to establish a communication. Batteries of guns and mortars were instantly began, within five hundred yards of the enemy's works: and, on the 25th, the gun-battery of four twenty-four pounders, another with two howitzers, and two mortar-batteries, were opened, and kept up a constant and heavy fire; which was returned, by the enemy, from eleven pieces of cannon. On the 26th, trenches were opened, and new batteries began, within a few yards of the glacis.

"The enemy, on finding our approach so rapid, sent out terms, which I rejected *in toto*; and offered, in return, the inclosed terms of capitulation, which the French general agreed to, and signed the following morning at six o'clock. The French garrison marched out this morning, at three; and, grounding their arms, proceeded to Naples, under the escort of four hundred English marines, and two squadrons of General Acton's cavalry.

"In performing this service, I feel much indebted to Captains Hallowell and Oswald; to whose abilities and exertions, I attribute the reduction of the place in so short a time; as they staid night and day in the field, to forward the erecting of the batteries. I also beg leave to recommend Lieutenant-Colonel Strickland and Major Cresswell, the officers and marines, for their constant and unremitted attention; as well as the officers and men of her most faithful majesty, the Queen of Portugal. The Russian forces, under Captain Builie, rendered every assistance. Generals Acton and De Boucard, and Colonel Gams, merit much for their zeal in chearfully performing all the different services that arose. Colonel Tschudy's zeal merits great attention, for his constant readiness to send working parties to the batteries, as well as pushing his men forward on all occasions.

"To M. Monfrere, a volunteer gentleman from the Seahorse, whom I had the honour to recommend to your lordship's notice at St. Elmo, I feel indebted for his great ability and assistance as an engineer, which forwarded our operations much.

"Lieutenants Lowcay and Davis, who served as aides-du-camp to me, have also great merit; as well as Mr. Greig, an officer in the Russian service, serving in his majesty's ship under my command, whom I beg your lordship to recommend to the court of Petersburgh as a promising officer. Count di Lucci, chief of the etat-major, was unremitting in his attention. I have the honour to inclose your lordship a return of the ordnance, stores, and provisions, found in Capua, as well as a return of the garrison, not including Jacobins, which were serving with the French.

"I have the honour to be, &c.

"T. Troubridge."

"The Right Honourable Lord Nelson, K.B."

 The capitulation contained nine articles, like that of St. Elmo, which it in all other respects resembled. The ordnance was one hundred and eighteen pieces of cannon; and there were twelve thousand muskets, four hundred and fourteen thousand musket-cartridges filled, and sixty-seven thousand eight hundred and forty-eight pounds of powder. The French garrison consisted of a hundred and ninety-nine officers, and two thousand six hundred and eighteen non-commissioned officers and privates.
 The town and garrison of Gaieta, being under the same commander in chief as Capua, Monsieur Girardon, General of Brigade, was immediately after agreed to be surrendered without a siege, and an order to that effect was sent, on the 30th, to the Governor: on which account, the place having only been blockaded, all the French troops, consisting of eighty-three officers, and fourteen hundred and fifteen privates, were allowed to march out with their firelocks, bayonets, swords, and cartouch-boxes, without being deemed prisoners of war on their arrival in France. In other respects, the articles of the capitulation, which was signed by General Acton, Lord Nelson, and Monsieur Girardon, on board the Foudroyant, were very similar to those of Capua. There were sixty pieces of brass cannon, twelve iron, and thirteen mortars, with an immense quantity of powder and other garrison stores.
 On the 1st day of August 1799, the first anniversary of Lord Nelson's glorious victory off the Nile, his lordship had the inexpressible happiness of announcing to his king and country, the entire liberation of the kingdom of Naples from French anarchy; the restoration of it's worthy sovereign to his hereditary throne; and of

his numerous oppressed subjects, to the felicity of that benign and paternal protection which they had ever experienced under his Sicilian Majesty's mild and gentle sway.

This agreeable intelligence was communicated in the two following letters: one, to the commander in chief, Lord Keith; the other, to Evan Nepean, Esq. Secretary to the Admiralty.

"Foudroyant, Bay of Naples,
1st August 1799.

"MY LORD,

"I have the honour to transmit you a copy of Captain Troubridge's letter to me, and the capitulation of Capua and Gaieta, &c. Too much praise cannot be given to Captain Troubridge, for his wonderful exertion in bringing about these happy events, and in so short a space of time. Captain Hallowell has also the greatest merit. Captain Oswald, whom I send to England with a copy of my letter, is an officer most highly deserving promotion. I have put Lieutenant Henry Compton, who has served as a lieutenant with me from January 1796, in the Perseus bomb, in his room, and whom I recommend to your lordship.

"I sincerely congratulate your lordship, on the entire liberation of the kingdom of Naples from a band of robbers; and am, with the greatest respect, my lord, your, &c.

"Nelson."

"Right Honourable Lord Keith, K. B."

"Foudroyant, Naples Bay,
1st August 1799.

"SIR,

"I have the honour to transmit you copies of my letter to the commander in chief, with it's several enclosures: and most sincerely congratulate their lordships on the entire liberation of the kingdom of Naples from the French robbers; for by no other name can they be called, for their conduct in this kingdom. This happy event will not, I am sure, be the less acceptable, from being principally brought about by part of the crews of his majesty's ships under my orders, under the command of Captain Troubridge. His merits speak for themselves. His own modesty, makes it my duty to state that, to him alone, is the chief merit due. The recommendation bestowed on the brave and excellent Captain Hallowell, will not escape their lordship's notice, any more than the exceeding good conduct of Captain Oswald, Colonel Strickland, and Captain Cresswell, to whom I ordered the temporary rank of major; and all the officers and men of the marine corps: also, the party of artillery, and the officers and men landed from the Portuguese squadron.

"I must not omit to state, that Captain Hood, with a garrison of seamen, in Castle Nuovo, has for these five weeks very much contributed to the peace of the capital; and Naples, I am told, was never more quiet than under his directions.

"I send Captain Oswald, of the Perseus bomb, with this letter; and I have put Lieutenant Henry Compton, who has served with me ever since January 1796, as a lieutenant, into the Perseus: and I beg leave to recommend these two officers, as highly meriting promotion.

"I have the honour to be, &c.

"Nelson."

"Evan Nepean, Esq."

In his lordship's private letter to Earl Spencer, of the same date, which accompanied the dispatches to England, he thus expresses himself—"I certainly, from having only a left hand, cannot enter into details which may explain the motives that actuate my conduct, and which may be necessary for a commanding officer who may wish to have every subject of duty detailed by those under his command. My principle, my dear lord, is—to assist in driving the French to the devil, and in restoring peace and happiness to mankind. I feel, that I am fitter to do the action, than to describe it; therefore, briefly, all the French being forced to quit this kingdom, and some order restored, two more ships of the line are to sail this evening for Minorca, which I will take care of." Having thus demonstrated that he was embracing the earliest opportunity to comply with Lord Keith's former orders, his lordship proceeds to state that he is going to send five hundred marines, with six hundred excellent Swiss, for the attack of Civita Vecchia, and to assist the insurrection in the Roman state: the sea part of this business to be under the direction of Captain Louis of the Minotaur, and the land part under Captain Hallowell of the Swiftsure; assisted by an excellent officer, Captain Cresswell of the marines, whom it has been necessary to give the temporary rank of major, which he wishes the board to confirm. His lordship also trusts to the earl's goodness, for the promotion of Lieutenant Compton. At the time of writing this letter, Lord Nelson had not heard that the French and Spanish fleets were returning to Brest; for he congratulates the earl on the happy arrival of the combined fleets at Cadiz; having, he says, been fearful that, as they had escaped the vigilance of Lord Keith, they would get to Brest. On the state of affairs at Naples, his lordship remarks that, his Sicilian Majesty, having settled a certain degree of order, will return to Palermo on the 7th. "I send you," adds his lordship, "a letter of Sir John Acton to me, which gives reasons for continuing the cardinal at the head of affairs in this country. My opinion of him has never altered. He is now only lieutenant-general of the kingdom; with a council of eight, without whose consent no act is valid: but, we know, the head of every board must have great weight. This man must soon be removed; for all about him have been, and are, so corrupt, that there is nothing which may not be bought. Acton, and Belmonte, seem to me the only uncorrupted men in the kingdom."

Lord Nelson's opinion of Cardinal Ruffo has been already seen, in his letter to Captain Troubridge: his lordship used facetiously to denominate him, the Great Devil who commanded the Christian Army; and, though he did not seriously think him a traitor, he probably considered him as not altogether incorruptible. To an ambitious cardinal, the tiara might have proved a dangerous temptation.

Captain Louis, who had been sent to the French governor of the fortress of Gaieta, with the terms of capitulation entered into between Lord Nelson and the commandant of Capua for the surrender of Gaieta, was to have immediate possession of the gates; and, within twenty-four hours, to embark the garrison. Some objections, however, being raised by the governor, which he expressed in writing, Captain Louis was induced to send them to his lordship; who instantly returned, for answer, that he was hurt, and surprised, the capitulation had not been complied with. "It shall be," said his lordship, "and the commander has agreed to it. I have not read your paper inclosed. You will execute my orders, or attack it. The Fellow ought to be kicked, for his impudence."

This French governor, it seems, with true Gallic insolence, had the audacity to require, among other unreasonable conditions, that they should embark horses for France, as well as carry away all the pillaged property; but Lord Nelson was not thus to be trifled with. "The greatest care," said his lordship, in a letter of the 3d of August, to Captain Darby, "is to be taken that no property, which they did not bring with them into the country can be theirs, or is suffered to be carried away. We are to send them to France: and will, properly; but, not as they dictate. As to horses, it is nonsense; as well might they say— *We will carry a house*! If the fellow is a scoundrel, he must be threshed."

A letter of this date, however, from Captain Louis, informed his lordship that the matter was settled; in answer to which, he thus expresses himslef—"i was sorry that you had entered into any altercation with the scoundrel. The capitulation once signed, there could be no room for dispute. There is no way of dealing with a Frenchman, but to knock him down. To be civil to them, is only to be laughed at, when they are enemies."

We tremble, in this age of refinement, for the fate of so rough a sentiment; but, perhaps, we ought rather to tremble for that of the age which is become so refined. It will, at least, not be disputed, by posterity, that no man ever knew better than Lord Nelson, how to deal properly with Frenchmen.

Besides assisting the councils of his Sicilian Majesty, with regard to the necessary arrangements for Naples, Lord Nelson was actively engaged in making a proper distribution of the squadron under his command, and directing the various operations already commenced, or in immediate contemplation. He had already ordered the Bellerophon, Captain Darby, and the Zealous, Captain Hood, to Minorca: and Captain Martin, in the Northumberland, was now detached, with the San Leon, Captain Harward, with orders to proceed off Civita Vecchia; looking out for Captain Nisbet of the Thalia, who had been seen cruizing off that place, and was to join them. From thence, Captain Martin had instructions to proceed into Leghorn Roads, and send a boat on shore for intelligence respecting the affairs of the north of Italy, and the situation of the allied armies: and, should he fall in with Captain Foote, of the Seahorse, to take that officer under his orders; and, proceeding to the Gulph of Genoa, co-operate with Field-Marshal Suwarrow, for the annoyance of the enemy, and the good of the common cause.

The following kind letter, which was written by Lord Nelson to Captain Nisbet, at this period, will evince the truly paternal anxiety which his lordship felt for the welfare of his son-in-law,

"Foudroyant, Naples Bay,
3d August 1799.

"MY DEAR SIR,

"I herewith inclose you a letter received some days ago: and, on
the receipt of this, you will keep a good look out for the
Northumberland, who is coming your way; and join her as soon as you

can, Captain Martin having letters for you. I am sorry to find, you have been cruizing off Civita Vecchia; I was in hopes of your being on the north coast of Italy: but, I am persuaded, it was done for the best. I here inclose you the copy of a letter, sent open to me, from Mr. Smith, at Constantinople; respecting some supplies furnished La Bonne Citoyenne, at the Dardanelles: and request, that you will give the necessary directions to have it settled; or explain it to me, that it may be settled. Mr. Tyson has written to the purser, Mr. Isaacson, to desire he will draw out bills for the amount; and fresh vouchers for your signature, and the settlement of his account.

"I am, wishing you every success, your's very affectionately,

"Nelson."

"Captain Nisbet."

This letter cannot require any comment; it must produce decisive convictions in the mind of every intelligent reader, respecting the true characteristics of both parties. It forms, indeed, a genuine picture of paternal solicitude.

On the 5th of August, Lord Nelson wrote to inform Lord Keith, as well as Earl Spencer and the Board of Admiralty, that being then about to proceed, in the Foudroyant, with his Sicilian Majesty on board, for Palermo; and, finding it necessary the command of the squadron in Naples Bay, and along the coast, should be left with an officer above the rank of post-captain—especially, as the Russian and Turkish squadrons were soon expected in the bay—he had thought it right to give Captain Troubridge an order to wear a broad red pendant at the main top-gallant mast-head of the Culloden, which he hoped their lordships would, respectively, approve and confirm.

Having thus generously promoted his friend Troubridge, he left under the command of the new commodore, besides the Culloden, the Audacious, Goliath, and Swiftsure, British line of battle ships, with two Portuguese, and smaller vessels of war: directing him to co-operate with Cardinal Ruffo, the lieutenant-general of the kingdom of Naples, in all things necessary for it's safety, and the peace and quiet of the capital; with liberty, should he find it necessary, to detach a part of the squadron along the Roman coast, to the northward, as far as Leghorn, in order to prevent the French from carrying off the plunder of Rome.

This and every other requisite arrangement being completed, for the peace and security of his Sicilian Majesty's Neapolitan dominions, and the due distribution of the British squadron under Lord Nelson's command, his lordship immediately sailed for Palermo, with the king and his principal ministers, and his friends Sir William and Lady Hamilton; all impatient personally to acquaint the queen with the particulars of those joyful events which had filled every bosom with sensations of the purest delight. Her majesty, indeed, had been regularly apprised of the various transactions, immediately as they occurred: but, in an affair of such variety and importance as the recovery of a wrested kingdom from foreign and domestic enemies, ten thousand little occurrences, often most powerfully interesting to souls of genuine grandeur, and forming the chief charm for minds of a delicate and tender susceptibility, may be supposed to have attracted those who were present amidst these impressive scenes, absolutely incommunicable by the most practised and facile pen, and only to be successfully detailed with the many adventitious aids of personal elocution. The feelings of the king, as he benignantly eyed his noble benefactors; of the illustrious hero, and his two estimable friends, who were the honoured objects of his majesty's just regards; must be left to the conception of the reader: it would be difficult to decide, which enjoyed, on this occasion, the greatest portion of substantial felicity; the grateful monarch thus happily restored to his rightful throne, or the generous friends who had so disinterestedly and successfully accomplished the arduous task of replacing him.

Fraught with these dignified sentiments, they no sooner arrived off Palermo, on the 8th inst. than the queen, and royal offspring, sympathetically replete with equally exalted sensations, and who had impatiently awaited the happy return of his majesty, came out, in the royal barge; attended by innumerable pleasure-boats filled with loyal Sicilians of all ranks, who hailed their beloved sovereign with acclamations of the sincerest joy. Her majesty, overwhelmed with delight, no sooner got on board the Foudroyant, than she embraced Lady Hamilton, who had respectfully hastened to receive the queen; and, at the same instant, hung round her ladyship's neck a rich chain of gold, to which was suspended a beautiful portrait of herself, superbly set in diamonds, with the motto—"Eterna Gratitudine!"—"Eternal Gratitude!"—inscribed at the back of the picture. To Lord Nelson, her majesty also united with the king in the highest degree of grateful regard which it is possible for language to convey. He was addressed as their preserver, their deliverer, their restorer; and it was easy to perceive that, even when they were silent, their great minds meditated some noble reward. Nor were the substantial services of Sir William Hamilton, though of a less brilliant nature than those of his heroic friend, passed over without the most grateful acknowledgments of their Sicilian Majesties; whose interests that wise and worthy minister had uniformly promoted, for a long series of years, with a zeal little less ardent than that which he is well known to have constantly exerted for the honour and advantage of his own sovereigns, whom himself and lady so splendidly and munificently represented at the Neapolitan court.

A few days after their arrival at Palermo, Lord Nelson received the royal remuneration of his transcendent services, in a stile far surpassing any expectation which his lordship could possibly have formed on the subject; and of which, so rare is any excess of human gratitude, history scarcely affords a single similar instance.

Indeed, when Lady Hamilton, by desire of the Queen of Naples, first announced to his lordship, on the second day after their arrival, that it was the determination of his Sicilian Majesty to create him Duke of Bronte, and to confer on him all the valuable estate and princely privileges attached to that most distinguished and appropriate title; such were his lordship's nice notions of honour, that he positively protested against receiving any reward from that sovereign, for what he considered as a mere faithful discharge of the duty which he owed to his own. It was not the formal "Nolo episcopari!"—"I am unwilling to become a bishop, or to take on myself the episcopal character!"—of every new bishop; who is injudiciously constrained, by a singular perversion of propriety, to prepare for the exercise of the most sacred of all functions, by making a declaration which, though it ought, in a spiritual sense, to be strictly correct, is extremely subject, at best, to be considered as not altogether sincere: but, in truth, the spontaneous and felt sense of that dignified delicacy of honourable conduct, by which his lordship was ever directed; and of which persons of vulgar intellect, who are by no means fitted to form any just estimate of the actions of so exalted a character, will probably be weak enough still to doubt the actual existence. It is certain, nevertheless, that Lord Nelson resolutely held out against the acceptance of these elevated dignities, and their annexed emoluments, for two or three days, at least, notwithstanding all the intreaties of Sir William and Lady Hamilton: nor did this incomparable man finally agree to receive them—maintaining, to the last, that he could not do so without subjecting the purity of his motives, in what he had happily effected, to the opprobrium of unjust suspicion—till Lady Hamilton, at the express instance of the queen, solicited the inflexible hero, even on her knees, to consent to the wishes of these truly amiable and most munificent sovereigns; as requisite to demonstrate that, amidst the too rigid sense which he evidently entertained of what might seem to him proper for the maintenance of his own honour, he was not altogether unregardful of what the world, as well as themselves, must ever consider as absolutely necessary for the preservation of their's. The exquisite address of this argument, as suggested by her Sicilian Majesty, and pressed by the unaffected eloquence of her ladyship, was too powerful to be opposed. His lordship could offer nothing sufficiently substantial against such persuasive wisdom; and, being unable longer to reason, he could no longer continue to resist. Should the scornful insolence, that is ever awakened, in low and vicious minds, by even the slightest mention of virtuous deeds, endeavour to interpose the mean malignity of it's cold suspicions on hearing this recital; let the humbler bosom, that cherishes more generous sentiments, reflect but for a moment, that his lordship had recently risked even a disobedience of orders from his temporary commander in chief, while promoting the interests of their Neapolitan Majesties, and it will feel sufficient reasons for our hero's delicate repugnance to the ready acceptance of any undesired aggrandizement, however highly merited, on this particular occasion.

On the 13th, therefore, in consequence of this acquiescence, the King of Naples sent his lordship a superb diamond-hilted sword, with a most affectionate letter; thanking him for having reconquered his majesty's kingdom, and again placed him on the throne of his ancestors. The value of this present, estimated at four thousand guineas, was incalculably enhanced by the very appropriate circumstance of it's being the identical sword which had been given to the King of Naples, by Charles the Third, on that monarch's memorable departure to Spain, accompanied by the following most remarkable declaration—"With this sword, I conquered the kingdom which I now resign to thee. It ought, in future, to be possessed by the first defender of the same; or, by him who shall restore it to thee, in case it should ever be lost." At the same time, Lord Nelson received an official letter from his Excellency the Prince Di Luzzi, informing him that his Sicilian Majesty had that day been graciously pleased to create his lordship Duke of Bronte, in Sicily, and to confer on him all the valuable estate and privileges attached to that most honourable title.

When it is considered, that the word *Bronte* signifies, in the Greek language, *Thunder*; that the fabulous forger of the thunder of Jupiter was said to be one of the Cyclops, named *Bronte*, who resided at Etna in the Island of Sicily, where the Dukedom of Bronte is situated; and that the military guard of honour, appertaining to the Dukes of Bronte, still actually wear, in allusion to the fabled Cyclops, sons of Neptune and Amphitrite, who had one large eye in the middle of their foreheads, the representation of an eye on the front of their caps; there could not, every person must admit, have been a more appropriate dignity bestowed on our incomparable hero, by his Sicilian Majesty, than that which he had thus liberally and judiciously been induced to confer.

Lord Nelson, penetrated with unutterable gratitude, by his majesty's most generous munificence, instantly wrote the following letter to the minister who had made this interesting communication.

"Palermo, 13th August 1799.

"SIR,

"I have this moment received the honour of your excellency's letter, conveying to me his Sicilian Majesty's most gracious approbation of my conduct; and, also, that his majesty had been pleased to confer upon me the title of Duke of Bronte, together with the estate attached to it. I request that your excellency will lay me, with all humility, and full of gratitude, at his majesty's feet: express, to him, my attachment to his sacred person, the queen, and royal family; and that it shall be the study of my life, by following the same conduct which has gained me his royal favours, to merit the continuance of them.

"I sincerely thank your excellency for the very handsome manner in which you have executed the royal commands; and believe me, with the highest respect, your excellency's most obliged and obedient servant,

"Bronte Nelson".

"His Excellency Prince Di Luzzi."

Immediately after, his lordship penned also the following admirable letter for the sovereign by whom he had been thus bountifully honoured, which was instantly transmitted to that generous monarch.

"Palermo, 13th August 1799.

"SIRE,

The bounty of your majesty has so overwhelmed me, that I am unable to find words adequate to express my gratitude: but it shall be my study to continue in the same line of conduct which your majesty has been pleased to approve, and to mark with such very extraordinary proofs of your royal favour; and which has also gained me the approbation of my own most gracious sovereign, your majesty's most faithful ally. That the Almighty may pour down his choicest blessings on your sacred person, and on those of the queen and the whole royal family, and preserve your kingdoms in peace and happiness, shall ever be the fervent prayer of your majesty's faithful servant,
Bronte Nelson.
On the morning of this day, while Lady Hamilton was at the palace with the queen, who had purposely invited that lady early, two coach loads of the most mag-

nificent and costly dresses, were secretly sent to her house, with a richly jewelled picture of the king, worth a thousand guineas, for her ladyship; and another picture of his majesty, of the same value, for Sir William Hamilton. The whole of the presents on this occasion received by Sir William and his lady, from their Sicilian Majesties, were estimated at full six thousand guineas.

Lord Nelson had, in these few days, so completely detached the squadron under his command to the several destinations, that his own flag was now flying on board the Samuel and Jane transport; yet, even thus situated, so confident were their majesties, and their Sicilian subjects, that there could be nothing to fear while they possessed even the person of our invincible hero, not the smallest alarm was either felt or expressed on the occasion.

The Foudroyant, indeed, which had accompanied two Portuguese ships of the line to Captain Ball at Malta, was only intended to remain there a few days, with some hope of quickening the surrender of that island by the appearance of such a force; and, on the 14th, his Sardinian Majesty having requested a ship to carry him and his family to the continent, in a letter received from his minister by our grand protector of kings, his lordship was constrained to order the Foudroyant on that important service. This letter also solicited the kind and powerful interference of our hero, to obtain, from the Bey of Tunis, some modification of the very severe terms to which his Sardinian Majesty had been under the necessity of agreeing, but found it impossible immediately to raise the sum stipulated from his distressed people for the ransom of their fellow-subjects. Though his lordship could not but feel almost hopeless of success in any requisition of pecuniary forbearance from a Barbary State, he did not hesitate a single moment in making the attempt, by writing both to Mr. Magra and the Bey of Tunis, with his customary diplomatic dexterity and address. Having done this, his lordship thus answered the letter of his Sardinian Majesty's minister, Count Chilembert.

"Palermo, 16th August 1799.

"SIR

"I was yesterday honoured with your excellency's letter of August 11th. The situation of the poor people taken by the Bey of Tunis is shocking to humanity, and must sensibly touch the royal heart: but I will not attempt to cherish a hope, that the bey will abate one zequin of the sum fixed in the convention of June the 21st; and I very much doubt, if a longer time than that fixed by the convention, and witnessed by six friendly consuls, will be granted. However, I have, I can assure your excellency, no difficulty in sending a letter to Mr. Magra, his Britannic Majesty's consul, covering one to the bey; to say, that I am confident such a mark of his goodness will be highly acceptable to the great king, my master.

The Chevalier Marechal is gone towards Malta, after the Foudroyant; and, I hope, she will be at Cagliari in three days after this letter: I have, therefore, only to intreat, that every thing for the service of his majesty may be ready to put on board the moment she anchors. I send the Foudroyant, as she is my own flag-ship, and the first two-decked ship in the world. I would send more ships, but the service of the civilized world requires every exertion; therefore, I have not the power to send another ship of war. A very fine brig I have directed from Naples, to assist in carrying his majesty's attendants; and, as a much less ship has carried a much more numerous royal family, I trust, their majesties will not be pressed for room. I beg that your excellency will lay me at their majesties feet, and assure them of my sincere desire to be useful for their service; and believe me, with the greatest respect, your excellency's most obedient servant,

"Bronte Nelson.

"There is a Russian squadron in the bay; but they are not, in the smallest degree, under my orders."

"His Excellency Compte Chilembert."

The Russian squadron mentioned in the above postscript had arrived at Palermo the preceding day, as appears from the following letter to the celebrated Russian general, Field-Marshal Suwarrow.

"Palermo, 16th Aug. 1799.

"MY DEAR FIELD-MARSHAL,

"Yesterday, brought me your excellency's letter of July 30th; and four galliots are ordered, by his Sicilian Majesty, to protect provisions, &c. for the use of your army, under the orders of my friend Captain Martin. I have ordered another frigate and brig to join the squadron on the Riviere of Genoa. I wish, I could come to you myself; I shall truly have a pleasure in embracing a person of your exalted character; but, as that cannot be at present, I only regret I cannot send you more ships. Rear-Admiral Katzow is here, with three sail of the line and a frigate; but, they are not under my orders or *influence*. May God bless you, my honoured friend! and believe me, for ever, your attached friend,

"Bronte Nelson."

In a long letter, of this day's date, to Admiral Duckworth, Lord Nelson says—"In Naples, every thing is quiet; but the cardinal appears to be working mischief against the king, and in support of the nobles: sooner, or later, he must be removed, for his bad conduct. We are dying with heat, and the feast of Santa Roselia begins this day; how shall we get through it!" Then, mentioning the honours and gifts from the King of Naples, his lordships says, respecting the dukedom of Bronte, "the title, of course, I cannot assume, without the approbation of our king; which, I now hear, has been some time desired." His lordship, it appears, had just received medals for his captains; for he says—

> "Darby and Hood, I hope, have long joined you. Pray, be so good as to deliver to them the medals, with my best regards. Our dear lady," he adds, "has been very unwell: and, if this fete, to-night, does not kill her, I dare say she will write to you to-morrow; for, there is none she respects more than yourself. Good Sir William is much better for his trip. Make my best regards to Sir James St. Clair. I really have not the power of writing, and I am really blind; but, whilst I have life," concludes this excellent, indefatigable, and friendly hero, "believe me, my dear admiral, your obliged and affectionate
>
> "Nelson."

His lordship might well be weary, on this sultry day; the festivity of which he so little regarded, that he was actually employed, from morning till night, in writing and dictating letters and orders. In the evening of this day, Lord Nelson received information that the Russian and Turkish squadrons, from Corfu, had arrived at Messina; and, on the 18th, sent the copy of a letter just received from Lord Keith, who had quitted the Mediterranean in pursuit of the combined fleets, to Admiral Uschakoff, commander in chief of the Russian squadron, who had retaken the Leander at Corfu, mentioning an order from the British Admiralty for the restoration of that ship. His lordship, however, not having received this order, apologized for being unable to send it: and stated, very properly, that it was to be presumed the courts of Petersburgh and London had decided on the restoration of the Leander; as the Admiralty would not, otherwise, have sent such orders to the commander in chief, and appointed officers to that ship. Captain Drummond, his lordship observed, who would wait on his excellency with these letters, was appointed to the temporary command of the Leander; and requested that he might be favoured with directions to the officer commanding at Corfu, for assistance in fitting out and manning the said ship, so as to enable him to proceed with it to Minorca.

On the 19th, his lordship wrote to Commodore Troubridge, acquainting him that Lord Keith was in pursuit of the combined fleets, which had been seen off Cape St. Vincent's the 24th of July; that the British fleet passed the Straits on the 30th; and that the Earl of St. Vincent sailed for England, in the Argo, on the 31st. His lordship also mentions, that he has just received great news from Egypt. The siege of Acre was raised on the 21st of May; and Bonaparte, leaving all his cannon and sick behind, had got again to Cairo. The La Forte French frigate had been taken by the English La Sybille, but that poor Captain Coote had been killed; "and here," says his lordship, "we must shed a tear for dear Miller! By an explosion of shells, which he was preparing on board the Theseus, him and twenty-five others were killed; nine drowned, by jumping overboard; and forty-three wounded." After observing that, if Commodore Troubridge cannot immediately proceed against Civita Vecchia, he is to collect all his ships; and, the moment the Russians appear, to join his lordship, for the purpose of proceeding to Gibraltar, by the way of Palermo, where the necessary provisions may be obtained—"Your letter of the 13th," he concludes, "is just arrived. The Neapolitans must manage their own Jacobins; we have, thank God, done with them."

Sir Sidney Smith having transmitted to Lord Nelson, as his superior in command, the account of his splendid atchievements in the defence of Acre, and the total defeat and discomfiture of Bonaparte on that memorable occasion, his lordship immediately wrote the following congratulatory epistle to Sir Sidney; whose important dispatches he afterwards forwarded to England, accompanied by a public letter to Mr. Nepean, as they were afterwards published in the London Gazette.

"Palermo, 20th Aug. 1799.

"MY DEAR SIR,

"I have received, with the truest satisfaction, all your very interesting letters to July 16th. The immense fatigue you have had, in defending Acre against such a chosen army of French villains, headed by that arch-villain Bonaparte, has never been exceeded; and the bravery shewn by you, and your brave companions, is such as to merit every encomium which all the civilized world can bestow. As an individual, and as an admiral, will you accept of my feeble tribute of praise and admiration, and make them acceptable to all those under your command? I have returned the Cameleon, that your lieutenant might have a good sloop; which, I hope, Lord Keith will approve: and, in every thing in my junior situation in the fleet, you may be assured of my readiness to do what you can wish me. I hope, Alexandria is long before this in your possession, and the final blow given to Bonaparte; but, I hope, no terms will ever be granted for his individual return to Europe. Captain Stiles will tell you all our news here; and good Sir William Hamilton tells me, he thinks that he has told you the heads of all. In short, all is well, if Lord Keith falls in with the combined fleet. I think, you had better order the Theseus to Mahon; and I will endeavour to send you either a good sloop, or a small frigate. The factory at Smyrna, in my opinion, have written a very improper letter to you. I do not like the general stile of Mr. Wherry's letters, they too much talk of government affairs. It is our duty to take care of the Smyrna trade, as well as all other, and it never has yet been neglected; but Great Britain, extensive as her navy is, cannot afford to have one ship lay idle. Be assured, my dear Sir Sidney, of my perfect esteem and regard, and do not let any one persuade you to the contrary: but my character is, that I will not suffer the smallest tittle of my command to be taken from me. But, with pleasure, I give way to my friends; among whom, I beg, you will allow me to consider you: and, that I am, with the truest esteem and affection, your, &c.

"Nelson.

"Sir Sidney Smith."

This excellent letter not only makes amends for all former asperities, but forms a most noble eulogium on the merits of Sir Sidney Smith; who, it must be confessed, had entitled himself, by his skill and valour, even to this proudest of all possible panegyrics from the first of heroes.

The Russian admiral not complying with Lord Nelson's request, as to the restoration of the Leander, his lordship immediately addressed the Chevalier Italinskoy, the Russian minister at the court of their Sicilian Majesties, on the subject: informing him that, whenever the admiral chose to send the Leander to Minorca, the ship would be received. "But," says his lordship, "after even my word not being taken, by his excellency, I cannot again subject myself to a refusal of giving up the Leander, agreeable to the intention of the emperor; though the form of order, on this occasion, was not arrived." His lordship also sent Captain Drummond, with the particulars of this refusal, to Lord Keith; observing, that he should now wait till the Russian admiral sent the Leander to Mahon. Captain Drummond was desired, on failure of meeting with Lord Keith, to proceed immediately to England, and deliver his lordship's letter to the secretary of the Admiralty, acquainting him with the cause of his arrival.

On the 28th, Lord Nelson transmitted to Captain Hope, at the request of his Sicilian Majesty, a diamond ring of considerable value: for having, as it was expressly stated, embarked his Majesty and the Prince Royal in his barge, on the night of December 21, 1798; and which his majesty desired might be accepted, by Captain Hope, as a mark of his royal gratitude. This, and other similar presents of rings and gold boxes, were sent by Sir John Acton, to Sir William Hamilton, from his Sicilian Majesty; with a request that his excellency would have the goodness to present them to the Duke of Bronte, that he might distribute them according to the note enclosed, and in the name of his Sicilian Majesty, as a small mark of his royal gratitude to the several English commanders. The pleasure which this agreeable task afforded Lord Nelson's excellent heart, may be judged of by the following effusion of it's feelings, addressed to Captain Hood on the occasion. "My dear Hood, I never had greater pleasure, than in executing his Sicilian Majesty's orders, for sending you a box from his majesty; and, as the dispatch expresses it—To Captain Hood, for services in the Gulph of Naples, and at Salerno; for his operations on shore, and his care of the castles of Naples." In afterwards describing these presents from his

Sicilian Majesty, on writing to England, his lordship informs Mr. Nepean, that each of the captains had a very valuable gold box, set round with diamonds. In the centre of that given to Commodore Troubridge, was his majesty's portrait; and, to him, he also gave an elegant ring. In the centre of the others, were his majesty's cypher of f.r. neatly set in diamonds. His majesty, he adds, has also presented Captain Thomas Masterman Hardy, his lordship's captain in the Foudroyant, with an elegant box, set round with a double row of diamonds, and his portrait in the centre, and an elegant diamond ring; and, to Mr. Tyson, his lordship's secretary, a diamond ring of great value.

Transient, however, seem to have been all the felicities of his lordship's most eventful life. The happiness which he enjoyed, in seeing the companions of his cares and successes thus rewarded with truly royal munificence; while he felt himself remunerated, beyond his proudest hope or expectation; the pleasing sensations which he must necessarily have experienced on beholding the vast and magnificent preparations to celebrate their united atchievments on the anniversary of receiving, at Naples, the first intelligence of the glorious victory off the Nile, which had arrived on the 3d of the preceding September; were not permitted to remain undisturbed in his ever anxious bosom, even for a few days.

On the 31st, his lordship received letters from Malta, which gave birth to most extraordinary suspicions. The agonized feelings of his heroic mind are not to be described; but, nothing could for a moment divert him from the painful discharge of it's duty. In a state of inconceivable agitation, he wrote the following letter to Sir John Acton.

"Palermo, 31st Aug. 1799.

"MY DEAR SIR,

"I send your excellency a letter from Captain Ball, of his majesty's ship Alexander, with two papers enclosed. I cannot bear the thought of what the papers convey; but it is my duty, as a British admiral, to ask of your excellency an explanation of this very extraordinary business--which, I trust in God, is entirely false, as far as relates to his Sicilian Majesty and Prince Luzzi! If this man is an unauthorized person, his majesty will have no difficulty in approving of my condemning him as a spy; and, as such, ordering him to be hanged. But, what shall I say, if Prince Luzzi has authorized this man to enter La Vilette, and to communicate with the enemy? I must say, that the minister has betrayed his trust; for I never will believe, that their Sicilian Majesties could treat in such a manner his Britannic Majesty, my royal master. On your excellency's communication of his Sicilian Majesty's pleasure, depends the line of conduct which my duty will call upon me to perform. I have the honour to be, with the greatest respect, your excellency's obedient servant,

"Bronte Nelson."

"His Excellency, Sir John Acton, Bart."

Happily, this alarm turned out to be unfounded; but the circumstance serves, nevertheless, to assist in demonstrating the jealous attention of his lordship to whatever might be supposed capable of affecting either the national honour or his own. In a few days, having fully investigated the affair, he wrote thus to Captain Ball—"My dear Ball, Mr. Alos is, doubtless, a scoundrel. He had persuaded some here, that he had an interview with Vaubois; which, I believe, is a lie: and, as to his conduct with the Maltese, it was, probably, to shew his consequence. I am sure, the good queen never had a thought of any under-hand work against us; therefore, I would recommend sending him here with a kick in the breech, and let all the matter drop."

In a letter of this date, August 31, Lord Nelson thus laments, to Commodore Troubridge, the situation in which he finds himself. "Our joint exertions," he says, "have been used, to get the king to go to Naples; but, of no avail; the Austrians will be there before him. I do not expect any of the Russian troops this some time to come. I am, indeed, sick and tired of this want of energy; and, when I find the impossibility of being longer useful, I will retire from this inactive service." He complains, also, to Lord Spencer, in a letter written about this time, of the uncomfortableness of his situation: for, he says, plain common sense points out that the king should return to Naples; but, nothing can move him. "Believe me," his lordship adds, "I shall do my best, in all circumstances. But, I am almost blind; and, truly, very unwell; and, which does not mend matters, I see no king in Europe really assisting these good monarchs, but our gracious sovereign."

In this unenviable state of mental anxiety, and corporeal lassitude, was our justly renowned hero, at the period of those preparations being completed, which were calculated to display him, in the view of an enraptured people, as the greatest and most felicitous of mortals; nor did his admirable heart, amidst all it's oppressions, reject a temporary participation in the bliss which was so amply provided for his enjoyment,

On the 3d of September, their Sicilian Majesties gave their splendid Fete Champetre in the royal gardens at Palermo, to celebrate the recovery of the kingdom of Naples under the auspices of Lord Nelson. A grand temple of Fame was erected, on this occasion; in which were three figures, the size and exact resemblance of life, beautifully modelled in wax. The centre figure represented Admiral Lord Nelson, Duke of Bronte, dressed in a full British uniform; as conducted, by a figure of Sir William Hamilton, to receive from the hand of a third, resembling Lady Hamilton in the character of Victory, the laurel wreath of triumph which adorned the hero's brow. Before the steps of this temple, their Sicilian Majesties, with all the royal family, stood ready to receive the three illustrious characters thus represented; and, on their approach, after publicly embracing them, the king, with his own hand, took the laurel wreath from the wax figure, and placed it on the head of the real hero, who wore it during the whole of the entertainment. Sir William, and his lady, were also presented with similar investments; the queen thus honouring her ladyship, and his majesty Sir William. On the robe of the figure of Victory were embroidered the names of all those heroes, in particular, who had fought at the battle of the Nile; and, on various Egyptian pyramids, placed around the several temples of the garden, were inscribed the names of the most distinguished English, Neapolitan, Russian, and Turkish, heroes of the war, with appropriate verses to each. Their majesties received the company; which consisted of some of the principal nobility of Naples as well as of Palermo, with all the British, Russian, and Turkish, officers of the respective squadrons. Prince Leopold, their majesties youngest surviving son, then nine years of age, who was educating for the navy, did the honours of the evening, in his midshipman's uniform: and all the three princesses, as well as the consort of the hereditary prince, and most other ladies, wore some ornament allusive to Lord Nelson and his victories round their necks. The entertainment commenced with a most brilliant and magnificent fire-work: representing the English and French fleets at Aboukir, the ever-memorable battle off the Nile, and the total defeat of the French; terminating with the explosion of L'Orient, and the blowing up of the tri-coloured flag. The queen, at this representation, said to Cadir Bey, the Turkish admiral—"On this day, last year, we received from Lady Hamilton intelligence of this great man's victory; which not only saved your country, and our's, but all Europe!" After the fire-works, a cantata was performed, entitled the Happy Concord. This piece, which was written purposely on the occasion, expressed the general joy for the deliverance of the two Sicilies; loyal wishes for the prosperity of their sovereigns, and the royal family, as well as for those of their worthy allies; and particular acknowledgments to the British hero. The music was most excellent; and all the opera band, with Senesino at their head, sung—"Rule Britannia!" and "God save the King!" in which they were joined by the whole assembly, who had been previously drilled to the English pronunciation.

About the time of this grand festival, an unfortunate affray between the Turkish seamen and some of the Sicilians, occurred at a tavern, in Palermo; and was carried to such an excess, that many men of both countries lost their lives on the occasion. The quarrel originated in the superstition of the Sicilians; who, like all the vulgar Italians, when they address the Turks, rudely tell them, that they are not Christians, but beasts. The Turks, after getting on board their ships, continued to wrangle among themselves; and were, at length, in such a state of mutiny, that Cadir Bey, their commander in chief, became greatly terrified. Lord Nelson, however, being made acquainted with the affair, and having a great friendship for this Turkish admiral, immediately offered him his services; and, the next day, very calmly going on board, accompanied by Sir William and Lady Hamilton, speedily quelled the mutiny. It appears, however, to have soon again broken out: having been excited, it is said, by Patrona Bey, who was desirous of supplanting Cadir Bey; but who, not very long afterwards, had rendered himself so obnoxious to the men whom he thus endeavoured to delude, that they suddenly rose on him, and literally cut him to pieces. It was well, therefore, that the generous friendship of Lord Nelson had impelled him to pen a letter to the Grand Signior, previously to Cadir Bey's departure, that he might protect this worthy man from any misrepresentation respecting the fatal affray with the Sicilians; as, without such a powerful advocate, it is highly probable that Cadir Bey would have lost his situation, if not his life: instead of which, he obtained the merited approbation of the Grand Signior, by this epistle; which was inclosed in a letter to the Captain Pacha—and a copy of it also sent to Spencer Smith, Esq. the minister at Constantinople—of the same date. The letter to the Grand Signior was expressed in the following terms.

"Palermo, 10th Sept. 1799.

"SIRE,

"I trust, that your Imperial Majesty will permit the servant of your most faithful ally to bear his testimony to the good conduct of your Admiral Cadir Bey.

"I can assure your majesty, that ships in higher order cannot be, than those under his command; and the little disturbance which has arose in this place has not been owing to any want of attention from your majesty's admiral.

"Cadir Bey is with me every day; and a better man does not live in the world, or a better officer. He is my brother; and I am, in the truest sense of the words, your majesty's attached and faithful servant,

"Bronte Nelson."

"To his Imperial Majesty, the Grand Signior."

His lordship, in writing to Earl Spencer, a few days before, thus states the difference between the Russian and Turkish commanders in chief. "The Russian admiral," says he, "has a polished outside, but the bear is close to the skin: he is jealous of our influence; and thinks, whatever is proposed, that we are at the bottom. The Turk, who is by no means a fool, on the contrary, has more natural sense than the other; is our brother; and, I am sure, there is not a thing that we could desire him to do, which he would not instantly comply with. I make use of the word *we*," adds his lordship; "because Sir William and Lady Hamilton have more merit in gaining the affection and implicit confidence of Cadir Bey, and his officers, than I have."

On the 12th, Lord Nelson writes to Rear-Admiral Duckworth—"The Russian admiral has told me, his ships *cannot* keep the sea in winter; and I see no *desire* to go to sea in summer." Then, mentioning the state of some of the ships at Minorca, reported to be unfit for active service, his lordship says—"To keep them lying at Mahon, appears to me to be a waste of public money. My mind," proceeds this great and most considerate commander, "is fixed, that I will not keep one ship in the Mediterranean, that is not fit for *any* service during the winter; those half fit, drain us of all the stores, and render us all useless: you have acted on this principle, in sending the Aurora and Dolphin; and it is my *particular* desire, that you continue it. I beg you will write to the Admiralty, of my intentions to keep no ships but what are fit for service in the Mediterranean; and, I am sure, the king will save by the measure being adopted on stations so near England. I am aware of the argument, which may be used against my plan; viz. our seamen get no good by going to England: to which, I perfectly agree. But, the ships left here with me are beyond all common refit; nor can they be furnished with stores, not having any foundation to be kept up: and what would be an ample supply to keep up a squadron, is really nothing in our situation."

To Sir James St. Clair Erskine, also at Minorca, in a letter of the 13th, his lordship writes—"I see, with pleasure, that you do not envy me my good fortune. The field of glory is a large one, and was never more open to any one, than at this moment to you. Rome would throw open her gates, and receive you as her deliverer; and the pope would owe his restoration to the papal chair to a *heretic*. This is the first great object; as it would not only be the compleat deliverance of Italy, but restore peace and tranquillity to the torn to pieces kingdom of Naples: for such an occasion, a part of the garrison of Messina might be taken. The next great object, is the reduction of Malta; and, in any other moment than the present, it would be a most important one. Vaubois only wants a pretence, to give up: his sole hope is that, in the next month, he may escape with the ships." General Fox, however, being hourly expected at Minorca, Sir James did not judge it proper to lessen the garrison; and, says his lordship, in a letter to Sir Thomas Troubridge, "enters upon the difficulty of the undertaking in a true soldier way."

These difficulties, however, were in a very few days completely surmounted by Sir Thomas Troubridge: for, on the 20th of September, a capitulation was entered into by that commander, who was then blockading Civita Vecchia, on the part of Great Britain and her allies, with the General of Division Gamier, commander in chief of the French troops, and those of Italy and other allies then in the Roman Republic in a state of siege; which terminated in the surrender of the fort and town of Civita Vecchia on the 29th in the afternoon, and of Rome and St. Angelo two hours after midnight. Civita Vecchia, Corneto, and Tolfa, containing five thousand troops, were taken into possession by two hundred marines and seamen of the Culloden and Minotaur; and General Bouchard, with the troops of his Sicilian Majesty, took possession of Rome: but the French general refused to treat with any other than a British commander.

It was the wish of Lord Nelson, that Commodore Troubridge should himself have every advantage of transmitting to England the dispatches on this occasion: being generously desirous of giving all the glory to this favourite officer; who, accordingly, wrote the following letter to Mr. Nepean.

"Civita Vecchia, 5th Oct. 1799.

"SIR,

"In obedience to orders from Lord Nelson, I have the honour to send you, for their lordships information, a copy of the articles of capitulation I have made with the French General Garnier, to clear the Roman state. As I knew the French had all the valuables of the Roman state packed up ready for embarking, and the coast of Civita

Vecchia forming a deep bay, with hard west south-west gales and a heavy sea, which prevented the blockade from being so close as was necessary to prevent the enemy from carrying off those truly valuable articles; I, therefore, thought it best to grant the liberal terms I have, to get them out of this country, where they have committed every excess possible. I trust, what I have done, may meet their lordships approbation. I beg you to represent to their lordships, that I received every assistance from Captain Louis; who went to Rome, and arranged the evacuation and taking possession of that place, with General Bouchard, with great ability and exertion, and much to my satisfaction.

I have the honour to be, &c. T. Troubridge.

Evan Nepean, Esq."

Lord Nelson informed Earl Spencer, in a private letter, as well as the Admiralty Board in a public one to Mr. Nepean, that he had desired Commodore Troubridge to send extracts of all his letters to him, as temporary commander in chief of the Mediterranean fleet, with the terms on which the French evacuated the Roman state. "I sincerely congratulate your lordship," concludes Lord Nelson to Earl Spencer, "on this event, so honourable to our country; for the French would treat with no country but Britain."

It was, certainly, a most singular circumstance, that Rome should thus be reduced by a naval force: and it appeared to be the more remarkable, as it fulfilled what was now called a prophecy, which had been pronounced on our hero's first arrival at Naples after his glorious victory off the Nile; in which it had been said, *that his lordship should take Rome by his* ships. This prophecy, however, it seems proper to remark—the author having no desire to encourage the growth of superstition, or to degrade the dignity of historical research by dazzling weak powers of perception with the fascinative influence of the marvellous—was considered, at the time of it's being pronounced, as nothing more than a mere harmless Hibernicism; originating in the zeal of Father M'Cormick, a very honest and worthy Irish priest, who had come from Rome to Naples, disgusted at the enormities of the French. This good and loyal man, in the ardent warmth of congratulating Lord Nelson on his stupendous victory, triumphantly exclaimed—"And your lordship shall, before long, take Rome, too, with your ships!" A declaration which, it may be supposed, was heard with far less gravity than it was uttered, though now converted into a prophetic anticipation of the event. This honest Irish pastor, though not regarded as a prophet by Lord Nelson, was so well known to be a pious and faithful priest, that his lordship, who was for ever studying how he could best serve all persons of merit who came in his way, afterwards recommended him to the present Pope, in a letter which was written, expressly for that purpose, by Lady Hamilton.

So active was Lord Nelson in all his operations, that he no sooner received information of the successes of Commodore Troubridge, than he instantly drew his attention to other objects. In a letter of the 1st of October, his lordship says—"If it is necessary to leave a few of your and Louis's marines, do it, and one or two of the small craft for the protection of the trade; but I want, certainly, all the line of battle ships, and such of the small craft as are not absolutely wanted there. My intention is, to go almost directly to Minorca, and arrange a proper naval defence for that island; and to try and get troops to finish the business of Malta, which the French intend to relieve. Five polacres, and two Venetian ships, are loading provisions and stores; therefore, I wish to fix our ships on the spot most likely to intercept them: at Lampedosa and Cape Bon, and in the track from Toulon to Ajaccio. These are my ideas; for, as to blockading Toulon for so few ships, they would escape, the first north-west wind, if the whole fleet was there. I need only say, to you, these are my objects, for you to support me; which it is my pleasure always to acknowledge."

His lordship afterwards repeats the full confidence which he feels, that the commodore, knowing what is necessary, will come as soon as he can; "for," says his lordship, "our business is never done."

Lord Nelson had already sent information to the Marquis De Niza respecting these supplies for Malta, which were preparing at Toulon, with directions for intercepting them; but, by letters from Lisbon, just received, the Portuguese squadron was now ordered to return home. Anxious, therefore, to prevent the intended relief from reaching Malta—over the people of which island he had, a few days before, obtained the honour, for his friend Captain Ball, of being regularly appointed Chief, by his Sicilian Majesty—he inclosed the particulars of this information to General Acton, and urged the necessity of having part of the English garrison at Messina, as well as of the Russian squadron and troops, ordered immediately to Malta; observing that, if Malta was relieved, all our forces got together could not take it, and the commencement of a new blockade would become useless. "Nor," says his lordship, "would this be the worst consequence; for all the Barbary cruizers would here have their rendezvous, and not a vessel of his Sicilian Majesty's could put to sea: and, Great Britain and Russia not being at war with those powers, the case would be dreadful, and ruinous, to the subjects of his Sicilian Majesty. I have," concludes his lordship, "stated the situation, under mature reflection; and have only to request, that it maybe taken into immediate consideration."

In the mean time, Lord Nelson wrote to the Marquis De Niza, inculcating the necessity of not obeying his orders to return home. "I have," says his lordship, "received a letter from Don Roderigo de Souza, saying that, as the squadron under your orders were not now necessary in the Mediterranean, his royal highness had directed their return. On this belief, your orders are founded; but, as the contrary is the fact—for your services were never more wanted than at this moment, when every exertion is wanting to get more troops of English and Russians to Malta—I must, therefore, most positively desire, that your excellency will not, on any consideration, withdraw one man from the shore, or detach any ship down the Mediterranean. I send you an order, to justify your excellency's not complying with his royal highness's orders; and, I am confident, he will approve of my conduct."

While his lordship was indefatigably engaged in obtaining every aid for the reduction of Malta, information arrived, that thirteen French and Spanish sail of the line, one of them a three-decker, had been seen on the coast of Portugal. He immediately, therefore, wrote to hasten Commodore Troubridge, and sent also to Sir Sidney Smith: informing them, that he should sail next day, the 5th of October, for Mahon; and, probably, to Gibraltar. "If," says his lordship, to Commodore Troubridge, "I can but get a force to fight these fellows, it shall be done quickly. I am in dread for our outward bound convoys; seven hundred sail, under a few frigates, in England, thinking all the force was at Brest. I need only say, get to Mahon as quick as possible, that we may join." Accordingly, having sailed from Palermo, he wrote the following letter to Captain Ball.

"Foudroyant, at Sea,
5th Oct. 1799.

MY DEAR BALL,

"I fervently hope, that Niza has got hold of the French ships from Toulon. As that business is over, I have only to hope the best: This day, by his Sicilian Majesty's orders, a letter is wrote to Messina, to request General Graham to get to Malta with five hundred men. The Russian Admiral is wrote to, to go with at least seven hundred. A corps of Russian grenadiers are also expected at Leghorn, for Malta. If Niza has been successful, all will end well. Ever your's, most faithfully,

"Nelson."

"I am not well; and left our dear friends, Sir William and Lady Hamilton, very unwell."

"Captain Ball, Chief of the Maltese."

His lordship had, this day, fallen in with the Salamine brig; which brought him a letter from Captain Darby at Minorca, stating that a fleet of twenty vessels, among which were two sail of the line and several frigates, had been seen steering to the south-east on the 29th of September. These, his lordship was of opinion, could only be the two Venetian ships from Toulon, with a convoy for Malta; and, as the Marquis De Niza had seven sail of the line, one frigate, and three sloops, he had hopes that the greatest part of them would be taken.

On the 12th, having arrived off Port Mahon; and left orders with Captain Darby, who had come on board the Foudroyant, for Commodore Troubridge, with some other ships to follow, his lordship proceeded on his voyage to Gibraltar. Between Port Mahon and Majorca, however, Lord Nelson fell in with the Bull-dog, ten days from Rear-Admiral Duckworth, at Gibraltar; who, giving little or no credit to the report of the ships seen off Cape Ortegal, and Sir Edward Berry, from Lisbon, assuring his lordship that the information was entirely disbelieved there, the squadron returned to Minorca.

On the 14th, his lordship wrote a long letter to Rear-Admiral Duckworth; in which are some interesting passages, relative to Captain Nisbet. "I send you down," says his lordship, "the Bellerophon; who, Darby says, and I believe truly, is in good order, and fit to stand fair winter's service. The Thalia also goes with him: I wish I could say any thing in her praise, inside or out. You will receive an order for holding a court-martial on the lieutenant of marines. Perhaps, you may be able to make something of Captain Nisbet; he has, by his conduct, almost broke my heart. The ship, I believe, wants some little matter doing to her. If so, I wish Inglefield would bring her out of the mole as soon as possible; and if, after all our pains, no good can be got out of either ship or captain, send the Thalia to England with some of the convoys; or send her any where out to try. I wished to have placed him with my friend Cockburne; but, alas! he will not let me do for him what my heart wishes." This letter mentions the propriety of getting a list of all vessels taken since the 1st of August, Lord Keith having arrived in Torbay on the 17th. Custom, his lordship observes, will point out, whether they are to be considered as the only two flag-officers in the Mediterranean; and freights of money, by the Earl of St. Vincent's acting, belong to the commander in chief. "Whether that is so, or no," says his lordship, "we shall never differ about; my only wish is, to do as I would be done by." After detailing the particulars of his proceedings since leaving Palermo, and stating his future intentions, particularly with regard to Malta, his lordship concludes with observing—"Captain Buchanan has just told me, that you wish to put two young men into the Port Mahon; and, that Lord St. Vincent had intended you should name all the officers for her. Believe me, I would not, on any consideration, do less than was intended by the earl; therefore, I beg you will send up all officers you like, and I will leave acting orders for them with Captain Buchanan."

In a letter to Mr. Nepean, dated Port Mahon, October 15, 1799, Lord Nelson also details his late proceedings and intentions with regard to Malta; which, if not speedily forced to surrender, will call for the attention of more ships than he may have the power of placing there, and necessarily cramp other requisite services.

The Chichester storeship, Captain Stevens, his lordship observes, is going with the officers of the Leander to Corfu, having now the Russian admiral's order for that ship's delivery; and he has no doubt that Captain Stevens, who appears an excellent seaman, will very soon get her to Minorca. "This island," says his lordship, "is in such a state of security as to bid defiance to any force Spain can send against it; and, if General Fox was not hourly expected, Sir James would go with me to the attack of Malta, with fifteen hundred good troops." In another letter, of the same date, addressed to Earl Spencer, his lordship says, "I have considered the security of his Sicilian Majesty's dominions as very near the heart of the king: this makes the reduction of Malta of the very utmost importance, and to accomplish which is now, in Italy, the dearest object I have in view." Lord Nelson mentions that, Sir Edward Berry having joined the Foudroyant, by the Bull-dog, he has put Captain Hardy into the Princess Charlotte; and, mustering a few men, intends taking her with him to sea. "My friend Hardy," says his lordship, "will make a man of war of her very soon; and I make it my earnest request that, if Captain Stephenson is not sent out to her, Captain Hardy may be allowed to remain in her, and receive an Admiralty commission."

This letter, too, is remarkable for containing, a request in favour of his worthy elder brother, Maurice Nelson, Esq. "I have given," says his lordship, "my brother, belonging to the Navy Office, a strong letter of recommendation to your lordship, that he may be appointed a Commissioner of the Navy. I mention the circumstance, that you may be aware such a letter is coming; and prepared, I most earnestly hope, to meet my wishes."

On the 23d of October, Lord Nelson returned to Palermo, where he found letters from Sir Sidney Smith; to which he, next day, returned the following interesting answer.

"Palermo, 24th Oct. 1799.

"MY DEAR SIR,

"When I arrived here, yesterday, from Mahon--having been down the Mediterranean to look out for a French and Spanish squadron, which had been on the coast of Portugal, but returned to Ferrol---I received all your letters by the Turkish corvette, which is arrived at Messina. The details you have given me, although unsuccessful at Aboukir, will by all military men ever reflect upon you, and your brave companions, the highest honour; and I beg you will tell all those whose conduct you have so highly approved, that their merits--even of the lowest--will be duly appreciated by me: for which reason, I have given all the promotion, and shall continue to do it, if they deserve it, amongst them. All the arrangements for your young men are filled up as you desired; and, my dear Sir, you shall ever find that, although I am jealous of having a particle of my honour abridged, yet that no commanding officer will be so ready to do every thing you wish. We have but little, here, of stores; but I have stripped the Foudroyant of every thing. At Mahon, there is nothing. But, your demands, with a bare proportion for the Theseus, goes to-morrow for Gibraltar; and, although I am pretty sure you will not receive half what your ships want, I shall urge Inglefield to send you every thing he can. You will have heard, probably, that Lord St. Vincent still retains the Mediterranean command; and that I am, by order, acting till his return: therefore, I have not the power of giving commissions, or any thing more than acting orders. As to getting Neapolitan gunboats to you, there are many reasons against it. In the first place, they have none fit for such a voyage. This is enough; but, was this not sufficient, it would be a thing impossible. I believe, we are as bad a set to deal with, for real service, as your Turks. Mr. Harding has sent me word, he does not chuse to return to Egypt; for which, he is a fool. Your brother will, of course, tell you all our good news from Holland and Germany; and, I hope, the King of Prussia has joined the coalition. May peace, with a monarchy in France, be soon given to us! I have just got a report, which appears to have some foundation, that Bonaparte has passed Corsica in a bombard, steering for France. No crusado ever returned with more humility. Contrast his going out in L'Orient, &c. Again, be assured that I place the greatest confidence in all you do; and no commanding officer shall ever have more attention to all your wants and wishes, than will your, &c.

"Nelson."

"Sir William Sidney Smith, Knt."

Lord Nelson had, also, on his return to Palermo, received a letter from his friend, Lord Minto; which, he observed in his answer, gave equal pleasure to Sir William, Lady Hamilton, and himself. "Yesterday," says his lordship, writing on the 24th, "your whole letter was read to the queen. I am charged to say every thing which is grateful, and thankful, on her majesty's behalf. But, I know, I need not say much; as she intends, I believe, to write you herself. We all have the most affectionate regard for your public and private character; and I should do injustice to my friends, was I to attempt to say my regard exceeded their's. My conduct, as your's, is to go straight and upright. Such is, thank God, the present plan of Great Britain; at least, as far as I know: for, if I thought otherwise, I should not be so faithful a servant to my country, as I know I am at present. As I shall send you my letters to Mr. Nepean and Lord Spencer, they will speak for themselves: therefore, I will only say, believe I am the same Nelson as you knew Captain of the Agamemnon; and, more than ever, your attached and faithful friend."

The pleasurable sensations excited by Lord Minto's most kind and friendly communications, were succeeded by the most racking anxieties respecting Malta. Fresh orders had arrived for the recall of the Portuguese squadron; and Captain Ball could with difficulty keep the distressed islanders from joining the French. Lord Nelson, in a state of distraction, wrote letters to the Marquis De Niza, deprecating his departure; and consoled Captain Ball with hopes of assistance, which he strained every nerve to obtain from all possible sources. The following most urgent epistle to Sir James St. Clair Erskine, on this occasion, will not only convey the state of his lordship's feelings to every intelligent reader, but elucidate the genuine principles on which his lordship ventures to advise a departure from the strictness of etiquette in the discharge of military duties.

"Palermo, 26th Oct. 1799.

"MY DEAR SIR JAMES,

"I am in desperation about Malta. We shall lose it, I am afraid, past redemption, I send you copies of Niza's and Ball's letters; also, General Acton's: so that, you will see, I have not been idle. If Ball can hardly keep the inhabitants, in hopes of relief by the five hundred men landed from our ships; what must be expected, when four hundred of them, and four sail of the line, will be withdrawn? And, if the islanders are forced again to join the French, we may not find even landing a very easy task; much less, to get again our present advantageous position. I therefore intreat, for the honour of our king, and for the advantage of the common cause, that whether General Fox is arrived, or not, at least, the garrison of Messina may be ordered to hold post in Malta, till a sufficient force can be collected to attack it; which, I flatter myself, will in time, be got together. But, while that is effecting, I fear our being obliged to quit the island; therefore, I am forced to make this representation. I know, well enough, of what officers in your situation can do. The delicacy of your feelings, on the near approach of General Fox, I can readily conceive; but, the time you know nothing about. This is a great and important moment; and the only thing to be considered-- Is his majesty's service to stand still for an instant? I have no scruple in declaring what I should do: that, knowing the importance of possessing Malta, to England and her allies; that, if even two regiments were ordered from Minorca, yet it must be considered--for which the officer must certainly be responsible--was the call for these troops known at home, would not they order them to proceed where the service near at hand so loudly calls for them? This is the only thing, in my opinion, for consideration. If we lose this opportunity, it will be impossible to recal it. If possible, I wish to take all the responsibility. I know, my dear Sir James, your zeal and ability; and, that delicacy to General Fox, has been your sole motive for not altering the disposition of the troops: but, I hope, General Fox is with you; and, I am sure, from his character, he will approve of my feelings on this subject. If he is not, I must again earnestly entreat that, at least, you will give directions for Colonel Graham to hold Malta till we can get troops to attack La Valette. May God direct your councils, for the honour of our king and his allies, and to the destruction of the French, is the fervent prayer of, &c.

"Nelson."

At the same time, addressing a letter to Commodore Troubridge, who he had reason to suppose was at Minorca, his lordship says—"My letter to Sir James St. Clair, if this finds you at Mahon, will shew you what I feel about Malta." After again describing apprehended consequences, and expressing his hope that General Fox is arrived, and that Sir James will lay all circumstances before him, his lordship continues—"I know Sir James to be a most fair, honourable, and zealous officer; and I earnestly hope, that you will have the carrying him and fifteen hundred troops to Malta. If, alas! all my arguments are in vain, against *orders—not knowing our situation here*—or the delicacy of the approach of General Fox; then, it is only for me to grieve, and intreat of you to come here, and bring the Northumberland—that, at least, I may prevent supplies getting in: and, for this purpose, I shall be under the distressing necessity of taking as many ships as possible from Minorca; which, I assure you, would hurt me very much."

On the 28th, his lordship detached the Minotaur, and even the Foudroyant, to join the Marquis De Niza off Malta; intreating him, not to withdraw a man from the island, even on the arrival of the Russians. "Again, and again," writes his lordship, "I desire—for which, you may be certain, I hold myself responsible—that you will not, on any consideration, withdraw a single man belonging to your squadron from the island."

Scarcely a day now passed, that Lord Nelson did not send some information to Captain Ball, for the purpose of inspiriting his depressed hopes in the conduct of this arduous undertaking; and, certainly, the indefatigability of his lordship, in labouring to obtain every requisite aid for the accomplishment of this important object, was impossible to be surpassed, and has probably never been equalled. Every risk, the purity of his heroic mind was prepared to encounter; every honour, it's dignified humility was desirous of yielding to all who should assist in the enterprize.

In one of these letters, he says—"I have begged, almost on my knees, for money, for the present subsistence of the Maltese who bear arms." In another, a day or two after—"The court have all the inclination; but, to my knowledge, they have not cash enough for the common purposes of the government!" In a third, the day following—"The King of Naples has sent four thousand ounces, to assist the poor islanders who bear arms." His lordship adds, that this will do for the present; and, that the large sum required must come from the three allied courts. In a future letter, Lord Nelson observes, that this sum of four thousand ounces, was taken, for it was no where else to be had, from their Sicilian Majesties children, with the hope of being replaced with the money which Lord Grenville had so handsomely promised to the Marquis Circello. "The enormous expences," writes his lordship to Earl Spencer, "incurred within the last eight months, have drawn the king's chest very low; but, his majesty has never failed giving every thing I could ask."

On the 31st of October, Lord Nelson, fully resolved that nothing should, on his part, be neglected, for the attainment of Malta, or the advantage of it's temporary chief, wrote a long epistle to the Emperor of Russia, as Grand Master. In which, he details the principal operations of this protracted siege; the various difficulties which had occurred, and those which still existed: with the admirable address, fortitude, and perseverance, of Captain Ball, in conciliating the inhabitants, relieving their necessities, and animating their nearly extinguished hopes; whose merits his lordship most earnestly recommended to the notice of his Imperial Majesty. His lordship had before applied for the order of Malta, for his friend Ball, in a letter to Sir Charles Whitworth; but, not having received any answer, he says, in a letter to Captain Ball, "I have now gone to the fountain head."

While Lord Nelson was thus earnestly solicitous to obtain honours for his meritorious friend, he little imagined that he should, in two or three days, be gratified by the acquisition of a new and most distinguished one conferred on himself. This, however, actually and very unexpectedly happened: for a Turkish corvette, which had probably reached Messina about the time when his lordship was writing the above letter in favour of his brave friend, brought from Constantinople Abdur Amand, a special messenger, sent by the Grand Signior, who arrived at Palermo on the 3d of November, and was charged with an additional manifestation of the Sublime Porte's friendly esteem for our incomparable hero. This gentleman, on that day, presented to Lord Nelson, as an honourable gift from his imperial master, the Grand Signior, a magnificent diamond star, or medallion; in the centre of which, on blue enamel, were represented the Turkish crescent and a star. This valuable present was accompanied by an elegant letter from the Grand Vizier, dated the 9th of September: in which it was announced, that the Grand Signior had been pleased to order Lord Nelson a medallion, which his Imperial Majesty was desirous should be worn on his lordship's breast, as a mark of esteem for his kindness to Osman Hadgi—a noble Turk, who had accompanied Lord Nelson from Alexandria, and to whom his lordship was much attached by the strongest ties of friendship—as well as for the interest which his lordship on all occasions took in the prosperity of the Sublime Porte. From the nature of this rich gift, and the respectful manner in which it was delivered by Abdur Amand, his lordship was induced to consider it as constituting him, in conjunction with the former insignia, First Knight of the Order of the Imperial Turkish or Ottoman Crescent. In a most respectful answer to the Grand Vizier, Lord Nelson says—"I intreat that your excellency will present, with the most profound gratitude, my thanks to the emperor, for this new and distinguished honour conferred upon me. I have placed it on my coat, on my left side, over my heart. I cannot say, however flattering this mark of favour is to me, that I can in any manner serve the Sublime Porte more than I have done; for, it has ever been with all my soul. But this mark of favour shews, in the strongest light, that the smallest services are watched, and most magnificently rewarded, by his Imperial Majesty; whose life, may God prolong, with health and every other earthly happiness: and may he give me opportunities of shewing my gratitude, by risking my life for the preservation of the smallest grain of sand belonging to the Ottoman empire; and may the enemies of his Imperial Majesty fall into dust, by the wise councils of your excellency!"

His lordship also wrote a similar letter to the Captain Pacha; in which he did not forget the kindest recommendation of his friend Cadir Bey, and general remembrances to all the admirals and captains serving under that worthy commander. Earl Elgin, and Mr. Spencer Smith, both now at Constantinople, were likewise most respectfully addressed by his lordship. To the former, he modestly writes—"Having yesterday received such a mark of the Grand Signior's favour, I have been puzzled how to express myself properly. I must, therefore, trust to your excellency's goodness for supplying my deficiency of language." To the latter, he returns thanks for all his goodness to his lordship, both public and private; sends him some sherry and sugar, but can neither get a drop of Madeira nor claret in the island, or even in all Italy: and concludes with desiring affectionate remembrances to his brother, Sir Sidney, whenever he writes; for whom, his lordship observes, he has just sent "a large cargo of good things."

The pleasure, however, of this unexpected honour from the Grand Signior, was insufficient to preserve the susceptible heart which it covered, from corroding cares, and painful anxieties, for his country and his friends. He wanted not, indeed, for personal and private causes of vexation and regret: but these, though they were perpetually preying on his constitution, seldom called forth his complaint; and scarcely ever were even mentioned, except to a very few of his most select friends.

One of the first disappointments, after this recent honour, was the arrival of Captain Stephenson, to take the command of the Princess Charlotte; by which, his lordship feelingly observes, in a letter of the 7th, to Captain Ball, "poor Hardy was consequently turned adrift." He had, at this time, too, received a mortifying letter from General Sir James St. Clair Erskine: mentioning, that the twenty-eighth regiment was ordered to England; and that he was sure General Fox, who was every moment expected, would not, on any consideration, break his orders, for any object. With this disagreeable information, his lordship could not bring his mind yet to acquaint Captain Ball. On the contrary, he affects to anticipate, in the letter above mentioned, that he expects the answer from Minorca will be unfavourable to both their wishes; and expresses his intention of going to Naples, for assistance from the Russians and his Sicilian Majesty. He then, with exquisite kindness and address, introduces the extract of a letter from Earl Spencer; which liberally states, that

Captain Ball, by his unparalleled vigilance and exertion, had indeed shewn himself worthy of the friendship with which Lord Nelson had honoured him. "I only send this, my dear Ball," says his lordship, "to shew that I do not forget my friends: as to honouring you, that is not in my power; but to render you justice, is my duty."

In the mean time, his lordship had, on the preceding day, thus expressed himself to Earl Spencer, on the subject of attention to orders, in consequence of this refusal of troops from Minorca—"Much, my dear lord, as I approve of strict obedience to orders—even to a court-martial, to enquire whether the object justified the measure—yet, to say that an officer is never, for any object, to alter his orders, is what I cannot comprehend. The circumstances of this war so often vary, that an officer has almost every moment to consider—What would my superiors direct, did they know what is passing under my nose? The great object of the war is—Down, down, with the French! To accomplish this, every nerve, and by both services, ought to be strained. My heart is," says this excellent man and true hero, "I assure you, almost broke, with that and other things." Then, speaking of the state of the blockade, he says—"If the enemy get supplies in, we may bid adieu to Malta. This would compleat my misery; for, I am afraid, I take all services too much to heart. The accomplishing of them is my study, night and day."

It is a singular circumstance, and merits high consideration, that while Lord Nelson thus strongly urges the necessity for both services to be equally strained; Sir Sidney Smith was most feelingly complaining, in letters dated off Rhodes, 29th September 1799, of the want of a cordial co-operation in General Koehler: who seems to have regarded Sir Sidney's gallant exploits on land as an improper interference with the military department; and to have made the subject of a long and formal complaint, what all the world has agreed to consider as fairly entitling him to immortal honour. On the receipt of these letters, which are written with a noble confidence in the kind and generous sanction of his lordship, Lord Nelson immediately wrote the following excellent letter to the Duke of Clarence. It certainly has, being addressed to a brother sailor, some strong professionalism; but it delicately claims, nevertheless, for Sir Sidney's conduct, the most decided approbation and applause, from a very competent judge of the duties of the profession.

"Palermo, 9th Nov. 1799.

"SIR,

"I beg leave to present to your royal highness, Captain Hardy, late of the Foudroyant: an officer of the most distinguished merit; and, therefore, highly worthy of your notice. He will tell you of all my arduous work in this country; and, that all my anxiety is, at present, taken up with the desire of possessing Malta. But, I fear, notwithstanding all my exertions, that I shall not get any British troops from Minorca: without which, the business will be prolonged, perhaps, till it is relieved; when all the force which we could collect would be of little use, against the strongest place in Europe. I am anxiously waiting the arrival of General Fox; and hope he will not consider the order for the removal of one or two regiments, of such great consequence as the reduction of Malta, by keeping them for two months longer in the Mediterranean. On the one hand, they must, in England, or on the continent, be like a drop of water in the ocean. By staying here, and employed, they would liberate us from our enemy close to our door; gratify the Emperor of Russia; protect our Levant trade; and relieve a squadron of our ships from the service: besides giving us one eighty-gun ship, two forty-gun frigates, a Maltese new ship of the line ready for sea, and two frigates. With these in the scale, I cannot comprehend that a moment can be lost in deciding. But, Sir, I find, few think, as I do--that, to obey orders, all perfection. To serve my king, and to destroy the French, I consider as the great order of all, from which little ones spring; and, if one of these little ones militates against it--(for, who can tell exactly, at a distance?)--I go back to obey the great order, and object; to *down*, *down*, with the damned French villains! Excuse my warmth; but my blood boils at the name of a Frenchman. I hate them *all*; royalists and republicans.

"My late letters from Egypt are, that Sir Sidney Smith is hurt at the notorious cowardice and want of discipline in the Turkish army; and I find, that General Koehler does *not approve* of such irregular proceedings, as naval officers attacking and defending fortifications. We have but one idea; to get close along-side. None but a sailor, would have placed a battery only a hundred and eighty yards from the Castle of St. Elmo: a soldier must have gone according to art, and the zig-zag way; my brave Sir Thomas Troubridge went straight, for we had no time to spare. Your royal highness will not believe, that I mean to lessen the conduct of the army. I have the highest respect for them all. But General Koehler should not have wrote such a paragraph in his letter. It conveyed a jealousy which, I dare say, is not in his disposition.

"May health and every blessing, attend your royal highness, is the constant prayer of your attached and obliged servant,

"Bronte Nelson."

Lord Nelson had, as it may be seen, signed his letters to foreigners as Duke of Bronte, from the time of obtaining that honour; but this epistle to the Duke of Clarence was one of the first in which he ever prefixed the word Bronte to his name when addressing any British subject. It is probable, therefore, that he had, about this time, received his sovereign's recognition of that Sicilian title.

Though his lordship had hitherto been unsuccessful in his repeated applications for troops at Minorca, he continued still to offer new reasons why they ought to be sent. With the most unwearied exertions, did this great man constantly labour for the promotion of whatever related to the honour or advantage of his king, his country, and his friends; and his assiduities never relaxed, till he had secured the accomplishment of his object. He tried, in particular, on this occasion, for the possession of Malta, all the arts of that powerful eloquence which flowed so naturally from his pen; and he might well say, as he did, in a letter of the 10th of November, to Mr. Nepean, "it has been no fault of the navy, that Malta has not been attacked by land; but we have neither the means ourselves, nor influence with those who have the power." In short, the history of this protracted siege, including all the military and political perplexities with which our hero's naval operations were entangled, would alone form a volume of no inconsiderable magnitude.

It appears that, about this time, suspicions were entertained, by Sir John Acton, respecting our intentions with regard to Malta; which first manifested themselves in a remark addressed to Lord Nelson, that the flag of the order was to be hoisted, instead of the three flags, when that island should be taken. This observation, he remarks, in a letter immediately written to Sir John, dated at Palermo, 18th November 1799, seems to convey, that his sentiments of respect for his Sicilian Majesty's flag were lessened. "I send you," says his lordship, with that noble frankness, and prompt decision, for which he was ever remarkable, "two papers, on which my order to good Captain Ball was founded. If I have erred, it is not too late to call back my order; and, if you think so, I shall be happy to meet your excellency, and the minister of England and Russia, on this subject. There is not, I can assure you, that man on earth, who would so strongly unite the two monarchs whom we serve as myself; and may perdition seize the wretch who would do the least thing towards lessening that harmony! And could it ever happen, that any English minister wanted to make me an instrument of hurting the feelings of his Sicilian Majesty, I would give up my commission sooner than do it. I am open to your excellency; and, I think, you are so to me. The interests of our sovereigns require it; and, I am sure, that we both only think of uniting the courts of London and Naples still closer together. I am placed in such a situation—a subject of one king, by birth; and, as far as is consistent with my allegiance to that king, a voluntary subject of his Sicilian Majesty—that, if any man attempted to separate my two kings, by all that is sacred, I should consider even putting that man to death as a meritorious act! Therefore, my dear Sir John, never, never, for a moment, think that I am capable of doing any thing but endeavouring to exalt the glory of their Sicilian Majesties."

Nor was this the only prejudice which malevolence seems now to have been secretly exciting against our hero. Though it has been sufficiently seen, that his lordship's indefatigable endeavours for the possession of Malta, which were never surpassed, either in activity or address, had constantly in view the merited aggrandizement of his persevering, brave, and conciliating friend, Captain Ball—for whom he had implored both emoluments and honours, which no consideration on earth could ever have induced him to solicit for himself—some apprehensions of our hero's diminished regard had been malignantly insinuated into the bosom of that worthy commander: as appears from the following expressions, which occur in a letter written to him by Lord Nelson on the 24th of November 1799. "My dear Ball, I love, honour, and respect you; and no persons ever have, nor could they, were they so disposed, lessen you in my esteem, both as a public officer and a private man: therefore, never let such a thought come into your head; which was never more wanted to be clear from embroils, than at this moment." Then, fortifying his perseverance with assurances that Commodore Troubridge is immediately coming with ships, and Colonel Graham with troops, he thus affectionately proceeds—

> "But, my dear friend, your holding your post so long as you have, is matter of the greatest credit to you;" and, with unexampled kindness, concludes with thus arming his friend against the worst--"If you are forced to quit the island, it cannot lessen your exertion or abilities; and do not let such an event, should it unfortunately happen, depress your spirits for a moment: and believe me, as ever, your obliged and affectionate friend,
>
> "Bronte Nelson."

These unpleasant events did not fail momentarily to affect his lordship's sensibility, and with more permanency his health. In every excess of anxiety, or even of joy, his heart continued to suffer a renewal of that agony which it had first experienced during his search after the French fleet destined for Egypt; and such were the ever-shifting scenes of his active life, that he was seldom, for many days together, exempted from the effects of it's influence, by the occurrence of one or other of these causes.

As if it were not enough, that his mind was perpetually harrassed with professional cares, he had private and domestic sources of inquietude The former, he could freely impart to his numerous friends and in some degree fellow-sufferers;

but the latter was scarcely communicable to any, and no one could be implicated in the same identical cause of distress. Even the very quality in which he surpassed, perhaps, every commander, even by sea or land, that of keeping up a punctual and widely-extended correspondence, did not, at this oppressive period, entirely preserve him from censure. He received, what he calls, in a familiar letter to his friend Rear-Admiral Duckworth, of the 27th November 1799, "a severe set-down from the Admiralty, for not having written, by the Charon, attached to a convoy; although," adds his lordship, "I wrote, both by a courier and cutter, the same day. But I see, clearly, that they wish to shew I am unfit for the command. I will readily acknowledge it; and, therefore, they need have no scruples about sending out a commander in chief." In this letter, his lordship tells Rear-Admiral Duckworth, that he approves very much of his calling at Algiers. "I am aware," says he, "that the first moment any insult is offered to the British flag, is to get as large a force as possible off Algiers, and seize all his cruizers; but if, in such a contest, any English vessel is taken, I know what will be said against me, and how little support I shall experience. But, my dear admiral, where the object of the actor is only to serve faithfully, I feel superior to the smiles or frowns of any board." His lordship afterwards concludes—"Sir William and Lady Hamilton desire their kindest regards. I am nearly blind; but things go so contrary to my mind, *out* of our profession, that truly I care not how soon I am off the stage." In a postscript, his lordship does not forget to add—"Pray, do not let the Admiralty want for letters of every occurrence."

His lordship wrote, on the same day, a serious and respectable justification of his conduct, to Mr. Nepean; in which he observes, how perfectly conscious he is, that want of communicating where and when it is necessary, cannot be laid to his charge. After stating, that he actually wrote to Mr. Nepean, as well as to Earl Spencer, by a Neapolitan courier, who left Palermo on the very day the Charon sailed, he spiritedly says—"I own, I do not feel that, if cutters and couriers go off the same day, that it is necessary to write by a convoy. I know the absolute necessity of the board's being exactly acquainted with every thing which passes; and they, I beg, will give me credit for attention to my duty. As a junior flag-officer," he observes, "of course, without those about me—secretaries, interpreters, &c.—I have been thrown into a more extensive correspondence than ever, perhaps, fell to the lot of any admiral; and into a political situation, I own, out of my sphere. It is a fact, which it would not become me to boast of, but on the present occasion—I have never, but three times, put my feet on the ground, since December 1798; and, except to the court, that till after eight o'clock at night I never relax from business. I have had, hitherto," concludes his lordship, "the board knows, no one emolument, no one advantage, of a commander in chief."

In a letter written to Earl Spencer next day, the 28th, this exalted man, after observing that General Fox orders Colonel Graham not to incur any expence for stores, or any other articles but provisions, asks—"What can this mean? But I have told Troubridge, that the cause cannot stand still for want of a little money. This would be, what we call—penny wise, and pound foolish. If nobody will pay it," nobly adds our hero, "I shall sell Bronte, and the Emperor of Russia's box; for I feel myself above every consideration, but that of serving faithfully. Do not, my dear lord," he most pathetically concludes, "let the Admiralty write harshly to me; my generous soul cannot bear it, being conscious it is entirely unmerited!" The reader of sensibility will not fail to feel this very affecting deprecation; and to lament, that it should ever have been necessary.

On the day following, however, Lord Nelson had the satisfaction of receiving eight thousand ounces from his Sicilian Majesty, for the relief of the poor Maltese; which his lordship immediately sent to Captain Ball, by the Perseus bomb; and, determined that nothing in his power should be wanted, he not only took on himself, from the discouraging circumstance of General Fox's orders to Colonel Graham, to augment his numerous other occupations, by becoming a commissary for these troops, but actually pledged Bronte for twelve thousand ounces—six thousand six hundred pounds—should any difficulty arise in the payments.

On the 19th, Lord Nelson having been informed, by his friend Sir William Hamilton, that the principal inhabitants of Rome, and other professors and admirers of the fine arts, were about to erect, in that city, a grand monumental testimony of their gratitude to his lordship, for having delivered the country, as well as those valuable treasures of art and antiquity which had for ages formed it's proudest boast, from the tyranny and rapacity of French cruelty and barbarism, he immediately addressed the following letter to Mr. Fagan, an ingenious artist at Rome, who had so handsomely made the communication of this pleasing intelligence, through Sir William, and with whom the design of that honourable intention appears to have chiefly originated.

> Palermo, 19th Dec. 1799.
>
> "DEAR SIR,
>
> "Sir William Hamilton has been so kind as to communicate to me the distinguished honour intended me by the inhabitants, by you, and other professors and admirers of the fine arts at Rome, to erect a monument. I have not words sufficient to express my feelings, on hearing that my actions have contributed to preserve the works which form the school of fine arts in Italy, which the modern Goths wanted to carry off and destroy. That they may always remain in the only place worthy of them, Rome, are and will be my fervent wishes; together with the esteem of, dear Sir, your most obliged servant,
>
> "Bronte Nelson."

Had the several powers of the continent taken the constant advice of his lordship, cordially to unite, in resolutely opposing the French pillagers of principle as well as property, these rare productions of the Greek and Roman schools of art would not since have found their way to Paris, nor the projected grand rostral column have finally failed equally to honour Rome and our immortal hero.

On the 17th of December, the Phaeton, Captain Morris, arrived from Constantinople; having, by desire of the Ottoman ministry, brought two Turkish ministers, one for Tunis, and the other for Algiers, to be landed by Captain Morris, in his way down the Mediterranean. These Turkish gentlemen brought Lord Nelson a very elegant letter from the Grand Signior; accompanied by a drawing of the Battle of the Nile, and another of the hero himself: "a curious present," pointedly says his lordship, in writing next day to Earl Spencer; "but highly flattering to me, as it marks that I am not in the least forgotten."

At this time, too, Lord Nelson received, from the inhabitants of Zante, through the hands of Mr. Speridion Forresti, the very elegant and flattering presents of a sword and cane; accompanied by a most kind and respectful letter, in which they express their grateful acknowledgments to his lordship, for having been the first cause of their liberation from French tyranny. This, though true, his lordship observed, in a very affectionate answer, was such an example of gratitude as must for ever do them the highest honour; and begs that Mr. Speridion Forresti, by whom he transmits it to them, will have the goodness to express, in fuller terms than any words which his lordship can find, his sense of their kindness, and of the wish to prove himself farther useful to them. The cane was mounted in gold, with a single circle of diamonds; the value of which was rendered incalculable, by the circumstance of the inhabitants having declared that it was their wish to have added another circle, but that they had no more diamonds in the island.

His lordship's letter to the Grand Vizier, in return for the presents and epistle from the Grand Signior, was as follows.

"Palermo, 22d Dec 1799.

"SIR

Were I to attempt, by words, to express what I felt on receiving the imperial present of the drawing of the Battle of Aboukir, and the highly flattering letter wrote by your excellency in obedience to the imperial command, I should feel myself unequal to the task. Therefore, I can only beg your excellency to express, in words most adapted to convey my gratitude to his imperial majesty, my sense of the extraordinary high honour conferred upon me, by a present more valuable than gold or jewels; as they may come only from the hand of a great monarch, while this can only flow from the benevolent heart of a good man. That the Almighty may pour down his choicest blessings on the imperial head, and ever give his arms victory over all his enemies, is the fervent prayer, and shall ever be, as far as my abilities will allow me, the constant exertion, of your excellency's obliged servant,

"Bronte Nelson."

In a letter to Earl Elgin, then ambassador at Constantinople, his lordship thus expresses his grateful attachment to the Turks. "They," says he, "do me but justice, in believing that I am always alert to do them every kindness; for, as no man ever received greater favours from the Sublime Porte, so no one shall be more grateful." His lordship sincerely regrets the escape of Bonaparte; and remarks, that those ships which he had destined for the two places where Bonaparte would certainly have been intercepted, were—from the Admiralty's thinking, doubtless, that the Russians would do something at sea—obliged to be at Malta and on other services, in which he also thought the Russian admiral would have assisted: "therefore," he adds, "no blame lays at my door." The Vincejo sloop, however, his lordship says, had a few days before taken a vessel from Egypt, with General Voix, and seventy-five officers; and that Captain Long was happy enough to save the dispatches, which had been thrown overboard with a weight insufficient to instantly sink them. These dispatches represented the extreme distress of the French army in Egypt; and he expresses his hope, that the Sublime Porte will never permit a single Frenchman to quit Egypt. "I own myself," says his lordship, in that severe spirit of Antigallicanism for which he was ever so remarkable, "wicked enough, to wish them all to die in that country they chose to invade. We have scoundrels of French enough in Europe, without them." It is contrary to his opinion, he repeats, to allow a single Frenchman, from Egypt, to return to France, during the war; nor would he subscribe any paper giving such permission. "But," concludes his lordship, "I submit to the better judgment of men."

To Spencer Smith, Esq. now secretary of the embassy, his lordship writes in a similar strain—"I have read, with pleasure, all that has passed in Egypt, between Bonaparte, Kleber, and the Grand Vizier; and I send Lord Elgin some very important papers, which will shew their very deplorable situation: but I cannot bring myself to believe they would entirely quit Egypt; and, if they would, I never would consent to one of them returning to the continent of Europe during the war. I wish them to perish in Egypt; and give a great lesson to the world, of the justice of the Almighty."

On the 23d of December, his lordship received information from Sir Thomas Troubridge, that the Culloden, in going into the Bay of Marsa Scirocco, in the Island of Malta, to land cannon, ammunition, &c. from Messina, for the siege, had struck on a rock, and was greatly damaged. The rudder, and great part of the false keel, were carried away; and the rudder would have been lost, but for Sir Thomas's timely exertion in getting a hawser reeved through it. The pintles were all broken; and the ship was steered to the anchorage, with the sails, in a safe but leaky state. In answer to his friend Troubridge, respecting this unfortunate accident, Lord Nelson says—"Your resources never fail; and you would contrive something, I dare say, if the ship's bottom was knocked out."

In another letter of the 2d of January 1800, his lordship, who is incessantly labouring, at all points, to obtain every requisite for the reduction of Malta, and for the relief of the distressed natives, writes thus—"I cannot get the frigate out of the mole; therefore, I must learn to be a hard-hearted wretch, and fancy the cries of hunger in my ears. I send you orders for the different governors: you will see, they are for the supply of the army and navy; therefore, whatever Graham and you send for will, if possible, be granted. I hope the Russians will sail, this north-east wind; and it is my intention to give you all a meeting, the moment the Foudroyant arrives."

On this day, too, his lordship wrote letters to Portugal: containing the kindest praises of the Marquis De Niza, and the several officers and men of the Portuguese squadron under his command; which were, at length, returning home, in obedience to orders, on being relieved by Sir Thomas Troubridge's arrival at Malta. One of these letters contained particular recommendations of promotion for Captains Thompson, Welch, and De Pinto. "When," says his lordship, "I mention my brother, and friend, Niza, I must say, that I never knew so indefatigable an officer. During the whole time I have had the happiness of having him under my command, I have never expressed a wish that Niza did not fly to execute."

On the 6th of January, his lordship learned that his prediction to Rear-Admiral Duckworth, of what had been intended respecting the command of the Mediterranean fleet, was completely verified, by the approach of Lord Keith; who now signified, in a letter to Lord Nelson, that he was coming to Sicily. The effect which this event, though not unsuspected, must have produced on his lordship's mind, is less difficult to be conceived, than expressed. He had already met with sufficient impediments to the execution of his designs, most of which were just happily surmounted; but a paramount difficulty seemed now arising, against which he might be disarmed of all power to perform any thing efficient. The general aspect of his public situation, at this period, is concentrated by his own skilful hand, in the following professional letter, which he immediately wrote to Lord Keith; but his exalted and superior mind disdained to discover, in such a communication, the state of his own private feelings.

"Palermo, 7th Jan. 1800.

"MY DEAR LORD,

Last night, I received your letters, and orders, to December 14th, from November 30th; all of which, I shall endeavour to obey: and, with the greatest pleasure, to give you the state of the squadron, and of affairs on this side of Minorca. I shall begin in the east. My last accounts from thence were by the Phaeton, Captain Morris; and, as your lordship will probably see him, I shall only say, that I have not heard immediately from Sir Sidney Smith since September the 7th. At Constantinople, they heard he was communicating with the Grand Vizier, at Gaza, respecting the French army. The ships with him are, Theseus and Cameleon; but the Bulldog is directed to go to him, till the Smyrna convoy is ready to return. I have lately sent provisions, and some few stores, all we had, for those ships; and I have written to Duckworth, and Inglefield, to send particularly for those ships. What Turkish ships of war Sir Sidney Smith has under him, I know not; but, I am told, there are several. The Turkish admiral, Captain Morris tells me, who served under him, had his head taken off, for leaving the port of Alexandria open, and permitting the escape of Bonaparte. I would have kept up a more constant communication with Egypt; but, I have never had the benefit of small vessels. At Corfu, General Villete is arrived, and raising two regiments of Albanians. Our consul there, Mr. Speridion Forresti, is a very able man; and, from thence, the passage of an express, by land, to Constantinople, is twelve days. To get to Malta--which has kept, for sixteen months, every ship I could lay my hands on fully employed; and has, in truth, broke my spirits for ever--I have been begging, of his Sicilian Majesty, small supplies of money and corn, to keep the Maltese in arms, and barely to keep from starving the poor inhabitants. Sicily has, this year, a very bad crop, and the exportation of corn is prohibited. Both Graham and Troubridge are in desperation, at the prospect of a famine. Vessels are here, loading with corn for Malta; but I can neither get the Neapolitan men of war, nor merchant vessels, to move. You will see, by the report of the disposition of the ships, what a wretched state we are in. In truth, only the Foudroyant and Northumberland are fit to keep the sea. The Russians are, on the 4th, arrived at Messina; six sail of the line, frigates, &c. with two thousand five hundred troops. It is not to be expected, that any one Russian man of war can, or will, keep the sea; therefore, the blockade by sea can only be kept up by our ships: and it is my intention, if the Foudroyant, or even a frigate, comes soon, to go for two days to Malta, to give the Russian admiral and general, Graham, Troubridge, and Governor Ball, a meeting; not only, on the most probable means of getting the French out, but also, of arranging various matters, if it should fall to our exertions. The Maltese have, Graham says, two thousand excellent troops; we have, soldiers and sailors, fifteen hundred; the Russians will land full three thousand. I hope, the Ricasoli may be carried; and, if it is, I think the French general will no longer hold out. What a relief this would be to us! If I cannot get to Malta very soon, I shall, from your letter, remain here, to give you a meeting and receive your orders. It is impossible to send, from Mahon, too many supplies of stores to Malta; sails, rope, plank, nails, &c. You can form no idea of our deplorable state, for the last year. In Sicily, we are all quiet. I have been trying, with Sir William Hamilton, in which the queen joins, to induce the king to return to Naples; but, hitherto, without effect. I must suppose, his majesty has reasons which I am unacquainted with. It has long been my wish, to send a small squadron on the coast of Genoa; for the Russian ships are of no use, to co-operate with the Germans: but, I have not them to send. La Mutine, I have directed to protect our trade about Leghorn; and to assist, as far as she is able, in giving convoy to vessels carrying provisions to the Austrian army. The report of the combined fleets being ready for sea, induced me to direct the Phaeton and Penelope to cruize between Cape Spartel and Cape St. Vincent; that I may have timely notice of their approach, if bound this way-- *which I believe*.

I have run over our present state; perhaps, too hastily: but, I am anxious not to keep the brig one moment longer than my writing this letter. With every sentiment of respect, believe me, my dear lord, your most obedient servant,

"Bronte Nelson."

To his Excellency, the Honourable Lieutenant-General Fox, at Minorca, his lordship on the same day wrote, that he would not suffer General Graham to want, if he could "beg, borrow, or steal, to supply him. Lord Keith," he adds, "is, I dare say, with you, at this moment; and, I am sure, all matters will be much better arranged with him than I have ability of doing. I have only the disposition to do what is right, and the desire of meriting your esteem." To Colonel Graham, at Malta, he also wrote, this day, as follows—"I hope to soon pay you a visit, and I only wish that I could always do all you ask me. It is certain, that you cannot go on at Malta, without money; therefore, I declare, sooner than you should want, I would sell Bronte. But, I trust, from General Fox's letter to me, that you will have his consent for ordering what money may be necessary. I send you all the Egyptian papers, for you, Ball, and Troubridge; and, if you like, in confidence, Italinskoy. Suwarrow is at Prague, with his whole army: ready to act with the Austrians, if they come to their senses; or, perhaps, against them. *Moreau* is at Vienna, treating for peace. What a state the allies bring us into! But, it is in vain to cry out; John Bull was always ill-treated. May a speedy success attend you!"

On the 14th, a new mortification occurred to his lordship. The Russian admiral, who had so long lingered at Naples, and recently arrived at Messina, with the intent, as was supposed, of at length going to Malta, sent notice that he was proceeding with his ships and troops to Corfu, and could not go to Malta. Lord Keith was, at this time, gone to station a squadron for the blockade of the port and coast of Genoa; and Lord Nelson, after arranging, with General Acton, a plan for sending two thousand six hundred troops, and encouraging his respective friends at Malta to persevere in their labours, under these and other comforting assurances, sailed in the Foudroyant, on the 16th, to concert measures for future operations with the commander in chief.

On the 23d, his lordship writes to Earl Spencer, from Leghorn, that he came thither to meet Lord Keith; and that they are going, together, to Palermo and Malta. "If," says his lordship, "Sir James St. Clair, or General Fox, had felt themselves authorized to have given us two thousand troops, I think that Malta, by this time, would have fallen; and our poor ships been released from the hardest service I have ever seen. The going away of the Russians, has almost done me up; but the King of Naples has ordered two thousand six hundred troops from Sicily, to assist Graham, and they are to be under our command. It is true, they are not good soldiers; but, they will ease our's in the fatigues of duty. The feeding the inhabitants of Malta, and paying two thousand of the people who bear arms, has been a continual source of uneasiness to my mind. His Sicilian Majesty has done more than it was possible to expect he had the ability of performing; for the resources of his kingdom are hardly yet come round, and his demands are excessive from all quarters of his dominions. Lord Keith will now be able to judge, with his own eyes and ears, and your lordship will see his report. The loyalty and attachment of their Sicilian Majesties to our king and country is such, that I would venture to lay down my head to be cut off, if they would not rather lose their kingdom of Naples, than hold it on terms from Austria and the French, by a separation from their alliance with England. There is not a thing which his majesty can desire, that their majesties of the two Sicilies will not have the greatest pleasure in complying with. I have, before, ventured on the character of their Sicilian majesties. The king is a real good man, but inclined to be positive in his opinion; the queen is certainly a great monarch, and a true daughter of Maria Theresa. I am just favoured with your letter of December 12th; which, although so entirely contrary to my expectations, cannot alter my respect for all your kindness. I am in debt, from my situation; but, time and care will get me out of it. Since May 1798, I have had all the expence of a commander in chief, without even the smallest advantage. Lord Keith," concludes his lordship, "shall find, in me, an officer ever ready to anticipate his wishes, so long as my health permits."

Though Lord Nelson does not absolutely complain of his then ill health, he was certainly much indisposed; and, but a few weeks before, had undergone a painful course of electricity, at Palermo, from which he entertained hopes of recovering the sight of his left eye.

On the 26th, his lordship sailed from Leghorn, and arrived safely at Palermo; from whence, in a few days, he proceeded to Malta, for the purpose of arranging the business of that important siege.

On the 12th of February, at sea, his lordship received the report of a survey held on the warrant-officers stores found onboard the Leander at the time, of it's being delivered up, with an account of those said to be supplied by the Russians while this ship was in their possession, which he inclosed to Lord Keith, as commander in chief; and, only six days after, being in company with the Northumberland, Audacious, and El Corso brig, fortunately captured Le Genereux, by which the Leander had been originally taken. The particulars of this pleasing event will be best described in his lordship's own words.

> "Foudroyant, at Sea, 10th Feb. 1800.
> Off Cape di Corso,
> Eight Leagues West of Cape Passaro;
> off Shore, Four Miles.
>
> "MY LORD,
>
> This morning, at day-light, being in company with the ships named in the margin, I saw the Alexander in chase of a line of battle ship, three frigates, and a corvette: and, about eight o'clock, she

fired several shot at one of the enemy's frigates, which struck her colours; and, leaving her to be secured by the ships astern, continued the chase. I directed Captain Gould of the Audacious, and the El Corso brig, to take charge of this prize. At half past one P.M. the frigates and corvette tacked to the westward; but the line of battle ship, not being able to tack without coming to action with the Alexander, bore up. The Success being to leeward, Captain Peard, with great judgment and gallantry, lay across his hawser, and raked him with several broadsides. In passing the French ship's broadside, several shot struck the Success; by which, one man was killed, and the master and seven men wounded. At half past four, the Foudroyant and Northumberland coming up, the former fired two shot; when the French ship fired her broadside, and struck her colours. She proved to be Le Genereux, of seventy-four guns, bearing the flag of Rear-Admiral Perree, commander in chief of the French naval force in the Mediterranean; having a number of troops on board, from Toulon, bound for the relief of Malta. I attribute our success, this day, to be principally owing to the extreme good management of Lieutenant William Harrington, who commands the Alexander in the absence of Captain Ball: and I am much pleased with the gallant behaviour of Captain Peard, of the Success; as, also, with the alacrity and good conduct of Captain Martin, and Sir Edward Berry. I have sent Lieutenant Andrew Thomson, First Lieutenant of the Foudroyant, to take charge of Le Genereux; whom I beg leave to recommend to your lordship, for promotion: and send her, under care of the Northumberland, and Alexander, to Syracuse, to wait your lordship's orders. I have the honour to be, my lord, your lordship's most obedient and most humble servant,

Bronte Nelson

The Right Honourable Lord Keith, K.B. &c."

His lordship, the next day, directed Captain Gould, of the Audacious, to proceed with the French prisoners for the harbour of St. Paul, in the Island of Malta; and, putting them on board any ship of war, or empty transport, he might find there, to return to the westward of Goza, where he was to cruize till farther orders.

Though Lord Nelson was much gratified by this capture, which reduced the number of French ships that had escaped at the battle off the Nile to the single one of Le Guillaume Tell, then blocked up at Malta, his health appeared daily on the decline. Still, however, his spirits seem to have remained lively; for, in writing on the occasion, to Palermo, he desires Prince Leopold will tell his august father, that he is, he believes, the first Duke of Bronte who ever took a French seventy-four.

Besides the French prisoners sent to Malta for the sake of compelling their countrymen to maintain them, and consequently to assist in the consumption of the provisions of the garrison, and thus accelerate it's surrender; there were a number of Moorish prisoners on board Le Genereux, subjects of the Bashaw of Tripoli. These Lord Nelson sent back to their own country; with letters to the bashaw, as well as to the British consul: the former of whom he assures, that he is happy in the opportunity of saving so many of his subjects from a French prison; and the latter, he requests, will not fail to impress on the bashaw's mind, that Nelson is never unmindful of his friends. "The bashaw," he adds, "was very good in supplying the El Corso with some rope, which was duly reported to me; and, for which, I beg, you will thank his excellency in my name."

On the 24th of February, off Malta, where his lordship found his health much affected, he wrote to Lord Keith, that it was impossible he could remain much longer there. "Without some rest," says his lordship, "I am gone. I must, therefore, whenever I find the service will admit of it, request your permission to go to my friends at Palermo, for a few weeks, and leave the command here to Commodore Troubridge. Nothing but necessity obliges me to write this letter." Finding, however, on the 28th, from the report of his friend Captain Ball, that the French ships were perfectly ready for sea, and would probably attempt to escape the first fair wind, he writes thus to Lord Keith—"My state of health is very precarious. Two days ago, I dropped with a pain in my heart, and I am always in a fever; but the hopes of these gentry coming out, shall support me a few days longer. I really desire to see this Malta business finished." The following passage, which occurs in another part of this letter, is highly characteristic—"The intended movements of their ships, is a convincing proof, to me, that the garrison has lost all hopes of a successful resistance, and I wish General Graham would make false attacks. I am no soldier; therefore, ought not to hazard an opinion: but, if I commanded, I would torment the scoundrels night and day."

Having waited till the 8th of March, with the vain expectation that the French ships would venture out, his lordship wrote to Lord Keith, that his health continued so bad, he was obliged, in justice to himself, to retire to Palermo for a few weeks, directing Commodore Troubridge to carry on the service during his necessary absence: and, in a day or two after, sailed for Palermo; where he did not arrive, having had a tedious passage, till the 16th.

On the 20th, his lordship writes to Lord Keith—"It is too soon to form any judgment of what effect it may have on my health; but, on the 18th, I had near died, with the swelling of some of the vessels of the heart. I know, the anxiety of my mind, on coming back to Syracuse in 1798, was the first cause; and more people, perhaps, die of broken hearts, than we are aware of." To Commodore Troubridge he writes, also, on this day, much in the same strain—"It is too soon to form an opinion whether I can ever be cured of my complaint. At present, I see but glimmering hopes; and, probably, my career of service is at an end: unless the French fleet should come into the Mediterranean, when nothing shall prevent my dying at my post. I hope, my dear friend, that your complaints are better. Pray, do not fret at any thing; I wish I never had: but my return to Syracuse, in 1798, broke my heart; which, on any extraordinary anxiety, now shews itself, be that feeling *pain* or *pleasure*." His lordship remarks, however, that he is an infidel about the Brest fleet again trusting themselves in the Mediterranean. The Russians, he observes, are certainly going to Malta; under commanders, both at sea and land, with whom all will be harmony. "You will have heard," continues his lordship, "that Mr. Arthur Paget is daily expected, to replace, for the present, Sir William; Comte Pouskin is also superseded by Italinskoy. In short, great changes are going on; and none, that I can see, for the better. I have not yet seen General Acton; but I am led to believe, that the king's not returning to Naples, *has* been entirely owing to the general. At present, perhaps, he has so much frightened him, that the act appears his own. *We, of the Nile*, are not equal to Lord Keith, in his estimation; and ought to think it an honour to serve under such a *clever man*." In concluding this letter, his lordship says—"Acton has, I am almost convinced, played us *false*."

In another letter to Sir Thomas Troubridge, dated on the 28th, his lordship says, that if the ships get away, he is certain the garrison will not hold out; and expresses his intention again to visit Malta, before he retires from the station. A courier, from Constantinople, he says, is just arrived: bringing intelligence, that the French treaty for quitting Egypt is ratified by the Porte; and, that the ministers of England and Russia have acquainted the Porte of the determination of the allies not to suffer the French army to return to Europe. His lordship then directs him to repeat the orders already given, for making the French from Egypt, under whatever protection they may be, come into some of the ports of the allies; for, on no consideration, must they be allowed to return to France. "I now," adds his lordship, "come to the most painful part of my letter, the loss of the Queen Charlotte, by fire. Lord Keith is safe; and, I hope, most of the officers and crew. She sailed from Leghorn at daylight of the 17th, with a strong land wind. She was, when five miles distant, discovered to be on fire; and, at noon, she blew up, about twelve miles from the light-house. This is the whole we know. Vessels were fearful, till after some time, to approach her; therefore, many poor fellows must be gone!"

In a very few days after this melancholy accident, Lord Nelson experienced one of the highest gratifications of his life, by the capture of Le Guillaume Tell. The first information of that important event was conveyed in the following note from Sir Edward Berry.

"Foudroyant, 30th March 1800.

"MY DEAR LORD,

"I had but one wish, this morning; it was for you. After a most gallant defence, Le Guillaume Tell surrendered, and she is compleatly dismasted. The Foudroyant's lower masts, and main topmast, are standing; but, every roll, I expect them to go over the side, they are so much shattered. I was slightly hurt in the foot; and, I fear, about forty men are badly wounded, besides the killed, which you shall know hereafter. All hands behaved as you would have wished. How we prayed for you, God knows, and your sincere and faithful friend,

"E. Berry."

On the 4th of April, his lordship having received farther particulars from Sir Thomas Troubridge, wrote thus to Mr. Nepean.

"Palermo, 4th April 1800.

"SIR,

"I have received no official reports, but I have letters from Commodore Troubridge, Captain Dixon, and Sir Edward Berry, telling me of the capture of the William Tell, on the morning of the 30th of March, after a gallant defence of three hours. The Lion and Foudroyant lost each about forty killed and wounded. The French ship is dismasted; the French Admiral, Decres, wounded; and the Foudroyant much shattered. I send Sir Edward Berry's hasty note. Thus, owing to my brave friends, is the entire destruction of the French Mediterranean fleet to be attributed, and my orders from the great Earl of St. Vincent are fulfilled. Captain Blackwood, of the Penelope, and Captain Long, of the Vincejo, have the greatest merit. My task is done; my health is finished; and, probably, my retreat for ever fixed--unless another French fleet should be placed for me to look after. Ever your most obedient humble servant,

"Bronte Nelson of the Nile."

"Evan Nepean, Esq."

The letter of Commodore Troubridge, above mentioned, contains the following particulars.

"Culloden, Marsa Scirocco,
1st April 1800.

"MY LORD,

"I most sincerely congratulate your lordship on the capture of Le Guillaume Tell, the thirteenth and last of the line of battle ships of the famous Egyptian squadron. I would have given one thousand guineas your health had permitted your being in the Foudroyant. I hear Le Guillaume Tell is dismasted, and Foudroyant little better. I have sent three top-masts, spare-sails, lower and top-gallant caps, spars, &c. to refit, and make jury-masts. As I do not feel authorized to send any of these prisoners away until I hear from your lordship, I have sent two transports to take them in. The Maltese seamen I shall divide; the miserable wretches that Vaubois was sending away as lumber, I mean to *return to him*, in his own way--put them on the glacis, and fire on them if they attempt to come away. I really think, the officers should not be permitted to go to France for some time. Their business was, to have returned with men and provisions. Suppose we could get them to Mahon, with orders to carry them to England in the convoy. As I shall see your lordship here soon, you can settle that then. The French wounded, I have ordered to be landed at Syracuse. If the Foudroyant is not ready, or in a state to fetch your lordship, what are your wishes? The other three ships are preparing to sail from Valette the first wind. Northumberland goes out, with my men, to-day. If the Foudroyant had not come as she did, Le Guillaume Tell would have beat all we had. The Penelope is the only effective ship; if she goes, we shall be badly off. Much credit is due to Captains Blackwood and Long; the latter, I beg your lordship to recommend to the commander in chief. Every thing shall be done, in my power. If the ships were here, I could soon refit them. My people begin to droop, from hard work; the prize still sticks to us. I long to get Diana and Justice to compleat the gang. In my former letter, I acquainted your lordship, that I every night placed a lieutenant, and three trusty men, with a night-glass, in a house close to the enemy's works, to watch the ships. The signals from them apprized the ships she was moving; and answered, fully, my expectations. Rely on all and every exertion in my power. I am so busy, I have not time to write you more at present. I have the honour to be, my lord, your lordship's most obedient humble servant,

"T. Troubridge."

"Right Hon. Lord Nelson, K.B. &c."

The following is Captain Dixon's official account of the action, transmitted to Sir Thomas Troubridge; and, as it contains much fuller particulars than his hasty private letter, which had been inclosed to Lord Nelson, it is here inserted instead of that communication.

"Lion, at Sea, off Cape Passaro,
31st March 1800.

"SIR,

"I have the honour to inform you that, yesterday morning, at nine o'clock, Cape Passaro bearing north half east, distant seven leagues, the French ship of war Le Guillaume Tell, of eighty-six guns, and one thousand men, bearing the flag of Contre-Admiral Decres, surrendered, after a most gallant and obstinate defence of three hours and a half, to his majesty's ships Foudroyant, Lion, and Penelope. To declare the particulars of this very important capture, I have to inform you, that the signal rockets and cannonading from our batteries at Malta, the midnight preceding, with the favourable strong southerly gale, together with the darkness which succeeded the setting of the moon, convinced me the enemy's ships of war were attempting to effect an escape: and which was immediately ascertained, by that judicious and truly valuable officer, Captain Blackwood of the Penelope; who had been stationed, a few hours before, between the Lion and Valette, for the purpose of observing closely the motions of the enemy. Nearly at midnight, an enemy's ship was descried by him; when the Minorca was sent to inform me of it, giving chase himself, and apprizing me, by signal, that the strange ships seen were hauled to the wind on the starboard tack. I lost not one moment, in making the signal for the squadron to cut, or slip; and directed Captain Miller of the Minorca, to run down to the Foudroyant and Alexander with the intelligence, and to repeat the signal. Under a press of canvass, I chased until five in the morning, solely guided by the cannonading of the Penelope; and, as a direction to the squadron, a rocket and blue light were shewn every half hour from the Lion. As the day broke, I found myself in gun-shot of the chase; and the Penelope, within musket-shot, raking her; the effects of whose well-directed fire, during the night, had shot away the main and mizen top-masts and main-yard. The enemy appeared in great confusion, being reduced to his head-sails, going with the wind on the quarter. The Lion was run close along-side, the yard-arms of both ships being just clear, when a destructive broadside, of three round shot in each gun, was poured in, luffing up across the bow, when the enemy's jib-boom passed between the main and mizen shrouds. After a short interval, I had the pleasure to see the boom carried away, and the ships disentangled; maintaining a position across the bow, and firing to great advantage. I was not the least solicitous, either to board or to be boarded: as the enemy appeared of immense bulk, and full of men, keeping up a prodigious fire of musketry; which, with the bow-chasers, she could, for a long time, only use. I found it absolutely necessary, if possible, to keep from the broadside of this ship. After being engaged about forty minutes, the Foudroyant was seen under a press of canvass; and soon passed, hailing the enemy to strike: which being declined, a very heavy fire, from both ships, broadside to broadside, was most gallantly maintained, the Lion and Penelope being frequently in situations to do great execution. In short, Sir, after an action, the hottest that probably was ever maintained by an enemy's; ship, opposed to those of his majesty, and being totally dismasted, the French admiral's flag and colours were struck. I have not language to express the high sense of obligation which I feel myself under to Captain Blackwood, for his prompt and able conduct, in leading the line of battle ships to the enemy, for the gallantry and spirit so highly conspicuous in him, and for his admirable management of the frigate. To your discriminating judgment, it is unnecessary to remark, of what real value and importance such an officer must ever be considered to his majesty's service. The termination of the battle must be attributed to the spirited fire of the Foudroyant; whose Captain, Sir Edward Berry, has justly added another laurel to the many he has gathered during the war. Captain Blackwood speaks in very high terms of the active and gallant conduct of Captain Long of the Vincejo, during the night; and I beg to mention the services of Captains Broughton and Miller. The crippled condition of the Lion and Foudroyant, made it necessary for me to direct Captain Blackwood to take possession of the enemy, take him in tow, and proceed to Syracuse. I received the greatest possible assistance from Lieutenant Joseph Paty, senior officer of the Lion; and from Mr. Spence, the master: who, together with the other officers, and ship's company, shewed the most determined gallantry. Captains Sir Edward Berry and Blackwood have reported to me the same gallant and animated behaviour in the officers and crews of their respective ships. I am sorry to say, that the three ships have suffered much in killed and wounded; and the loss of the enemy is prodigious, being upwards of two hundred. I refer you to the inclosed reports for farther particulars as to the state of his majesty's ships, and have the honour to remain, Sir, your's most truly,

Manly Dixon.

P.S. The Guillaume Tell is of the largest dimensions, and carries thirty-six pounders on the lower gun-deck, twenty-four pounders on the main-deck, twelve pounders on the quarter-deck, and thirty-two carronades on the poop."

Sir Thomas Troubridge."

Copious as the above account of this action may seem, the following affectionate letter of Sir Edward Berry, to Lord Nelson, relates so many interesting particulars of the contest, not elsewhere mentioned, and is so characteristically amiable, that it would be unpardonable to omit such a valuable document.

"Foudroyant, at Sea,
Cape Passaro North by East Eight or Nine Leagues.
30th March 1800.

"MY VERY DEAR LORD,

"Had you been a partaker with me of the glory, every wish would have been gratified. How very often I went into your cabin, last night, to ask you if we were doing right; for, I had nothing to act upon! I thought one ship had got out of La Valette, but I did not know which. The Minorca hailed me, after I had slipped; and said, Captain Blackwood *believed* an enemy's ship had passed on the starboard tack. The wind was south. I came aft, and considered for two minutes; which determined me to stand on the starboard tack, one point free. This was at three quarters past twelve. After hearing guns on shore, and seeing rockets thrown up, the night remarkably dark, could just carry single reefed topsails, top-gallant sails, gib, and maintopmast staysails. At one, heard guns to the eastward, saw false fires; then, some rockets. Put the helm up; brought those rockets, and false fires, to bear two points on the weather-bow; could then carry royal and top-gallant stay-sails, and reefed fore top-mast studding-sail. Got her to go ten and a half and eleven knots occasionally. Every now and then, saw the flashes of guns; kept steering a steady course, east north-east; set the lower studding-sail occasionally: frequently obliged to take in the royal and top-gallant stay-sails. We gained rapidly on the firing and rockets. Were convinced, at three o'clock, there was a running fight, of some sort. Thought it never would be day-light. Praying, earnestly, for you to fly on board. At last, day-light came. Saw a ship, firing into a ship with the main and mizen-topmast gone; and a ship going athwart her, firing. She wore, and the Lion was to leeward. At this time, her running rigging much cut, and appeared very ungovernable; firing, occasionally, at the William Tell; which I was surprised to see was not returned by the enemy, as they were within gun-shot. But it was not long, ere I had good reason to know that a most tremendous broadside was reserved for me. Began to shorten sail, hauled the main-sail up, and had every gun loaded with three round shot. She was on the larboard, I on the starboard, tack; I, therefore, steered as if meaning to go to windward of her: but, determined to go close to leeward, kept the weather leeches of the main and mizen topsail lifting; and, at six, backed the main topsail, running as close as possible, to avoid touching. I went on the gangway, and desired the French admiral, who I distinctly saw, to strike; which he answered, by brandishing his sword, and firing a musket at me; and fired a most tremendous broadside in, of round, grape, musketry, and langridge. The good effects of being so close, was manifest. It was only our sails and rigging that suffered considerably, as not one running rope was left. But, if what we received was tremendous, our return was furious; and not to be stood against, but by determined veterans. The obvious effects, silenced his musketry; but not the great guns: though we could distinctly hear the shot crash through and through her, and the mainmast began to totter. Fortunately, I kept way on the Foudroyant: and was, though with infinite difficulty, able to wear, and give him as compleat a dose from the larboard as we had done from the starboard side; and, down came his mainmast. The action then continued, with great obstinacy. A man, in the heat of the fire, nailed the French ensign on the stump of the mainmast. By this time, our fore topmast was over the side, main topsail down, yard shot away, mizen top-gallant mast and main-sail--indeed, every sail--in tatters. The enemy's mizen-mast was gone; which enabled him to wear, and draw ahead of us. His men were on deck, very active in clearing away the wreck, regardless of the fire; and they fixed a small French admiral's flag on the stump of the mizen mast, over another ensign nailed there, which seemed to bid defiance to us. At half past seven we had separated a little, our head to his stern. The Lion gave him many broadsides; but he preferred firing at us, when a gun would bear. I threw out the Penelope's pendants, who had just raked the enemy, and got her within hail; and begged that Blackwood would take me in tow, and get me once more close along-side the William Tell: which he was in the act of performing--for, when I watched a favourable moment to call the people from the main-deck guns, and filled the main-sail, and secured the mizen-mast; and, with a few rugs forward (the sprit-sail yard, jib-boom, &c. being all shot away) got her before the wind, and had the happiness to get once more close along-side of her, the action then began again, with more obstinacy than before. Our guns were admirably well served, and well directed, crashing through and through her. At eight, I began to think they were *determined* to sink, rather than surrender; as she began to settle in the water, till her fore-mast went over the side: when, in a few minutes after, the gallant Decres struck, having four hundred killed and wounded--so the prisoners report. I felt my heart expand, when I took this brave man by the hand; happy to find, he had survived so much honour. When you consider the superiority of three ships--the Lion, Foudroyant, Penelope, and the two brigs in company with the Strombolo; though the latter, of course, did not act, but it carried the appearance of numbers: on the other hand, the Lion was nothing to her, only three hundred men; but that, the French admiral did not know. In short, it seems as if he considered us his only *match*; and the happiness I have experienced, in proving it, on this occasion, is a circumstance that you, my friend, can participate in. They are feelings that are familiar to you; I, happily, caught them from your lordship: and let me beg of you, on this occasion, to accept my tribute of gratitude. It is to you, I owe my success; and, by a strict observance of your order, I arrived exactly in time. I sent Lieutenant Bolton to take possession of the prize; but, as I had great difficulty in floating one boat, Captain Blackwood's officer got there before him. The admiral, of course, he carried to the Lion, being the commodore; but, I hope, our officers will get promoted for it. You will see, the letter I have written you on the subject, is with a view of your inclosing it to Lord Spencer, if you approve of it. You know how to distribute my best wishes and regards to all your party; and that I am, my very dear lord, your affectionate, and faithful,

"E. Berry.

"No accident by powder, but one bad cartridge, which did not communicate with any other. Performed divine service, at two, and returned thanks to Almighty God for the victory. I only write about this ship; having nothing to say officially, from our idea it would be wrong."

On the 8th, Lord Nelson wrote, officially, to Lord Keith, the following letter, relative to this happy event.

"Palermo, 8th April 1800.

"MY LORD,

"I have the happiness to send you a copy of Captain Dixon's letter to Commodore Sir Thomas Troubridge, informing him of the capture of the William Tell. The circumstances attending this glorious finish to the whole French Mediterranean fleet, are such as must ever reflect the highest honour to all concerned in it. The attention of the commodore, in placing officers and men to attend the movements of the French ships, and the exactness with which his orders were executed, are a proof that the same vigour of mind remains, although the body, I am truly sorry to say, is almost worn away. Then come the alacrity of the Vincejo, Captain Long, and other sloops of war. The gallantry and excellent management of Captain Blackwood, of the Penelope frigate: who, by carrying away the enemy's main and mizen topmasts, enabled the Lion to get up; when Captain Dixon shewed the greatest courage, and officer-like conduct, in placing his ship on the enemy's bow, as she had only three hundred men on board, and the enemy one thousand two hundred and twenty. The conduct of these excellent officers enabled Sir Edward Berry to place the Foudroyant where she ought, and is the fittest ship in the world, to be--close along-side the William Tell; one of the largest and finest two-decked ships in the world: where he shewed that matchless intrepidity, and able conduct, as a seaman and officer, which I have often had the happiness to experience, in many trying situations. I thank God, I was not present; for it would finish me, could I have taken a sprig of these brave men's laurels. They are, and I glory in them, my darling children; served in my school; and all of us caught our professional zeal and fire, from the great and good Earl of St. Vincent!

"I am confident, your lordship will bestow the promotion in the properest manner; therefore, I have done nothing in that respect: and, on this occasion, I only beg leave to mention, that Governor Ball would be much flattered by the command of the William Tell; and Captain Ormsby, a volunteer in the Penelope, would be happy in filling her for him, during his very necessary attendance at Malta; and, in complying with their request, your lordship will highly oblige your most obedient servant,

"Bronte Nelson of the Nile.

"Right Honourable Lord Keith, K.B. &c."

His lordship also wrote, this day, to Earl Spencer, the following very feeling letter.

"Palermo, 8th April 1800.

"MY DEAR LORD,

"I send you Sir Edward Berry's letter, and am sure your lordship will not be sparing of promotion to the deserving. My friends wished me to be present. I have no such wish; for a something might have been given me, which now cannot. Not for all the world, would I rob any man of a sprig of laurel; much less, my children of the Foudroyant! I love her, as a fond father a darling child, and glory in her deeds. I am vain enough to feel the effects of my school. Lord Keith sending me nothing, I have not, of course, a free communication. I have wrote to him, for permission to return to England, when you will see a brokenhearted man! My spirit cannot submit, patiently. My complaint, which is principally a swelling of the heart, is at times alarming to my friends; but not to, my dear lord, your obliged and faithful

Bronte Nelson of the Nile.

"If I may again say it--what would I feel, if my brother was a commissioner of the navy; for ever, grateful!"

"Earl Spencer."

The effect of this agreeable event on Lord Nelson's spirits, had it been followed by other pleasing circumstances, might possibly have recruited his lordship's health; but a long succession of felicity, was what he never on earth enjoyed. In a few days, without any previous notice, his friend Sir William Hamilton was suddenly superseded by the arrival of Mr. Arthur Paget, as himself had recently been by Lord Keith. This circumstance effectually determined him immediately to quit the station. Resolved not to begin either with new men, or new measures, Mr. Paget had no sooner delivered his credentials, than his lordship, though still much indisposed, immediately sailed for Malta; with hopes of getting that business also brought to a conclusion before his return home. Sir William and Lady Hamilton accompanied his lordship on this occasion; having agreed, that they would afterwards proceed to England together. The Queen of Naples, it may be presumed, was greatly affected at thus beholding the cherished friends of herself, her family, and country, suddenly torn away from situations which they had filled with so much honour to themselves, and with such advantage to the interests of the two allied sovereigns. Nor could the good sense of the king fail to feel some apprehensions, that a change might prove for the worst, which was not possible to be for the better; though his envious ministers are supposed to have inspired him with flattering hopes, which he was never afterwards happy enough to see realized. Her majesty, indeed, felt such alarm, even for the safety of the country, under any other protectors than those whose abilities, zeal, and fidelity, had been so long and so beneficially experienced, that she determined to take her three daughters, with her son Prince Leopold, to their sister, the empress, at Vienna; and, accordingly, while her estimable friends were gone to Malta, the queen was making preparations for accompanying them, in their way to England, as far as that imperial city.

At the time of Lord Nelson's first conveying the King and Queen of Naples to Palermo, three Spanish ships had taken refuge in that port; two of them most immensely rich, being laden with quicksilver for the use of the South American mines, and the third a man of war to protect them. There, however, from the period of his lordship's arrival, they had continued snugly to remain; appearing rather disposed to rot in the mole, than venture out to sea with a certainty of being captured. The Spanish commander was no stranger to Lord Nelson's circumspection; who, it will be readily imagined, was often observed to cast a longing eye on such desirable booty: and his lordship's good-humoured remarks on the excessive politeness of the fearful Spaniard, whenever they met, were highly diverting to his friends. About the 20th of April, however, just before his lordship sailed for Palermo, some strong indications had been manifested, of a design in these ships to attempt getting off. He had, therefore, instantly, sent judicious instructions for intercepting them to the squadron at Minorca, as well as ordered express-boats on the spot to be sent in all directions with the necessary information for their being pursued, and had consequently little doubt that they must be immediately captured, should they happily venture to depart.

Lord Nelson, and his friends, on arriving at Malta, were received with the most rapturous joy. The flag of Le Guillaume Tell was presented to his lordship, by the gallant captors; with a kindly affectionate address, on thus delivering the trophy which marked the completion of his glorious triumph over every French ship which had been encountered at the battle off the Nile: and the grand illuminations which took place, on visiting Governor Ball's villa at St. Antonia, where his lordship and friends remained two days, so greatly alarmed the French, who were unable to penetrate the cause, that they attempted to make a sortie, but were instantly driven back.

About the 8th of May, amidst these pleasing attentions of his gallant brethren in arms, and the grateful inhabitants who owed so much to his lordship's protecting influence, he received letters from England which filled him with extreme concern. He learned, by these, that his noble friend, the Earl of St. Vincent—who had accepted a challenge sent by Sir John Orde, immediately after his return home, for having appointed his lordship, instead of himself, the senior officer, to the command of the squadron which had so successfully destroyed the French fleet; an intended duel, happily prevented by the interposition of the law, and the still stronger efficacy, it is said, of a positive royal injunction—now made a claim to prize-money, as commander in chief, after having quitted the Mediterranean station on account of ill health. His lordship, who always felt warmly, vehemently protested against the admission of this claim, in a powerful protest, addressed to his confidential friend, Mr. Davison. It is to be lamented that this unfortunate affair, which was afterwards litigated, and finally decided against the earl, should have in any degree abated that ardent friendship which had, so much to their reciprocal honour and advantage, as well as to the benefit and glory of their country, heretofore subsisted between the two first naval heroes in the world!

Information, it appears, had reached Lord Keith, so long since as the beginning of April, respecting the intention of these Spanish ships at Palermo: for Lord Nelson, in a letter dated on board the Foudroyant, at Malta, 10th May 1800, observes that he has received his lordship's intelligence from Mahon, of the 3d of April, on that subject, which is perfectly correct; and had already ordered that, in case of their preparing to leave the port, express-boats should be sent in all directions with the necessary information for their being pursued, as well as written to Mahon on the occasion. These ships, however, it may be proper here to remark, though they could not elude the vigilance of Lord Nelson, who had narrowly watched them for upwards of seventeen months, certainly effected their escape from Palermo, very shortly after his departure; and, to his lordship's infinite mortification and regret, arrived safely in Spain, long before he reached England.

After remaining about a month at Malta, and being fully convinced, from the arrangements then made, that it must soon fall, his lordship returned to Palermo; as, notwithstanding his earnest wishes for the possession of that important island, he did not chuse to be present at the time of it's actual surrender, lest his friend Ball should thus lose the chief honour of the conquest. Besides concerting plans for the speedy reduction of this island, his lordship, during his stay there, was busily engaged in politely closing his numerous public correspondences with the allied powers, the Barbary states, and the respective British envoys, &c. at the various courts.

On arriving at Palermo, the latter end of May, every preparation was made, by his lordship, and Sir William and Lady Hamilton, for immediately going to England. One of the chief objects of his lordship's attention, had been to promote, by all possible means, the general and individual prosperity of Bronte; by enriching the country with the improvements of agriculture, and preserving the people from oppression. He selected, with this view, a governor, of unimpeachable honour, and of uncommon abilities in directing agricultural operations. The name of this gentleman was Graffer; and he had, already, for some time, acted in that capacity, highly to the satisfaction of his lordship. The following letter to Sir John Acton, occasioned by some interesting communications from Mr. Graffer, not only affords a satisfactory proof of that gentleman's integrity, but a fine picture of his lordship's ever anxious regard to the comfort of those who had claims on his powerful and benign protection.

"Palermo, 2d June 1800.

"SIR,

My object, at Bronte, is to make the people happy, by not suffering them to be oppressed; and to enrich the country, by the improvements of agriculture. For these reasons, I selected Mr. Graffer, as a proper person for governor; as his character for honesty is unimpeachable, and his abilities as an agriculturist undeniable: and yet, it would appear, that there are persons who wish, for certain reasons, to lessen the king's most magnificent gift to me; and, also, to make the inhabitants of that country more miserable than they were before the estate came into my possession. Several people who have hired farms, on the contract of not letting them to what we in England call middle-men, have already done so;

and I am told, that I either have been, or am to be, induced to consent that a superior, or rather that all Bronte causes, should be tried at Palermo. Now, as this is a measure so repugnant to justice, and which must heap ruin on those it is my wish to render happy, I intreat that, except such causes as the present laws of Sicily oblige to resort to some superior court, it may never be imagined that I will consent to do an unjust act. It is possible, from my not reading Italian, that I may sign a very improper paper--(which God forbid!)--if men in whom I place confidence lay it before me for my signature. In his majesty's most gracious gift of Bronte, has been omitted the word Fragile a farm belonging to me. The reasons of this omission are, I fear, too clear; and, at a future day, I may lose it, and his majesty not retain it. These are, in brief, the letters of Mr. Graffer. I have, therefore, by his desire, to request his majesty to grant me the following favours--First, that the farm of Fragile may be inserted in the patent; secondly, that a billet-royale may be granted, to annul the present contract of the feuds of St. Andrea and Porticella. I send your excellency copies and extracts of Mr. Graffer's letters, which prove him an honest and upright man. In arranging these matters for me, it will be an additional obligation conferred upon your excellency's most obedient and obliged

"Bronte Nelson of the Nile."

These requests were readily granted by his Sicilian Majesty; who had, this morning, transmitted his lordship the statutes of the order of St. Ferdinando, accompanied by such expressions of kindness as made the most sensible impression on his lordship's mind, and filled his heart—to use his own phrase—with affection, pleasure, and gratitude. Under these impressions, our hero was desirous of presenting a gold medal to the king, as a small but sincere testimonial of his esteem and regard; he sent one, therefore, accompanied by the following letter.

Palermo, 2d June 1800.

"SIRE,

"The Almighty, who granted to my legitimate sovereign's arms the battle of the Nile, impressed your majesty with a favourable opinion of me; which has led your royal heart to grant me the most distinguished honours, and a fortune which I never had an idea of expecting. I presume, therefore, to request that your majesty will permit to lay on your table a gold medal, highly flattering to your majesty's devoted and faithful

"Bronte Nelson of the Nile."

"His Sacred Majesty, the King of the Two Sicilies."

His lordship had intended to quit Palermo on the 4th of June; but, owing to disagreeable news from Vienna, respecting the successes of the French, the queen waited a few days longer. On the 8th, however, her majesty, with the three princesses, and Prince Leopold; Sir William and Lady Hamilton; Prince Castelcicala, who was going to England on a special mission; and a numerous train of royal attendants, &c. were embarked on board the Foudroyant and Alexander, which immediately proceeded to Leghorn. After a quick but tempestuous passage, during which his lordship was so extremely ill as to be at one time considered in a very dangerous state, they arrived in Leghorn Roads on Saturday evening, the 14th of June; with so fresh a gale from the west, that the ships had sometimes gone more than eleven miles an hour. The weather continuing bad, they were unable to land till the 16th; when Lord Nelson steered his launch, which conveyed the queen and royal family on shore, where they were received with all possible honours. The Governor of Leghorn first conducted his illustrious guests to the cadethral; and afterwards to the palace, where the queen and royal family took up their temporary residence, while Lord Nelson and his friends were accommodated at the British consul's. Intelligence of the unfortunate defeat of the Austrians having just arrived, the queen was prevented from pursuing her journey by land, as had been originally intended; and Lord Nelson, and his friends Sir William and Lady Hamilton, were pledged not to quit the royal family till they should be in perfect security. The Queen of Naples, on landing safely at Leghorn, presented our hero with a rich picture of the king; at the back of which were the initials of her own name in diamonds, inclosed with branches of oak and laurel intertwining each other, composed of diamonds and emeralds. Sir William Hamilton, at the same time, received the gift of a gold snuff-box, with a picture of the king and queen set round with diamonds; and Lady Hamilton a most superb diamond necklace, with cyphers of all the royal children's names, ornamented by their respective hair: the queen observing, that she considered herself as indebted to her ladyship for the safety of them all, by having been the means of enabling Lord Nelson to fight the glorious battle off the Nile, and thus become their protector. In writing to Sir John Acton, from Leghorn, his lordship says, after mentioning the queen's agitation, on account of the unfavourable news—"Your excellency will assure his majesty, in which join Sir William and Lady Hamilton, that nothing shall make us quit the queen and royal family, until *all is safe*. and their future plans are *perfectly* and securely settled. On every occasion," adds his lordship, "I only wish for opportunities of proving to their majesties my desire to shew my gratitude for the numerous favours, honours, and magnificent presents, they have heaped upon me." Lord Nelson now first heard of the attempt on our sovereign's life, by Hatfield, the lunatic, who fired a pistol at the king from the pit of Drury Lane Theatre, on the 15th of May 1800. "The Queen of Naples," says his lordship, writing to Lord Keith, on the 18th of June, "waits here, with impatience, news from the armies; for, if the French beat, I have only to return with my sacred charge: but, a very few days must decide the question. What a sad thing," feelingly exclaims our hero, "was the attempt on our good king's life! But, from what I hear, it was not a plan of any Jacobin party, but the affair of a madman."

After remaining about a month at Leghorn, his lordship was called early out of bed, one morning, by a message from the palace, informing him of an insurrection of the people. The French army being then at Lucca, only twenty-four miles distant, the populace had assembled in great force, with arms snatched from the arsenal, and expressed their determination to secure the queen and royal family, for the purpose of detaining Lord Nelson also; as they knew, they said, that he would not depart without her majesty, and they wanted him to lead them against the French, whom they were resolved to attack under the command of the invincible hero. It was with the utmost difficulty, that his lordship, with Sir William and Lady Hamilton, could force their way to the palace, through the assembled multitude; where the queen, and royal offspring, appeared in a balcony, anxious for the approach of their friends and protectors. Lady Hamilton, however, had the address to gain over one of the ringleaders; by assuring him that Lord Nelson was their friend, and wished to deliver his sentiments as soon as he could reach the palace, where the queen waited his arrival. Having, at length, by this man's assistance, penetrated to the balcony of the palace, Lady Hamilton, at the request of Lord Nelson, who was unable to speak the Italian language, addressed the populace in his lordship's name. Her ladyship began, accordingly, by remonstrating on the impropriety of thus violently surrounding an amiable and illustrious queen, and her royal offspring, whose powerful and sovereign protector was in a distant country, with weapons of war in their hands; and positively declared, that his lordship would not hold the smallest communication with them, unless every man demonstrated the rectitude of his intentions, by immediately returning his arms to the public arsenal. This was attended with all the desired effect: the insurgents signified their acquiescence, by repeated shouts of approbation; and instantly proceeded to deposit their arms in the place from whence they had been so indiscreetly taken. The queen, and royal family, in the mean time, being exceedingly terrified, retreated on board the Alexander; from whence they landed in the night, and set off for Florence, distant sixty-two miles, in their way to Ancona. His lordship, and friends, followed next morning; the whole forming a train of fourteen carriages, and three large baggage-waggons.

After remaining two days at Florence, where they also received the most respectful attentions, they proceeded to Ancona, a journey of about four days. Here they continued nearly a fortnight; and then embarked, in two Russian frigates, for Trieste. After a voyage of four or five days, in very boisterous weather, they arrived there on the 1st of August 1800; being the second anniversary of his lordship's glorious victory off the Nile.

At this, as well as every other place, they were received with universal rejoicings, and experienced every mark of honour; but the queen and Sir William Hamilton had both caught violent colds on board the Russian ship, followed by a dangerous degree of fever, which confined them upwards of a fortnight, and considerably alarmed their friends. From Trieste, the queen, immediately on her recovery, departed for Vienna: and Lord Nelson, with Sir William and Lady Hamilton, two days afterwards; accompanied by Mr. Anderson, the British vice-consul, who offered his services in conducting them thither, being perfectly familiar with that particular route, through the provinces of Carniola, Carinthia, Stiria, and into Austria.

His lordship, and friends, having travelled to Vienna, in about a week from the time of leaving Trieste, were privately introduced to their imperial majesties, by the Queen of Naples, who had arrived two days before them. The empress afterwards held a grand circle, to receive her royal mother publicly: when Lord Nelson, and Sir William Hamilton, were also publicly presented by their friend Lord Minto, the British ambassador; and Lady Hamilton, by Lady Minto. On the day after Lord Nelson's arrival, the party having intended to quit Vienna almost immediately, and none of them understanding the German language, Mr. Oliver, an English linguist residing in that city, was engaged by his lordship, to act as confidential secretary and interpreter, and accompany them to England; this gentleman having been long known to Sir William Hamilton, who had many years before recommended him to be employed, occasionally, by the King of Naples, in procuring carriages, horses, curious animals, and various other articles of pleasure and amusement, from London. The very flattering attentions universally paid to Lord Nelson and his friends, added to the slow recovery of Sir William from the consequences of his recent indisposition, and the unwillingness which they all felt to accelerate their affecting separation from the good queen, detained them in the fascinations of this charming city six weeks. So attractive was our hero, wherever he went, that his presence drew all the best company thither: and the proprietors of the several theatres, alarmed at his lordship's confining himself, for a few nights, to one of them in particular, protested all the rest were deserted; and that they should be entirely ruined, unless he kindly condescended to visit them by turns, which he accordingly promised, and faithfully performed. The journey, which had proved too fatiguing for his friend, Sir William Hamilton, seems to have nearly restored our hero to perfect health; who, on his first arrival at Leghorn, had been so extremely indisposed, as to be four days out of seven confined to his bed. In truth, besides the salutary changes of air, in the different climates thus rapidly passed, from the excessive enervating heats and sultry breezes of Italy, to the corroborating cool temperature of the Austrian refreshing gales; his lordship's ever active mind felt now not only delivered from the thraldom of a controuled and perplexed command, but was invigorated by the boundless admiration he beheld, at each stage of his progress, and through every varying country which he travelled, affectionately and respectfully tendered to it's indubitable and transcendent worth: even the barriers, like our turnpikes, were all thrown open on his approach, and the whole company, sanctioned by the hero's presence, permitted gratuitously to pass. Such public testimonies of universal esteem, could not fail to exhilarate his heart, and fortify it against the depressive influence of any deficient kindness where he felt himself still more entitled to receive it. To enumerate all the instances of affectionate respect which his lordship and friends experienced while at Vienna, would be quite an impracticable task. Some of them, however, must by no means be omitted.

The Prince and Princess of Esterhazy invited them to their delightful palace at Eisenstadt, one of the frontier towns of Hungary, about forty miles from Vienna. Here they were entertained, for four days, with the most magnificent and even sovereign state. A hundred grenadiers, none of them under six feet in height, constantly waited at table, where every delicacy was sumptuously served up in profusion: a grand concert, too, was given in the chapel-royal, under the direction of the chief musician, the celebrated Haydn; whose famous piece, called the Creation, was performed on this occasion, in a stile worthy of that admirable composer, and particularly gratifying to those distinguished amateurs of musical science, Sir William Hamilton and his most accomplished lady. The prince and princess had, a few years before, during a residence of several months at Naples, received such polite attentions from, and been so splendidly entertained by, Sir William and his lady, that they repeatedly promised to evince their gratitude, should the opportunity ever offer; which now happily occurred, and was nobly embraced, to the extreme gratification of all parties.

The Archduke Albert, the emperors uncle, formerly Governor of the Low Countries, gave a grand dinner to his lordship and friends, at the Au Gardens, near Vienna: which was likewise honoured with the presence of the Elector of Cologne, another uncle of his imperial majesty; the Prince of Wirtemberg; his brother, the

Governor of Vienna; all the foreign ministers; and about fifty other persons of the first nobility.

An aquatic fete was also given by the Count Bathiani, on the Danube, within a mile of Vienna; where Lord Nelson was particularly invited to see some experiments made with a very large vessel, which had been projected and constructed by the count, having machinery for working it up against the powerful stream of that rapid torrent. This vessel had been so splendidly prepared for the reception of the illustrious guests, that it would not have disgraced a congress of sovereigns. The party were served with coffee, fruits, cakes, ices, &c. in the utmost profusion, and were much pleased with their entertainment; but his lordship did not appear to consider the count's plan, though prodigiously ingenious, as likely to answer the intended purpose. The pleasure of the day was considerably enhanced, by their having previously formed a fishing-party, and dined on what they caught by angling, which was Sir William Hamilton's favourite diversion, at Bridgid Au, near the Au Gardens; two long-boats having conveyed the company to that charming place, with an excellent band of music.

Arnstein, too, the banker, at Vienna, a most opulent, liberal, munificent, and benevolent Jew, whose family may be considered as the Goldsmids of Germany, gave a grand concert, and splendid supper, to his lordship and friends; at which all the foreign ministers and principal nobility were present.

Though the Queen of Naples insisted on defraying all sorts of expences incurred by his lordship and friends during their stay at Vienna, whither they had so handsomely escorted her—and who had, accordingly, every thing prepared for them at the palace, and regularly sent—they constantly purchased, without her majesty's knowledge, whatever they might happen to want. Mr. Oliver, being one day informed that the Champagne was nearly exhausted, went immediately in search of a fresh stock. It being a prohibited article at Vienna, the merchant whom he applied to, observed that he did not sell it. Mr. Oliver then asked, where he could procure some, as he feared his lordship would have none at table. "What!" said the merchant, "do you want it for the great Lord Nelson?" On being answered in the affirmative, he immediately replied—"Then you shall take as much as you like; for, no man on earth is more welcome to any thing I have." Mr. Oliver took only two bottles, as the owner positively refused to receive any money from his lordship;

who, with his usual benignity of heart, on being informed of this generous act, immediately invited the merchant to dine with him next day.

At the earnest request of the Queen of Naples, their departure from Vienna had been put off for several days; when it could no longer be protracted, this dreaded separation took place at the imperial palace of Schoenbrun, situated on the river Wien, which gives name to the city of Vienna, from whence the palace is only two miles distant. The queen was prodigiously affected, and earnestly intreated Lady Hamilton to return with her to Naples. Sir William, too, her majesty remarked, when he had transacted his business in England, whither he was for that purpose accompanying his illustrious friend, would find the soft climate of Italy far more congenial to his constitution than the damp atmosphere of his own native country. Neither Sir William, nor his lady, however, could listen to any arrangement which must subject them to even a temporary separation from each other. Their domestic happiness, notwithstanding the very considerable disparity of age, was ever most exemplary; and it seems probable, that the amiable demeanour of Lady Hamilton, whose tender regard for Sir William could not fail to excite the admiration of every virtuous visitor, first gave birth to that ardent friendship by which Lord Nelson unquestionably felt himself attached to her ladyship. When the Queen of Naples found, that nothing could induce Sir William to leave his lady behind, her majesty immediately wrote an instrument, appointing Lady Hamilton to receive, for her eminent services, an annuity of one thousand pounds a year. This, however, Sir William positively objected to her ladyship's accepting. He maintained, that he could not suffer his lady to take it, without subjecting them both to unmerited suspicions at home; and her ladyship, impressed with similar sentiments, instantly tore the paper in pieces. The Queen of Naples, however, persisting in her desire to promote, if possible, the interests of her estimable and beloved friends, now penned an elegant epistle to her Britannic majesty, in which she is said to have recommended Sir William and Lady Hamilton as worthy of receiving every possible honour.

The travelling party, who proceeded from Vienna, on the 26th of September 1800, with Lord Nelson, and Sir William and Lady Hamilton, including domestics, consisted of seventeen persons. The Archduke Charles had written to his aunt, the Queen of Naples, soon after her arrival, intreating that Lord Nelson might be requested to visit him at Prague, in the way to Dresden; being himself so extremely ill, that he was unable to pay the British hero his respects at Vienna, as had been his most earnest wish. His lordship, accordingly, on arriving at Prague, the capital of Bohemia, had an immediate interview with that great military hero. He was accompanied, as usual, by his friends Sir William and Lady Hamilton, to the palace; and was so delighted with the archduke, that he said, when he got into the carriage, returning to their hotel—"This is a man after my own heart!" The next day, being the anniversary of our hero's birth, Michaelmas-day 1800, the Archduke Charles gave a grand entertainment; verses written for the occasion were published in the newspapers; and the whole city was illuminated. Sir William Hamilton politely remarked, at this festival, with one of these two renowned heroes on each side of him, that he had then the honour to be between the greatest naval and the greatest military character in Europe.

On the following day, Lord Nelson departed for Dresden, the capital of Saxony; and, after a few stages, quitting the direct road, turned off towards the Upper Elbe, for the purpose of embarking at Leitmeritz, and proceeding down that celebrated river: a circuitous but agreeable route, to which his lordship had been recommended, that he might escape the rough and dangerous passes, and stoney roads, of the dreadful mountain and limitropic barrier of Peterswald, which extends to within two stages of Dresden. His lordship was much amused by this freshwater voyage; and viewed with delight the stupendous rocks of basaltes through which the Elbe here securely wound it's way, amidst scenes of such impressive grandeur. In two days they reached Dresden, and took up their residence at the Great Hotel: where they were immediately visited by Mr. Elliot, the British minister; who is a brother of Lord Minto, our hero's early, great, and invariable, friend. Prince Xavier, the Elector of Saxony's brother, came also, the same day, to pay his grateful respects to Sir William and Lady Hamilton, in return for their polite attentions to his highness while at Naples, where he had been for two months entertained by their excellencies; as well as to be introduced to our immortal hero, whom he was induced emphatically to denominate, on this occasion, "*the Glory of the World*."

A message having been sent, from the elector, that the celebrated Dresden Gallery would be open for the inspection of his lordship and friends, Sir William's love of the arts soon led them thither; and the ladies of the electoral court, who had given orders to be informed when they should arrive, contrived to gratify their curiosity, by thus gaining a sight of our hero, previously to his public introduction. The party remained eight days at Dresden, while two gondolas were fitted up with chambers, and other conveniences, to convey them to Hamburgh; having a small boat attached to one of them, for the purpose of sending occasionally on shore. During the time of making these preparations, there was a grand entertainment given to them at court; they visited all public places; and accepted invitations to dine with the different foreign ministers.

The company having embarked with the English coach, baggage, and eleven male and female servants, they quitted Dresden, and proceeded to Magdeburg. At every place where they touched, assembled crowds lined the shore; all so anxious to see the British hero, that they are said to have remained, in many different stations, two or three days and nights, purposely to behold him pass. At Magdeburg, where they landed, and remained one whole day, the King of Prussia had ordered a guard of honour to attend his lordship. The curiosity of the crowd was here so great, that the master of the hotel where the party were entertained, gained no inconsiderable sum of money, by permitting the people to mount a ladder, which enabled them to view the hero and his friends through a small window. On leaving Magdeburg, in the evening, they were still more numerously attended than they had been at landing, in the morning; and the multitude testified their delight, by every customary expression of joy.

Lord Nelson, who had never, till this journey, experienced the pleasures of travelling by any inland navigation, was anxious to behold, and inquisitive to know, every thing. When night came on, his lordship and Sir William Hamilton often amused themselves, by playing together their favourite game of cribbage: and, not unfrequently, while passing down this river, was the hero's busy mind actively employed in forming new plans for future naval attacks; the operations of which, he fully demonstrated to his admiring friends, by instantaneously sketching rough and hasty illustrations of his ideas, must necessarily prove so decisively successful, that the affair off the Nile, the hero maintained, would hereafter be considered as nothing. Mr. Oliver, his lordship's confidential secretary and interpreter, who had, during the whole of this voyage, been occasionally dispatched on shore with a servant, in the small boat rowed by two men, was landed within two stages of Hamburgh, to take a post-carriage; announce their approach; and prepare the apartments for their reception, which had been hired by the British consul: and, on the twelfth day after quitting Dresden, the party arrived safely at Hamburgh, where they were greeted with the most rapturous rejoicings.

The people of all descriptions, in this motley city, hailed our hero with the most perfect unity of sentiment; and, at the theatres, and other public places, even the hat with the Gallic tri-coloured cockade of republicanism was waved with exultation and applause, on beholding the chief champion of royalty and prime protector of kings. Such was the acknowledged glory of all his public actions, and such the universal sense of respect for the various known virtues of his private character, that every good and great mind aspired to claim for itself the privilege of regarding him as a brother. The honours which his lordship here received were greater, perhaps, than had ever been before paid to any individual by the joyful inhabitants of this then free commercial city. The grand governing bodies, every illustrious personage, and all the most opulent merchants, vied with each other in testifying the happiness they felt on thus having the first hero of the world among them.

At a grand fete given by the English merchants to Lord Nelson and his friends, his lordship, after dinner, addressed the company, consisting of all the principal people of Hamburgh, in a very admirable speech, expressive of the high sense which he entertained of their indulgent regards: and having, a few days before, been to visit the British consul at Altona, who was a brother of his friend Captain. Cockburne, from whence his lordship, with Sir William and Lady Hamilton, had not returned to Hamburgh till after the gates had been long closed, and were consequently under the necessity, of waiting a considerable time before permission could be obtained for admitting them into the city; his lordship, ingeniously adverting to the circumstance, remarked that he had happily experienced a specimen of the difficulties which the French were likely to encounter, should they ever approach the gates of Hamburgh; and trusted that the worthy inhabitants would always be found ready as obstinately to defend them against their worst enemies, as they had recently done against their most sincere friend. Lord Nelson, at this fete, lost one of the large diamonds from the grand sword given to him by the King of Naples; which, notwithstanding the greatly boasted security of property, from the depredations of theft, in this well-governed city, was never afterwards recovered by his lordship. The merchants, however, much to their honour, would have replaced it by another of equal value, at the expence of eight hundred pounds, but his lordship could not be induced to accept any gift on such an occasion.

Among the numerous interesting occurrences while Lord Nelson and his friends remained at Hamburgh, there are some which seem to merit particular notice, as highly illustrative of amiable characteristics both in our hero himself and the generality of the different persons to whom they also relate.

A venerable clergyman, apparently between seventy and eighty years of age, was perceived one morning by his lordship, with a large book under his arm, anxiously looking towards the door of his apartment, with the most expressive solicitude depicted in his countenance. His lordship, immediately, with his ever prompt kindness and humanity, desired Mr. Oliver to enquire what was the object of his wish. Having learned, that he was the pastor of a place forty miles distant, who had travelled thus far with his parochial bible, in the first leaf of which he wanted the immortal hero to inscribe his name, his lordship instantly admitted him into his presence; readily complied with his request; and then, taking him kindly by the hand, heartily wished the patriarchal and spiritual shepherd a safe return to his rural flock. The aged and pious minister suddenly dropped on his knee: fervently imploring Heaven to bless his lordship, for so generously condescending to indulge his wish; and solemnly declaring that he should now be happy till it pleased God to call him, when he would die contented, having thus done homage to, and obtained favour from, "*the Saviour of the Christian World.*"

Another circumstance, of still greater singularity, occurred at Hamburgh, relative to a wine-merchant. This gentleman, who was likewise more than seventy years of age, and of a very respectable appearance, had requested to speak with Lady Hamilton. Her ladyship, accordingly, condescendingly admitted him to a private audience; when he informed her, through the medium of Mr. Oliver, who interpreted for both parties, that he had some excellent old Rhenish wine, of the vintage of 1625, and which had been in his own possession more than fifty years. This, he said, had been preserved for some very extraordinary occasion; and one had now arrived, far beyond any he could ever have expected. In short, he flattered himself that, by the kind recommendation of her ladyship, the great and glorious Lord Nelson might be prevailed onto accept six dozen bottles of this incomparable wine: part of which, he observed, would then have the honour to flow with the heart's blood of that immortal hero; a reflection which could not fail to render himself the most fortunate man in existence, during the remainder of his days. His lordship being informed of these curious particulars, immediately came into the apartment, and took the old gentleman kindly by the hand, but politely declined his present. He was, however, finally persuaded to accept of six bottles, on condition that the worthy wine-merchant should dine with him next day. This being readily agreed, a dozen bottles were sent; and his lordship, jocosely remarking that he yet hoped to have half a dozen more great victories, protested he would keep six bottles of his Hamburgh friend's wine, purposely to drink a bottle after each. This his lordship did not fail to remember, on coming home, after the battle of Copenhagen; when he "*devoutly drank the donor*." It is said, that this winemerchant, soon after Lord Nelson had first taken him by the hand, happening to meet with an old friend, who was about to salute him in a similar way, immediately declined the intended kindness, and said he could not suffer any person to touch the hand which had been so highly honoured by receiving that of Lord Nelson. Certain it is, that this man felt so overcome by his excessive sensibility, that he literally shed tears of joy during the whole time he was in our hero's presence.

At a grand public breakfast, given to Lord Nelson and his friends, by Baron Berteuil, formerly the French ambassador at the court of Naples, the celebrated General Dumourier was introduced to his lordship. Lord Nelson, notwithstanding his general aversion to Frenchmen, had a favourable opinion of this able and intelligent officer; and said to him, that he hoped they should both, in future, fight hand in hand for the good cause: adding, as there was then some prospect of General Dumourier's being employed in the British service, that there was no person, if we were to have joint operations by sea and land, with whom he would sooner act. The general was so overpowered by this generosity and grandeur of soul in our hero, that he could only articulate—"Great Nelson! brave Nelson! I am unable to speak. I cannot make any reply to your goodness!" His lordship, finding the circumstances of General Dumourier very humble, for a man of his merits, kindly sent him a weighty purse, next day, by Mr. Oliver, to whom the general feelingly expressed the utmost thankfulness.

While Lord Nelson remained at Hamburgh, he received, one morning, a very extraordinary visit. An Englishman, of gentlemanly address, called on his lordship, and requested to speak with him in private. Sir William Hamilton, conceiving the stranger's appearance to be suspicious, particularly as he held one hand under his coat, advised his lordship not to withdraw. Our hero replied that, though he had never before differed with Sir William in opinion, he must decidedly do so now. He felt conscious, be said, that he had done no ill; and, therefore, dreaded none. He then, with firmness, bade the stranger follow him into another apartment; who soon gave his lordship to understand, that he was no less a personage, than the famous Major Semple, of swindling notoriety. With a considerable degree of feeling, he detailed his miserable situation: an outcast from society; in the deepest distress; avoided, and despised, by every body. Lord Nelson protested, that he had not expected the honour of such a visit; but, nevertheless, returning to Sir William and Lady Hamilton, and mentioning who it was, kindly asked—"What shall we do for the poor devil?" They accordingly gave him, between them, a purse of twenty guineas: his lordship tenderly remarking, that he seemed a man of talents; who had, probably, from some first error of early life, unchecked by friendly advice or assistance, finally sunk into a state of, perhaps, irrecoverable ignominy.

His lordship, on arriving at Hamburgh, had written for a frigate, to convey him and his friends to England; but, as it was not sent, he hired a packet at Cuxhaven, which was sent up the river, as far as the villa of Mr. Power, about five miles from Hamburgh: where the party embarked; and, after a voyage of five days, in very stormy weather, arrived off Yarmouth, on Thursday the 6th of November.

A pilot immediately came out, on beholding them in the offing; but, awed by his sense of danger, and the consideration of who and what were on board, he was afraid to undertake getting the vessel in. Lord Nelson, who thought a seaman ought not to fear any thing, asked him if it were not his trade; and, immediately ordering him a glass of liquor, said it would inspirit him to take the ship over the bar, where the pilot had expressed his opinion there was by no means a sufficient depth of water. His lordship, however, was resolved that the experiment should be tried: and, accordingly, they got safely into the harbour; though not without a considerable degree of that horrible grating of the ship's bottom, while forcing it's way through the sands, which so often thrills those who navigate this perilous road. The weather being bad, his lordship and friends, on landing, went into a carriage; from which the shouting multitude, who had hailed his arrival, instantly detached the horses, and drew them to the Wrestlers Inn. All the ships in the harbour hoisted their colours, and every honour was paid to his lordship by Admiral Dickson, the then commander of the fleet. The Mayor and Corporation of Yarmouth immediately waited on his lordship with the freedom of the town; which, in consequence of his eminent services, had been previously voted. With the blundering fatality, however, that seldom fails to mark some member in almost every town-corporate, on any extraordinary occasion, when the usual oath was tendered to his lordship, who placed his left and only hand on the book, the officer who administered it incautiously exclaimed—"Your right hand, my lord!" His lordship, with a good-humoured smile, mildly reminded him that he had no right hand. The surrounding company, however, were less merciful; and not only indulged an immediate hearty laugh at his expence, but sarcastically fastened on him, for ever after, the unfortunate phrase— *"Your right hand, my lord!"* In the mean time, all the troops quartered in the town paraded before the inn, with their regimental band; paying every military honour to his lordship, and firing *feux de joie*. The corporation, after presenting Lord Nelson with the freedom, went in procession, with his lordship, to church; whither he was also attended by all the naval officers on shore, as well as the principal inhabitants, who joined his lordship in this public thanksgiving to the Almighty, on thus landing in his native country. At night, the whole town was illuminated, bonfires were kindled, and discharges of musketry and ordnance continued till midnight. On quitting the town, next day, the corps of Volunteer Cavalry, commanded by William Palgrave, Jun. Esq. now Collector of the Customs at the port of Yarmouth, and who had paid his lordship and friends the most polite attentions, unexpectedly drew up, saluted, and followed the carriage; not only to the town's end, but as far as the extreme boundary of the county of Norfolk: a mark of respect, which too sensibly impressed his lordship, ever to be forgotten; and, accordingly, he never afterwards went to Yarmouth, without making his first visit to Mr. Palgrave.

In Suffolk, his lordship was no less honoured than in his native county. The people of Ipswich came out to meet him, and dragged the carriage a mile into town; and, on his leaving it, drew it three miles out. When his lordship was Captain of the Agamemnon, he had felt desirous to be returned member for this town, and some leading men of the then corporation had been consulted by a friend. The terms, however, were such as could not be listened to; and his lordship, shrewdly observing that he would endeavour to find a preferable path into parliament—meaning, no doubt, that which so honourably conducted him into the House of Peers, instead of the House of Commons—wrote to his sister, Mrs. Bolton, that there might a time come, when the people of Ipswich would think it an honour for him to have ever represented them; a time which, most certainly, had now long since arrived.

At Colchester, in Essex, and every other place through which his lordship passed, he was received with similar demonstrations of joy, and experienced every respectful attention.

On Sunday, the 9th, his lordship arrived in London; and immediately proceeded to Nerot's Hotel, King Street, St. James's; where Lady Nelson, and his lordship's venerable father, who were just arrived from Norfolk, had taken up their residence. His lordship, who was dressed in a full uniform, with three stars on his breast, and two gold medals, was welcomed by repeated huzzas from a prodigious crowd, who had followed the carriage from the moment they knew who was arrived. These affectionate testimonies of public regard, were most courteously returned by his lordship, who bowed continually to the enraptured multitude. Every eye beamed with pleasure to behold him; every heart exulted in the possession of such a hero; every tongue implored blessings from Heaven on the honoured protector of his country. If these were the obvious feelings of those who could boast no nearer affinity than that of being the fellow-subjects of this exalted man, what was not to be expected from such as were closely allied to him by the ties of blood: the father, from whom he derived his existence; the wife, whom he had so disinterestedly selected from society, to participate in all his earthly honours and enjoyments? That his worthy father did, indeed, receive him with a heart which overflowed with paternal love, is not to be doubted: to the Christian and the father, however, was he indebted for the ardent and sincere embrace; while the tear of rapture was blended with that of regret, drawn by imputations of apprehended private guilt dreadfully detracting from the honourable list of his son's known public virtues. The duteous hero, unconscious of crime, happily perceived not, in his beloved father, any symptoms of suspicion. At the obvious coldness of her ladyship, however, the warmth of his affectionate heart felt a petrifying chill, which froze for ever the genial current of supreme regard that had hitherto flowed with purity through the inmost recesses of his soul. This is a topic which must, for evident reasons, be touched with a tender hand. Woe to the woman who, wedded to a man with superlative merits, whatever they may be, which are acknowledged and admired by all the world, feels alone insensible of her husband's transcendent worth! Where there is genius, the warmth of affection is seldom wanting; if it be not returned with ardour, it kindles into a fierce and dangerous flame. Lady Nelson's ideas were so little congenial with those of his lordship, that she is said never to have asked him a single question relative to that glorious victory which had so astonished the world. On the contrary, all the scandalous insinuations, and licentious remarks, with which the Jacobinical foreign journalists had filled their pestiferous pages, relative to our hero and his friends in Italy, and which had found their way into the most thoughtless and depraved of our own newspapers, were preserved for his lordship's immediate amusement. Without introducing the reader behind the sacred veil of the connubial curtain, let it suffice to say, that Lord Nelson rose at an early hour, and went to visit Sir William and Lady Hamilton; where, at least, he was always sure to behold the actual existence of conjugal happiness. He related, in a few words, the nature of his situation; and assured Sir William that, such was his misery, it would be mercy to dispatch him. These amiable friends did all they could to tranquilize his perturbed spirits; and their soothing consolations succeeded, at length, in calming the tempest by which his feeling bosom was so cruelly agitated. A temporary reconciliation was soon effected; the contrariety of sentiment, however, between the parties, gave but little hope of it's ever proving permanent. In the mean time, as the 9th of November happened this year to be Sunday, the Lord-Mayor's day, in London, was kept on Monday the 10th; and Lord Nelson, being particularly invited to the civic festivity, joined the procession in it's return. His lordship was accompanied by his inseparable friend, Sir William Hamilton; it having been long mutually agreed, between them, that they would never visit any place where both were not equally welcome. The carriage had no sooner reached the top of Ludgate Hill, than the citizens took out the horses, and drew him to Guildhall; the ladies, from the windows, all the way round St. Paul's Church-yard, along Cheapside, and down King Street, waving their handkerchiefs as the hero passed, and using every other expression of admiration and applause. After a most sumptuous dinner, to which the company sat down at six o'clock, had been succeeded by the usual toasts, a very elegant sword, richly ornamented—the handle being of solid gold, covered with blue enamel, and studded with diamonds, the guard supported by anchors, with the figure of a crocodile, as emblematical of the battle off the Nile—and which had been voted, as formerly mentioned, immediately after receiving information of that glorioas victory, was presented to his lordship by Richard Clarke, Esq. Chamberlain of the City of London; who, at the same time, delivered the following address.

"LORD NELSON!

"In chearful obedience to a unanimous resolution of the right honourable the lord-mayor, aldermen, and commons, of the city of London, in common-council assembled, I present your lordship with the thanks of the court, for the very important victory obtained by a squadron of his majesty's ships under your command, over a superior French fleet, off the mouth of the Nile, on the 1st of August 1798: a victory, splendid and decisive; unexampled in naval history; and reflecting the highest honour on the courage and abilities of your lordship, and your officers, and the discipline and irresistible bravery of British seamen; and which must be productive of the greatest advantages to this country, and to every part of the civilized world, by tending to frustrate the designs of our implacable enemy, and by rouzing other nations to unite and resist their unprincipled ambition.

"As a farther testimony of the high esteem which the court entertains of your lordship's public services, and of the eminent advantages which you have rendered your country, I have the honour to present your lordship this sword.

"The consequences of the action I am thus called upon to applaud, are perhaps unequalled in the history of mankind. A numerous army, which had triumphed in Europe over brave and veteran troops, commanded by officers of the most established reputation, landed in

Egypt, under the command of him who now sways the Gallic sceptre, with designs of the most ambitious and extensive nature. One of their objects, as acknowledged by themselves, was to annihilate, by degrees, the English East-India trade; and, finally, to get into their possession the whole commerce of Africa and Asia. Such were the gigantic views of our implacable foe; and such confidence had they in the fleet which conveyed them, and in the station which it took on the coast of the devoted country, that it bade defiance to the whole navy of Britain: but, at this momentous period, the Almighty directed your lordship, as his chosen instrument, to check their pride, and crush their force as a maritime power during the present contest. The circumstances attending this grand display of providential interposition and British prowess, must interest the feelings of every Englishman. Had a space been chosen, to exhibit to the world a struggle for superiority in nautical skill, and personal valour, between the two greatest naval powers of the globe, none could have been more happily selected. The three grand divisions of the ancient world were witnesses; and the shores which had beheld the destruction of the Persian navy by the Greeks, and the heroic acts of Sesostris, now resounded with the echo of British thunder. To your lordship belongs the praise of having added glory to such a scene: the heroes we applaud, would themselves have applauded us; and he who, ages since, led his three hundred against an almost countless host, might on that proud day have wished himself a Briton.

"The thanks of your country, my lord, attend you; it's honours await you: but, a higher praise than even these imply, is your's--In the moment of unexampled victory, you saved your country: in the next moment, you did still more--you exemplified that virtue which the heathen world could not emulate; and, in the pious--"*Non nobis Domine!*" of your modest dispatches, you have enforced a most important truth--that the most independant conqueror felt, in the most intoxicating point of time, the influence and protection of Him whom our enemies, to their shame and ruin, had foolishly and impiously defied. May that same Power, my lord, ever protect and reward you! May it long, very long, spare to this empire so illustrious a teacher, and so potent a champion!"

To this highly respectable address, Lord Nelson instantly replied—

"SIR,

"It is with the greatest pride, and satisfaction, that I receive, from the honourable court, this testimony of their approbation of my conduct: and, with this very sword,"[Holding it up, in his only hand] "I hope soon to aid in reducing our implacable and inveterate enemy to proper and due limits; without which, this country can neither hope for, nor expect, a solid, honourable, and permanent peace."

His lordship was highly gratified with his city reception, on this day of annual festivity. He was ever a great friend to the grand display of a London Lord-Mayor's shew: not on account of the pageantry and parade of such a public spectacle; but, as he expressed himself to his friends, for the sake of it's beneficial effects on youthful minds. It was, he contended, a holiday without loss of time: since the hope of one day riding in the gilt coach of the Lord Mayor, excited a laudable emulation in the breast of every ingenuous city apprentice, which made them afterwards apply themselves, with redoubled diligence, to the business of their respective masters; and, by thus fixing them in industrious habits, could not fail of proving finally advantageous to themselves.

Not only the city of London, but the whole nation, through every gradation of rank, from the sovereign on the throne to the occupier of the humblest hut gratefully regarded the hero of the Nile as the person to whom they were chiefly indebted for the security and comfort they enjoyed; and there was, perhaps, scarcely a house which his lordship could enter, in the British dominions, or even those of our allies, where he would have been welcomed with a less affectionate aspect than his own.

Having taken up his residence in Dover Street, he naturally wished to enjoy the society of his nearest and dearest relatives; from whom he had, in the discharge of his professional duties, been so long divided. Few of these, however, had, during his lordship's absence, met with any excess of respectful civilities from her ladyship; and, of course, though now affectionately invited, their visits by no means appeared to augment her felicity. Lady Nelson's nerves could not bear the constant presence of his lordship's young nephews and nieces; while his lordship, fond of virtue in every shape, never felt happier than when surrounded by the amiable children of his brother and sisters. Here was another want of unison in sentiment; and, consequently, a considerable source of discord. It will be sufficient, to hint a few such unhappy incongruities of disposition, to account for that extreme deficiency of harmony between the parties which afterwards led to a separation by mutual consent. The present Earl and Countess Nelson, there can be no doubt, will long remember the mortifying *hauteur* which they so often experienced from her ladyship, even at their brother's table, as well as on other occasions, where they were then deemed of insufficient consequence to appear in company with so lofty a personage as their elevated sister-in-law, over whom they now triumph in rank: such are the fluctuations of fortune; such, not unfrequently, the salutary checks to the career of a vain ambition.

Lady Nelson unfortunately regarded all his lordship's relations as the natural enemies of her son; whom she seems, unaccountably, to have considered as the rightful heir of her husband's honours. This improvident young man, however, far from conciliating his father-in-law's esteem, had insulted him with more grossness than his lordship ever experienced from any other person; and, consequently, estranged himself, as much as possible, from his heart. Had any other human being acted exactly in the same manner, it is not improbable that his life might have paid the forfeiture. What a source was this, too, for domestic inquietude! In short, without any charge of criminality against her ladyship, the unfortunate tempers of herself and son, so little accordant with that of his lordship, conduced to render our hero, amidst all the honours he was every where deservedly receiving, the most miserable mortal in existence. After one of those too frequent domestic broils, by which his life was embittered, this exalted man, of whom the world was scarcely worthy, had wandered all night, through the streets of London, in a state of absolute despair and distraction. He rambled as far as the city; perambulated Fleet Market, Blackfriars Bridge, &c. and, exhausted with fatigue, as well as overpowered by mental suffering, reached the house of Sir William Hamilton, in Grosvenor Square, about four in the morning; where, having obtained admittance, he threw himself on the bed of his alarmed friends, in an agony of grief much too poignant for expression. The soothing voice of friendship; the sympathetic tenderness of such congenial minds; and the manifest interest which they felt in the affecting recital which his lordship ventured to unbosom; all assisted, by degrees, to calm the tremendous hurricane in his perturbed breast. After his lordship was refreshed, and had taken a little rest, his friend, Sir William, persuaded him to seek that happiness in his professional pursuits, which it seemed unlikely be would ever find at home; and, that very day, it is said, his lordship offered his services at the Admiralty, where they were gladly accepted.

On the 1st of January 1801, he was elevated to the rank of Vice-Admiral of the Blue: and, on the 9th, ordered to hoist his flag on board the San Josef, of a hundred and twelve guns, one of the Spanish prizes taken by himself in the battle off Cape St. Vincent, and then lying at Plymouth Dock; which he accordingly did, on the 17th of the same month.

On the 28th, his lordship received orders to put himself under the command of his old friend, the Earl of St. Vincent; and, as soon as the San Josef should be in all respects ready for sea, to proceed with that ship to Torbay.

In the mean time, the memorable Quixottical insanity of the Russian Emperor Paul, having operated, with the intrigues of France, to produce an intended naval confederacy of the northern nations against the maritime power of Great Britain, it was wisely determined, by the then British government, instantly to crush a design pregnant with such alarming consequences. For this purpose, a powerful fleet was now fitting out, under Admiral Sir Hyde Parker; which, while it conveyed to the triple league of the Danes, the Swedes, and the Russians, the most unequivocal desire of preserving peace, on the part of Great Britain, should carry with it the fearless front of a decided readiness to commence, if necessary, immediate hostilities.

Lord Nelson having consented to go out second in command, on this grand

and most important expedition, came to London, for a few days, previously to his departure: when his lordship learned, with no small degree of surprise, that Lady Nelson had given up the house, and was retired to Brighthelmstone. His astonishment, at thus finding himself without a house or home, is not easy to be described. He hastened to his friend Sir William Hamilton, and most pathetically represented his situation. Sir William embraced him—"My dear friend! while I have a house, you can never want one." Then, conducting him to his lady—"Emma," exclaimed Sir William, "Lord Nelson says, he has no home. I say, he has, while I have one; what say you?" Her ladyship replied, that she was exactly of the same opinion. Lord Nelson opposed this arrangement, on account of the slanders of the world: but Sir William Hamilton, with a noble disdain of malevolence, felt sufficiently satisfied of the virtue in which he confided; and Lady Hamilton, who never opposed Sir William in any thing, without affecting to raise squeamish objections, readily signified her acquiescence. Lord Nelson then dropped on his knee, and piously appealed to Heaven, as witness of the purity of his attachment; and, with similar solemnity, they each, reciprocally, vowed an equally disinterested and indissoluble friendship. Such was the bond of that sincere amity which, whatever may be said, the individuals who compose the world will generally be inclined to estimate, as they always do on such occasions, according to the larger or lesser degree of vice or virtue which they respectively find in their Own hearts. From this moment, it was agreed that, while his lordship should be in England, they would constantly reside together: and, as no power on earth could have now prevailed on Lord Nelson again to live with his lady, who had carried her resentments much farther, in several respects, than it is thought necessary on this occasion to particularize, deeds of separation were soon after prepared and executed by mutual consent; the negociation of which was kindly undertaken by Alexander Davison, Esq. his lordship's confidential friend.

While Lord Nelson, the second in command, was thus seeking to escape infelicity, by a separation from his lady, which he had fully resolved should be brought to a conclusion previously to his return from this expedition; his old friend, Sir Hyde Parker, the commander in chief, was equally desirous of securing happiness, prior to his departure, by the immediate possession of a young wife. This difference in the state of their respective domesticities by no means operated to disturb their harmony; though, doubtless, his lordship was rather in the greatest hurry to be gone.

The few days while Lord Nelson remained in London were chiefly engaged at the Admiralty; where, happily, his mind was so much absorbed by the consideration of public affairs, and the formation of due professional arrangements, that his domestic concerns found fewer intervals for their unwelcome intrusion. Even while at the house of his friend Alexander Davison Esq. in St. James's Square, transacting his own private business, so intent was his lordship on the public service that, when he mentioned, at the first proposal of the Copenhagen expedition, his intended going under Sir Hyde Parker—"If," added his lordship, "I had the chief command, I know well enough what I would do." Then, observing that his knowledge of the Cattegat was rather imperfect, and that he should therefore wish to see a correct chart, he requested Mr. Davison would immediately send for one to Mr. Faden's shop at Charing Cross. This being done, he said that government could spare only twelve ships for the purpose; and, after examining the chart a very few minutes, he positively marked on it the situations of those twelve ships exactly as they were afterwards placed on that memorable occasion. This extraordinary anecdote of Lord Nelson, his biographer had the honour to receive from Mr. Davison's own lips, in the very parlour where the circumstance occurred; and it affords an admirable proof of our hero's wonderful promptness and decision, as well as of his ardent zeal for the service of his country.

His lordship's flag had been shifted to the St. George, a second rate of ninety-eight guns; the San Josef, which he left at Torbay, being unfit for the intended service in the north seas. After joining part of the squadron at Spithead, they proceeded to Yarmouth, where the whole armament, consisting of fifty-two sail of various descriptions, unfortunately lessened by the loss of the Invincible of seventy-four guns, which struck on a shoal off Winterton, having been assembled, and fully prepared, took their departure on the 12th of March 1801.

Early in the morning of the 18th, land was discovered; and next day, about noon, the British fleet made the Scaw, or Scagen, the first general rendezvous. This low point of sandy and apparently barren land, which is the most northernly part of the peninsula of North Jutland, is eleven or twelve leagues distant from Marstrand Island on the Swedish shore. At both these points, the Danes and Swedes have respectively erected light-houses; for the support of which, all vessels passing the Sound, or entering the Swedish ports, are required to contribute: the entrance between the Scaw Lights and the Cattegat being considered as the entrance to the Cattegat. As it was well known, that the Danes were making every possible effort to obstruct the passage of the Sound, and render Copenhagen inaccessible to the approach of gun-vessels, much surprise was expressed, at the fleet's not being ordered to pass the Cattegat, with a strong north north-west wind, so highly favourable to such a design. The commander in chief, however, was probably deterred, by the nature of his instructions, from committing the country, by a forcible passage of the Sound, till the effect of Mr. Vansittart's pacific propositions, who had preceded the fleet, on board a frigate with a flag of truce, should be first fairly ascertained. This gentleman having reached Elsineur the 20th of March, proposed to the Danish court, in conjunction with Mr. Drummond, the British minister at Copenhagen, the secession of Denmark from the northern alliance; the allowance of a free passage to the British fleet through the Sound; and an abandonment of the system of sending convoys for the protection of Danish merchant vessels. These proposals being instantly rejected, the two British plenipotentiaries received passports for their return.

In the mean time, the officers and crew of the fleet, by foul winds, with heavy falls of sleet, snow, and rain, added to a chilling cold, which they particularly experienced from the 21st to the 24th, suffered considerable fatigue. This, with the delay, had a tendency to damp the ardour of the enterprise; and Lord Nelson, aware of all the consequences, would gladly have discarded much of that diplomatic etiquette which finally proved, as he had from the first supposed it would do, quite unimpressive with the Danes. Still less did he regard the discouraging suggestions of ignorant and designing pilots, whose exaggerated accounts of the difficulties to be surmounted, when the commander in chief had resolved on forcing the passage of the Sound, represented the enterprise as more practicable, and less hazardous, by the circuitous passage of the Great Belt. Though Lord Nelson's mind could not be thus induced to fluctuate, and was decidedly for the immediate passage of the Sound, when the Great Belt appeared to be preferred—"Let us, then, go by the Great Belt!" said the hero. Impatient for action, he was desirous of proceeding by any way which might soonest lead to the object.

On the 26th, at day-break, the fleet got under weigh, and stood to the westward; for the purpose, as was generally imagined, of passing the Great Belt; and Captain

Murray, of the Edgar, who had, the preceding summer, surveyed that entrance to the Baltic with a degree of precision hitherto unknown, tendered his services for the purpose. The facility with which this passage might be effected, by the aid of so active and intelligent an officer, where the Danes had only a single guard-ship, left little room to doubt that it would be adopted. This, however, was not done. Several vessels from the Baltic, on this and the following day, passed the Sound, under Prussian colours; and they were permitted to proceed, notwithstanding it was then sufficiently ascertained that Prussia had also acceded to this confederacy against Great Britain.

On the 27th, Sir Hyde Parker, acting under his instructions, dispatched a flag of truce, with the following note, to the Governor of Cronenberg Castle,

> "From the hostile transactions of the Court of Denmark, and sending away his Britannic Majesty's Charge d'Affaires, the commander in chief of his majesty's fleet is anxious to know what the determination of the Danish Court is--and whether the commanding officer of Cronenberg Castle has received orders to fire on the British fleet as they pass into the Sound?--as he must deem the firing; of the first gun a declaration of war on the part of Denmark.
>
> "Hyde Parker."

To these enquiries, this answer was returned by the Danish Governor.

> "I have the honour to inform your excellency, that his Majesty, the King of Denmark, did not send away the Charge d'Affaires; but that, on his own demand, he obtained a passport. As a soldier, I cannot meddle with politics; but, I am not at liberty to suffer a fleet, whose intention is not yet known, to approach the guns of the castle which I have the honour to command. In case your excellency should think proper to make any proposals to the King of Denmark, I wish to be informed thereof before the fleet approaches nearer to

the castle.

"Heer Stricker."

After receiving the above reply, the British commander in chief immediately sent notice to the Danish Governor—That, finding the intentions of the Court of Denmark to be hostile against his Britannic Majesty, he regarded his excellency's answer as a declaration of war; and, therefore, agreeable to his instructions, could no longer refrain from hostilities, however repugnant it might be to his feelings: but that, at the same time, the admiral would be ready to attend to any proposals of the Court of Denmark, for restoring the former amity and friendship, which had for so many years subsisted between the two courts. During these negociations, an officer of distinction, high in favour with the crown prince, coming on board the admiral, with a verbal answer to one of our proposals, and finding some difficulty in expressing, with sufficient accuracy, the sentiments of his court, was requested to communicate them in writing; when, a pen being brought for this purpose, which happened to be ill pointed, he held it up, and remarked, with a sarcastic smile—"If your guns are not better pointed than your pens, you will make little impression on Copenhagen." Certain it is, that the Danes, who were conscious of having taken every precaution which science could suggest for the defence of their country, entertained very little doubt that the British fleet would be compelled to retire, should it even venture to make an attack. The Sound was protected, on the Swedish side, by the fort of Helsingberg; and, on that of Denmark, by the Castle of Cronenberg: each of them garrisoned with forces very sufficient to withstand any attack. Besides this formidable opposition, numerous strong batteries were erected on the Danish shore, through the tremendous fire of which it was thought quite impracticable for any hostile fleet to pass. As for Copenhagen, it was, from the excellent state of it's ancient fortresses, the different batteries recently constructed, and the numerous well-disciplined troops by which they were manned, considered as absolutely impregnable.

On the 28th, the order to prepare for battle was received, as usual, by the British tars, with the loudest acclamations of joy; and they were soon convinced, that the passage of the Sound had been at length decided on. Nothing was now wanting to their felicity, but the appointment of a popular leader: and, happily for their country, and even for those who opposed them, this service was allotted to Lord Nelson; who, for that purpose, had judged it advisable to shift his flag on board the Elephant, commanded by his gallant and judicious friend, the Honourable Captain Thomas Foley.

The ships were now cleared for action, with an alacrity and expedition almost incredible: and, on the 30th, the wind having become favourable, the British fleet weighed, and formed the order of battle, Lord Nelson leading the van-division; and all safely passed the Sound, the celebrated Key of the Baltic, in about four hours, without having received the smallest damage from any of the Danish artillery. The only casualty, indeed, of this day, happened on board the Isis; where six or seven men were killed or wounded, by the bursting of a lower-deck gun. It is to be observed, however, that the Swedish batteries were very prudently silent, which afforded our ships an opportunity of keeping at a sufficient distance from the shore of Denmark; where a heavy and well-supported fire had commenced, from the whole line of their positions, at half-past six in the morning, when the Monarch, which had the honour of leading the fleet, appeared sufficiently advanced to be nearly within their range: a compliment which was soon returned, and with far better effect, on the town of Elsineur, by the leading ships, as well as by some of those which composed the centre and rear divisions.

The Danes, from a long received opinion in Europe, that the possession of Cronenberg Castle gave them an uncontrouled command of the passage of the Sound, have exacted, for more than a century, the undisputed right of levying contributions on all vessels trading to and from the Baltic, in proportion to the value of the cargoes: an imposition so sanctioned by time, that they considered any augmentation to the works as superfluous; and, relying on the co-operation of the Swedes, had fortunately neglected to render the approach more difficult, by forming a line of floating-batteries.

The channel of the Sound offers a prospect of very singular interest. On the right, appear the territories of Denmark; the islands of Saltholm and Amak, with part of Zealand; and Copenhagen, the capital of the kingdom, nearly in the front. The shore of Denmark presents a continued succession of fertile plains, umbrageous woods, rich meadows, rural mansions, neat villas, and embellished gardens; while the Swedish side chiefly exhibits, with much excellent pasture, a mountainous and picturesque coast. The island of Nuen, too, famous for the Observatory of the celebrated Tycho Brahe, fails not to attract the attention of every curious voyager: from whence the eye, looking back, perceives the fortresses of Elsineur, Cronenberg, and Helsingberg, apparently unite, bounding a vast lake to the north; but, on advancing, immediately descries the ocean, and the whole extent of the plain of Copenhagen, with it's capacious port crouded by vessels, and it's highly cultivated environs. On the side next the sea, this city, which is visible at the distance of several miles, presents itself in all it's magnificence; and the Gothic towers, with which it abounds, greatly engage the attention of every spectator, as well by the loftiness of their spires, as by the variety of their pleasingly grotesque decorations. The fortresss of Fredericstadt, supported on one side by the batteries of one of the arsenals, defends the entrance of the harbour: where there is, also, another battery; and where, as at this period, in case of necessity, a number of flat-bottomed boats, and floating-batteries, may likewise be stationed.

It appears that Sir Hyde Parker had, with the soundest discretion, now left every thing, but the nominal chief command, to our hero; who, with his usual alertness on all important occasions, lost not a single moment in preparing for the grand attack of the Danish capital. "The attempt," observes an ingenious eye-witness, said to be Mr. Fergusson, surgeon of the Elephant, "was arduous in the extreme; no common mind durst have conceived it, but it was suited to the exalted heroism of his. As his was the invigorating spirit of the counsel that planned the attack; so, in the execution, he only could have commanded success." During the interval which preceded the battle, the passage to the scene of action being very little known, and extremely intricate, his lordship had the soundings accurately made under his own eye and observation, and the several buoys laid which were to direct the passage of the fleet; the vast fatigue of this employ was too much for his tender constitution, and had nearly proved fatal, but he was happily re-invigorated by his excessive zeal. With the most indefatigable attention, did he prescribe every measure to be adopted by all ranks and degrees under his command; and there was no possible position that could have been contrived by the enemy, for which he was not effectually prepared, "I could only admire," says Mr. Fergusson, modestly disclaiming nautical science, "when I saw the first man in all the world spend the hours of the day and the night in boats; and wonder, when the light shewed me a path, marked by buoys, which was trackless the preceding evening." It had been agreed, with Sir Hyde Parker, that his lordship should proceed with twelve ships of the line, and all the frigates, bomb-ketches, fire-ships, and other vessels, to Draco Point, a short distance from Copenhagen, for the purpose of making his final dispositions for the attack; waiting, there, the favourable effect of a wind to the southward: and the commander in chief was to weigh anchor, with his division, whenever his lordship should proceed to the immediate scene of action; thus menacing, by his advance, the Crown Batteries, together with four ships or hulks which lay near for the protection of the arsenal, as well as covering any vessels which might happen to be disabled in an attack where they must necessarily be so prodigiously exposed. Being now fully prepared, his lordship, with that truly Christian spirit which, in direct opposition to the puritanic cant of piety, was ever far more manifested by his actions than expressed by his lips, devoutly exclaimed—"Thank God, for having enabled me to get through this difficult and fatiguing part of my duty: which has, really, worn me down; and is infinitely more grievous to me, than any resistance I can experience from an enemy!"

The subsequent circumstances, as described by Mr. Fergusson, are so very characteristically detailed, that they cannot fail highly to interest every reader—"On the 1st of April, in the afternoon," says this ingenious gentleman, "we took our departure from the main body of the fleet, then lying about four miles below Copenhagen; and coasted along the outer edge of the shoal called the Middle Ground, till we doubled it's farthest extremity, when the squadron cast anchor. This shoal, of the same extent as the sea-front of the town, lies exactly before it, at about three quarters of a mile in distance. The interval between it and the shore has deep water, and is called the King's Channel. There the Danes had arranged their line of defence, as near the town as possible. It consisted of nineteen ships and floating-batteries, flanked at the lower extremity by two artificial islands in the mouth of the harbour, called the Crown Batteries, and extended for about a mile along the whole extent of the town, leaving intervals for the batteries on shore to play. As our anchor dropped, at eight in the evening, Lord Nelson emphatically called out, that he would fight them the moment he had a fair wind. It came with the morning; and the signal to prepare for battle, floated from our mast-head. He had spent the whole night in consultation. The gallant and ever to be lamented Captain Riou never left him. Captain Hardy, too, was there, of course; and the brave and the good Captain Foley. To mark the spirit which the presence and example of Lord Nelson never failed to inspire, Captain Hardy, as soon as it became dark, had ventured along the enemy's line, in the smallest sized boat; and, as he went so near that the noise of throwing the lead might have discovered him, he used a long pole, or rod, on which he marked the depth of the water. About half past nine in the morning, the signals of the different ships having been made, repeated, and answered, we had the mortification to see the Agamemnon get upon the edge of the shoal, on the first attempt to leave her anchorage, where she remained immovable. A similar misfortune followed, in succession, to the Russell and Polyphemus; and the Jamaica frigate, with a convoy of gun-boats and small craft, having fallen in with a counter-current, made the signal of inability to come forward. A mind less invincible than Lord Nelson's, might have been discouraged. Though the battle was not began, yet he had approached the enemy; and he felt that he could not retreat, to wait for reinforcements, without compromising the glory of his country. His soul, too, was ever superior to common discouragements; and, the signal to bear down still kept it's place. His agitation, during these moments, was extreme. I never shall forget the impression that it made upon me! It was not, however, the agitation of indecision; but of ardent, animated patriotism, panting for glory, which had appeared within his reach, and was vanishing from his grasp. The Edgar, at last, led in. I shall not attempt to describe the scene that ensued, for language has not the power. We were received with the fire of more than a thousand guns! No sooner had all the ships got into their stations, than the countenance of our chief brightened, and his good-humour flowed. As the fire rolled, his conversation became joyous, animated, elevated, and delightful; for, confident of victory, he knew that his deck was, at that moment, the most glorious theatre of human nature. For an hour, the battle raged. Our fire was regular, distinctive, and terrible; that of the enemy was becoming desultory and ill-directed. When the signal-lieutenant called out, that number 39, (to discontinue the action) was thrown out by the commander in chief, then about four miles off, Lord Nelson refused to believe it: but, when he was again assured, he exclaimed—"Then, damn the signal; take no notice of it, and hoist mine for closer battle: that is the way I answer such signals!" It flew, at the word; and every ship engaged respected it as soon as seen. He again exclaimed—"Now, nail mine to the mast!" and, turning to Captain Foley, with admirable good-humour said—"Foley, you know I have lost an eye, and have a right to be blind when I like; and, damn me, if I'll see that signal!"—pointing to Sir Hyde Parker's ship. At a quarter before three in the afternoon, the victory was compleat; the whole Danish line, that was drawn up before the town, having struck their colours, after a dreadful defence, and their ships becoming untenable. The Elephant, the flag-ship, about an hour before, in veering away cable, to get opposite the Crown Batteries, had stuck on a small middle shoal, and remained fast: the same misfortune had happened to the Defiance; and, I believe, one more besides. To board the prizes was difficult; or, rather, impossible: for, being under the batteries of the town, no boat could approach them. Lord Nelson, therefore, sent a flag of truce, with the following letter—

> "Lord Nelson has directions to spare Denmark, when no longer resisting; but, if the firing is continued on the part of Denmark, Lord Nelson will be obliged to set on fire all the floating-batteries he has taken, without having the power of saving the brave Danes who have defended them.
>
> "Nelson and Bronte,
>
> "Vice-Admiral, under the command of
> "Admiral Sir Hyde Parker.
>
> "Dated on board his Majesty's ship Elephant, Copenhagen Roads,
> "April 2, 1801.
>
> "To the Brothers of Englishmen, the Danes."

"It may be farther characteristic of his lordship, to mention that, when a wafer was brought for the above letter, he said—"No; bring me wax, and a match: this is no time to appear hurried and informal." An unfounded idea has prevailed, that the flag of truce was sent to cover his own ships, which would inevitably have been destroyed if the Danes had not been cajoled into an armistice; and the victory is, thereby, converted into a defeat: but the victory was too decisive, to be thus ravished from his grasp. The enemy were compleatly horrified and dismayed, at the carnage and ruin which a dreadful contest of five hours had involved them in. The batteries of the town were too far distant, to have much effect even upon the ships aground; Sir Hyde Parker, with the rest of the fleet, could soon have approached; and, as to the Crown Batteries, which alone were to be dreaded, the following disposition was made for carrying them—As the flag of truce left the admiral's ship, fifteen hundred of the choicest boarders, who had been selected from the whole fleet previously to the action, descended into fifty boats, thirty men in each boat. These boats were to be commanded by the Honourable Colonel Stewart, and Captain Freemantle. The moment it could be known, that the flag of truce was refused, the boats were to have pushed for the batteries. The fire of every gun in the fleet would have covered their approach; a few minutes would have carried them there; and let any one ask himself, what defence was to be expected from five hundred raw Danish soldiers, on an ill-built battery, that gave no cover—fatigued, besides, by the carnage of a terrible battle—against such assailants, flushed with victory, and irresistible in courage." It may, however, be proper to remark, that we could have done little more than spiked the guns; as these batteries, being within the range of the fire of the citadel, were not possible to have been long retained.

The following note, in answer to that sent on shore by Lord Nelson, was brought in a flag of truce from Copenhagen, by General-Adjutant Lindholm.

> "His Royal Highness, the Crown Prince, has sent me,
> General-Adjutant Lindholm, on board, to his Britannic Majesty's
> Vice-Admiral, the Right Honourable Lord Nelson, to ask the
> particular object of sending the flag of truce?"

Though Sir Frederic Thesiger, formerly a commander in the Russian service, and who had been recommended, by Earl Spencer, to accompany Lord Nelson as what is absurdly denominated, with a very reprehensible spirit of Gallicism to introduce into the British navy, the admiral's aide-de-camp, had carried the flag of truce, with Lord Nelson's note, and was authorized verbally to enlarge on the humanity of it's import, some suspicions appear to have been entertained as to the true nature and extent of his lordship's object; and, therefore, General-Adjutant Lindholm was thus commissioned to procure a farther explanation in writing. His lordship, accordingly, addressed to the Government of Denmark the following reply.

> "Lord Nelson's object in sending the flag of truce, is humanity. He, therefore, consents that hostilities shall cease, till Lord Nelson can take his prisoners out of the prizes; and he consents to land all the wounded Danes, and to burn or remove his prizes.
>
> "Lord Nelson, with humble duty to his royal highness, begs leave to say, that he will ever esteem it the greatest victory he ever gained, if this flag of truce may be the happy forerunner of a lasting and happy union, between his own most gracious sovereign and his majesty the King of Denmark.
>
> "Nelson and Bronte.
> "Elephant, 2d April 1801."

The Danish government, now wisely satisfied of Lord Nelson's sincerity, immediately invited him on shore, that a conference might be held with the King of Denmark, for arranging the preliminaries of an amicable treaty; and his lordship, without hesitation, visited Copenhagen in the afternoon of this very day.

On landing at the quay, the carriage of a respectable merchant, by whom it had been purposely sent, was respectfully offered to his lordship: the royal carriage, intended for our hero's conveyance, not having arrived sufficiently soon; owing to the suddenness of his arrival, and the vast press of people who had assembled to behold him. Much has been said, respecting the temper of this prodigious multitude, on first seeing the British hero among them: some protesting, that the conqueror of their country in the morning, was hailed, in the afternoon, as their guardian angel—which, all things considered, he perhaps well deserved to have been; while others maintain, that the people's fury was so excessive, and their knowledge of his lordship's views so imperfect, that they were with difficulty restrained from absolutely tearing in pieces the pacific hero who had thus, inspired by the most humane and generous sentiments, fearlessly ventured his person among them. It may be very difficult, and cannot on this occasion prove of much importance, to ascertain the exact truth; which seldom resides in extremes, and is not always found precisely in the centre, where dull and formal gravity is ever induced alone to seek it. Whatever might seem the momentary bias of the mob, they unquestionably proceeded to no actual outrage; and it is universally agreed, that the Danes, of all ranks, were no sooner made acquainted with our hero's humane and generous motives, than they greeted him with every testimony of the truest admiration and regard.

Lord Nelson having walked to the royal palace of the Octagon, the crown prince received him in the hall; conducted him up stairs; and presented him to the king, whose very infirm state is said to have greatly affected our hero's sensibility. The preliminary objects of this impressive interview having been arranged, with every appearance of reciprocal sincerity, his lordship readily accepted an invitation to partake of some refreshment with the crown prince. During the repast, Lord Nelson spoke in raptures of the valour of the Danes; and he is asserted to have declared that, though the French fought bravely, they could not have stood one hour the fight which the Danes had maintained for four. "I have been," observed his lordship, "in one hundred and five engagements, in the course of my life, but that of to-day was the most terrible of all." It is added, that he particularly requested the crown prince would introduce him to a very young officer, whom he described as having performed wonders during the battle, by attacking the Elephant immediately under the lower guns. This proved to be a youth of seventeen, named Villemoes: whom the hero, on his being presented, immediately embraced with the affection of a brother; and delicately intimated, that he ought to be made an admiral. The crown prince, with peculiar felicity, instantly replied—"If, my lord, I were to make all my brave officers admirals, I should have no captains or lieutenants in my service." This heroic stripling had volunteered the command of a sort of raft, called a praam, carrying twenty-four guns, and a hundred and twenty men; on which, having pushed off from shore, in the fury of battle, he got under the stern of his lordship's ship, below the reach of the stern-chasers, and fired with considerable effect. The British marines, however, made terrible slaughter among these brave fellows; many of whom were soon killed, but their young commander still remained at his post, surrounded by the slain, till the announcement of the truce. The crown prince has since presented this youth with a medallion commemorative of his gallantry, and appointed him to the command of the royal yacht in which his royal highness makes his annual visit to Holstein.

On the day following, Lord Nelson addressed the official account of this great victory to Sir Hyde Parker, his commander in chief.

"Elephant, off Copenhagen,
3d April 1801.

"SIR,

"In obedience to your directions, to report the proceedings of the squadron named in the margin--[the Elephant, Defiance, Monarch, Bellona, Edgar, Russell, Ganges, Glatton, Isis, Agamemnon, Polyphemus, and Ardent, ships of the line; the Amazon, Desiree, Blanche, and Alcmene, frigates; the Dart, Arrow, Cruiser, and Harpy, sloops; the Zephyr, and Otter, fire-ships; the Discovery, Sulphur, Hecla, Explosion, Zebra, Terror, and Volcano, bombs; with eight gun-brigs]--which you did me the honour to place under my command, I beg leave to inform you that, having by the assistance of that able officer Captain Riou, and the unremitting exertions of Captain Brisbane and the masters of the Amazon and Cruiser in particular, buoyed the channel of the Outer Deep and the position of the Middle Ground, the squadron passed in safety, and anchored off Draco the evening of the 1st: and that, yesterday morning, I made the signal for the squadron to weigh; and to engage the Danish line, consisting of seven sail of the line, ten floating-batteries mounting from twenty-six twenty-four pounders, to eighteen eighteen pounders, and one bomb-ship, besides schooner gun-vessels. These were supported by the Crown Islands, mounting eighty-eight cannon; four sail of the line, moored in the harbour's mouth; and some batteries on the island of Amak.

"The bomb-ship, and schooner gun-vessels, made their escape; the other seventeen sail are sunk, burnt, or taken, being the whole of the Danish line to the southward of the Crown Islands, after a battle of four hours.

"From the very intricate navigation, the Bellona and Russell unfortunately grounded: but, although not in the situation assigned them, yet so placed as to be of great service. The Agamemnon could not weather the shoal of the Middle Ground, and was obliged to anchor: but not the smallest blame can be attached to Captain Fancourt; it was an event to which all the ships were liable. These accidents prevented the extension of our line by the three ships before mentioned: who would, I am confident, have silenced the Crown Islands, the two outer ships in the harbour's mouth, and prevented the heavy loss in the Defiance and Monarch; and which unhappily threw the gallant and good Captain Riou (to whom I had given the command of the frigates and sloops named in the margin--[the Blanche, Alcmene, Dart, Arrow, Zephyr, and Otter]--to assist the attack of the ships at the harbour's mouth) under a very heavy fire. The consequence has been, the death of Captain Riou, and many brave officers and men in the frigates and sloops. The bombs were directed, and took their stations, abreast of the Elephant, and threw some shells into the arsenal. Captain Rose, who volunteered his services to direct the gun-brigs, did every thing that was possible to get them forward, but the current was too strong for them to be of service during the action; but not the less merit was due to Captain Rose, and--I believe--all the officers and crews of the gun-vessels, for their exertions.

"The boats of those ships of the fleet who were not ordered on the attack, afforded us every assistance; and the officers and men who were in them, merit my warmest approbation.

"The Desiree took her station in raking the southernmost Danish ship of the line, and performed the greatest service.

"The action began at five minutes past ten. The van led by Captain George Murray of the Edgar, who set a noble example of intrepidity, which was as well followed up by every captain, officer, and man, in the squadron. It is my duty to state to you, the high and distinguished merit and gallantry of Rear-Admiral Graves.

"To Captain Foley, who permitted me the honour of hoisting my flag in the Elephant, I feel under the greatest obligations; his advice was necessary, on many important occasions, during the battle. I beg leave to express how much I feel indebted to every captain, officer, and man, for their zeal and distinguished bravery on this occasion. Colonel Stewart did me the favour to be on board the Elephant; and himself, with every officer and soldier under his orders, shared with pleasure the toils and dangers of the day.

"The loss, in such a battle, has naturally been very heavy. Amongst many other brave officers and men who were killed, I have, with sorrow, to place the name of Captain Moss, of the Monarch, who has left a wife and six children to lament his loss; and, among the wounded, that of Captain Sir Thomas Boulden Thompson, of the Bellona.

"I have the honour to be, with the greatest respect, Sir, your most obedient humble servant,

"Nelson and Bronte."

The above letter being transmitted to England by Sir Hyde Parker, inclosed in his dispatches to government, was afterwards published in the London Gazette, preceded by the following public letter from the commander in chief.

"Copenhagen Roads, 6th April 1801.

"Sir,

"You will be pleased to acquaint the Lords Commissioners of the Admiralty, that since my letter of the 23d of March, no opportunity of wind offered for going up the Sound, until the 25th; when the wind shifted, in a most violent squall, from the south-west to the north-west and north, and blew with such violence, and so great a sea, as to render it impossible for any ship to have weighed her anchor. The wind and sea were even so violent, as to oblige many ships to let go a second anchor to prevent them from driving, notwithstanding they were riding with two cables an end; and, by the morning, the wind veered again to the southward of the west. On the 30th of last month, the wind having come to the northward, we passed into the Sound with the fleet; but not before I had assured myself of the hostile intention of the Danes to oppose our passage. After anchoring about five or six miles from the Island of Huen, I reconnoitred, with Vice-Admiral Lord Nelson and Rear-Admiral Graves, the formidable line of ships, radeaus, pontoons, galleys, fireships, and gun-boats, flanked and supported by extensive batteries on the two islands called the Crown; the largest of which was mounted with from fifty to seventy pieces of cannon. These were again commanded by two ships of seventy guns, and a large frigate, in the inner road of Copenhagen; and two sixty-four gun ships, without masts, were moored on the flat on the starboard side of the entrance into the arsenal. The day after, the wind being southerly, we again examined their position, and came to the resolution of attacking them from the southward. Vice-Admiral Lord Nelson having offered his services for conducting the attack, had some days before we entered the Sound shifted his flag to the Elephant; and, after having examined and buoyed the outer channel of the Middle Ground, his lordship proceeded, with the twelve ships of the line named in the margin--[Elephant, Defiance, Monarch, Bellona, Edgar, Russell, Ganges, Glatton, Isis, Agamemnon, Polyphemus, and Ardent]--all the frigates, bombs, fire-ships, and all the small vessels; and, that evening, anchored off Draco Point, to make his disposition for the attack, and wait for the wind to the southward. It was agreed, between us, that the remaining ships with me, should weigh at the same moment his lordship did, and menace the Crown Batteries and the four ships of the line that lay at the entrance of the arsenal; as, also, to cover our disabled ships, as they came out of action.

"I have, now, the honour to inclose a copy of Vice-Admiral Lord Nelson's report to me of the action on the 2d instant. His lordship has stated so fully the whole of his proceedings on that day, as only to leave me the opportunity to testify my entire acquiescence and testimony of the bravery and intrepidity with which the action was supported throughout the line. Was it possible for me to add anything to the well-earned renown of Lord Nelson, it would be by asserting that his exertions, great as they have heretofore been, never were carried to a higher pitch of zeal for his country's service. I have only to lament, that the sort of attack, confined within an intricate and narrow passage, excluded the ships particularly under my command from the opportunity of exhibiting their valour: but I can with great truth assert, that the same spirit and zeal animated the whole of the fleet; and I trust, that the contest in which we are engaged will, on some future day, afford them an occasion of shewing that the whole were inspired with the same spirit, had the field been sufficiently extensive to have brought it into action.

"It is with the deepest concern, I mention the loss of Captains Moss and Riou; two very brave and gallant officers, whose loss, as I am well informed, will be sensibly felt by the families they have left behind them: the former, a wife and children; the latter, an aged mother. From the known gallantry of Sir Thomas Thompson, on former occasions, the naval service will have to regret the loss of the future exertions of that brave officer, whose leg was shot off. For all other particulars, I beg leave to refer their lordships to Captain Otway; who was with Lord Nelson in the latter part of the action, and is able to answer any questions that may be thought necessary to put to him. A return of the killed and wounded you will receive herewith."

KILLED.

Officers	20
Seamen, Marines, and Soldiers	234-254

WOUNDED.

Officers	48
Seamen, Marines, and Soldiers	651-699
Total killed and wounded	953

After a week's negotiation, during which Lord Nelson daily went on shore, and greatly endeared himself to the virtuous of all ranks, for his amiable frankness, generosity, and honour, the following treaty was signed and sealed, as the basis of returning amity between Great Britain and Denmark.

"The Danish Government on the one hand--and Admiral Sir Hyde Parker, Knight, Commander in Chief of his Britannic Majesty's Forces in the Road of Copenhagen, on the other--being, from motives of humanity, equally anxious to put a stop to the farther effusion of blood, and to save the City of Copenhagen from the disastrous consequences which may attend a farther prosecution of hostilities against that city, have mutually agreed upon a Military Armistice, or Suspension of Arms. His Danish Majesty having, for that purpose, appointed Major-General Ernest Frederic Walterstorff, Chamberlain to his Danish Majesty, and Colonel to a Regiment; and Adjutant-General Hans Lindholm, Captain in his Danish Majesty's Navy; his Commissioners for agreeing about the terms of the said Armistice--and Admiral Sir Hyde Parker, Knight, having, with the same view, duly authorized the Right Honourable Horatio Lord Nelson of the Nile, Knight of the most honourable Order of the Bath, Duke of Bronte in Sicily, Knight of the Grand Cross of the Order of St. Ferdinand and of Merit, and of the Imperial Order of the Ottoman Crescent, Vice-Admiral in the Fleet of his Britannic Majesty; and the Right Honourable William Stewart, Lieutenant-Colonel in his Britannic Majesty's service, and commanding a detachment of his Britannic Majesty's forces embarked--the said Commissioners have met this day; and, having exchanged their respective powers, have agreed upon the following terms--

"ARTICLE I.

"From the moment of the signature of this armistice, all hostilities shall immediately cease, between the fleet under the command of Admiral Sir Hyde Parker, and the City of Copenhagen, and all the armed ships and vessels of his Danish Majesty in the road or harbour of that city; as, likewise, between the different islands and provinces of Denmark, Jutland included.

"ARTICLE II.

"The armed ships and vessels belonging to his Danish Majesty shall remain in their present actual situation, as to armament, equipment, and hostile position; and the treaty, commonly understood as the treaty of Armed Neutrality, shall, as far as relates to the co-operation of Denmark, be suspended while the Armistice remains in force.

"On the other side, the armed ships and vessels under the command of Admiral Sir Hyde Parker, shall in no manner whatsoever molest the City of Copenhagen, or his Danish Majesty's armed ships and vessels on the coasts of the different islands and provinces of Denmark, Jutland included; and, in order to avoid every thing which might otherwise create uneasiness or jealousy, Sir Hyde Parker shall not suffer any of the ships or vessels under his command to approach within gun-shot of the armed ships or forts of his Danish Majesty, in the road of Copenhagen. This restriction shall not, however, extend to vessels necessarily passing and repassing through the Casper or King's Channel.

"ARTICLE III.

"This armistice is to protect the city of Copenhagen, as also the coast of Denmark, of Jutland, and islands included, against the attack of any other naval force which his Britannic Majesty may now, or hereafter, during it's remaining in force, have in those seas.

"ARTICLE IV.

"The fleet of Admiral Sir Hyde Parker shall be permitted to provide itself at Copenhagen, and along the coasts of the different islands and provinces of Denmark, Jutland included, with every thing which it may require for the health and comfort of it's crews.

"ARTICLE V.

"Admiral Sir Hyde Parker shall send on shore all such subjects of his Danish Majesty as are now on board the British fleet under his command; the Danish government engaging to give an acknowledgment for them, as also for all such wounded as were permitted to be landed after the action of the 2d instant, in order that they may be accounted for in favour of Great Britain, in the unfortunate event of the renewal of hostilities.

"ARTICLE VI.

"The coasting trade carried on by Denmark along all such parts of her coast as are included in the operation of this armistice, shall be unmolested by any British ships or vessels whatever, and instructions given accordingly by Admiral Sir Hyde Parker.

"ARTICLE VII.

"This armistice is to continue, uninterrupted by the contracting parties, for the space of fourteen weeks from the signature hereof; at the expiration of which time, it shall be in the power of either of the said parties to declare a cessation of the same, and to recommence hostilities, upon giving fourteen days previous notice.

"The conditions of this armistice are, upon all occasions, to be explained in the most liberal and loyal manner, so as to remove all ground for farther dispute, and facilitate the means of bringing about the restoration of harmony and good understanding between the two kingdoms.

"In faith whereof, we, the undersigned commissioners, in virtue of our full powers, have signed the present armistice, and have affixed to it the seal of our arms.

"Done on board his Britannic Majesty's ship the London, in Copenhagen Roads, April 9, 1801.

"Nelson and Bronte.
"William Stewart.
"Ernest Frederic Walterstorff.
"Hans Lindholm.

"In pursuance of my abovementioned authority, I ratify this document with my hand--

"Frederic.

"Ratified by me--

"Hyde Parker, Admiral and Commander in Chief of his Britannic Majesty's Fleet."

The Danes had great reason to be satisfied with the liberality of this armistice; the conditions of which certainly were, on our part, most strictly performed. It will appear that, on the part of Denmark, this was not precisely the case. Lord Nelson's conduct, however, at once firm and conciliating, procured justice to his country without again resorting to arms. The first blow had been struck by Denmark, and she had suffered for her rashness and temerity. Even in passing the Sound, her guns evinced the disposition, but happily possessed not the power, to injure the British fleet. A very heavy fire was kept up by the Danes, but none of our ships received a shot. In the mean time, we had several bomb-ships firing on the town of Elsineur, the shells from which killed upwards of a hundred and fifty people on shore. At Copenhagen, still more confident in their strength, they had made every arrangement for the destruction of our fleet, but no preparation for the defeat of their own. Shielded by nature with dangerous shoals, and fortified by art with powerful batteries, they seemed rather to invite, than to dread, any hostile attack. They reflected not, that the hero coming against them was no less expert as a navigator than as a warrior, and scarcely more a seaman than a soldier. Happily his heroic heart was replete with humanity, and his dreadful ability to shed human blood only surpassed by his ardent desire to spare it's unnecessary effusion. The Danes, trusting to the strength of their grand line of defence, composed of eighteen ships, block-ships, floating-batteries, &c. which were all, in a few hours, sunk, burnt, or taken, had neglected to engage surgeons for their wounded defenders; who were found bleeding to death, on boarding the different captured vessels, in prodigious numbers, and afforded a shocking spectacle of horror to our brave but humane seamen. To preserve his fellow creatures from wanton destruction, the hero's flag of truce unfurled; a pause was thus obtained; reason had time to operate; and the basis was immediately laid for a renewal of that amity which had happily prevailed, for a long series of years, between the two nations, though anciently the fiercest foes.

The news of this victory was received in England with the utmost rejoicing; nor did the temper of the people fail to participate in their favourite hero's generous sentiments towards the brave but vanquished Danes. They considered Denmark as having been unwillingly dragged into the confederacy; they admired the patriotic courage of her misdirected sons; and generously lamented the cruel necessity of thus compelling them to relinquish a league, which had for it's object, beneath the artful veil of a generous love of liberty, that has sufficiently deluged the earth with blood, the unjust and absurd view of destroying the maritime power of Great Britain, by which the freedom of the, seas is alone preserved to the honourable commerce of all civilized nations.

On the 16th of April, the Earl of St. Vincent, then First Lord of the Admiralty, made a motion in the House of Peers—and Mr. Addington, now Lord Sidmouth, then Chancellor of the Exchequer, in the House of Commons—of thanks to Sir Hyde Parker, Lord Nelson, Rear Admiral Graves, and the rest of the officers, seamen, and marines, for their very exemplary bravery displayed in the great and glorious victory atchieved at Copenhagen; which were carried, in both houses, with acclamations of unanimous applause. The Duke of Clarence observed, of his old friend, Lord Nelson, whom he ever loved and revered, that fortune seemed to back his courage and intrepidity, in every enterprise he engaged; and acknowledged his own obligations, as a prince of the blood, to the gallant commanders, and to the whole fleet, for the accomplishment of a victory which, probably, in it's effects, would restore the possessions on the continent to his family, together with the peace and security of the British empire, and of Europe. About a month afterwards, Lord Nelson was elevated to the rank of Viscount of the united kingdom of Great Britain and Ireland, by the name, stile, and title, of Viscount Nelson of the Nile, and of Burnham-Thorpe in the county of Norfolk; an additional honour which was generally and justly considered, at the time, and must ever be regarded by posterity, as by no means equal to his high deserts.

In the mean time, immediately after signing the convention with Denmark, Russia and Sweden remaining still unattacked, Sir Hyde Parker had proceeded to the eastward, with such ships as were in a condition for service: leaving Lord Nelson at Copenhagen, with orders to repair his damaged ships, and dispose of the prizes; after which, he was to follow the commander in chief, and assist in accomplishing the other designs of this very important expedition. The repairs were not long compleating, and the prizes were soon disposed of; of the latter, all but one—the Holstein of sixty-four guns—were found entirely unfit for service, and immediately destroyed. Even this solitary remain of the Danish formidable line of defence, was only judged worthy of being commissioned as an hospital-ship in the British fleet; yet villainy and weakness united to wrest from our hero the honour of a compleat victory, even on the spot where it had been felt as well as witnessed.

Lord Nelson, after the battle of the 2d of April, had returned with his flag to the St. George; and, on the 16th, was ready to proceed after the commander in chief, who had entered the Baltic, and greatly alarmed the Russians, Prussians, and Swedes. Most of the squadron of his lordship, however, touched the ground, in their passage through the narrow and shallow channel which divides the islands of Amak and Saltholm, and two or three of them actually sticking fast for a short time, he was detained, even after they did pass, to have the St. George lightened, which drew still more water than the rest, by taking out the guns, and putting them on board an American ship. While this was effecting, the report of the Swedish fleet being out, with an intention to join that of Russia, then lying at Revel, reached his lordship. The instant he received this intelligence, though it was then a very cold evening of that climate, he descended into his gig, or smallest boat; and, after being so exposed on the water several hours, got again on board the Elephant, the former bearer of his flag and triumph. Lord Nelson, in his extreme haste to quit the St. George, had neglected to take his boat-cloak; but he would not lose a moment in returning for it, notwithstanding the inclemency of the weather and the great distance he had necessarily to go. A master of one of the ships, who was ordered to attend, earnestly pressed his lordship's acceptance of a great coat which he had brought for himself. This, however, was as kindly refused, as it had been affectionately tendered—"I thank you," said the hero, "very much; but, to tell you the truth, my anxiety, at present, keeps me sufficiently warm." Soon afterwards, his lordship asked—"Think you, that the British fleet has quitted Bornholm? If it has," continued he, without waiting for a reply, "we must follow it to Carlscrona." His lordship had arrived about midnight; and, the next day, saw the Swedish armament safely sheltered under the numerous forts and batteries erected on the island at the entrance of Carlscrona; where, as he suspected, it had taken timely refuge from the British fleet. Sir Hyde Parker, while on his voyage to Revel, having gained intelligence of the intended junction of the Swedish fleet with that of the Russians against which he was proceeding, had immediately steered his course for the Island of Bornholm, with the hope of intercepting the Swedes; but the commander, warned by the Danish disaster, wisely retreated from the danger of a similar encounter, by returning into port with the utmost precipitation.

Scarcely had Lord Nelson quitted Copenhagen, where he could not but have endeared himself to every virtuous heart, by his amiable liberality of disposition—bountifully rewarding youth of promise in the national military schools of the

Danes, as if he had been dealing honours among the deserving of his own country, and every way displaying the superior cast of his dignified soul—when he learned that Olfert Fischer, the Danish commander in chief, had officially published the following shamefully partial account of this indisputably great and glorious victory, as transmitted to his Royal Highness the Crown Prince.

DANISH OFFICIAL ACCOUNT OF THE BATTLE OF COPENHAGEN.

"On the 1st of April, at half past three in the afternoon, two divisions of the English fleet, under the command of Vice-Admiral Lord Nelson, and a rear-admiral, weighed anchor, and stood eastward, and by the south of the middle passage of the road, where they anchored. This force consisted of twelve ships of the line; and several large frigates, gun-boats, and other smaller vessels; in all, thirty-one sail.

"On the 2d of April, at three-quarters past nine in the morning, the wind south-east, both the vessels to the south and the vessels to the north of the middle road, weighed anchor. The ships of the line, and heavy frigates, under Lord Nelson, steered for the Konigstiefe, to take their stations, in order, along the line of defence confided to me. The gunboats, and small vessels, took their stations near the town; and the division of Admiral Parker, consisting of eight ships of the line, and some small vessels, steered with a press of sail southwards, to the right wing of defence.

"At half past ten, the foremost ship of Admiral Nelson's division passed the southernmost ship of the line of defence. I gave those ships that were within shot the signal for battle. The block-ships, Provesteen, and Wagner, and immediately after these the Jutland, between which and the block-ship Dannebrog, the leading English ship of seventy-four guns fixed her station, by throwing out one of her rear-anchors, obeyed the signal, by a well directed and well supported fire. By degrees, the rest of the ships came up; and, as they sailed past, on both sides of the ships already at anchor, they formed a thick line: which, as it stretched northward to the ship of the line the Zealand, engaged not more than two-thirds of the line of defence committed to me; while the Trekroner--or Three Crowns Battery--and the block-ships Elephanten and Mars, with the frigate Hielperen, did not come at all into the action.

"In half an hour, the battle was general. Ten ships of the line, among which was one of eighty guns, the rest chiefly seventy-fours, and from six to eight frigates, on the one side: on the other, seven block-ships; of which, only one of seventy-four, the rest of sixty-four and under; two frigates; and six smaller vessels. *This was the respective strength of the two parties*. The enemy had, on the whole, *two ships to one*: and the block-ship Provesteen had, besides a ship of the line and the rear-admiral, two frigates against her; by which she was raked the whole time, without being able to return a shot.

"If I only recapitulate, *historically*, what your highness, and along with you a great portion of the citizens of Denmark and Europe, have seen, I may venture to call that an unequal combat, which was maintained, and supported, for four hours and a half, with unexampled courage and effect--in which the fire of the superior force was so much weakened, for an hour before the end of the battle, that several of the English ships, and particularly Lord Nelson's, were obliged to fire only single shots--that this hero, himself, in the middle and very heat of the battle, sent a flag of truce on shore to propose a cessation of hostilities--if I also add, that it was announced to me, that two English ships of the line had struck; but, being supported by fresh ships, again hoisted their flags--I may, in such circumstances, be permitted to say, and I believe I may appeal to the enemy's own confession, that in this engagement Denmark's ancient naval reputation blazed forth with such incredible splendor, that I thank Heaven all Europe are the witnesses of it!

"Yet the scale, if not equal, did not decline far to the disadvantage of Denmark. The ships that were first and most obstinately attacked, even surrounded by the enemy, the incomparable Provesteen, Wagner, and Jutland, fought till almost all their guns were dismounted; but these vessels were obliged to give way to superior force, *and the Danish fire ceased along the whole line from north to south*.

"At half past eleven, the Dannebrog ship of the line, which, lay along-side Admiral Nelson, was set on fire. I repaired, with my flag, on board the Holstein, of the line, belonging to the north wing; but the Dannebrog long kept her flag flying, in spite of this disaster. At the end of the battle, she had two hundred and seventy men killed and wounded.

"At half past two, the Holstein was so shattered, and had so many killed and wounded, and so many guns dismounted, that I then carried the pendant to be hoisted instead of my flag, and went on shore, to the battery of the Three Crowns, from whence I commanded the north wing; *which was slightly engaged with the division of Admiral Parker*, till about four o'clock, when I received orders from your royal highness to put an end to the engagement.

"Thus, the quarter of the line of defence, from the Three Crowns to the frigate Hielperen, was in the power of the enemy; and the Hielperen, finding herself alone, slipped her cables, and steered to Stirbfeir. The ship Elven, after she had received many shots in the hull, and had her masts and rigging shot away, and a great number killed and wounded, retreated within the Crowns. The gunboats, Nyebrog and Aggershuus--which last towed the former away, when near sinking--ran ashore, and the Gurnarshe floating-battery, which had suffered much, together with the block-ship Dannebrog, shortly after the battle, blew up.

"Besides the visible loss the enemy have suffered, I am convinced, their loss in killed and wounded is considerable. The advantage the enemy have gained by their victory, too, consists merely in ships which are not fit for use, in spiked cannon, and gunpowder damaged by sea-water.

"The number killed and wounded cannot yet be exactly ascertained; but I calculate it, from sixteen to eighteen hundred men. Among the former, it is with grief that I mention the captains of the block-ship Infoedstratten and the frigate Kronbrog, Captain Thura and First-Lieutenant Hauch, with several other brave officers: among the wounded, the commander of the Dannebrog; who, besides other wounds, has lost his right hand.

"I want expression, to do justice to the unexampled courage of the officers and crews. The battle itself can only enable you to form an idea of it.

"Olfert Fischer."

The honourable mind of Lord Nelson indignantly revolted at the meanness conspicuous in this account; and he was resolved to chastise the pusillanimous malignity which it was so clumsily adapted to cover, by addressing the following letter, through General-Adjutant Lindholm, to the Crown Prince of Denmark, that his royal highness might see his lordship's sense of such a wretched attempt to deprive our hero of the honour of a victory, and screen the Danish commander in chief, himself, from the dreaded shame of a defeat not in itself by any means disgraceful.

"St. George, at Sea,
22d April 1801.

"MY DEAR SIR,

"Commodore Fischer having, in a public letter, given an account to the world of the battle of the 2d, called upon his royal highness as a witness to the truth of it. I, therefore, think it right to address myself to you, for the information of his royal highness; as, I assure you, had this officer confined himself to his own veracity, I should have treated his official letter with the contempt it deserved, and allowed the world to appreciate the merits of the two contending officers. I shall make a few, and very few, observations on this letter. He asserts the superiority of numbers on the part of the British; it will turn out, if that is of any consequence, that the Danish line of defence, to the southward of the Crown Islands, was much stronger, and more numerous, than the British. We had only five sail of seventy-fours, two sixty-fours, two fifties, and one frigate, engaged; a bomb vessel, towards the latter end, threw some shells into the arsenal. Two seventy-fours, and one sixty-four, by an accident, grounded; or the Crown Islands, and the Elephanten and Mars, would have had full employment: and, by the assistance of the frigates--who went to try, alone, what I had directed the three sail of the line who grounded to assist them in--I have reason to hope, they would have been equally successful as that part of the British line engaged. I am ready to admit, that many of the Danish officers and men behaved as well as men could do, and deserved not to be abandoned by their commander. I am justified in saying this, from Commodore Fischer's own declaration. In his own letter, he states that, after he quitted the Dannebrog, she long contested the battle. If so, more shame for him to quit so many brave fellows! *Here* was no manoeuvering, it was downright fighting; and it was his duty to have shewn an example of firmness becoming the high trust reposed in him. He went in such a hurry, if he went before she struck--which, but for his own declaration, I can hardly believe--that he forgot to take his broad pendant with him, for both pendant and ensign were struck together; and it is from this circumstance, that I claimed the commodore as a prisoner of war. He then went, as he says, on board the Holstein--the brave captain of which did not want him--where he did not hoist his pendant. From this ship, he went on shore, either before or after she struck, or he would have been again a prisoner. As to his nonsense about victory, his royal highness will not much credit him. I sunk, burnt, captured, or drove into the harbour, the whole line of defence to the southward of the Crown Islands. He says, he is told that two British ships struck. Why did he not take possession of them? I took possession of his as fast as they struck. The reason is clear, that he did not believe it. He must have known the falsity of the report, and that no fresh British ships did come near the ships engaged. He states, that the ship in which I had the honour to hoist my flag fired, latterly, only single guns. It is true; for steady and cool were my brave fellows, and did not wish to throw away a single shot. He seems to exult, that I sent on shore a flag of truce. Men of his description, if they ever are victorious, know not the feel of humanity. You know, and his royal highness knows, that the guns fired from the shore could only fire through the Danish ships which had surrendered; and that, if I fired at the shore, it could only be in the same manner. God forbid, that I should destroy an unresisting Dane! When they became my prisoners, I became their protector. Humanity alone, could have been my object; but Mr. Fischer's carcase was safe, and he regarded not the sacred call of humanity. His royal highness thought as I did. It has brought about an armistice; which, I pray the Almighty, may bring about a happy reconciliation between the two kingdoms. As I have not the names of all the ships correct--only of the thirteen, including the seven sail of the line which struck, remained at anchor, and fell into my possession after the battle--I shall, therefore, be very much obliged to you, for a correct list of their names; and the number of men, if possible to be obtained, on board each, and the numbers sent from the shore during the action. My earnest wish is, to be correct; and believe me, dear Sir, with great esteem, your most obedient servant,

"Nelson and Bronte."

"General-Adjutant Lindholm."

Whatever severity may appear in this retort, it's, justice would be with difficulty refuted. The answer of General-Adjutant Lindholm apologizes, with very considerable address, for the commander in chief; but that honourable officer's reasoning is also tinctured with as much national partiality as is consistent with a due regard to truth. This is no uncommon effect of patriotic zeal in the best minds, and may be traced even in that of our hero.

"Copenhagen, 2d May 1801.

"MY LORD!

"Your lordship has imposed upon me a very painful task, by desiring me to communicate to his Royal Highness the Crown Prince the contents of that letter with which your lordship has favoured me the 22d of April; and in which you have treated Commodore Fischer with a severity which, as a brother officer, I cannot but think too great, indeed, I conceive, that your lordship has felt a certain degree of displeasure at that incorrectness which you have thought to find in Commodore Fischer's official report; but your lordship did not fully consider, at that moment, that he himself might have received incorrect reports: a fatality to which every commander in chief is exposed. I flatter myself, from your lordship's well-known candour and indulgence, that you will not think it presuming in me, or contrary to the respect I feel for your lordship, if I take the liberty of offering you some few observations in vindication of the conduct of Commodore Fischer. But, first, let me have the honour to assure your lordship, that I have not communicated to that officer your letter of the 22d of April; and that, what I take the liberty of offering your lordship, is absolutely my private and individual opinion.

"Your lordship thinks, that Commodore Fischer has over-rated the forces by which he was attacked, and under-rated his own; or, that he wrongly asserts the superiority of numbers on the part of the British. I must confess, that I am now, as I have always been, of opinion, that the squadron with which your lordship attacked our southern line of defence, say all those ships and vessels lying to the southward of the Crown Battery, was stronger then than that line. I will say nothing about our not having time sufficient to man our ships in the manner it was intended: they being badly manned, both as to number and as to quality of their crews, the greatest part of which were landmen; people that had been pressed, and who never before had been on board a ship or used to the exercise of guns. I will not mention our ships being old and rotten, and not having one-third of our usual complement of officers; I will confine myself to the number of guns, and from the ships named in your lordship's official report: and there I find, that your squadron carried one thousand and fifty-eight guns, of much greater calibre than our's; exclusive of carronnades, which did our ships so much injury; also, exclusive of your gun-brigs and bomb-vessels.

"Now, I can assure your lordship, upon my honour, that to my certain knowledge the number of guns on board of those eighteen ships and vessels of our's which were engaged (including the small ship the Elbe, which came into the harbour towards the end of the action) amount to six hundred and thirty-four, I have not included our eleven gun-boats, carrying each two guns, as a couple of them only had an opportunity of firing a few shot. Nor need I to mention the Crown Battery, on which sixty-six guns were mounted, as that battery did not fairly get into action, and only fired a few random shot.

"When Commodore Fischer left the Dannebrog, that ship was on fire, had many killed, several of it's officers wounded, and otherwise suffered much. It was, I conceive, the duty of the commander, to remove his broad pendant to another ship; and he went on board the Holstein, from whence he commanded the line of defence; and where he remained two hours, his broad pendant flying on board the said ship. When this ship was mostly disabled, the Commodore went to the Crown Battery, which also was under his command. He would, in my humble opinion, have been justified, from the wound he received on his head, to quit the command altogether, when he left the Dannebrog; and no blame could ever have attached, for it, to his character as a soldier. I have given myself every possible pain, to be informed whether Commodore Fischer's pendant has been removed before or after the ship struck; and the officers all agree, in declaring, that the broad pendant has been replaced by a captain's pendant, both on board the Dannebrog and the Holstein, previous to those ships hauling down their ensign. It is even remarkable that, on board the Dannebrog, the man who had taken down the broad pendant, and hoisted the captain's pendant, was killed when coming down the shrouds, and fell upon deck with the commodore's pendant in his hand.

"I do not conceive that Commodore Fischer had the least idea of claiming as a victory what to every intent and purpose was a defeat: he has only thought, that this defeat was not an inglorious one; and, that our officers and men displayed much bravery and firmness, against force so superior in every respect. Your lordship's report, and your letter to me, proves it. I confess, that your lordship took all the vessels opposed to you; except five, carrying together eighty-six guns. I am of opinion, with your lordship, that three ships of seventy-four guns each would have been a hard match for the Three Crowns Battery; but, they certainly would have been forced to go away.

"As to your lordship's motive for sending a flag of truce to our government, it can never be misconstrued; and your subsequent conduct has sufficiently shewn, that humanity is always the companion of true valour. You have done more; you have shewn yourself a friend of the re-establishment of peace, and good harmony, between this country and Great Britain. It is, therefore, with the sincerest esteem, I shall always feel myself attached to your lordship; and it is with the greatest respect I have the honour to subscribe myself, my lord, your lordship's most obedient and most humble servant,

"H. Lindholm."

On these respective letters, the judicious part of mankind will judge for themselves. We need not have blushed for a Lindholm, but we have reason to glory in our Nelson. Olfert Fischer, notwithstanding the arguments of his able apologist, must always be considered as having been superabundantly solicitous for the safety of his own person: in leaving two different ships, by his own confession, while the respective crews continued fighting; and finally retiring, to continue his command, under cover of a powerful battery on shore. His roundly asserting, that we had two ships for one, and that he was told two English ships had struck; his ungenerous and distorted application of Lord Nelson's noble acknowledgment of the general bravery of the Danes; and the low source of solace that he finds in disingenuously limiting the advantage gained by the victory to the possession of a few wretched wrecks, without at all appreciating the grand political consequences which it so fully accomplished; exhibit, in the whole, a disposition meanly selfish, conspicuously sordid, and deplorably deficient in all the most lofty qualities of mind. What a contrast to our immortal Nelson! whose single sentence, in his letter of rebuke for this man—"God forbid that I should destroy an unresisting Dane! When they became my prisoners, I became their protector!"—deserves to be charactered with letters of diamonds on the shrine destined to cover the hero's hallowed remains.

Lord Nelson did not think it necessary to differ with his friend Lindholm, an undoubted man of honour, about punctilious particulars. To his own mind, however, or that of an enemy, he would not abate a particle of what he had asserted. The following statement is copied from a private memorandum of his lordship's, in which he acutely turns the scale of superior force against the Danes.

> "Lindholm ought to have omitted the guns of the Russell, Bellona, Agamemnon, Amazon, Alcmene, Blanche, Dart, and Arrow; as the two first were aground; and, although within random shot, yet unable to do that service expected from seventy-four gun ships. The Agamemnon was not within three miles; the others, frigates and sloops, were exposed to a part of the Crown Battery and the ships in the other channel, but not fired upon by the eighteen sail drawn up to the southward of the Crown Islands. Therefore, sixty-six guns are to be taken from the British, and a hundred and sixty-six guns added to the Danes: viz. sixty-six, Crown Batteries--(I think, there were eighty-eight)--and a hundred for the batteries on Amack; besides random shot from the ships in the other channel, citadel, &c. Therefore, the account ought to stand thus--

Guns, by Lindholm's account	1058
Deduct, as above	366

British force in action	692

Danish force, by Lindholm's account	634
Add, I say, at least	166
Danish force	800
British force	692
Superiority of the Danes	108"

Though Lord Nelson could not have rested without satisfying himself of the precise fact, he saw no necessity for entering into any altercation, on so trivial a topic, with General-Adjutant Lindholm. He contented himself, therefore, with immediately closing the subject, by the following very liberal reply.

St. George, May 3d, 1801.

"MY DEAR LORD,

"I was yesterday evening favoured with your reply to my letter of the 22d of April; and I have no scruple in assuring you, that if Commodore Fischer's letter had been couched in the same manly and honourable manner, I should have been the last man to have noticed any little inaccuracies which might get into a commander in chief's public letter; and if the commodore had not called upon his royal highness for the truth of his assertions, I never should have noticed his letter. You have stated, truly, the force which would have been brought into action, but for the accidents of their getting aground; and, except the Desiree frigate, no other frigate or sloop fired a gun to the southward of the Crown Islands. I have done ample justice to the bravery of nearly all your officers and men; and, as it is not my intention to hurt your feelings, or those of his royal highness--but, on the contrary, to try and merit your esteem--I will only say, that I am confident you would not have wrote such a letter. Nothing, I flatter myself, in my conduct, ought to have drawn ridicule on my character from the commodore's pen; and you have borne the handsomest testimony of it, in contradiction to his. I thought then, as I did before the action, and do now, that it is not the interest of our countries to injure each other. I am sorry that I was forced to write you so unpleasant a letter; but, for the future, I trust that none but pleasant ones will pass between us: for, I assure you, that I hope to merit the continuation of your esteem, and of having frequent opportunities of assuring you how I feel interested in being your sincere and faithful friend,

"Nelson and Bronte."

"Adjutant-General Lindholm."

After a correspondence between Vice-Admiral Cronstadt, Adjutant-General for the Swedish Fleet and Commander in Chief at Carlscrona, with Sir Hyde Parker, which terminated in assurances of a pacific tendency, Russia remained the only object now worthy of any serious regard. The Baltic fleet wintering in two divisions, at the two great naval arsenals of Revel and Cronstadt, and the ships in the former station being locked in by the ice several weeks longer than at the latter, it was then about the time when it might be possible to get into Revel. For that port, therefore, the British fleet immediately steered: but was met by a dispatch-boat, on the 22d of April, from the Russian Ambassador at Copenhagen, announcing the death of the Emperor Paul; and bearing conciliatory propositions from Alexander the First, who had succeeded to the imperial dignities of all the Russian empire. Sir Hyde

Parker, on receiving this intelligence, immediately returned into anchorage near Copenhagen: a measure which by no means met the approbation of Lord Nelson; who well knew that, in order to negociate with effect, at critical periods, force should always be at hand, and in a situation to act. The British fleets, he conceived, ought to have held a position between the two Russian squadrons; so as to have prevented the possibility of their effecting a junction, should their pacific dispositions prove otherwise than sincere.

On the 5th of May, Sir Hyde Parker having been recalled, Lord Nelson was appointed to be commander in chief; but his health was now so greatly impaired, and his spirits were so much depressed, that he received it with little hope of being able long to enjoy it's advantages. However, not another moment was lost: for, after requiring an explicit declaration that the British trade should not be molested by Sweden, in his absence, nine sail of the line immediately weighed anchor; and proceeded, with his lordship, towards Revel. He wished for farther satisfaction respecting the friendly disposition of the Russians; and thought the best method of putting it to proof, was that of trying how he should be received in one of their ports. On the passage, every possible opportunity was embraced for arranging, with the different commanders, plans of conduct to be adopted in the event of either finding the Russians friendly or hostile. There was a sincere desire for peace, but not the smallest dread of war. His lordship, however, no sooner approached the port of Revel, which he had determined to enter, than he learned, to his extreme mortification, that the state of the ice had permitted the escape of the Russian fleet to Cronstadt, on the 10th of May, being three days prior to his arrival. Lord Nelson was disappointed, but not disconcerted. An amicable correspondence was commenced; the governor and forts were saluted; he was permitted to anchor in the outer port; and, an invitation from shore being readily accepted by our hero, he was entertained with the greatest respect and attention by the governor, admiral, and all the Russian officers, at Revel. It appears, however, that the suspicions of some less honourable minds had been excited, on the occasion, to a height of considerable alarm; and, a letter having been received, on the 16th, from the Comte de Pahlen, censuring his lordship for thus visiting the Gulph of Finland, he was resolved immediately to prevent the effect of all malevolent misrepresentations, by returning to join the squadron off Bornholm, where he had left Captain Murray with seven sail of the line.

In a letter to his Excellency Earl Carysfort, dated on board the St. George, off Gothland, May 19th, 1801, in which his lordship incloses a copy of his correspondence with the Comte de Pahlen, he says—"You will have your opinion, as I have mine, that he never would have wrote such a letter, if the fleet had been at Revel in April. Mine was a desire to mark a particular civility; which, as it was not treated in the way I think handsome, I left Revel on Sunday the 17th, and here I am. From all the Russian officers at Revel, I received the most attentive behaviour; and, I believe, they are as much surprised at the answer as I was. Sir Hyde Parker's letter on the release of the British merchant ships has not been answered. I hope, all is right: but seamen are but bad negociators; for, we put to issue in five minutes, what diplomatic forms would be five months doing." He observes that, though he feels sensible all which he sends in this letter is of no consequence; still he knows, from experience, that to be informed there is nothing particular passing, is comfortable. "Our fleet," he adds, "is twenty-two sail of the line, and forty-six frigates, bombs, fire-ships, and gun-vessels; and, in the fleet, not one man in the hospital-ship. A finer fleet," his lordship exultingly concludes, "never graced the ocean!" Such, however, was his lordship's ill state of health, that he had, on the day of quitting Revel, written home for permission to relinquish the command, that he might try and re-establish it, by immediately returning to England; being unable, at present, as his lordship stated, to execute the high trust reposed in him, with either comfort to himself, or benefit to the state.

Captain Murray, having been relieved from his station, by a squadron under Rear-Admiral Totty, met Lord Nelson, with four sail of the line, off the north end of Gothland; and, on the 23d, at three in the morning, his lordship joined the rear-admiral off Gothland. He left him, however, the same evening; and, having sent the Ganges, Defence, and Veteran, to water in Kioge Bay, anchored next day off Rostock. His lordship had now not only received letters from the Russian government of an indisputably amicable tendency, but his Imperial Majesty, Alexander the First, with a wisdom and candour which do him the highest honour, absolutely sent Admiral Tchitchagoff for the purpose of holding a confidential communication with the British commander in chief. His lordship, accordingly, in a conference with this brave and worthy Russian admiral, soon became satisfied that the emperor, like his own most gracious sovereign, was sincerely disposed to enter into an amicable arrangement, and they respectively exchanged written documents to that effect; thus proving, that two honest and wise seamen are by no means such bad pacific negociators as might be imagined. Nor was this all; for, on the 26th, Lord Nelson received an invitation to visit the Emperor Alexander, in a letter from the Comte de Pahlen, which also apprised his lordship that the British merchant ships, unjustly detained by his imperial majesty's late predecessor, were now ordered to be liberated. To this pleasing communication, his lordship instantly returned the following answer, by the Russian lugger which brought his letter from the count.

"St. George, Rostock Bay,
10 o'clock at night, 26th May 1801.

"SIR,

"I am this moment honoured with your excellency's flattering letter of May 6, O.S. and I assure you, that his imperial majesty's justice has filled the idea I had formed of his excellent heart and head; and, I am sure, the handsome manner in which the embargo has been taken off the British shipping, will give the greatest pleasure to my good and gracious sovereign. I am truly sensible of the great honour done me, by the invitation of his imperial majesty; and, at a future time, I hope to have the pleasure of presenting my humble duty. I have now only to pray that a permanent (which must be honourable) peace, may be re-established between our gracious sovereigns; and, that our august masters reigns may be blessed with every happiness which this world can afford: and I beg that your excellency will believe, that I am, with the highest respect, your most obedient and very humble servant,

Nelson and Bronte.

His Excellency the Comte de Pahlen."

There could now be no sort of doubt, that a peace with the northern powers must soon be concluded on terms honourable to all parties. The Danes, however, though so liberally treated, appear to have been somewhat sore from the wounds which their temerity had invited. Sweden, through the whole business, sagaciously kept as much as possible aloof: ready to meet the evils of war, if necessary; but prudently prefering to avoid them, while this might be effected without dishonour. Such, happily, was also the disposition of Russia, from the moment of the frantic Paul's demise; as well as that of the British government, which had been forced into a state of hostility with those whom they were ever desirous of considering only as friends. Nations sincerely so disposed, have only thoroughly to understand each other, and the sword need seldom quit it's scabbard. With respect to Denmark, however, though a positive peace was every hour expected by his lordship, he found it necessary, at the beginning of June, to remind some of her governors of the conditions of the armistice. In a letter of June 11th, to Rear-Admiral Totty, his lordship writes—"A week, from this date, all must be settled, one way or the other. Reports say, that victuallers are laying at Yarmouth, ready to sail; probably, they are waiting the issue of Lord St. Helen's negociation at St. Petersburgh. In Denmark, we shall no longer find an enemy; they have too much to lose, by the renewal of hostilities.

At this moment, generally speaking, they hate us; but they are determined not to give up their colonies, ships, &c. In this nation, we shall not be forgiven our having the upper hand of them. I only thank God we have, or they would try and humble us to the dust." In this letter, his lordship says, to the worthy rear-admiral—"I feel much flattered at your kind wishes for my remaining with the fleet: but, although my health is perfectly re-established; yet, as the Admiralty cannot know it, I trust that they have had consideration to my situation, and directed another admiral to supersede me. Sir Thomas Graves is represented to be getting better; but, as yet, is unable to get out of his cabin." In a preceding letter to Admiral Totty, speaking of the indisposition of his worthy friend, is the following interesting passage, admirably illustrative of the characteristically affectionate regards of these most brave and excellent men. "Sir Thomas Graves is still very ill: so much so, that he begged *I would not* go and see him; as the pleasure he had in seeing me, did him harm when he was left." The pain, too, which he knew could not fail to be felt by his sympathetically susceptible friend, doubtless formed an equally strong reason for dreading those visits, in the breast of the rear-admiral, though he had the kind precaution to conceal that cause. Can we wonder, that such men should be invincible!

On the 13th of June, Lord Nelson received permission for his return to England; and immediately thanked the Lords of the Admiralty, in an answer addressed to Mr. Nepean, for the very flattering and handsome manner in which their lordships had expressed their acquiescence with his request of the 17th of May. Having received, at the same time, a commission from his majesty, to invest his friend Rear-Admiral Graves with the military order of the Bath, his lordship performed that ceremony, on board the St George, next day, in the following manner.

> "His Majesty's Ship St. George, Kioge Bay,
> June 14, 1801.
>
> "A chair was placed on the gratings of the skylight, on the quarter-deck, with the royal standard suspended over it, shewing the king's arms. The chair was covered with the union flag; a guard was ranged on each side the quarter-deck, consisting of the marines, and a detachment of the rifle corps; and the captains of the fleet attended in their full-dress uniforms. The royal standard was hoisted the moment of the procession's beginning, which took place in the following order--Lord Nelson came up the ladder in the forepart of the quarter-deck, and made three reverences to the throne; he then placed himself on the right-hand side of it. Captain Parker, bearing the sword of state, being that which was presented to Lord Nelson by the captains of his majesty's fleet who fought under his command at the battle of the Nile, followed Lord Nelson, and placed himself on his right side, a little in advance; making three reverences to the throne, and one to Lord Nelson. His lordship's secretary, Mr. Wallis, then followed, bearing in his hand, on a sattin cushion, the ensigns of the order, and making similar reverences to the throne and to Lord Nelson. Captain Parker then read the Duke of Portland's order to Lord Nelson; which being ended, Rear-Admiral Graves was introduced between Captains Hardy

and Retalick, making three reverences to the throne, and one to Lord Nelson. The rear-admiral then kneeled down; and Lord Nelson, in the name of his majesty, laid the sword on the shoulders of the rear-admiral. The knight-elect then arose; and, bending his body a little forward, Lord Nelson, with the assistance of Captains Hardy and Retalick, put the ribbon over the new knight's right shoulder, and placed the star on his left breast. His lordship then pronounced the following speech on the occasion--

"Sir Thomas Graves! Having fulfilled the commands of his majesty, by investing you with the ensigns of the most honourable and military order of the Bath, I cannot but express how much I feel gratified that it should have fallen to my lot to be directed to confer this justly merited honour and special mark of royal favour upon you; for I cannot but reflect, that I was an eye-witness of your high merit, and distinguished gallantry, on the memorable 2d of April, and for which you are now so honourably rewarded. I hope that these honours conferred upon you, will prove to the officers in the service, that a strict perseverance in the pursuit of glorious actions, and the imitation of your brave and laudable conduct, will ever ensure them the favours and rewards of our most gracious sovereign, and the thanks and gratitude of our country."

"At the conclusion of this speech, the procession retired in the same manner as it came; except that the new knight went first, making one reverence to Lord Nelson, and three to the throne.

"The moment the ribbon had been placed over Sir Thomas Graves's shoulder, the signal being made preparative, the whole fleet fired a salute of twenty-one guns; when the ceremony was finished, the standard was hauled down. The troops and marines, on hoisting it, had presented their arms, and the drums beat a march. The troops kept their arms presented during the ceremony; and, on the standard's being hauled down, a march was likewise beat."

A few days after, having concluded his epistolary correspondences, and arranged other requisites, both with the fleet and on shore, his lordship resigned the command to Admiral Sir Charles Morice Pole, who had been sent out to relieve him, and immediately sailed for England. On the day preceding his departure, however, Lord Nelson took leave of the fleet, by issuing the following public orders—

"St. George, in Kioge Bay,
18th June 1801.

"Lord Nelson has been obliged, from the late very bad state of his health, to apply to the Lords Commissioners of the Admiralty for leave to return to England, which their lordships have been pleased to comply with. But Lord Nelson cannot allow himself to leave the fleet, without expressing to the admirals, captains, officers, and men, how sensibly he has felt, and does feel, all their kindnesses to him: and, also, how nobly and honourably they have supported him in the hour of battle, and the readiness which they have shewn to maintain the honour of their king and country on many occasions which have offered; and, had more opportunities presented themselves, Lord Nelson is firmly persuaded they would have added more glory to their country. Lord Nelson cannot but observe, with the highest satisfaction which can fill the breast of a British admiral, that--with the exception of the glaring misconduct of the officers of the Tygress and Cracker gun-brigs, and the charges alledged against the lieutenant of the Terror bomb---out of eighteen thousand men, of which the fleet is composed, not a complaint has been made of any officer or man in it; and he cannot but remark, that the extraordinary health of this fleet, under the blessing of Almighty God, is to be attributed to the great regularity, exact discipline, and chearful obedience, of every individual in the fleet. The vice-admiral assures them, that he will not fail to represent to the Lords Commissioners of the Admiralty their highly praise-worthy conduct; and, if it please God that the vice-admiral recovers his health, he will feel proud, on some future day, to go with them in pursuit of farther glory; and to assist in making the name of our king and country beloved and respected by all the world."

On the 1st of July, his lordship landed at Yarmouth, where he was received with universal joy. He had no sooner arrived, than his humane heart led him to visit the hospitals which contained such of his brave fellows as had been wounded in the late battle. He enquired, with parental solicitude, into the state of their health, tenderly soothed their sufferings, generously relieved their necessities, and kindly encouraged their hopes. On his leaving the town, the volunteer cavalry assembled; and escorted his lordship to Lowestoffe, a distance of eleven miles.

Lord Nelson being much indisposed when he reached Sir William Hamilton's house in Piccadilly, where his friends had assembled to meet him, a party was formed, consisting of Sir William and Lady Hamilton, the present Earl and Countess Nelson, with their son and daughter, now Lord Merton and Lady Charlotte, and Captain Parker, to go with his lordship, for change of air, and variety of scene, as far as Box Hill, near Dorking, in Surry, where they remained a few days; and then accompanied him to the Bush Inn, at Staines, in Middlesex. Here they continued about a week; and afterwards visited Mrs. Maurice Nelson, at Laleham, only two miles distant from Staines. This unfortunate lady, relict of his lordship's then recently deceased elder brother, has for many years been afflicted with total blindness. Lord Nelson now kindly condoled with her; and generously made up the small pittance left by his brother, whom he most tenderly loved, a regular annuity of two hundred pounds, besides providing for immediate exigences. It is greatly to be regretted, that his lordship's repeated solicitations for Mr. Maurice Nelson's advancement had been so little regarded, that this worthy gentleman, though almost his whole life in the Navy Office, was only elevated to the situation of a principal clerk about four months prior to his decease.

With his health considerably improved by this rural excursion, Lord Nelson returned to London; and, on dining with Mr. Addington, then Chancellor of the

Exchequer, was informed, by the minister, that nothing could satisfy the people, who were in a state of continual alarm at Bonaparte's immense preparations for the threatened invasion of our country, but his lordship's immediately taking the home command. Though the nature of the French armament, which consisted chiefly of innumerable gun-boats, rendered the attack of their flotilla a species of petty warfare apparently too trivial for the attention of our heroic admiral, it was sufficient for him to be assured that his services were requisite for the safety or welfare of his country, to obtain an immediate acquiescence; however humble, hazardous, or unprofitable, the nature of the proposed employ. His friends, however, were desirous that he should receive, on the occasion, some positive benefit. His lordship alledged, with great truth, that he was one of the worst negociators on earth for himself, and seemed disinclined to tender any conditions; but Lady Hamilton urging him to obtain, at least, an entailment of his titles on the family, which would take nothing out of the national purse, and yet preserve his merited honours to the most remote posterity, he ventured, at length, to solicit that small favour, which was very readily granted.

In consequence of this arrangement, Lord Nelson was appointed commander in chief of a powerful squadron, employed between Orfordness and Beachy-Head: together with the entire flotilla of gun-brigs, fire-ships, bomb-ketches, and vessels of every other description; and all the sea-fencibles embodied within the same district, with all the boats, vessels, and other floating defences, on board of which they might be required to act. His lordship, accordingly, hastened to Sheerness, and hoisted his flag on board L'Unite frigate of thirty-two guns. Having, with his accustomed activity, directed the respective stations of the several ships there under his command; he sailed, in a very few days, for the Downs: and it is remarkable that, on his passage from the Nore, instead of pursuing the usual course, and proceeding through the King's Channel, he resolved on attempting a passage hitherto deemed impracticable for ships of war—an experiment which he judiciously considered, at this particular period, as well worthy of trial—and, having compleatly succeeded, it has ever since been properly called Nelson's Channel.

On the 29th of July, at night, Lord Nelson arrived in the Downs, and immediately hoisted his flag on board the Leyden of sixty-four guns; but shifted it, two days after, to the Medusa frigate of thirty-two. Not a moment was now lost in making every preparation for a formidable attack on the French flotilla, by the assistance of which we were menaced with the invasion of the myriads of troops that lined the shore of the enemy from Brest to the Texel. Fearful, however, of our approach, they had been particularly careful to fortify their coast swarming with soldiers, by the erection of innumerable strong batteries, having furnaces for preparing red-hot shot, and adapting every other contrivance to annoy their dreaded assailants and protect themselves. From the moment it was known that Lord Nelson had undertaken the home command, every apprehension of a French invasion was changed into the wish that such an attempt might instantly be made, and there was, perhaps, scarcely a man, woman, or child, in the united kingdom, who now longer felt the smallest fear of an event which had lately excited so much general alarm. With a promptness inconceivable, his lordship planned every species of precautionary defence, while engaged in executing his offensive operations: and it is anxiously hoped, that his excellent defensive arrangements, made on this occasion, though happily not then needed, will be carefully treasured in the archives of the Admiralty, for immediate adoption, should any attempt ever be made, by a rash and powerful enemy, to approach the British shores; who may thus be vanquished, by our immortal hero, in a future and even distant age.

The French flotilla prepared at Boulogne had of late been considerably increased by reinforcements from Calais; and it was found difficult for the British cruizers to prevent, with certainty, or even safety, such small vessels as these gun-boats from stealing along the shore. They were, therefore, become extremely numerous, and it was judged prudent to attempt lessening their number by capture or demolition. Every thing being prepared with these intentions, his lordship, on the 1st of August 1801, being the third anniversary of his glorious victory off the Nile, sailed from the Downs, and stood over to the coast of France.

On the 2d, having arrived off Boulogne, twenty four armed vessels were perceived at anchor outside the port; the boasted gun-boats seemed, to his lordship, incapable of being rowed, in the smoothest water, more than a mile and a half an hour. The enemy, alarmed at the approach of the British armament, were labouring hard to erect new batteries; but the wind being too far to the northward for our bombs to go on the lee-shore, this attack, by way of experiment, did not commence till the 4th. The following official account of it's success was immediately transmitted to England, by his lordship.

> "Medusa, off Boulogne,
> 4th August 1801.
>
> "SIR,
>
> The enemy's vessels, brigs, and flats (lugger-rigged) and a schooner, twenty-four in number, were this morning, at day-light, anchored in a line, in front of the town of Boulogne. The wind being favourable for the bombs to act, I made the signal for them to weigh; and throw shells at the vessels, but as little as possible to annoy the town. The captains placed their ships in the best possible position; and, in a few hours, three of the flats, and a brig, were sunk: and, in the course of the morning, six were on shore, evidently much damaged. At six this evening, being high water, five of the vessels which had been aground hauled with difficulty into the mole, the others remained under water. I believe, the whole of the vessels would have gone inside the pier, but for want of water. What damage the enemy may have sustained, beyond what we see, is impossible to tell. The whole of this affair is of no farther consequence, than to shew the enemy that they cannot, with impunity, come outside their ports. The officers of the artillery threw the shells with great skill: and I am sorry to say, that Captain Fyers, of the Royal Artillery, is slightly wounded in the thigh by the bursting of an enemy's shell; and that three seamen are also wounded. One more of the enemy's flats is this moment sunk.
>
> I am, Sir, &c.
> "Nelson And Bronte."
>
> "Evan Nepean, Esq."

This attack seems to have been chiefly intended to ascertain what might be hereafter effected with a force particularly adapted to the nature of the service, founded on some degree of actual experience. His lordship was, therefore, far less disappointed by the event, than might generally be imagined. To prevent the commanders of the bomb-vessels from being discouraged, who had really deserved better success, his lordship thus complimented them on the occasion.

"Medusa, off Boulogne,
Aug. 5th, 1801.

"Lord Nelson has reason to be very much satisfied with the captains of the bombs, for the placing of their vessels yesterday. It was impossible they could have been better situated; and the artillery officers have shewn great skill in entirely disabling ten of the armed vessels out of twenty-four opposed to them; and many others, Lord Nelson believes, are much damaged. The commander in chief cannot avoid noticing the great zeal and desire to attack the enemy in a closer combat, which manifested itself in all ranks of persons; and which Lord Nelson would gladly have given full scope to, had the attempt at this moment been proper; but the officers, and others, may rely that an early opportunity shall be given them for shewing their judgment, zeal, and bravery. The hired and revenue cutters kept under sail, and performed the duty entrusted to them with, a great deal of skill.

"Nelson and Bronte."

On the day following, Lord Nelson quitted the French coast, and repaired to Margate Roads; leaving, however, a sufficient force off Boulogne to watch the motions of the enemy, and the gun-boats and smaller vessels of his fleet in the Downs. While every possible effort was making to prepare for a most vigorous attempt on the flotilla at Boulogne, his lordship, by visiting Harwich for a few days, endeavoured to divert the attention of the enemy, and induce them to suppose that he was now going against Flushing, really meant to be the next object of attack. By this stratagem, both services were actually, at the same time, in a state of constant preparation. Having arranged matters at Harwich, his lordship returned to the Downs; from whence, on the 15th, he again stood over to Boulogne, with a force now augmented to seventy sail, including vessels of all descriptions. The French, however, had been equally alert in guarding against an expected second blow; and, to the total discomfiture of the enterprize, as well as the loss of many of our brave men, though to their own eternal ignominy, it was discovered, when too late, that these threatening invaders had literally chained down all the vessels of this boasted flotilla to the shore, in dread of their being carried off by the British assailants. Of this unfortunate affair, which failed from a cause that could scarcely have been suspected, by a brave man, in even the most pusillanimous enemy, the following copious dispatches from Lord Nelson to the Admiralty, including the reports of the several commanders of divisions as transmitted through Mr. Nepean, will afford a very full and particular description.

"Medusa, off Boulogne, 16th Aug. 1801.

"SIR,

"Having judged it proper to attempt bringing off all the enemy's flotilla moored in the front of Boulogne, I directed the attack to be made in four divisions of boats for boarding, under the command of Captains Somerville, Parker, Cotgrave, and Jones, and a division of howitzer-boats under the command of Captain Conor, of his majesty's ship Discovery. The boats put off from the Medusa, at half past eleven last night, in the best possible order; and, before one o'clock this morning, the firing began: and I had, from the judgment of the officers, and the zeal and gallantry of every man, the most perfect confidence of compleat success--and which I have no doubt would have been according to my expectations--but owing to the darkness of the night, with the tide and half tide, which must always make the attacks in the night, on the coasts of the channel, very uncertain, the divisions separated; and from all not arriving at the same happy moment with Captain Parker, is to be attributed the failure of success. But I beg to be perfectly understood, that not the smallest blame attaches itself any where; for, although the divisions did not arrive together, yet each (except the fourth, which could not be got up before day) made a successful attack on that part of the enemy they fell in with, and actually took possession of many brigs and flats--particularly, the commodore. But the vessels being, as I am informed, chained to the, shore, but certainly hauled on shore, as the commodore's brig had less under her bottom than could support her, the moment the battle ceased on board, such vollies upon vollies of musketry were fired, directed on their decks, the enemy being perfectly regardless of their own men, who must have suffered equally with us, that it was impossible even to remain on board to burn them. But allow me, who have seen much service this war, to say, that more determined, persevering courage, I never witnessed; and, that nothing but the impossibility of being successful, from the causes I have mentioned, could have prevented my having to congratulate their lordships on bringing off the enemy's flotilla: and, although, in value, the loss of such gallant and good men is incalculable; yet, in point of numbers, it has fell short of my expectations. I must also state, that greater zeal, and ardent desire, in the whole of the officers and crews, in the numerous vessels under my command, to distinguish themselves by an attack on the enemy, were never shewn: and the commanders and crews of the hired and revenue cutters vie with their brethren of the navy; the whole of whose boats were employed, and the commanders of the Hunter and Greyhound cutters volunteered their services.

"Among the many gallant men wounded, I have, with the deepest regret, to state the heavy loss I have sustained, by the grievous wounds of my gallant good friend, and able assistant, Captain

Edward Thomas Parker, my aid-de-camp; also of Lieutenant Frederic Langford, my flag-lieutenant, who has served with me many years; and who were both wounded, in attempting to board the French commodore. To Captain Gore, of the Medusa, I feel the highest obligations; and, when their lordships look at the loss of the Medusa on this occasion, they will agree with me, that the honour of my flag, and the cause of their king and country, could never have been placed in more gallant hands. Captain Bedford, of the Leyden, with Captain Gore, very handsomely volunteered their services to serve under masters and commanders: but, it would not have been fair to the latter; and I only mention it, to mark the zeal of those officers. From the nature of the attack, only a few prisoners were made; a lieutenant, eight seamen, and eight soldiers, are all which were brought off. Herewith, I send you the report of the several commanders of divisions, and also a return of killed and wounded, &c.

I have the honour to be, &c.

"NELSON AND BRONTE."

"P.S. Captain Somerville was the senior master and commander employed.

"Evan Nepean, Esq."

The letters received by his lordship from the several commanders of divisions, and transmitted by him to England, with his own public letter, were as follow.

FIRST DIVISION.

"Eugenie, off Boulogne,
16th Aug. 1801.

"MY LORD,

"In obedience to your lordship's directions to state the proceedings of the first division of boats which you did me the honour to place under my command, for the purpose of attacking the enemy's flotilla in the Bay of Boulogne, I beg leave to acquaint you that, after leaving the Medusa last night, I found myself, in getting ashore, carried considerably, by the rapidity of the tide, to the eastward of the abovementioned place; and, finding that I was not likely to reach it in the order prescribed, I gave directions to the boats to cast each other off. By so doing, I was enabled to get to the enemy's flotilla a little before the dawn of day: and, in the best order possible, attacked, close to the pier-head, a brig; which, after a short contest, I carried. Previous to so doing, her cables were cut; but I was prevented from towing her out, by her being secured with a chain: and, in consequence of a very heavy fire of musketry and grape-shot, that was directed at us from the shore, three luggers, and another brig, within half pistol shot, and not seeing the least prospect of being able to get her off, I was obliged to abandon her, and push out of the bay, as it was then compleatly day-light. The undaunted and resolute behaviour of the officers, seamen, and marines, was unparalleled; and I have to lament the loss of several of those brave men, a list of whom I inclose herewith.

I have the honour to be, &c.
P. Somerville."

SECOND DIVISION.

"Medusa, off Boulogne,
16th Aug. 1801.

"MY LORD,

"After the compleat arrangement which was made, the perfect good understanding and regularity with which the boats you did me the honour to put under my command left the Medusa, I have an anxious feeling to explain to your lordship the failure of our enterprize, that on it's outset promised every success. Agreeable to your lordship's instructions, I proceeded, with the second division of the boats under my direction, the half of which was under the direction of Lieutenant Williams, senior of the Medusa, to attack the part of the enemy's flotilla appointed for me: and, at half past twelve, had the good fortune to find myself close to them; when I ordered Lieutenant Williams, with his subdivision, to push on to attack the vessels to the northward of me; while I, with the others, run alongside a large brig off the mole head, wearing the commodore's pendant. It is at this moment, that I feel myself at a loss for words to do justice to the officers and crew of the Medusa, who were in the boat with me; and to Lieutenant Langford, the officers and crew of the same ship, who nobly seconded us in the barge until all her crew were killed or wounded: and to the Honourable William Cathcart, who commanded the Medusa's cutter, and sustained the attack with the greatest intrepidity, until the desperate situation I was left in obliged me to call him to the assistance of the sufferers in my boat. The boats were no sooner alongside, than we attempted to board: but a very strong netting, traced up to her lower yards, baffled all our endeavours; and an instantaneous discharge of her guns, and small arms from about two hundred soldiers on her gun-wale, knocked myself, Mr. Kirby the master of the Medusa, and Mr. Gore a midshipman, with two thirds of the crew, upon our backs, into the boat; all, either killed or desperately wounded. The barge, and cutter, being on the outside, sheered off with the tide: but the flat-boat, in which I was, hung alongside; and, as there was not an officer or man left to govern her, must have fallen into the hands of the enemy, had not Mr. Cathcart taken her in tow, and carried her off.

"Mr. Williams led his subdivision up to the enemy with the most intrepid gallantry, took one lugger, and attacked a brig; while his crew, I am concerned to say, suffered equally with ourselves: nearly the whole of his boat's crew were killed or wounded. Lieutenant Paley, who commanded the Medusa's launch, and the Honourable Mr. Maitland, midshipman, were severely wounded; and Mr. William Bristow, master's mate in the Medusa's cutter under Lieutenant Steward, was killed.

"I now feel it my duty to assure your lordship, that nothing could surpass the zeal, courage, and readiness, of every description of officers and men under my command; and I am sorry that my words fall short of their merit, though we could not accomplish the object we were ordered to. I have the honour to be, &c.

"Edward T. Parker."

THIRD DIVISION.

Gannet, 16th Aug. 1801.

"MY LORD,

"On the night of the 15th inst. the third division of boats, which I had the honour to command, assembled on board his majesty's ship York, agreeable to your lordship's directions; and, at eleven, P.M. by signal from the Medusa, proceeded, without loss of time, to attack the enemy's flotilla off Boulogne, as directed by your lordship. As I thought it most advisable to endeavour to reduce the largest vessel first, I lost no time in making the attack; but, in consequence of my leading the division, and the enemy opening a heavy fire from several of the batteries, thought it advisable to give the enemy as little time as possible, cut the tow-rope, and did not wait for the other boats, so that it was some little time before the heavy boats could get up. I received so many shots through the boat's bottom, that I soon found her in a sinking state; and, as it was not possible to stop so many shot-holes, was obliged, with the men, to take to another boat; and have the pleasure to acquaint your lordship that I received particular support from the boats of his majesty's ship York, which soon came up with the rest of the division I had the honour to command. But, finding no prospect of success, and the number of men killed and wounded in the different boats, with the constant fire from the shore of grape and small-arms, thought it for the good of his majesty's service to withdraw the boats between two and three in the morning; as we could not board her, although every effort was made.

I have the honour to be, &c.
Isaac Cotgrave."

FOURTH DIVISION.

"His Majesty's Ship Isis,
16th Aug. 1801.

"MY LORD,

"In consequence of directions received from your lordship, I last night, on the signal being made on board the Medusa, left this ship, with the boats of the fourth division, formed with two close lines, and immediately joined the other divisions under the stern of the Medusa; and, from thence, proceeded to put your lordship's orders into execution, by attacking the westernmost part of the enemy's flotilla. But, notwithstanding every exertion made, owing to the rapidity of the tide, we could not, until near day-light, get to the westward of any part of the enemy's line; on approaching the eastern part of which, in order to assist the first division then engaged, we met them returning. Under these circumstances, and the day breaking apace, I judged it prudent to direct the officers commanding the different boats to return to their respective ships.

"I have the honour to be, &c.
Robert Jones.

"P.S. None killed or wounded on board any of the fourth division."

DIVISION OF HOWITZER-BOATS.

Discovery, off Boulogne,
Aug. 6, 1801.

"MY LORD,

"I beg leave to make the report to your lordship of the four howitzer-boats that I had the honour to command in the attack of the enemy last night. Having led in, to support Captain Parker's division, keeping between his lines until the enemy opened their fire on him: we keeping on towards the pier, until I was aground in the headmost boat; then opened our fire, and threw about eight shells into it. But, from the strength of the tide coming out of the harbour, was not able to keep off the pier-head; but continued our fire on the camp until the enemy's fire had totally slackened, and Captain Parker's division had passed without me. I beg leave to mention to your lordship, that I was ably supported by the other boats. Captain Broome, and Lieutenant Beem, of the Royal Artillery, did every thing in their power to annoy the enemy. The other officers of artillery were detached in the other four howitzer-boats.

"I have the honour to be, &c.
John Conn."

* * * * *

Return of Killed and Wounded in the Boats of his Majesty's Ships and Vessels, on the attack of the French Flotilla, moored before Boulogne, 16th of August 1801.

KILLED	4 Officers.	33 Seamen.	7 Marines.
WOUNDED	14	84	30
TOTAL	18	117	37

Total, Killed and Wounded, 172.

The circumstances unfolded in the above letters very sufficiently account for the failure of success, while they demonstrate how well it had been merited. Lord Nelson was, doubtless, in some degree disappointed, for he had hoped to destroy or bring off all their boasted flotilla. He consoled himself, however, with reflecting that, if little advantage had been gained, there was, on his part, no loss of honour; while the enemy owed their security to the disgraceful resource of being constrained to chain their vaunted vessels for invading our country to the shores of their own.

His lordship was scarcely returned to the Downs, from this expedition, when he had the honour of receiving, from the First Lord of the Admiralty, his old friend the Earl of St. Vincent, a most kind and affectionate letter, dated the 17th of August 1801, from which the following is an extract—

> "It is not given us, to command success; your lordship, and the gallant men under your orders, certainly deserve it: and I cannot sufficiently express my admiration of the zeal and persevering courage with which this gallant enterprize was followed up; lamenting, most sincerely, the loss sustained in it. The manner in which the enemy's flotilla was fastened to the ground, could not have been foreseen. The highest praise is due to your lordship; and all, under your command, who were actors in this gallant attempt."

Lord Nelson immediately issued the following general orders to all who had fought under his command on this occasion.

"Medusa, Downs, 18th Aug. 1801.

"Vice-Admiral Lord Nelson has the greatest satisfaction in sending to the captains, officers, and men, under his command, that were employed in the late attempt on the enemy's flotilla off Boulogne, an extract of a letter which he has received from the First Lord of the Admiralty; not only approving of their zeal and persevering courage, but bestowing the highest praise on them. The vice-admiral begs to assure them, that the enemy will not have long reason to boast of their security; for he trusts, ere long, to assist them in person, in a way which will compleatly annihilate the whole of them. Lord Nelson is convinced that, if it had been possible for men to have brought the enemy's flotilla out, the men that were employed to do so would have accomplished it. The moment the enemy have the audacity to cast off the chains which fix their vessels to the ground, that moment, Lord Nelson is well persuaded, they will be conducted, by his brave followers, to a British port, or sent to the bottom.

"Nelson and Bronte."

Such were the consolations of these great and congenial minds. They had nothing with which to upbraid themselves; no cause of censure in any of the brave men employed on the occasion; nor the smallest doubt of success, with the same measures, and the same men, wherever success might be possible. The chief source of sorrow which afflicted the breast of our hero, was commiseration for the sufferings of the many gallant men who were now languishing, on the bed of anguish, with dreadful and dangerous wounds received in the action. At the hospital, his lordship was a constant attendant; this, indeed, had ever been his humane practice. He tenderly enquired into the state of their wounds, and poured the balm of sympathetic solace into their agonized minds. On beholding a brave fellow, whom he particularly recollected, and kindly asking what injury he had received, his lordship was informed that he had lost an arm. "Never mind that," said the hero; "I have lost an arm, too; and, perhaps, shall shortly lose a leg: but, my good fellow, they can never be lost in a better cause, than in the defence of our country." This had a wonderful effect, not only on the man particularly addressed, but all his fellow-sufferers around; several of whom exclaimed, that they should disregard their being wounded, if they were not thus prevented from accompanying his lordship in another attack on the enemy.

While Lord Nelson was engaged in these services off Boulogne, the new concessions of his majesty, with regard to the extensions of his lordship's titles and honours, had been published in the London Gazette, on the 4th and 12th of August 1801. The first, announcing his creation to the dignity of Baron of the United Kingdom of Great Britain and Ireland, by the name, stile, and title, of Baron Nelson of the Nile, and of Hilborough in the county of Norfolk, with remainders: and the second, that Lord Viscount Nelson had been permitted, by his Majesty's warrant, dated 7th January 1801, to adopt, for himself and heirs, the title of Duke of Bronte, with the fief of the Dutchy annexed thereto; and, also, to receive the Great Cross of the Order of St. Ferdinand and of Merit, all conferred on him by Ferdinand IV. King of the Two Sicilies.

The original of the creation of Lord Viscount Nelson, before Baron of Burnham Thorpe in the county of Norfolk, to the Barony of Hilborough in the same county, is expressed in terms at once so highly honourable to the sovereign from whom they proceeded, and to his lordship, in whose just praise they are thus publicly addressed by his Majesty to the whole world as well as to posterity, that it is judged proper to give a complete and correct copy of this curious and interesting document to the reader, as obtained from the office of the royal signet.

CREATION OF VISCOUNT NELSON, BARON HILBOROUGH, WITH REMAINDERS.

"His Majesty is graciously pleased, in consideration of the great and important services that renowned man, Horatio Viscount Nelson, hath rendered to his King and Country, and in order to perpetuate to the latest posterity the remembrance of his glorious actions, and to incite others to imitate his example, to grant the dignity of a Baron of his united kingdom of Great Britain and Ireland to the said Horatio Viscount Nelson, Knight of the most Honourable Order of the Bath, and Vice-Admiral of the Blue Squadron of his Majesty's Fleet--Duke of Bronte in Sicily, Knight of the Grand Cross of the Order of St. Ferdinand and of Merit, and of the Imperial Order of the Crescent--by the name, stile, and title, of Baron Nelson of the Nile, and of Hilborough in his county of Norfolk: to hold, to him, and the heirs male of his body lawfully begotten; and, in default of such issue, to his trusty and well-beloved Edmund Nelson, Clerk, Rector of Burnham Thorpe in his county of Norfolk, father of the said Horatio Viscount Nelson, and the heirs male of his body lawfully begotten; and, in default of such issue, to the heirs male of the body of Susannah, the wife of Thomas Bolton, Esq. and sister of the said Horatio Viscount Nelson, lawfully begotten and to be begotten, severally and successively, one after another, as they shall be in seniority of age and priority of birth; and, in default of such issue, to the heirs male of the body of Catharine, the wife of George Matcham, Esq. another sister of the said Horatio Viscount Nelson, lawfully begotten and to be begotten, severally and successively, one after another, as they shall be in seniority of age and priority of birth; with all rights, privileges, pre-eminences, immunities, and advantages, thereunto belonging. And a clause is inserted, declaring it to be his Majesty's royal will and pleasure, that the persons who shall hereafter succeed to the said title and dignity of Baron Nelson of the Nile, and of Hilborough aforesaid, shall take and use the surname of Nelson only."

In a note accompanying the above copy of this creation with remainders, it is observed, that the words therein scored under with red, and which are here printed in Italic characters, appear to be new, and are not inserted in common creations.

Immediately on Lord Nelson's arrival in the Downs, from off Boulogne, he had sent to request that Sir William and Lady Hamilton, with the present Earl and Countess Nelson, would hasten to Deal, for the purpose of attending on their esteemed friend Captain Parker, whose dreadful wounds afforded but little hope of his recovery, and tendering their kind offices to the rest of the brave sufferers.

In the mean time, his lordship had again sailed from the Downs, on Sunday the 23d of August; and was joined off the North Foreland, by the squadron from Margate, with a view of trying what might be effected against Flushing. The whole of this fleet, when united off West Capel, consisted of thirty-four sail, from sixty-four guns to fourteen, including three bombs and three fire-vessels; and, after consulting pilots, "who made use," his lordship observed, in his letter to Mr. Nepean, "of many *ifs*," with regard to being able to approach the enemy, or even get the ships safely back again, he was determined to satisfy his own mind, by going on board the King George hired cutter, Mr. Yawkins master, the 25th in the morning; who carried his lordship up the Welling Channel four or five leagues from his ships, and within about three of the enemy. From this distant observation, by himself and Captain Gore, joined to the local knowledge of Mr. Yawkins, he could not think himself justifiable in proceeding farther with the business; though he liberally acknowledged the admiration which he felt of the zeal of Captain Owen, in the anxious desire of that able officer to get at the enemy. The hazard, it appeared, was far greater, and the object, from the few ships there, considerably less, than had been imagined.

On the 27th, Lord Nelson returned to the Downs, in the Medusa; and, next day, hoisted his flag on board the Amazon. His worthy old friend, Admiral Lutwidge, being port-admiral at Deal, and residing there with his excellent and truly amiable lady, an indissoluble friendship was formed between them and Sir William and

Lady Hamilton. The gallant and good Captain Parker, having been under the necessity of submitting to an amputation of his thigh, suffered the most excruciating tortures for about a month; and then died, with the most magnanimous and pious resignation, surrounded by these estimable friends, who had contributed to afford him every solace of which his dreadful state was susceptible. As the French, now attacked on their own shores, seemed likely soon to accept propositions of peace, Lord Nelson thought it advisable to purchase a pleasant rural retreat, where he might enjoy the benefit of good air, and yet be "within hail of the Admiralty." Sir William Hamilton, therefore, was requested to search out a spot adapted to their joint establishment: and, shortly after his return to London, learning that Merton Place, in Surry, about eight miles distant from Westminster Bridge, was to be disposed of, he immediately bought this estate; which was expeditiously prepared for their mutual reception, under the guidance of that classical and elegant taste for which Sir William and Lady Hamilton were both so peculiarly distinguished. The site of this house and grounds is said to have been part of the ancient abbey lands of Merton, situated within about two hundred and fifty yards of the present remaining abbey wall; and, in digging to effect the various improvements, many old coins, and other antiquities, have been occasionally dug up. Though this place was familiarly denominated a farm, by our hero and his friends, it had been, for many years before, the respectable seat of Sir Richard Hotham. The ground, however, was certainly very contracted on one side of the house, being there little more than sufficient to bound the moat by which it was unpleasantly surrounded. Whatever could be effected, in such limits, was soon arranged; and, as the autumnal season's advancement probably reminded them of the spoliage which must speedily be expected to ensue in the general verdure of the scene, innumerable evergreens were most judiciously planted throughout the grounds; including a modest portion of those laurels, beneath the shade of which the transcendent merits of the heroic possessor so abundantly entitled him to repose. By pursuing this excellent management, the charming gardens of Merton, in their enlarged state, preserve a considerable degree of comfort and beauty throughout the rigours of the severest winter.

    Lord Nelson heard, daily, the progress which was making at the farm, and it afforded him a pleasure of which he stood greatly in need. His health was, at this time, very indifferent, and he suffered severely from the cold winds of the autumnal equinox. Though, however, the preliminaries of peace were now signed, he could not obtain leave of absence from the Admiralty, to try the good effects of a little retirement at his new dwelling, till the 22d of October, and then only for ten days. As if this were not sufficient, he was agitated by the estrangement of his father's affections, in consequence of the recent separation from Lady Nelson; and pestered with anonymous threatening letters, in a way very similar to those supposed to have been written by Mr. Barnard to the great Duke of Marlborough. Every means were tried, by the friends of his lordship, to detect the writer of these infamous incendiary epistles, but without the desired effect. They, however, gave the hero himself very little anxiety: he considered them, probably, as nefarious attacks on his purse, through the medium of his character, and treated every menace they contained with the most sovereign contempt. Such, however, was our hero's filial reverence of parental authority, that he could by no means regard his father's censure as a matter of light importance, though he felt conscious of his own innocence and integrity. This, indeed, was truly a source of sorrow; and he resolved fully to satisfy his venerable parent's every scruple, and convince him how cruelly he had been wronged by false and scandalous reports.

Early on the 22d of October, Lord Nelson quitted the Amazon, in the Downs; and, immediately landing at Deal, set off post for Merton. On arriving at this small village, it is a singular fact that, being asked by the post-boy, which was the house; his lordship could only reply, that he knew no more than himself. It was, however, soon found; and never was man more delighted, than our hero, at beholding his new residence. Every glowing feature of his amiable friends spoke the welcome which was felt by each heart, as the various beauties of this little spot were pointed out to his inquisitive eye. He viewed all with admiration and astonishment, so greatly did it surpass every idea which he had formed. "Is this, too, mine?" he repeatedly asked, as he was shewn the different parts of his estate; the house, the gardens, the dairy, &c. He was particularly charmed with the admirable contrivance of a commodious subterranean passage, formed beneath the high road, and leading to the beautiful and extensive plantation walks with which the fields and kitchen gardens, on that side, are so agreeably environed; this estate, among others in that neighbourhood, having been formerly severed, in consequence of an act of parliament for intersecting it by a new road to Epsom. "Oh, Sir William!" exclaimed his lordship, embracing his most worthy friend, when he had seen the whole, "the longest liver shall possess it all!" Lord Nelson was never a man of words; the memory of this engagement, when he afterwards made his will, has conveyed the beautiful villa of Merton Place to Lady Hamilton.

The peace that at this period ensued, happily prevented any necessity for his lordship's return to the fleet, which was soon after paid off. In the attainment of this peace, it will be the province of every historian who duly considers the entire combination of causes and effects, justly to appreciate the merits of our hero; who, however, was, by no means of opinion that it could prove of any very long duration, till the restless ambition of Bonaparte should be still more efficaciously checked.

His lordship was ever affectionately attached to his Royal Highness the Prince of Wales; as well as to the Duke of Clarence, and all the other royal brothers: he was fully sensible, too, of the brilliant political abilities of some of the chief members of the opposition, and felt sincerely desirous of seeing them fairly devoted to the service of the country. He regarded, however, what was universally deemed "the honest administration of Mr. Addington," the present Lord Sidmouth, as entitled to all the support which he could render men who not unworthily enjoyed a high degree of their sovereign's confidence and favour. No considerations of private friendship could ever induce him to unite in any systematic opposition of his majesty's ministers. He was, he said, the King's servant; and would, in every way, defend him with his best abilities. His lordship joined not in any condemnation of the peace; which he regarded, with many other intelligent persons, as an experiment worthy the trial. Of national honour, he conceived, nothing was sacrificed; and, except Malta, little was given up, which could be any just subject of regret. Even Malta itself, of which he so well knew all the value, and which could probably never have been wrested from France without his lordship's wonderful address and perseverance in obtaining aids for effecting it's reduction, he declared was, in his estimation, scarcely worth the trouble and expence of preserving, could we be certain that it might never fall into the hands of our enemies. The speeches of Lord Nelson, in parliament, on this and other popular topics, demonstrate great senatorial ability, with a profound knowledge of our political and even commercial interests. Such a potent coadjutor was well worth cherishing, and Mr. Addington appears to have been very properly of that opinion.

Lord Nelson, on surveying his new domains, felt vastly desirous of filling up the moat, and extending the grounds on that side of the house where the space was so exceedingly contracted. He had, accordingly, applied by letter, dated the 25th of October 1801, to William Axe, Esq. of Birchin Lane, London, who was proprietor of the small intervening field which alone separated Merton Place from the narrow lane at the end of the abbey wall, to be favoured with the purchase of it, on equitable terms; and though that worthy gentleman, in the handsomest manner, for which Lord Nelson ever after highly respected him, paid all possible attention to the wish of his lordship; a churlish farmer, who was Mr. Axe's tenant, on lease, of the whole adjoining estate, where he had acquired a considerable fortune, opposed so many objections, and evinced so rude and unaccommodating a disposition, notwithstanding his lordship had condescendingly treated him with every courtesy, that the object was not accomplished till his lordship, about a year and half afterwards, purchased the whole farm, consisting of a hundred and fifteen acres; which Mr. Axe liberally consented to sell for the very moderate sum of eight thousand pounds.

In November, the Reverend Mr. Nelson came to Merton, on the pressing invitation of his ever duteous son. The meeting was truly affecting; and terminated, as it ought, in a thorough conviction, that his lordship had been most shamefully slandered. Indeed, on an entire eclaircissement, it became manifest that the grossest part of the slander which had been cruelly levelled against our hero was so self-evidently false, and really impracticable, that a very small degree of consideration made the worthy and venerable father blush for the credulity which had contributed to criminate our hero; whose private life, all circumstances duly considered, was to the full as unsullied as his public character. He saw the happy family with whom his heroic son was so agreeably domesticated; and witnessed the pure felicity of those amiable friends, with a rapture which conveyed the highest satisfaction to his heart. He perceived the kindest attentions to his son's happiness in every act of all around him: and their success, in the joy now constantly diffused over his countenance; beaming in every glance of his eye, and speaking in every accent of his tongue. He beheld his great and good son happy, and blessed and loved the friends who made him so. "Merton," he said, "is the *Mansion of Peace*, and I must become one of the inhabitants. Sir William and myself are both old men, and we will witness the hero's felicity in retirement." Such was the intention of this virtuous and pious parent; who had, however, been long so habituated to passing his winters at Bath, that he could not, at once, wean himself of the custom: but he never resided with Lady Nelson, as has been falsely reported, from the moment he was convinced of his illustrious son's having been so egregiously misrepresented. Apartments, in the mean time, were actually prepared for him at Merton Place; and it was agreed that, after wintering at Bath, he should, in May, come to reside wholly with his son and Sir William and Lady Hamilton: but, unfortunately, the salubrity of Bath proved insufficient to prolong his valuable life even till that period, for he died at his own apartments in that city, on the 26th of April 1802, in the seventy-ninth year of his age: lamented by every person who had ever known him, with the deepest veneration and regret, for the blameless sanctity of his amiable manners, the agreeable cheerfulness of his admirable disposition, and the warm benevolence of his excellent heart.

The loss of such a father, though at an age when it was to be expected, could not but be sensibly felt by the amiable offspring whom he left behind. Lord Nelson, ever tender as an infant in all that regards the soft affections, lamented his father's death with a grief so poignant, that its effect had nearly proved fatal to himself.

About the middle of July, Sir William Hamilton being desirous that Lord Nelson should accompany him into Wales, for the purpose of viewing Milford Haven, and the improvements at Milford, which the Honourable Mr. Greville had made on his uncle Sir William's estate, under the powers of an act of parliament passed in 1790, a party was formed, consisting of his lordship, Sir William and Lady Hamilton, and Dr. Nelson, the present earl, with his lady and son. In compliment to his heroic friend, Sir William had resolved to establish, at Milford, a fair, or annual festival, on the 1st of August; and his nephew, the Honourable Mr. Greville, kindly undertook to make every requisite preparation for receiving them on the joyous occasion.

The party reached Oxford the first day, being Wednesday, the 21st of July; where, by appointment, they were met by Mr. and Mrs. Matcham, with their eldest son, George Matcham, Jun. Esq. The Oxonians received his lordship with great joy; and, on Thursday, the freedom of the corporation was presented to Lord Nelson in a gold box, by Richard Weston, Esq. mayor of that city, who addressed his lordship, on the occasion, in a very respectful speech; and Lord Nelson expressed, in the warmest and strongest terms, his high sense of the honour, and his earnest wishes for the happiness of the city, and the prosperity of the public service. On Friday morning, in full convocation, the university not only complimented Lord Nelson, and his friend Sir William Hamilton, with the honorary degree of LL.D. but liberally admitted his lordship's brother, the present earl, who had already taken his degree of D.D. at Cambridge, *ad eundem*—that is, to the same honour in Oxford. Lord Nelson, and Sir William Hamilton, were severally presented by Dr. Blackstone, Vinerian Professor of Law; and the Reverend William Nelson, of Christ's College, and Doctor of Divinity in the University of Cambridge, by Dr. Collinson, Lady Margaret's Professor of Divinity. Nothing, in short, could surpass the respect experienced by his lordship and friends at Oxford; from whence, highly gratified, they the same day proceeded to Woodstock, with an intention of viewing Blenheim.

It might have been expected, that his Grace the Duke of Marlborough, himself descended from a British hero of the first class, and inhabiting a magnificent palace, the honourable boon of his country, would have joyfully availed himself of the opportunity thus afforded by the presence of a man certainly not inferior to his own heroic ancestor, so near as even at Oxford, and politely requested the honour of entertaining such a guest. This, however, had not been done; and Lord Nelson, with his friends, put up at an inn in Woodstock; from whence they went to Blenheim, as strangers, for the purpose of viewing the internal attractions of art, in that grand but ponderous national pile. The family never made their appearance; but sent a servant with refreshments, which Lord Nelson proudly refused. As the duke was at home, his lordship thought, no doubt, that he ought, at least, to have come forward. Sir William Hamilton said that, if the shade of the Great Marlborough could arise, he would have done the honours to the victor of Aboukir, a greater victor than himself! Lady Hamilton finely remarked—with a spirit and energy forcibly depicting the grand character of that superlative mind which renders her, at once, the idol and idoliser of transcendent genius and valour—that "the splendid reward of Marlborough's services, was because a woman reigned, and women had great souls: and I," says her ladyship, for these are her own matchless words, "told Nelson that, if I had been a queen, after the battle of Aboukir, he should have had a principality, so that Blenheim Park should have been only as a kitchen garden to it! The tears came into his eyes, and he shook Sir William and me by the hand; saying, that he was content to have done his duty by the country, and the people, that he loved, and he hoped we should ever approve his conduct; but that, yet, he had not half done, for there were two or three beds of laurels in the Mediterranean to be gathered."

It was in this way, that these exalted friends of their country, and of each other, consoled themselves on all occasions, where they met with any of that incivility or ingratitude, which few persons of eminent worth fail to experience in the world. That the Duke of Marlborough should have come forward, and welcomed the hero to Blenheim, cannot well be disputed; but his grace, who is said to be of a shy and retiring disposition, could not, it seems probable, prevail on himself to forego the ceremonials of introductory etiquette, and might thus give considerable offence to his lordship and friends, without intending them the smallest personal disrespect.

The party, next morning, set off for Gloucester, where they were received with the usual demonstrations of joy, by all ranks of the inhabitants. The bells were immediately rung; and multitudes eagerly crouded before the King's Head Inn, to view the hero who had atchieved so much for his country. During the party's short stay, they visited the cathedral, and the county prison, with both of which his lordship expressed himself highly pleased; particularly, with the extent and convenience of the latter, and the described system of it's internal regulations. On Sunday morning, Mr. and Mrs. Matcham, with their son, returned to Bath; while his lordship, and the remainder of his party, proceeded to Ross.

They entered this town amidst bell-ringing, and the acclamations of the people; and, after breakfasting at the Swan Inn, where horses had been ordered to convey them to Monmouth, finding they might be accommodated with boats, and preferring the excursion by water, for the sake of viewing the beautiful scenery on the banks of the Wye, they walked through the beautiful gardens belonging to Walter Hill, Esq. to the banks of that river, attended by a vast number of people, who decorated the boat provided for his lordship and friends with laurels, and exhibited every other demonstration of respect and joy.

It was no sooner known at Monmouth, that the party were making this excursion down the Wye, than its shores were lined with spectators, and the river covered with boats; and, when those accompanying his lordship appeared, shouts of joy burst forth, and the guns on the celebrated Kymin were fired. At landing, they were received by the corporation, who had come out to meet them, and by whom the hero was complimented in an appropriate address; for which, as well as for the recent honours conferred on him, in making him a burgess of their ancient borough, together with his friend, Sir William Hamilton, and enrolling his name among the illustrious chiefs in the Kymin Naval Temple, he returned his most heartfelt acknowledgments. They were preceded, on their way into town, by the bands of the Monmouth and Brecon militia, playing "God save the King!"—"Rule, Britannia!" and other popular tunes. After dinner, his lordship paid his respects to Thomas Hollings, Esq. the mayor; and then walked out in the town, for the purpose of viewing whatever seemed worthy of notice, constantly surrounded by innumerable spectators, all anxious to behold the hero, and pay him their tributary acknowledgments. His lordship being engaged, for next day, at Crickhowell, with his friend Admiral Gell, was under the necessity of declining the kind invitation of the mayor and corporation, to dine with them on Monday; but promised to pass a day at Monmouth on his return, of which they should have previous notice.

After spending the day with Admiral Gell, they went on to Brecon, where the joy of the people surpassed all description. The deputation of farmers was affecting. They said, addressing the hero—-"My lord, you have saved us. While you was losing your limbs, and shedding your blood, for us, we slept soundly with our wives; and our lands, and children, were protected by your brave vigilance. Accept our thanks; these tears will tell you that we feel!" and the men wept like children. The town was illuminated; and one man exclaimed—"Now, I could die in peace; I have seen our saviour, and brave defender!"

Nothing particular occurred to the party, after leaving Brecon, till they arrived at Milford; where the hero of the Nile, and his friends, were received with enthusiastic rapture. Sir William Hamilton had not, for many years, visited his numerous tenants; and they were proud to behold their paternal friend leagued in so strict an amity with the first hero in the world. Sir William was delighted to see his dear friend at Milford, and to shew him off to every body; and every body was charmed with the pleasing affability of the illustrious hero. Lord Nelson often mentioned his progress through South Wales to Milford, as an affecting contrast of the genuine enthusiasm of natural character, to the cold expression of ministerial approbation by which his reception had been marked on his return from the Mediterranean, when Lord Keith was sent to take the chief command of the fleet in those seas.

The corporate towns, villages, nobility, and gentry, on the line through which his route was directed, vied with each other to detain him, that their neighbours might participate in the joy they felt on the arrival of the hero. In many places, it was not possible to avoid their generous importunity; and these kind attentions, which so honourably testified national gratitude, were accepted, by his lordship, as the most gratifying recompences of his public service.

The 1st of August being made the great day at Milford, the Honourable Mr. Greville had invited all the nobility and gentry of the county of Pembroke to welcome the hero and his friends at this intended annual festival. A rowing match, fair day, and shew of cattle, were established for ever at Milford, in honour of the victory off the Nile. All the most respectable families twenty miles round, with a prodigious concourse of the humbler classes, came to see their beloved hero. Mr. Bolton, his lordship's brother-in-law, too, determined to be present on the occasion, arrived at Milford, that very morning, from Norfolk. It proved, all together a most interesting scene. After dinner, Lord Nelson, with admirable address, gave "Captain Foley!" as his toast: a friend and brother officer, he said, than whom there was not a braver or a better man in his majesty's service. He had been with him in all his chief battles; deserved to participate in every honour; and was, his lordship had the pleasure to add, in that respectable company, not only a Welshman, but a native of the county of Pembroke. It need scarcely be added, that this toast, so honourable both to his lordship and Captain Foley, and so gratifying to the principality and county, was received, and drank, with the most rapturous delight. At this public meeting, they had also the high satisfaction to hear, from his lordship's lips, the result of his judicious observations on the matchless harbour which that county embosoms. Lord Nelson had fully examined it's entrance, and its qualities; and now declared, that he considered Milford Haven, and Trincomale in the East Indies, as the two finest harbours he had ever beheld. The obstacles which had hitherto impeded the employment of so important an appendage as this to the empire, appeared merely artificial, and would speedily be removed when once fully known. The rapid results of individual exertion had already, in fact, proved this, by bringing the mails to the water-side, rendering the custom-house shore accessible to ships of burden, and establishing daily packets to and from Ireland; so that nothing more was now wanting, to render Milford Haven, projecting into and separating the St.

George's and the Bristol channels, the only safe sea-port on the west coast of Great Britain for commerce, as well as a port of refuge and of call: but, when viewed in relation to Ireland, it became the central port of the empire; particularly, as a bonding port. The American settlers, by their character and ability, had been enabled to send eight ships to the South Seas, and thus established the whale fishery. He had, himself, he acknowledged, supposed that the danger and natural defects of this port justified the official prejudice which, since the year 1757, has been attached to Milford Haven; but, the fortifications being now properly abandoned, as incapable of defending the harbour, the qualities of the port, stated in the petition of British merchants, and in the report of the Committee of the House of Commons, he had, on his own view, ascertained to be correct. He applauded the wise measure of Earl Spencer, to improve naval architecture at Milford; and was of opinion that, to apply, with oeconomy, the supply of timber on the sides of the Severn, for the purpose of building ships on the draughts of Mr. Barralleer at Milford, would do honour to the earl's views, and benefit to the service. He had critically examined the ships on the slips; and declared, that they ought to be models, of their class, for the British navy. Mr. Barralleer, an ingenious French ship-builder, who quitted Toulon, on it's evacuation by our forces, was well known to Lord Nelson. He had been fourteen months on board Admiral Goodall's ship; and his observations, during all that time, in British practice, had perfected Mr. Barralleer's principles of construction. At his lordship's suggestion, this ingenious naval architect has since prepared draughts for the largest classes of ships, the usual defects of which had been pointed out by Lord Nelson, and are there effectually remedied. The high tides of Milford Haven, it's vicinity to the forest of Dean, and the dock-yard being exempt from those interruptions by repairs to which Portsmouth and Plymouth must ever be devoted during war, are circumstances which, his lordship remarked, ought to render Milford Haven of the greatest use. Earl Spencer, indeed, had established the utility of the situation; and Mr. Barralleer, aware of prejudices among workmen who are required to deviate from their accustomed methods, had the precaution to initiate young natives of South Wales in his own modes of construction, and thus contrived to raise a sufficient number of able artificers. As to the practical use of Milford Haven, for the king's service, it was only requisite that it should be known; and for the commander of the channel fleet to give notice, that he considered Milford Haven as a port where he would detach some of his ships to victual and water: for, as his lordship observed, before Earl Spencer ordered ships to be built at Milford, not the smallest assistance could be obtained; and, indeed, what ship would go thither, while the agent-victualler resided in Bristol, and had no store for salt provisions at Milford?—which was, then, actually the case. Such obstacles, once noticed, must immediately vanish; and he would himself recommend the trial, if in command. It had been said, there were not sufficient pilots; but, his lordship observed, there soon would be, if the arrival of ships sufficient to maintain them might be reasonably expected. In short, the port of Milford was adapted to become of the greatest importance to Great Britain, not only in a naval and commercial view, but as an excellent position for packets to the westward. It would be particularly convenient, his lordship remarked, for single ships to go down channel, and rendezvous at Milford Haven, from whence they might at any time put to sea; either for the purpose of going off Brest, or stretching for the West Indies, when it was impossible for whole fleets to clear the channel, where they were now not unfrequently detained as long a time as would be requisite to make the whole voyage. Adverting to the example of his esteemed friend, Captain Foley, as a native of Pembrokeshire, his lordship remarked that, if government would only continue a fair encouragement to the port, the officers, the seamen, and the artificers, of the county of Pembroke, it could not fail to effect important services for the nation. His lordship concluded with observing, that he felt so happy at beholding such public benefits combined with the objects established on his friend Sir William Hamilton's estate, by prudence of plan, unremitted perseverance, and with small means, under the judicious arrangements of the Honourable Mr. Greville, that he would, if not on service, promise to return, as often as it should be in his power, to join them in celebrating the annual festivity thus established: and hoped that what he now publicly said, or had previously stated in private to his friends while surveying the port, would be remembered, for they were genuine truths; and he had already actually written to the minister, that he was in perfect admiration of this fine neglected port. Such is the substance of Lord Nelson's observations with regard to Milford Haven; the remembrance of which will, no doubt, long be cherished in the grateful bosoms of all who had the honour to hear him.

Sir William Hamilton left a fine whole-length picture of Lord Nelson, which had been painted at Vienna, to be preserved, for the perpetual gratification of visitors, by the occupier of the New Hotel, where his lordship and friends resided while at Milford.

After visiting Lord Cawdor, at Stackpoole Court; Lord Milford, at Picton Castle; Lord Kensington; Mr. Foley, brother of Captain Foley; and other noblemen and gentlemen in that part of the country, by all of whom they were sumptuously entertained; the party set out on their return from this highly satisfactory tour. At Haverfordwest, on going to visit Mr. Foley, the horses had been taken from Lord Nelson's carriage, and he was drawn through the streets by the populace; preceded by the Pembrokeshire militia, a troop of the Haverfordwest cavalry, and the flags of the different companies and societies, &c. While they were at Mr. Foley's, the mayor and corporation waited on his lordship, and presented him with the freedom of that ancient town. At Swansea, too, where he minutely examined the pier, pottery, and other places, while on a visit to Glasmont, the seat of John Morris, Esq. the carriage had been drawn through the town by a choice body of exulting tars; and, after being regaled with his friends, by the portreeve, his lordship, and Sir William Hamilton, were both presented with the freedom of Swansea.

On Wednesday evening, the 18th of August, after passing the day with Mr. Wells, owner of the celebrated Piersfield estate, the returning party arrived at the Beaufort Arms, Monmouth; Lord Nelson, on his way to Milford, having promised the mayor and corporation that he would again visit them. Next morning, amidst the ringing of bells, and preceded by a band of music, they set out, in a carriage with four horses, for the famous Kymin Pavillion; where they were not only received with enthusiasm by the company, but saluted by a discharge of cannon; the militia band playing—"God save the King!"—"Rule, Britannia!" &c. After taking breakfast in the banqueting-room, they proceeded to the Naval Temple, which his lordship surveyed with great attention. They then walked through the Beaulieu Grove: and, when they had sufficiently surveyed this delightful scene, in order to gratify the public curiosity, they walked back to Monmouth; receiving, as they passed, the grateful applauses of all ranks of people. At four o'clock, they sat down to an elegant dinner, at the Beaufort Arms, with the mayor, corporation, and most of the principal inhabitants. On the health of—"The Hero of the Nile!" being drank, his lordship arose; and, in an admirable speech, expressed his gratitude for their kind attentions.

Lady Hamilton sung two songs, with her usual scientific taste, and superior vocal excellence, which quite enraptured the whole company. "Words, indeed," says a writer in one of the provincial journals, on this occasion, would "but ill convey an idea of the life and spirit which this deservedly admired lady gave to the festive board! In short, the polite and engaging behaviour of Lord Nelson, as well as of Sir William and Lady Hamilton, impressed on the minds of the visitors the most unqualified respect and admiration of their characters." The meeting broke up at eight o'clock; his lordship and friends being engaged to pass the evening at the Honourable Colonel Lindsay's.

On Friday, after walking in the town, viewing the public buildings, &c. they set out for Ross; where a triumphal arch, ornamented with laurel and oak, and bearing an appropriate inscription, had been erected for the hero to pass through. From hence, they paid a visit to Rudhall, the seat of Thomas Westfaling, Esq. where, in the evening, there was a splendid ball and supper, to which all the principal families, for some miles round, were invited. A deputation from the mayor and corporation of Hereford, having waited on Lord Nelson, at Rudhall, requesting he would honour that city with his presence, his lordship obligingly consented; and, on Monday morning, proceeded thither. Being met by the populace, near the city, about twelve o'clock, they took the horses from his carriage, and drew the hero and his friends to the hotel; where they were received by his Grace the Duke of Norfolk, Recorder of Hereford. Shortly after, they proceeded to the town-hall; the militia band playing—"See, the conquering Hero comes!" Being introduced, by the Duke of Norfolk, to the corporation, who were waiting to receive his lordship, he was immediately addressed, by Lacon Lambe, Esq. town-clerk, in an appropriate speech, complimentary of the hero's splendid achievements during the war; and soliciting his acceptance of the freedom of the city, presented in a box cut from the *apple-tree*—"the pride of the country; and of whose noble juice," concluded Mr. Lambe, "many libations will not fail to be offered to the long health, prosperity, and happiness, of the great and glorious conqueror of the Nile!" Lord Nelson, respectfully putting the box to his lips, returned his sincere thanks, for an honour which, he said, he should never forget—that of having his name enrolled among the freemen of Hereford. It was true, he had stood forward in the defence of his king and country, in many engagements: yet the honour and renown, for the brilliant victories which the fleets under him had obtained, were not attributable to himself, but must be ascribed, first, to the Deity; and, next, to the undaunted courage, skill, and discipline, of those officers and seamen whom it had been his good fortune to command—not one of whom, he was proud to say, had ever in the least swerved from his duty. "Should this nation," concluded his lordship, "ever experience a state similar to that from which it has been recently extricated, I have not the slightest doubt, from the result of my observations during this tour, that the native, the inbred spirit of Britons, whilst it continues as firmly united as at present, is fully adequate successfully to repel any attack, either foreign or domestic, which our enemies may dare to make. You have but to say, to your fleets and armies—Go ye forth, and fight our battles; whilst we, true to ourselves, protect and support your wives and little ones at home." The impression made by this speech is inconceivable. The Reverend Mr. Morgan, canon-residentiary, also addressed his lordship, on the part of the bishop and clergy of the diocese; and, being charged, by the venerable bishop, to express his regret at being deprived, by extreme age and infirmity, of the honour of paying his personal respects to Lord Nelson in the town-hall, his lordship immediately replied that, as the son of a clergyman, and from having been bred up in a sense of the highest veneration for the church and it's able ministers, while he sincerely lamented the cause of absence, he conceived it a duty, which he would perform with the utmost willingness, to wait on his lordship at the episcopal palace. This, on returning from the hall, he accordingly did; and, soon after, the party proceeded to Downton Castle, near Ludlow, the seat of Richard Payne Knight, Esq.

On approaching near Ludlow, the populace took the horses from his lordship's carriage, and drew it into the town; and, at his departure, drew him out of town, in the same manner, on the road to Downton Castle.

After passing a few days with Mr. Knight, at his beautiful seat, and receiving the honorary freedom of the ancient borough of Ludlow, his lordship, on Sunday evening, the 29th of August, while on the road to Worcester, was met by a prodigious concourse of people, who hailed his approach with heart-felt acclamations; and, taking the horses from his carriage, drew it to the Hop-Pole Inn. The hero was greeted, as he entered the city, by lively peals from the different church bells, and many discharges of cannon; and joyfully saluted by innumerable spectators, in the streets, at the windows, and on the tops of houses, where they crouded to see him pass. In the course of the evening, his lordship frequently appeared at a window; and courteously bowed to the exulting crowd, with the most grateful condescension. Next morning, the illustrious guest, and his friends, preceded by a band of music, visited the famous Worcester china manufactory of Messrs. Chamberlains; and they demonstrated their approbation of it's beauty, by making considerable purchases. His lordship, in particular, left a large order for china, to be decorated in the most splendid stile, with his arms, insignia, &c. On returning to the inn, Lord Nelson was attended by the city officers, in all their formalities, for conducting his lordship and friends to the council-room in the town-hall; where the mayor and corporation were assembled, and had prepared an elegant collation. At the conclusion of this repast, the Right Honourable the Earl of Coventry, as Recorder of Worcester, on presenting his lordship with the freedom of that city, in an elegant china vase from Messrs. Chamberlains manufactory, thus addressed him—"My lord! As recorder of the ancient and loyal city of Worcester, an office of the most pleasing nature to myself, and honourable to your lordship, is now imposed upon me. I am requested, by that respectable and patriotic body which I have the honour to represent on this occasion, the corporation of this city, to solicit your lordship's acceptance, as a testimony of their high and grateful sense of your distinguished services, in defence of the people, liberty, and constitution, of this kingdom, and our most gracious sovereign, with the freedom of the city of Worcester." Lord Nelson, in a very masterly speech, complimented the corporate body, on the polite manner in which they had received him; and delicately expressed the pleasure which he felt from the sentiments entertained of him by the civil power of so ancient, so loyal, and so respectable a city, as that of Worcester. For loyalty, his lordship remarked, they had always stood in the foremost rank; and, to that patriotic spirit, he conceived, was to be ascribed the high estimation in which they held his public and personal services. He considered himself fortunate, that his exertions had been called forth in such perilous and disastrous times; as, he flattered himself, he had contributed to the protection of the best of constitutions, and the best of kings. At the same time, he was bound to acknowledge that, whatever honour might arise to himself, from his conduct in those trying scenes in which he had been engaged, he had certainly been supported by the most able, intrepid, and active officers, and by men of the most undaunted and enterprising courage. The merit ascribed to him, was more particularly due to the brave men who had been put under his orders; it was to them that the country was indebted, he only had the good fortune to command the heroes who had obtained those important successes. With such assistance, aided by that Providence who watches over righteous kings and states with paternal care, he did not hesitate to say, that this kingdom rested on a safe and solid basis; that nothing could shake it's foundation, but internal discord and divisions; that, as those whom he had now the honour of addressing, on to him so pleasing and flattering an occasion, had always, with such zeal and promptitude, expressed their attachment to their sovereign, they would, he hoped, persevere in that unanimity and order, which tend, as the best and most solid security, to the preservation of all kings and states. He had now, he said, the honour of being one of that body, as a public acknowledgment of the approbation with which they regarded his former services; and, should the exigence of the times, at any future period, call them again into action, the remembrance of that attention for which he had to thank them on the present occasion, would act as a stimulus to the exercise, if possible, of more ardent zeal and exertion, in the old and favourite cause, the defence of his king, and the protection of the constitution. His future conduct, his lordship concluded, would best evince his gratitude for the distinguished honours which had been conferred on him. The remainder of his life should be devoted to the service of his king and country; and, while he had a limb left, that limb should, if necessary, be cheerfully sacrificed in their defence.

After this noble and impressive speech, which was much and most deservedly admired, his lordship and friends quitted the hall, and went to see the cathedral; where they were received, and congratulated, by the Reverend Dr. Arthur Onslow, the dean, and clergy. Lord Nelson viewed the choir, monuments, &c. of this elegant structure, with evident marks of satisfaction; and expressed himself much flattered by the polite attentions which he had experienced at Worcester. Having received an express invitation from the High and Low Bailiffs of Birmingham, his lordship and friends, soon after one o'clock, departed for that celebrated place, in two post-coaches and four, with the drivers in bluejackets, and wearing ribbons of the same colour in their hats. Apprehensive of accidents, from the curiosity of so crouded a population as that of Birmingham, his lordship contrived to reach this town two hours sooner than expected. Accordingly, he was met with by but few people on the road; and arrived, without any tumult, at Styles's hotel. The intelligence, however, soon became general; the bells merrily rung; and a prodigious concourse of people assembled, all desirous of beholding the hero who had, they exclaimed, saved them and their little ones from destruction. His lordship kindly gratified them as much as possible, with a sight of his person, by repeatedly presenting himself at the window; and was as repeatedly greeted by the grateful and applausive shouts of the surrounding multitude, invoking Heaven's best blessings on the noble champion of his country. His lordship was immediately waited on, at the hotel, by James Woolley, Esq. the high bailiff; and Timothy Smith, Esq. the low bailiff: who politely thanked him, for the honour of accepting their invitation to "the toy-shop of Europe." His lordship, and friends, in the evening, went to the theatre, drawn by the shouting populace; and the house was so crouded, that many hundred persons were unable to obtain admission. On their entrance, "Rule, Britannia!" was played in full orchestra; and the whole audience, respectfully standing up, instantly testified, by their unanimously loud and long continued plaudits, the happiness which they experienced at thus seeing among them the renowned Hero of the Nile. On returning, at midnight, his lordship and friends were drawn back, by the people, through New Street, High Street, and Bull Street, to Styles's hotel, amidst a blaze of several hundred lighted torches. Next morning, his lordship and friends, accompanied by the high and low bailiffs, walked to view the manufactory of Mr. Clay, japanner in ordinary to his Majesty and his Royal Highness the Prince of Wales; the sword manufactory of Messrs. Woolley and Deakin; the button manufactory of Messrs. W. and R. Smith; the buckle and ring manufactory of Messrs. Simcox and Timmins; and the patent-sash manufactory of Messrs. Timmins and Jordan. They then went, drawn in their carriage by the populace, a prodigious multitude constantly attending, to Mr. Egerton's stained-glass manufactory, at Handsworth, where they were received by a party of beautiful young ladies, dressed in white, and who literally strewed the hero's ways with flowers. Here his lordship particularly admired a large window intended for Lady Masterman Sykes, and some works for Fonthill and Arundel. The party then proceeded to Mr. Boulton's matchless manufactory at Soho; and visited that ingenious gentleman, who was slowly recovering from a dangerous illness, in his bed-chamber. They then viewed the extensive coining apparatus; and were presented with several appropriate medals struck in their presence. On returning to the hotel, they found an elegant dinner, consisting of every delicacy the season could afford, provided by the high and low bailiffs: at which they were met by Heneage Legge, Esq. the high-sheriff; Dugdale Stratford Dugdale, Esq. one of the members for the county of Stafford; his lordship's esteemed friend Captain Digby, who had the honour of being selected to bring intelligence of his lordship's glorious victory off the Nile; with other naval and military officers, clergy, magistrates, &c. Lady Hamilton very condescendingly gratified the company with some charming songs. The bells rung most of the day: and, in the evening, his lordship and friends again visited the theatre; which was crouded with all the beauty and fashion of the neighbourhood, who gave them the most rapturous welcome. A respectable song, written for the occasion by Mr. Collins, was sung to the good old tune of "Hearts of Oak;" and his lordship and party were conveyed to and from the theatre, by the populace, in the same stile as they had been the preceding night. On Wednesday morning, again attended by the high and low bailiff, they proceeded, on foot, to inspect Mr. Radenhurst's whip manufactory, the extensive toy warehouse of Messrs. Richards, Mr. Phipson's pin manufactory, and Mr. Bissett's Museum. They concluded, by visiting the famous Blue-Coat Charity School, and were much pleased with the appearance of the children; they then returned to their hotel, and set out for Warwick, where they arrived the same evening.

The inhabitants of Warwick received his lordship and friends with every possible demonstration of joy. They were waited on by the mayor and corporation; and, after remaining till Friday morning, chiefly occupied in viewing Warwick Castle, the county-hall, churches, and other public buildings, went on to Coventry.

On arriving in the city of Coventry, where they were greeted with the usual public rejoicings, they were immediately attended by the mayor and corporation: and, after taking some refreshment, his lordship proceeded to pay his respects to Earl Spencer, at Althorpe Park, near Northampton; from whence, on Sunday, the 5th of September, the party returned to Merton.

This journey to Milford proved eminently beneficial to Lord Nelson. It had not only established his health; but exhilarated his feeling mind, and freed it from every depression. The affectionate sentiments of a grateful and virtuous people, spontaneously bursting from their hearts, communicated a glow to his heroic bosom, which inspired him with renovated vigour, and fortified him against all the lurking malignancy of mean envy and disappointed ambition.

When Lord Nelson came to town, from Merton, which he did almost daily during the sittings of parliament, Sir William Hamilton usually accompanied his noble friend for the transaction of his own private business, and they always returned together in the evening. These inseparable friends would visit no where without each other; and they often declared, that nothing but death should ever divide them. His lordship, fond of retirement, visited very few of his opulent neighbours: but there was scarcely a poor inhabitant of Merton, whose house he did not occasionally enter; where he would converse familiarly with the humble tenants, take the kindest notices of their little ones, and bountifully relieve their necessities. Among his select wealthy neighbours, the celebrated Abraham Goldsmid, Esq. of Morden, and his amiable family, ranked high in his lordship's estimation, as well as in that of Sir William and Lady Hamilton, and their reciprocal visits were frequent. A most liberal and unsolicited tender of pecuniary accommodation to Lord Nelson, by that worthy and disinterested gentleman, in the very origin of their acquaintance, bound his generous heart for ever to Mr. Goldsmid; whose mutually ardent amity, shining with undiminished lustre, still survives for all who were dear to his lordship.

On the 21st of December, when the famous bill of his noble friend, the Earl of St. Vincent, then First Lord of the Admiralty, for a commission of Naval Enquiry, which brought on such a train of important but unexpected consequences, and was pregnant with so many beneficial effects to the service, underwent a discussion in the House of Lords, at it's second reading, Lord Nelson made the following exquisite speech, in support of it's proposed objects—

"MY LORDS!

"In the absence of my noble friend, who is at the head of the Admiralty, I think it my duty to say a few words to your lordships, in regard to a bill of which the objects have an express reference to the interests of my profession as a seaman. It undoubtedly originates in the feelings of the Admiralty; that they have not the power to remedy certain abuses, which they perceive to be most injurious to the public service. Every man knows, that there are such abuses; and, I hope, there is none among us who would not gladly do all that could be constitutionally effected to correct them.

Yet, if I had heard of any objection, of weight, urged against the measures in the present bill, I should certainly have hesitated to do any thing to promote it's progress through the forms of this house. But, I can recollect only one thing with which I have been struck as possibly exceptionable in it's tenor. It authorizes the commissioners to call for, and inspect, the books of merchants, who may have had transactions of business with any of the boards, or prize agents, into whose conduct they are to enquire. But, the credit of the British merchant is the support of the commerce of the world; his books are not, lightly, nor for any ordinary purpose, to be taken out of his own hands. The secrets of his business are not to be too curiously pryed into. The books of a single merchant may betray the secrets, not only of his own affairs, but of those with whom he is principally connected in business; and the reciprocal confidence of the whole commercial world may, by the authoritative enquiry of these commissioners, be shaken. All this, at least, I should have feared, as liable to happen, if the persons who are named in the bill had not been men whose characters are above all suspicion of indiscretion or malice. I may presume it to be the common conviction of the merchants, that in such hands they will be safe: since they have made no opposition to the bill, in it's progress; and since they have offered no appearance against it, by counsel at your lordships bar. And, truly, my lords, if the bill be, thus, superior to all objection; I can affirm, that the necessities, the wrongs, of those who are employed in the naval service of their country, most loudly call for the redress which it proposes! From the highest admiral in the service, to the poorest cabin-boy that walks the street, there is not a man but may be in distress, with large sums of wages due to him, of which he shall, by no diligence of request be able to obtain payment; not a man, whose intreaties will be readily answered, with aught but insult, at the proper places for his application, if he come not with particular recommendations to a preference. From the highest admiral, to the meanest seaman, whatever may be the sums of prize-money due to him, no man can tell when he may securely call any part of it his own. A man may have forty thousand pounds due to him, in prize-money; and yet may be dismissed, without a shilling, if he ask for it at the proper office without particular recommendation. Are these things to be tolerated? Is it for the interest, is it for the honour, of the country, that they should not as speedily as possible be redressed? I should be as unwilling as any man, to give an overweening preference to the interests of my own profession; but I cannot help thinking that, under all the circumstances of the business, your lordships will be strongly disposed to advance this bill into a law, as speedily as may be consistent with the order of your proceedings, and with due preference of deliberation!"

Next day, in a committee of the whole house, on the third reading of this celebrated bill, the Duke of Clarence having suggested the propriety of instituting a distinct enquiry, under a particular act, into the abuses of prize-money, Lord Nelson expressed himself to be of the same opinion; but, though severely animadverting on the flagrant enormities of prize-agents, his lordship, nevertheless, candidly acknowledged, that there might be instances where the delays of the payment of prize-money resulted, not from the villainy of the agents, but from accidents by no means easily avoidable in the common course of human affairs. In regarding the naval interests of his country, Lord Nelson was not unmindful of it's commercial prosperity; in censuring criminal abuses, he was careful not to involve innocence with guilt.

Lord Nelson's love of humanity led him, in February 1805, on the trial of Colonel Marcus Despard, for high-treason, to bear the most honourable testimony to that officer's character: they had, his lordship said, formerly served together on the Spanish main; together been in the enemy's trenches, and slept in the same tent; and he had every reason to believe him a loyal man, and a brave officer. His lordship, however, was fully satisfied, in the end, that Colonel Despard had been guilty of the crime for which he was executed in Horsemonger Lane, Southwark, on the 21st of the same month. Lord Ellenborough, the learned judge before whom Colonel Despard was tried and convicted, on noticing, in his address to the jury, the circumstances of Lord Nelson's testimony, from the seat of justice which he so worthily fills, delivered this fine panegyric on our illustrious hero—"You have heard," said that manly, wise, and virtuous judge, "the high character given of the prisoner, by a man on whom to pronounce an eulogy were to waste words! But, you are to consider whether a change has not taken place, since the period of which he speaks. Happy, indeed, would it have been for him, if he had preserved that character down to this moment of peril!" Had there been a gleam of doubt, as to the guilt of the culprit, the jury would certainly have acquitted him in consequence of our hero's testimony as to his character; and such was, after all, it's influence on their minds, that when, in the usual form, they were asked whether he was "Guilty, or not guilty?" the foreman, though he replied—"Guilty;" immediately added—"but we earnestly recommend him to mercy, on account of his former good character, and the services he has rendered his country." No recommendation, however, the crime being so atrocious, and the guilt so manifest, could reasonably be expected to avail. It is said, though such disabolism can scarcely be credited, that attempts were made, on this occasion, by secret enemies of his lordship in very high rank, to prejudice characters still more elevated against him; and thus, as in some other respects, vilely insinuating that his most honourable and virtuous heart was tainted with the very vice which he ever held in the greatest abhorrence. Among the various gross imputations against his lordship, which the future historian may find registered in some of the preserved licentious public journals of blended facts and falshoods, and inconsiderately adopt, is that of the Hero of the Nile's having been so addicted to gaming, that he lost, at a single sitting, the whole he had gained, both pay and prize-money, during the year of that memorable victory: whereas, in truth, his lordship was so extremely adverse to this vice, that he had scarcely ever, in his life, entered any one of the fashionable gaming-houses; nor ever, as he repeatedly assured his friends, whom these base reports induced particularly to ask the question, won or lost even the trifling sum of twenty guineas! Notwithstanding this undoubted verity; there will, probably, always be found weak heads firmly believing, and vicious hearts basely pretending to believe, that this exalted man was actually of a gambling spirit. So difficult is it entirely to eradicate the rank but fertile growth of once disseminated calumny; which, sown in darkness, by the arch-enemy of mankind, springs up, and spreads it's pernicious influence, to check the fairer growth, and defeat the just hopes of the meritorious husbandman.

It has been already observed that, owing to the unaccommodating disposition of a neighbouring farmer, Lord Nelson had been unable to enlarge the grounds of his retirement at Merton, till he agreed to purchase the whole of Mr. Axe's estate. This, however, had been so far effected, at the latter end of the year 1802, that there wanted nothing, but certain legal formalities, for the conclusion of that business. His lordship and friends had already rendered Merton Place a little paradise, by their tasteful arrangements. They jointly directed the disposition of the most beautiful shrubs; and not unfrequently placed them in the earth, Sir William or Lady Hamilton assisting his lordship to plant them with his single hand. A small mulberry-tree, now only a few feet high, and standing in front of the house, not far distant from the canal, where it was fixed by Lord Nelson's own hand, may hereafter rival the celebrated mulberry-tree at Stratford upon Avon, planted by the immortal Shakspeare; the first dramatic bard, and naval hero, "take them for all in all," the world is ever likely to know. The prospect of immediately executing the desirable additional improvements in his lordship's estate, the plan of which had already been long contrived, was a source of considerable satisfaction to their anticipatory minds, as the spring season advanced. The purchase, indeed, was compleated the beginning of May 1803; but, events were now destined to occur, in the few intervening days, which rendered the possession of what had been so eagerly sought, of little value to either of the persons by whom it had been regarded as so sure a source of increased enjoyments.

Towards the latter end of March, Sir William Hamilton, then in his seventy-fourth year, suddenly felt himself more than usually indisposed. He was a gentleman of the most exalted understanding; and knew, perfectly well, from the nature of his sensations, that the period had arrived, when his corporeal dissolution must hourly be expected. This circumstance conveyed, to his excellent heart, no uncommon alarm: the serious contemplation of death, had not been deferred to the last moment of his existence; and he therefore beheld, without dismay, every step of it's awful approach. With a calmness which he was unable to communicate to his lady, he announced the solemn certainty; and declared his resolution immediately to leave Merton Place, lest he should, by dying there, render it an insupportable future abode to the feelings of his tender and illustrious friend. Sir William, on arriving at his house in Piccadilly, the 29th of March, instantly annexed the following remarkable codicil to his will—

"March 29,1803.

"The copy of Madame Le Brun's picture of Emma, in enamel, by Bone, I give to my dearest friend, Lord Nelson, Duke of Bronte: a small token of the great regard I have for his lordship; the most virtuous, loyal, and truly brave character, I have ever met with. God bless him! and shame fall on those who do not say--*Amen*."

The moment his lordship learned that Sir William Hamilton's physicians declared him to be in danger, he never once quitted him: but, during six nights, constantly sat up with his friend; who died, in the arms of Lady Hamilton, and with Lord Nelson's hand in his, on the 6th of April 1803. A few moments before Sir William's decease, he said to his lordship—"Brave and great Nelson, our friendship has been long, and I glory in my friend. I hope you will see justice done to Emma, by ministers; for you know how great her services have been, and what she has done for her country. Protect my dear wife; and may God bless you, and give you victory, and protect you in battle!" Then, turning to his lady—"My incomparable Emma," said he, "you have never, in thought, word, or deed, offended me; and let me thank you, again and again, for your affectionate kindness to me, all the time of our ten years happy union." Lord Nelson could scarcely be torn from the body of his friend. He requested Mrs. Nelson, now the Countess Nelson, immediately to take apartments for him: and begged her to tell Lady Hamilton, that it would not be right, now his friend was dead, to be an inmate of her ladyship's house; for it was a bad world, and her grief for the loss of her husband might not let her think of the impropriety of his continuing there. His lordship, accordingly, removed that evening to lodgings in Piccadilly.

It is remarkable that, the very day of Sir William's death, Captain Macnamara, Lord Nelson's old fellow-traveller when he visited France the latter end of the year 1783, killed Colonel Montgomery, and was himself shot through the left side by his antagonist, in a duel near Primrose Hill, Hampstead. They had been riding in Hyde Park, that morning, with each a Newfoundland dog; in whose first quarrelling and fighting, originated the dispute which so fatally terminated in the evening. Captain Macnamara was tried at the Old Bailey, on the 22d of the same month; but Lord Nelson, as well as his friends Lord Minto, Lord Hood, and Lord Hotham, giving him a most excellent character, though Judge Heath directed the jury to find a verdict of manslaughter, both from the evidence and the captain's own admission, they resolutely pronounced him—"Not guilty!"

Lord Nelson had not, now, been quite eighteen months at home; and, within less than the twelve last, his ardent hopes of a tranquil retirement with the friends he loved, had been twice cruelly chilled by the hand of death. Having lost the best of fathers, and the best of friends, with whom he was solicitous to have enjoyed his enlarged domains at Merton, before the incivility of a rude rustic, and the procrastinating formalities of legal conveyance, would permit him to possess the requisite additions for it's improvement. Indeed, without the aid of Sir William's income, the establishment at Merton Place, was already too great for Lord Nelson's slender fortune. It suited well enough their joint means, but was not adapted, individually, for either. However, even the possession of the whole had scarcely been obtained, and not at all occupied, when it was rendered useless to the hero; for, a renewal of the war being now inevitable, his transcendent abilities were instantly called for by the united voice of the nation.

On the 16th of May, little more than five weeks after the decease of his revered and regretted friend Sir William Hamilton, a message from his majesty announced to both houses of parliament the necessity for immediate war with France: and, the very next day, Lord Nelson, who had accepted the command of the Mediterranean fleet, departed for Portsmouth; from whence he sailed for Gibraltar, the day following, in the Amphion frigate, accompanied by the Victory of a hundred and ten guns, his lordship's flag-ship.

Previous to his departure, however, Lord Nelson, not unmindful of his dying friend's last request, had both written to, and waited on, Mr. Addington, respecting Lady Hamilton's pension; and this most honourable minister, as he has ever been generally esteemed, frankly told his lordship, that it certainly ought to be granted. Indeed, when it is duly considered, that Sir William Hamilton was the foster-brother of his present majesty, who always entertained for him the most affectionate regard; that he had, for thirty-six years, filled the character of British minister at the court of Naples, with a zeal and ability not to be surpassed, and with a munificent and splendid hospitality very rarely exercised; that his surviving lady, who constituted the chief felicity of his latter years, so contributed to promote all the best interests of her country, and all the dignity of a beloved husband who there held the honour of representing his sovereign, that the Queen of Naples, in a letter to his British majesty, dictated by the grateful feelings of her heart, expressly stated Lady Hamilton to have been—"her best friend and preserver! to whom she was indebted, certainly, for her life; and, probably, for the crown!" and that the pension of twelve hundred pounds a year, conferred on Sir William for his long diplomatic services, ceased at his death; added to the solicitations of such a man as Lord Nelson, and the avowal of so upright a minister as Mr. Addington: it must, certainly, appear evident that, if there had not been some very unaccountable neglect, or some most scandalous impediment, the just expectations of so many great and estimable characters, would long since have been satisfied by the grant of a liberal pension to Lady Hamilton; not only as the relict of such an honourable envoy, but for her ladyship's own individual public services to the country. What Lord Nelson thought on this subject, to the last hour of his most invaluable life, will necessarily be hereafter more particularly noticed.

Soon after his lordship's arrival at Gibraltar, while he was going up to Malta, in the month of June, for the purpose of collecting his ships, he wrote to Lady Hamilton that, when he was in sight of Vesuvius, his thoughts of his dear friend, Sir William, were so severe, that he had nearly fainted. Thus delicately tender were all the virtuous affections, in the bosom of this truly heroic man.

Though Lord Nelson was, now, established commander in chief, in some sense for the first time, the dread with which his name inspired the enemy rendered the service far too inactive for his lordship's taste. To watch the motions of a timid enemy, and wait the tedious periods of their venturing out, was to him a most irksome task. He disdained, however, any strict blockade of Toulon: but encouraged the boastful fleet, ignominiously skulking there, to come fairly forward; by always leaving them sufficient sea room; though he endeavoured to preserve over all their motions a constantly watchful eye. Month, after month, seemed sluggishly to pass away, in wearisome succession; though his lordship, whose mind was ever too alert for a state of actual supineness, kept continually cruizing about. He hoped that, at least, they might thus be encouraged secretly to detach a small squadron, which he had little doubt some of his brave fellows would soon contrive to pick up. In these cruizes, too, his lordship, at least, was certain of securing one object, ever the first regard of his heart, that of preserving the health of the men, without which no victory could be expected. His care, in this respect, was most unremittingly employed; and the following letter, written by Lord Nelson, at that period, to his friend and physician, the celebrated Dr. Moseley, of Chelsea Hospital, who has purposely favoured the biographer with a correct copy, will not only evince his lordship's indefatigable attention, and his very great skill and success, but prove otherwise considerably interesting.

"Victory, 11th of March 1804.

"MY DEAR DR. MOSELEY,

Yesterday, I received the favour of the 4th edition of your invaluable work on Tropical Diseases, &c. and, with it, your most kind letter: and, though I know myself not equal to your praises, yet I feel that my honest intentions for the good of the service have ever been the same; and, as I rise in rank, so do my exertions. The great thing, in all military service, is health; and you will agree with me, that it is easier for an officer to keep men healthy, than for a physician to cure them. Situated as this fleet has been, without a friendly port, where we could get all the things so necessary for us; yet I have, by changing the cruizing ground, not allowed the sameness of prospect to satiate the mind. Sometimes, by looking at Toulon, Ville Tranche, Barcelona, and

Roses; then running round Minorca, Majorca, Sardinia, and Corsica; and, two or three times, anchoring for a few days, and sending a ship to the last place for *onions*--which I find the best thing that can be given to seamen: having, always, good mutton for the sick; cattle, when we can get them; and plenty of fresh water. In the winter, it is the best plan to give half the allowance of grog instead of all wine.

"These things are for the commander in chief to look to; but, shut very nearly out from Spain, and only getting refreshments by stealth from other places, my command has been an arduous one.

"Cornwallis has great merit for his persevering cruize; but he has every thing sent him, we have nothing. We seem forgotten, by the great folks at home. Our men's minds, however, are always kept up, with the daily hopes of meeting the enemy. I send you, as a curiosity, an account of our deaths, and sent to the hospital, out of 6000 men. The fleet put to sea on the 18th of May 1803, and is still at sea; not a ship has been refitted, or recruited, excepting what has been done at sea, You will readily believe, that all this must have shaken me. My sight is getting very bad; but I must not be sick, until after the French fleet is taken, Then, I shall soon hope to take you by the hand, and have farther recourse to your skill for my eye.

"I am always glad to hear good accounts of our dear Lady Hamilton. That she is beloved, wherever she is known, does not surprise me; the contrary would, very much. I am sure, she feels most sincerely all your kindness.

"Believe me, for ever, my dear doctor, your much obliged friend,

Nelson and Bronte
Dr. Moseley, Chelsea Hospital."

The account of the very few persons who had died, or been on the sick list, transmitted as a curiosity in the above letter, having been unfortunately lost by Dr. Moseley, their exact number cannot be ascertained.

Notwithstanding the opportunities given by Lord Nelson for the French fleet to depart from Toulon, either in the aggregate, by detached squadrons, or even single ships, more than a year elapsed without any of them daring to quit the port. A solitary frigate, indeed, had occasionally appeared, but was soon chased back, and no stratagem seemed capable of inducing them to move. Among other contrivances to put them in motion, was that of sending two or three ships of the line, with a single frigate, off the harbour, while the main body of the fleet remained at a considerable distance out of sight.

On the 23d of May 1804, Admiral Campbell in the Canopus, accompanied by Sir Richard Strachan in the Donegal, and the Amazon frigate, were detached by Lord Nelson thus to reconnoitre the enemy; and, after being some hours as near the mouth of the harbour as their batteries would allow, had the pleasure to behold three line of battle ships, and three frigates, come out. Our ships immediately tacked, in order to draw them from the land; but only went under an easy sail, so that they soon came within random-shot. When the enemy began to fire, the people of the Canopus were just sat down to dinner; which they quietly took, and then returned their fire: meaning, now, to bring them to close action, though so far superior. At this moment, however, two more ships of the line, with another frigate, were perceived coming up fast to their assistance. This was too great odds, so near their own batteries, and our small squadron were obliged to sheer off, under a press of sail. The French pursued them, for some time, still keeping the advantage of sailing; but, fearful of following too far, by the time they were five leagues from Toulon, they were recalled, about three quarters of an hour past three, by their signal-post from the hill, and all stood in again. At six, the rear-admiral saw our fleet to leeward, and joined them at half-past nine. They had heard, indistinctly, the firing: and the Leviathan was, in consequence, detached toward Toulon; but had not proceeded far, before our ships were perceived on their return. This trivial affair was magnified, by the French admiral, Latouche Treville, who had so manfully ventured to pursue, a little way, with two eighty-fours, three seventy-fours, three forty-four frigates, and a corvette, our two eighty-fours and a single frigate, into a compleat discomfiture of the whole British fleet!

In the mean time, though Lord Nelson could in no way contrive effectually to decoy out the wary Gallic boasters, their commerce was not only distressed, but nearly annihilated; their privateers were taken; and the British flag waved, with proud defiance, throughout the Mediterranean, and was unopposed even on the coast of France. The city of London, sensible of what the experienced security of the British commerce owed to his lordship's services, though uninformed as to the precise mode in which the hero's operations were conducted, now transmitted to him, through the lord-mayor, their public thanks, voted on the 9th of April 1804, for his skill and perseverance in blockading the port of Toulon, so as to prevent the enemy's fleet in that quarter from putting to sea. This panegyric, however intended, was not at all relished by his lordship, who had never approved of the blockading system. "Praise undeserved," the hero probably thought, as well as the poet, "is censure most severe." Under some such impression, therefore, instantly on receiving the lord-mayor's letter, which unfortunately arrived the famous 1st of August, he wrote the following animated answer; spiritedly declining any acceptance of thanks from his fellow-citizens, in which his own services seemed so imperfectly recognized, and from which his brave coadjutors were unjustly excluded.

"Victory, August 1, 1804.

"MY LORD,

"This day, I am honoured with your lordship's letter of April 9th; transmitting me the resolutions of the corporation of London, thanking me as commanding the fleet blockading Toulon. I do assure your lordship, that there is not that man breathing, who sets a higher value upon the thanks of his fellow-citizens of London than myself; but I should feel as much ashamed to receive them, for a particular service marked in the resolution, if I felt that I did not come within that line of service, as I should feel hurt at having a great victory passed over without notice.

"I beg to inform your lordship, that the port of Toulon has never been blockaded by me; quite the reverse. Every opportunity has been offered the enemy to put to sea: for, it is there that we hope to realize the hopes and expectations of our country; and, I trust that they will not be disappointed.

"Your lordship will judge of my feelings, upon seeing that all the junior flag-officers of other fleets, and even some of the captains, have received the thanks of the corporation of London, whilst the junior flag-officers of the Mediterranean fleet are entirely omitted. I own, that it has struck me very forcibly; for, where the information of the junior flag-officers and captains of other fleets was obtained, the same information could have been given of the flag-officers of this fleet and the captains; and it was my duty to state, that more able and zealous flag-officers and captains do not grace the British navy, than those I have the honour and happiness to command. It likewise appears, my lord, a most extraordinary circumstance, that Rear-Admiral Sir Richard Bickerton should have been, as second in command in the Mediterranean fleet, twice passed over by the corporation of London: once, after the Egyptian expedition, when the first and third in command were thanked; and, now, again. Consciousness of high desert, instead of neglect, made the rear-admiral resolve to let the matter rest, until he could have an opportunity personally to call upon the lord-mayor to account for such an extraordinary omission; but, from this second omission, I owe it to that excellent officer, not to pass it by: and I do assure your lordship, that the constant, zealous, and cordial support, I have had, in my command, from both Rear-Admiral Sir Richard Bickerton and Rear-Admiral Campbell, has been such as calls forth all my thanks and admiration. We have shared together the constant attention of being more than fourteen months at sea, and are ready to share the dangers and glory of a day of battle; therefore, it is impossible that I can ever allow myself to be separated, in thanks, from such supporters.

"I have the honour to remain, with the very highest respect, your lordship's most faithful and obedient servant,

"Nelson and Bronte."

"To the Right Honourable the Lord Mayor."

During the remainder of the year, though there was scarcely a day which his lordship did not employ in endeavours to improve the natural supineness of his situation, very little occurred that calls for particular notice. A tedious detail of so many days of languid expectation, would be comparatively as oppressive to the reader, as the time thus passed proved to the hero himself and the many brave men under his command. The destruction, however, of a number of vessels at La Vandour, in Hieres Bay, was performed with such a display of hardihood and address, that it should, at least, receive honourable mention. This can be in no way so well effected, as by transcribing Lord Nelson's own words on the occasion—"The importance of the service," says his lordship, "may be but little; but, the determined bravery of Lieutenants Thompson, Parker, Lumley, and Moore, and the petty officers, seamen, and marines, employed under them, could not be exceeded." Nor must a small anecdote, highly honourable to our hero himself, fail also to be recorded. A seaman of his lordship's flag-ship, the Victory, on the 11th of September, fell from the forecastle into the sea; when Mr. Edward Flin, a volunteer, hearing the cry of a man overboard, instantly leaped from the quarter-deck, and had the good fortune to save him, notwithstanding the extreme darkness of the night, and the ship's being under sail. Next morning, Lord Nelson sent for Mr. Flin; and, presenting him with a lieutenant's commission, appointed him to the Bittern sloop of war, and afterwards procured the Admiralty's confirmation of his appointment.

The year 1805, rendered for ever too fatally memorable, commenced with presages of sufficiently active employ. The vast exertions of France for the augmentation of her navy, seemed to inspire a hope of being able, with the assistance of Spain, now forced into a war which that unfortunate court had so much reason to dread, at length, in the confidence of superior numbers, to hazard an encounter with the British fleet. This, however, was by no means to be rashly ventured: it would be necessary, they well knew, first to effect a junction of their united force; which was not easily accomplishable, while they were watched with such diligent circumspection by our indefatigable hero. The first operation, by which they sought to elude his vigilance, was that of risking a small squadron from Rochfort, under Rear-Admiral Missiessi; which, having got out unobserved by our cruisers, arrived safely in the West Indies, with the double view of pillaging our colonies, and assisting to relieve St. Domingo. In the mean time, another, but far more powerful squadron, was ready to seize the first convenient opportunity of slipping out from Toulon.

On the 15th of January, while Lord Nelson, who had no desire to restrain the enemy from putting to sea, was busily engaged in observing the whole line of the Italian, French, and Spanish coasts, from Palermo, Leghorn, Toulon, and Barcelona, to the Straits of Gibraltar, and picking up all the French and Spanish vessels which his cruisers could meet with in that wide extent of ocean, Admiral Villeneuve, with a formidable squadron, consisting of eleven sail of the line and two frigates, suddenly pushed out of Toulon harbour. The Seahorse, Lord Nelson's look-out frigate, accordingly, narrowly escaped being taken: and the Venus sloop of ten guns, with his lordship's dispatches, was actually captured; having, however, previously thrown the dispatches overboard. The Seahorse, instead of watching, at a safe distance, the course of the enemy's fleet, till their destination should have been in some degree ascertained, hastened to acquaint his lordship that they had sailed, without being able to afford the smallest additional information. This, indeed, was sufficient to call forth our hero's energies; but he was, at the same time, checked by the dread of proceeding in a wrong direction. Strong circumstances induced his lordship to suppose, that another attack on Egypt might possibly be intended by this armament; which, indeed, was the current report. He deemed it likely, however, that they might first, as they formerly did at Malta, make an insiduous attempt on Sicily, in their way to the grand scene of their perfidious operations. Actuated by the force of these reflections, Lord Nelson sent to apprize the Ottoman Porte, as well as the Commandant of Coron, that the Toulon fleet had sailed, having a considerable number of troops on board, with the probable intention of making a descent either on the Morea or on Egypt. He also dispatched, on the 25th, the Seahorse to Naples, and Le Tigre to Palermo, with similar intimations. Next day, the Phoebe joined the fleet; who had, on the 19th, seen a French eighty-gun ship get into Ajaccio, in Corsica, having lost all her topmasts, and being otherwise much crippled. This, it should seem, was the effect of that storm which, as it was afterwards found, had almost immediately occasioned the French armament's return to Toulon. His lordship, however, unaware of any such consequence, and deceived by the artful promulgation of false reports, kept running for Sicily; and, when in sight of Maritimo, sent Le Tigre, Captain Hallowell, to communicate with Sir John Acton at Palermo. Le Tigre joined next day, without any news whatever of the French. In the evening, the fleet passed round Strombolo, which burnt very strongly all night; and, having left the Sophia to cruize three days off Strombolo for information, and sent the Bittern to Tunis, proceeded for the Faro of Messina. On the 30th, off the Faro, his lordship was joined by the Seahorse from Naples; where, also, nothing had been heard of the French. At noon, on the 31st, having sent the Seahorse off Toulon, round Cape Corse, and Morgiana, to look into Elba, St. Fiorenzo, and Ajaccio, the fleet got through the Faro of Messina without any accident. On the 2d of February, they passed Candia; being unable, from the state of the wind and weather, to make that island: and, on the 5th, sent forward the Anson, with letters to the Governor of Alexandria; to the British resident, Major Bissett; and to the pro-consul, Mr. Briggs. Next day, his lordship saw the Arab's Tower; and, on the 7th, at seven in the morning, came within sight of Alexandria, but there were no ships in the port. His lordship immediately sent Captain Hallowell ashore, with duplicates of his letters, the Anson being unable to get up. At three o'clock, Captain Hallowell returned. The Turks, who were very much alarmed at the appearance of the fleet, had heard nothing of the French; and were in no condition to defend this most important place from an attack, by surprise, of even five hundred men. Such is the shocking supineness of these people! The Turks and Mamelukes were, however, at war; the former being in possession of Grand Cairo, and the latter of Upper Egypt. Immediately on the receipt of this intelligence, by Captain Hallowell, the fleet bore up, and made sail for Malta.

On the 11th, the Phoebe having joined off Candia, was dispatched to Malta with orders. At daylight, on the 19th, his lordship saw Malta; and, at eight in the morning, communicated with Vallette. The Phoebe made the signal for no information; and, at nine, the fleet bore away for Maritimo. The Superb picked up a boat, and made the signal for intelligence from Malta: but his lordship would not stop; for he wanted, he said, no intelligence, but where to find the French fleet. His anxiety, therefore, may be easily imagined. It was little less, in fact, than what he had formerly suffered, on his first vain pursuit to Alexandria. By a vessel met with, in the afternoon, eight days from Barcelona, his lordship now learned that the French fleet had returned to Toulon; wanting, however, at that time, three sail of the line and a frigate. On the 28th, while employed in watering the fleet, at Palla, in Sardinia, a letter arrived from Captain Munday of the Hydra, dated February 17th, who had reconnoitred the French fleet in Toulon on the 12th, when it consisted of seventeen sail.

On Thursday, the 7th of March, a cartel ship came into the fleet, then at anchor under Tolaro in the Isle of Rouse, with Captain Layman, the officers, and crew, of the Raven brig, which was wrecked off Cadiz, on the night of January the 29th. The Captain General of Andalusia, Lord Nelson was told, had treated them with the greatest kindness—"Which," generously exclaimed his lordship, "I will return, whenever fortune may put it in my power!" Having weighed, in the morning of the 8th, the fleet, at six in the evening, anchored in the Gulph of Palma; where a court-martial was held on the officers and crew of the late Raven brig, which passed a slight censure on the captain for not having approached the shore with greater caution. In the evening, the fleet beat out of Palma, and steered between Vache and the reef off Antioch. On the 12th, in the Gulph of Lyons, they were joined by the Active, Seahorse, and Juno; who had, the day before, seen the French fleet perfectly ready for sea. The Renown also joined that evening; on board of which, invalids, &c. were next day sent. It was a calm, all day; but, in the evening, light breezes springing up, the fleet stood out for St. Sebastian's. On the 16th, the Renown was dispatched for Gibraltar and England; on the 17th, the fleet was beating to the eastward, off Tarragona; and, on the 20th, in the afternoon, passed Minorca, standing for Sardinia, which they saw on the 23d in the evening, when his lordship sent the Juno with orders for the transports to join him. At sunset, on the 26th, the fleet anchored in the Gulph of Palma; where Lord Nelson found his old friend, Admiral Louis, in the Ambuscade, who had sailed from England the 16th of February. The whole of this night, and the three following days, were employed in clearing transports. On the 29th, the Seahorse brought intelligence that the French fleet were safe in port on Sunday the 24th. The day following, the signal was made to prepare for sea; and, our fleet having sailed from Palma, anchored at Palla, on the 31st in the evening. Next morning, April 1, at day-light, they commenced watering; and, at sun-set, every ship was compleat, and the fleet moved farther off shore. Their activity, his lordship remarked, was never exceeded. On the 3d, at day-light, they sailed from Palla; and, next morning, were joined by the Phoebe, with the signal that the enemy's fleet was at sea. At nine, Captain Capel went on board the Victory; and reported to his lordship, that he had seen the French fleet on Sunday morning at eight o'clock, and kept with them till sun-set, but lost sight of them during the night. Lord Nelson immediately sent the Ambuscade to Gaieta, and the Active to the coast of Africa, for intelligence respecting them. Next day, the Amazon and transports joined from Malta; and a Turkish corvette also arrived from Constantinople, with letters of gratitude from the Grand Vizier and the Capitan Pacha, to which his lordship immediately returned respectful answers. The Moucheron brig, too, having this day joined, from Malta, was sent to cruize seven days between Gaieta and Africa, and to call at Tunis for information. After clearing transports next day, and sending the Bittern to Gibraltar with dispatches, his lordship stood to the northward in the evening: and, the following morning, sent the Active to Cagliari, the Amazon to Naples, the Seahorse to Maritimo, and Le Tigre to Palermo, for information. The Active brought no news from the coast of Africa; but the Seahorse, returned from Maritimo with intelligence from the officer at the port, that fourteen ships of war had passed the island on the 28th of March, steering to the southward; and that two frigates had, on the 4th of April, also passed, steering to the northward: neither of which reports his lordship believed; and, in fact, they appear to have been totally false. In the evening, steering for Palermo, they were joined by the Ambuscade and Astrea, neither of whom had obtained any information of the enemy's fleet, though they had seen many vessels. On the 9th, having cleared transports, which arrived the preceding evening, they compleated the fleet to four months provisions and sixty days wine and spirits. Le Tigre joined next day, from Palermo: where they knew nothing of the French fleet's having sailed; but sent information that an expedition had left England, and that a Russian squadron was expected in the Mediterranean. This information led his lordship to suppose that the French fleet might, probably, with a view of intercepting them, be somewhere about Minorca; he stood, therefore, to the westward of Sardinia, in the hope of falling in with the enemy. The Hydra and Childers joined, this day, from Magdalena, but brought no intelligence. At sunset, seven leagues south of Maritimo, the Active also joined, from Cagliari; and informed his lordship, that the Ragusan consul had received a letter from St. Pierre's, giving him an account, brought by a Ragusan brig, which had arrived there from Marseilles, that the French fleet sailed from Toulon the 30th of March, having a great number of troops on board.

This intelligence turned out to be the fact. Admiral Villeneuve having succeeded in leading his dreaded antagonist to a safe distance, and compleated all his preparations for the grand design, which was that of forming a junction with the Spanish fleets, and then proceeding to the West Indies, had in truth left Toulon, on the 30th, with eleven sail of the line, a frigate, and two corvettes, in which were embarked ten thousand select troops under the command of General Lauriston. This armament first sailed to Carthagena; where the six ships expected to be ready, under Admiral Salcedo, not being quite prepared to join, and fearful of losing a moment's time, during the absence of Lord Nelson, Admiral Villeneuve pursued his course to Cadiz. There he had, for some time, been expected by Admiral Gravina, who was waiting his arrival with six Spanish sail of the line, and two thousand two hundred and eighty troops. On the approach of the French fleet off Cadiz, the 9th of April, Sir John Orde, who was blockading that port with five ships of the line, incapable of preventing their junction with the Spaniards, retired from his station; unpursued by the French fleet, which might easily have forced him into action. L'Aigle, a French ship of the line, which had been some time at Cadiz, immediately came out of the harbour; and was soon after followed by six Spanish sail of the line, and five frigates, under Admiral Gravina: when, having compleatly effected their junction, a strong easterly wind expeditiously carried them out of sight.

At this period, it has been seen, Lord Nelson had, from circumstances, supposed the Toulon fleet likely to be met with in the Sicilian seas. Having sent frigates, in all directions, to gain intelligence of the enemy, the moment it was ascertained that they had actually sailed, he was beating to windward, off the coast of Sardinia, on the 16th of April, when he was informed, by an Austrian vessel from Lisbon, that sixteen ships of war had been seen, the 7th inst. standing to the westward. His lordship, now, justly apprehensive that this must have been the French fleet, felt extremely uneasy, that they had thus eluded all his vigilance. His agony is not to be described; and he was only consoled, at length, by reflections that, in assuring himself of the safety of Naples, Sicily, the Morea, Egypt, and Sardinia, before he proceeded to the westward, he had certainly done what was perfectly right. "I must ever regret, however," writes his lordship, "my want of frigates which I could have sent to the westward; and I must also regret, that Captain Mowbray did not cruize until he heard something of the French fleet. I am unlucky, but I cannot exert myself more than I have done for the public service!"

In fact, the exertions of Lord Nelson, during the whole of this arduous and perplexing service, were inconceivably great. He had, besides the usual cares of a commander in chief, the very difficult task of conciliating a variety of discordant states, from whom he was under the necessity of drawing constant supplies of fresh provisions and other requisites, which they were deterred from affording by the dread of a powerful and unprincipled enemy, perpetually menacing them with destruction, whatever degrees of amity they might either possess, or profess, for this country. The address of our hero, in counteracting the enemy's designs, with what may be denominated diplomatic combat, and thus obtaining needful supplies as well as useful intelligence, has scarcely ever been equalled. In corresponding with the various powers with whom it was necessary thus to communicate, the abilities of the Reverend Mr. Alexander Scott, now Dr. Scott, from his acquaintance with most of the modern languages, proved eminently favourable to his lordship's views. This gentleman was not only chaplain of the Victory, but private and foreign secretary to Lord Nelson, who also often employed him in confidential communications on shore. They had known each other ever since the year 1793; when Mr. Scott was chaplain to Sir John Collins in the Mediterranean, and Lord Nelson captain of the Agamemnon. On the death of Sir John Collins, Captain Nelson asked Mr. Scott to go with him as his chaplain; which he was under the necessity of declining, having previously engaged to go with Sir Hyde Parker in the St. George. During the expedition to Copenhagen, Lord Nelson, not having his chaplain, Mr. Comyns, with him, borrowed Mr. Scott, then Sir Hyde Parker's chaplain and foreign secretary, to read prayers in his ship; and, on his lordship's going ashore, he chose Mr. Scott to accompany him, as secretary to the commission for arranging the convention:

the articles of which were, in fact, penned by this gentleman. Lord Nelson kindly advised Mr. Scott to subscribe the Convention with his name, as secretary; but he diffidently declined the honour: for which Lord Nelson greatly blamed him; and he has since often blamed himself, as his lordship predicted would one day be the case. From this period, Lord Nelson was always greatly attached to Mr. Scott, and constantly kept up a correspondence with him. He had then first asked this gentleman if he would attend him as his confidential foreign secretary, in case of his ever getting the Mediterranean command; which Mr. Scott readily promised to do, should his old friend, Sir Hyde Parker, "be laid on the shelf." Had the then war continued, that arrangement would have taken place. On the peace, Mr. Scott went to the West Indies: from whence he returned, just before the present war broke out, in a very deplorable state of health; having been struck by lightning, and severely wounded. He had, however, no sooner arrived in London, than Lord Nelson was at his bed-side: where the generously humane hero continually visited him, during his confinement; and, soon after, took him, in the Amphion, to the Mediterranean, on this expedition. It is somewhat remarkable, that his lordship's regular secretary, though no relation of this gentleman, should also be a Scott: the former, the Rev. Mr. Alexander Scott; and the latter, John Scott, Esq. So numerous were his lordship's correspondences, that both secretaries were often fully employed: his lordship, from the time of his having engaged Dr. Scott, constantly accompanying his original letters to foreign courts, by translations into the respective languages; a point of etiquette always highly gratifying to the power addressed, and frequently attended with other beneficial consequences. There was, in short, no point of probable advantage to his country, however minute it might appear, which Lord Nelson ever thought unworthy of his strict regard.

 On the 17th of April, in the evening, the Amazon brought a confirmation of the intelligence respecting the French fleet, from a vessel which had seen, on the 8th at noon, eleven sail of the line, four frigates, and three brigs, pass Gibraltar with their colours flying. To add to the mortification, westerly winds, and a heavy sea, prevented the British fleet's gaining any ground, either this or the following day. A vessel five days from Cadiz, still to augment his lordship's distress, now also informed the Amazon, that the Spanish squadron had joined the French, and were gone with them to the westward. Having appointed the general rendezvous at Gibraltar, his lordship sent every where to procure additional frigates. He also dispatched the Active to Ireland, the Channel fleet, and England, with an account of his intended pursuit of the enemy. His passage to Gibraltar was prodigiously impeded by continual foul winds, and heavy swells. "Nothing," writes his lordship, at this anxious period, "can be more unfortunate, than we are in our winds; but, God's will be done! I submit. Human exertions are absolutely unavailing. What man could do, I have done. I hope that the wind will come to the eastward. What ill fortune! but, I cannot help myself." Thus did the hero complain, and thus did he console himself.

On the 1st of May, near the coast of Barbary, he was joined by the Martin sloop, which sailed from Plymouth the 17th of April; and brought his lordship a letter from the Admiralty, dated the 15th, which informed him that five thousand troops were coming to the Mediterranean. On the 30th, at ten in the morning, the fleet anchored in Tetuan Bay; or, rather, in the little bay to the eastward of Tetuan, where there is a very fine river of fresh water. The day was chiefly employed in watering the fleet; and clearing a transport with wine, which had been brought out from Gibraltar. No information of the combined fleet was, however, obtained from thence, nor in letters dated at Lisbon the 27th; but it seemed generally credited, that they were gone to the West Indies. "Surely," exclaimed his lordship, "I shall hear something of them from Sir John Orde's cruizers; which he must, naturally, have sent after them!" Sir John, however, very unaccountably, had not taken any measures for ascertaining their course. On Sunday, the 5th, at eight in the morning, light easterly breezes springing up, the fleet weighed at ten; but, in the evening, the wind, having first shifted northerly, unfortunately came again fresh from the westward. At two in the afternoon, next day, the fleet anchored in Gibraltar Bay. At four o'clock, a Levanter came on: at six, the fleet again weighed; and, by midnight, they were abreast of Cape Spartel, where nothing had been heard of the enemy. In the evening of the 7th, having steered for Cape St. Vincent, Le Tigre was sent to call the transports left by Sir John Orde, who had sailed for England, out of Lagos Bay. On the 9th, Le Tigre returned with the transports; and the Amazon, arriving from Lisbon, brought intelligence, communicated by Admiral Knight, that Sir John Orde had joined the channel fleet. At nine, in the evening, the fleet anchored between Cape St. Vincent and Lagos Bay. The next day, and succeeding night, were busily occupied in clearing the transports, and compleating the fleet to five months. Early on the 11th, his lordship sent the Wasp, and the Doris transport, to England, with dispatches: at ten o'clock, the fleet weighed; at noon, were off Cape St. Vincent; and, at one, saw the convoy under Admiral Knight. They joined at four; and at six, parted company: Lord Nelson having given Admiral Knight the Royal Sovereign; which, he observed, would make him superior in force to any thing ready, either in Carthagena or at Cadiz. At seven o'clock, the Martin sloop was dispatched to Barbadoes; and, at the same time, his lordship likewise made all sail to the westward with his comparatively small fleet. The French had twelve ships of the line, a frigate, and two corvettes; the Spaniards, six sail of the line and five frigates; to say nothing of the Rochfort squadron: while the whole fleet under Lord Nelson consisted only of ten ships of the line and three frigates. The French had, also, upwards of ten thousand troops, and the Spaniards more than two. Notwithstanding this inferior strength, which would have deterred many a brave man from risking the responsibility of so hazardous an undertaking, Lord Nelson had resolved that he would follow them, as he emphatically expressed himself, "even to the Antipodes." The ships he had were well equipped, and his confidence in all the officers and men was precisely the same as they themselves felt in their adored commander—he believed them to be absolutely invincible. The ships which accompanied his lordship in this memorable pursuit, were—the Victory of a hundred and ten guns, Vice-Admiral Lord Viscount Nelson, Rear-Admiral Murray, and Captain Hardy; the Canopus of eighty, Rear-Admiral Louis, and Captain Austin; Le Tigre of eighty, Captain Hallowell; the Donegal of eighty, Captain Malcolm; the Spencer of seventy-four, the Honourable Captain Stopford; the Conqueror of seventy-four, Captain Pellew; the Superb of seventy-four, Captain Keates; the Belleisle of seventy-four, Captain Hargood; the Leviathan of seventy-four, Captain Bayntun; the Swiftsure of seventy-four, Captain Rutherford; the Decade frigate of thirty-six, Captain Stuart; the Amazon of thirty-eight, Captain Parker; and the Amphion of thirty-two, Captain Sutton.

His lordship, now in high spirits, since the destination of the enemy seemed evident, and the wind had shifted in his favour, jocosely remarked to his assembled captains—"There is just a Frenchman apiece for each English ship, leaving me out of the question to fight the Spaniards: and, when I haul down my colours, I expect every captain of the fleet to do the same; but, not till then."

Having got fairly into the trade winds, they run, on the 21st of May, in the last twenty-four hours, a hundred and ninety miles. The next day, they passed the tropic, vulgarly called crossing the line; when Neptune performed the usual ceremony, to the no small diversion of the fleet. There were, in the Victory alone, his lordship remarks, who highly enjoyed the scene, no less than five hundred persons by whom the tropic had never before been crossed.

On the 31st, at six in the evening, being within two hundred leagues of Barbadoes, the Amazon was sent forward for information.

On the 3d of June, at day-light, two Guinea ships, bound from Surinam to America, were seen to the westward; from whom intelligence was obtained, that they were told, the day before, by the Beaulieu frigate, that the French and Spanish squadrons had arrived at Martinico, but the African ships did not know the time of their arrival there. In the evening, a sloop of war was perceived, with the signal of intelligence to communicate; but, missing the Victory, his lordship would not shorten sail, as he knew nothing more could be communicated, than when the enemy's fleet had arrived at Martinico. Next morning, at day-light, Barbadoes was seen by the fleet, distant about ten leagues to the west; and, at eleven in the forenoon, his lordship received the salutes of Rear-Admiral Cochrane, and Charles Fort. The enemy's fleet, Lord Nelson was now informed, had arrived at Martinico on the 14th of May, with their men sickly: and, on the 28th, were seen to the windward of St. Lucia, standing to the southward; with the view, as was supposed, of attacking Tobago and Trinidada. General Sir William Myers, at Barbadoes, having very handsomely offered his lordship to embark with two thousand troops for the relief of those islands, the fleet anchored in Carlisle Bay; and, though very rainy, with squalls of wind, the embarkment immediately commenced, and was continued all night. In the morning, Le Curieux brig was sent forward, to look into Tobago; and Sir William Myers dispatched another vessel to General Prevost, at Dominica, to acquaint him with Lord Nelson's arrival.

The happy tidings of his lordship's approach expeditiously spread through all the West India islands. The enemy were not the last who heard this intelligence, which acted with double force against these marauders: it armed with resolution the defenceless inhabitants of even the least tenable situations, by inspiring them with hopes of a speedy and effectual aid to their own manly exertions; and filled with dread and horror those pusillanimous pillagers who had alone confided in their vast superiority of numbers, for the success of their plundering exploits, and now feared the avenging hand of our pursuing hero. Villeneuve, the Gallic fugitive from the Nile, no sooner gained intelligence that the victor on that occasion was likely soon to be once more at his heels, than he again made the most expeditious use of them in returning back from the scene of his paltry depredations; and, with his former good fortune, escaped the chastising hand of our hero, who continued every where seeking him in vain. His lordship, indeed, however aware of the dastardly disposition of the enemy, could scarcely think it possible for such a very superior force as the combined fleet thus timidly to fly before him.

Lord Nelson, in the mean time, having weighed; at eight in the evening, the fleet stood to the southward: and, at eight in the morning of the 6th of June, they saw Tobago. At two in the afternoon, abreast of Man of War Bay, Le Curieux joined; with information that an American had arrived at Scarborough the preceding day, the master of which said that he had been boarded, three days prior to his arrival, by the French fleet, then standing to the southward, and that they would, he supposed, pass Tobago as last night. This account, his lordship considered as a mere fabrication of the American: but, gaining no intelligence on which he could rely, he bore away to Trinidada; and, at midnight, bringing to off that island, sent the Pheasant to Toko for information. At four, next morning, his lordship bore up for the Bogasses; and, at sunset, anchored in the Gulf of Paria, but found that the enemy had not been heard of in the island. At day-light, an advice-boat brought letters from Captain Morrice at Barbadoes, giving an account of the capture of the Diamond Rock, with the little garrison by which it was defended: and stating, also, that the French and Spanish squadrons had not sailed from Martinico; but that, as the French commodore told him, the Ferrol squadron, of six sail of French, and eight of Spanish, arrived in Fort Royal on the 4th of June. This intelligence determined his lordship: who, at seven o'clock, sailed from Trinidada; and was at noon well out, clear of the Bogasses.

While his lordship was off Trinidad, with his usual gaiety and goodness of heart, he wrote to the governor, that he would rather he sent him a hogshead of *limes*, than a hogshead of *Joes*. With him, the health of his people was always the first object; his own individual wealth, ever the last.

At six in the morning of the 9th, he got within sight of Grenada; and, at noon, arrived off St. George's Bay in that island. A letter from General Prevost now informed his lordship, that the combined squadron had passed Dominica on the 6th of June; and, having gone to Guadaloupe, for the purpose of landing the troops and stores taken from thence, had been seen standing to the northward. Lord Nelson, on receiving this intelligence, having dispatched the Nelly to Antigua, and the Jason to Montserrat, for farther information, immediately stood to the northward, under a press of sail. The next day, at noon, between St. Lucia and Martinique, he sent a schooner to General Prevost: and, at eight the following morning, Tuesday, June 11, saw Guadaloupe; and spoke an American, from Boston, who gave no intelligence. At noon, the fleet got within sight of Montserrat; and, at two o'clock, saw the Jason, at anchor. The news from Montserrat was, that they had, on Saturday morning, the 8th, being only three days before, seen sixteen sail under Guadaloupe, beating to windward. His lordship, now, also beating up to windward, all night and the following day, anchored in St. John's Bay, Antigua, at sunset; which island, he learned, had been passed, on the 8th, by the French fleet standing to the north. Having, in the evening, sent Le Curieux, with dispatches, to England, his lordship, next morning, at day-light, landed the troops for the protection of the islands; got ready for sea; and sailed, at noon, with eleven ships of the line, three frigates, and a sloop of war: when the Kitty schooner joined, with the unpleasing information, that the French fleet had, on the 8th instant, captured it's whole convoy, consisting of fourteen sail. From four in the afternoon, till sunset, his lordship was within sight of Barbuda, still standing to the northward. "If," writes his lordship, this day, "I should ask an opinion where the enemy's fleet are gone, I should have as many opinions as there were persons. Porto-Rico, Barbadoes, Newfoundland, Europe. My opinion, from all the circumstances drawn into one point of view, with the best judgment I can form, is this—I think, that the whole or part of the Spaniards will go to the Havannah; and the rest of the fleet, to Cadiz and Toulon: and, upon this opinion, I am going to the Straits Mouth; unless I should alter it, from information gained."

Thus determined, every exertion was used, though with little hope, to overtake them, if possible, on their return; and, on the 14th, at noon, the fleet had run a hundred and thirteen miles from the Island of Barbuda, and a hundred and thirty from St. John's Bay, Antigua.

On the 18th, the Amazon communicated with a schooner; which had, on the

15th, at sunset, seen a fleet of twenty-two ships of war steering to the northward. On a computation formed from an examination of the schooner's then latitude and longitude, it appeared that the French fleet were, the night before, about eighty-seven leagues distant. His lordship, next day, forwarded the Martin to Gibraltar, and the Decade to Lisbon, with information of the enemy's return to Europe. At midnight, on the 21st, Lord Nelson saw three planks floating; which, he thought, came from the French ships: and, on the 23d, at dusk, a piece of a large ship's topmast had also passed by the Victory, but was not observed till too late to be picked up. Sir John Laforey, next morning, informed his lordship that, three days after they left Antigua, he had passed close by a bucket; which he supposed, by the make and wooden handle, to be French: also, a large chest, painted red.

From this period, till the 5th of June, the wind proved tolerably favourable; but they now, to use his lordship's expression, barely "crawled" about thirty miles every twenty-four hours. "My only hope is," writes the hero, "that the enemy's fleet are near us, and in the same situation." By a Spanish log and chart, taken out of a small bark from La Guira to Cadiz, his lordship found that the combined fleets went in sight of Cape Blanco, and passed over to the Salvages.

On the 9th, light breezes springing up, the fleet run eighty-eight miles; in the succeeding twenty-four hours, a hundred; and, the day after, a hundred and nineteen. The wind, however, now coming foul, his lordship expressed himself dreadfully apprehensive that the enemy would have too greatly the start of him. The Amazon, on the 13th, was detached to Gibraltar; and, the fleet having got into the Portuguese trade-winds, they run, next day, a hundred and forty-six miles.

On Wednesday, the 17th of July, at ten o'clock in the forenoon, they saw Cape St. Vincent, distant about nine leagues. By a friendly vessel from Rochfort, his lordship learned that the French squadron, of five sail of the line and four frigates, which had sailed from thence the 18th of January, returned from the West Indies on the 21st of May: having left Martinico about the middle of April; after taking several ships, and levying contributions at Dominica, St. Kitt's, Nevis, and Montserrat. The last twenty-four hours, the fleet went a hundred and twenty miles; making the whole run, from Barbuda, three thousand four hundred and fifty-nine miles. The run from Cape St. Vincent to Barbadoes, was three thousand two hundred and twenty-seven; making the run back only two hundred and thirty-two miles more than the run out: allowance to be made, however, for the difference of latitude and longitude between Barbadoes and Bermuda. The average of way daily made, on this almost unparalleled pursuit, was thirty-four leagues; wanting nine miles, only, in the whole.

At noon, the 18th, steering for the Straits Mouth, Admiral Collingwood passed to the northward, with three sail of the line and two or three frigates. Cape Spartel was then in sight; but no French fleet, or any information about them. "How sorrowful this makes me!" writes his lordship; "but, I cannot help myself." Next morning, at day-light, the fleet bore up for Gibraltar Bay; where, at eight o'clock, they securely anchored, but could gain no information of the enemy.

On Saturday, July the 20th, 1805, while the fleet were employed in compleating provisions and stores—"I went on shore," writes his lordship, "for the first time, since June 16, 1803; and, from having my foot out of the Victory, two years wanting ten days."

Having sent dispatches to England, and finished getting ready for sea, next day, Lord Nelson, on the following morning, ordered the Amphion to Sir Richard Bickerton, off Carthagena, and proceeded with the fleet to Tetuan; or, rather, to Mazin Bay, about eight miles to the south-east of Tetuan customhouse, where the river is very fine, and the situation peculiarly convenient for watering. Many of the ships got two hundred tons on board in a single day. Several bullocks were here purchased, and a considerable quantity of onions. At noon, on the 24th, having gained no intelligence, the fleet again weighed, and stood for Ceuta; but variable winds, and a thick fog, kept them all night in Gibraltar Gut. About four o'clock, next morning, the Termagant joined, with an account of the combined fleet's having been seen, the 19th of June, by the Curieux brig, standing to the northward. At eight, the Spaniards fired a few shot, from Tariffa, at the Victory; which, however, took no effect. At noon, they saw Admiral Collingwood's squadron; and Lord Nelson sent letters to the admiral, with arrangements for preventing the combined fleet from entering Cadiz, while his lordship proceeded to seek them nearer home. On the 26th, the Spartiate got on board the Victory; but, fortunately, neither ship suffered any material damage. Having traversed the Bay of Biscay, without discovering any thing of the enemy, his lordship, on the 28th, at day-light, came abreast of Cape St. Vincent; from whence, with faint hopes of finding them, he pursued his northerly course toward the north-west of Ireland, By foul winds, and very unfavourable weather, this proved a most tediously vexatious voyage. Unable, after all, to fetch Ireland, on account of the northerly winds, his lordship, in the afternoon of August 12, was informed by the Niobe, Captain Scott, three weeks from the channel fleet, that there had not, at that time, been the smallest intelligence of the enemy's arrival in any of the ports. He also learned, that they had not been heard of on the Irish coast. Having exhausted every rational conjecture with regard to their situation, he resolved on reinforcing Admiral Cornwallis with his squadron; lest the combined fleet of France and Spain should, by approaching Brest, either facilitate the escape of the squadron so long confined by this commander's blockade of that port, or place him aukwardly between two fires.

Accordingly, on the 15th, at six in the morning, Lord Nelson got within eighteen leagues of Ushant; and, at half past eleven, saw a fleet. At two in the afternoon, they exchanged private signals with the channel fleet; and, in the evening, his lordship, having detached the rest of his fleet, received orders from Admiral Cornwallis, as commander in chief, to proceed with the Victory and Superb to Portsmouth. His lordship now first gained information of Sir Robert Calder's having defeated the combined fleet from the West Indies, on the 22d of July, sixty leagues west of Cape Finisterre; which, at length, relieved him from the anxiety of suspence, though the action had been too indecisive compleatly to satisfy his lordship's mind. He regretted, exceedingly, that it had not been his own good fortune to encounter them; and felt less comforted, than he ought to have done, by the consideration, that this squadron, under Sir Robert Calder, had been sent out to intercept their return, in consequence of his, lordship's suggestions, judiciously transmitted to the Admiralty for that purpose, the moment he was satisfied that the combined French and Spanish fleet were on their return from the West Indies.

On the 17th, at day-light, his lordship was abreast of Portland; at noon, saw the Isle of Wight; and, at eleven at night, anchored off the Princesses Shoal. Having weighed next morning at day-light, they worked up to Spithead; and, at nine o'clock, anchored: just two years and three months from his lordship's arrival at Portsmouth. A contagious fever having recently made dreadful havoc at Gibraltar, where the ships touched, his lordship became subject to the quarantine regulations. However, after communicating, by signal, with the port-admiral, he addressed the following satisfactory declaration to the collector of the customs—

"Victory, Spithead, August 18, 1805.

"The Victory, with the fleet under my command, left Gibraltar twenty-seven days ago: at which time, there was not a fever in the garrison; nor, as Dr. Fellows told me, any apprehension of one. The fleet lately under my command, I left with Admiral Cornwallis on the 15th of August; at which time, they were in the most perfect health. Neither the Victory, nor the Superb, have on board even an object for the hospital; to the truth of which, I pledge my word of honour.

"Nelson and Bronte."

"To the Collector of the Customs, or those whom it may concern."

In consequence of these positive assurances, Lord Nelson was, at length, permitted to land; and, during the approach of his barge, a vast concourse of people, who had been assembling on the rampart from the moment his flag was first discovered, hailed the hero's approach with their loudest acclamations.

Intelligence of Lord Nelson's arrival in England had no sooner been received by Lady Hamilton and his nearest relatives, who were then passing a few weeks together at South End, than they hastened to Merton Place, where his lordship appointed to meet them. The delay in landing, made it late that afternoon before he could proceed thither: but, by travelling all night, he got to Merton at six o'clock in the morning of the 19th; where his friends had already assembled, in anxious expectation of beholding the beloved hero whose presence gladdened every virtuous heart.

His lordship, on undertaking this command, had quitted England so very expeditiously, that he could not be present at the Grand Installation of the Knights of the Bath, which took place in Westminster Abbey, on the 19th of May 1803, the day after his arrival at Portsmouth; and, consequently, was obliged to be installed by proxy. On this occasion, Lord Nelson had been represented by Captain Sir

William Bolton, son of the Reverend William Bolton, brother of Thomas Bolton, Esq. the husband of his lordship's eldest sister; to whose amiable daughter, now Lady Bolton, Sir William had the preceding evening been married, by special licence, at Lady Hamilton's house in Piccadilly.

The happy party now assembled at Merton Place, where the hero ever delighted to see his family around him, consisted of the present Earl and Countess Nelson, with Lord Merton and Lady Charlotte Nelson, their son and daughter; Mr. and Mrs. Bolton, with Thomas Bolton, Junior, Esq. and Miss Ann and Miss Eliza Bolton, their son and daughters; and Mr. and Mrs. Matcham, with their son George Matcham, Junior, Esq.

On the 20th, in the morning, Lord Nelson came to London; where he had the happiness to obtain that general approbation of his conduct, from persons of all ranks, which those who have not been eminently successful can rarely hope to experience. Indeed, the country seemed generally to participate in his lordship's disappointments, with a sympathy as honourable to the national character as to the hero so worthily applauded. It was felt, that he had exerted himself to the utmost; and that, notwithstanding he had been unable to meet with the enemy, his pursuit had relieved every anxiety from the consequences of their depredations, by forcing to fly before him a combined fleet of force nearly doubling his own. All apprehensions for our colonial settlements were quieted; and, though the small advantage gained by Sir Robert Calder had not much diminished their naval strength, or greatly augmented our own, this was no fault of his lordship, whose superior worth ever became more abundantly manifest on the intrusion of such comparisons. What his lordship would have done, with the same force, similarly situated, according to the general opinion, every where freely expressed, made the nation at large, as well as our hero himself, sincerely regret that he had not been fortunate enough to encounter them. In justice to Sir Robert Calder, however, it must be admitted, there are few naval actions so brilliant, that they might not have been rendered still more so by the presence of such a commander as Lord Nelson.

Immediately after his lordship's arrival in town, a meeting of the West India merchants was convened at the London Tavern; who, having met on the 23d, Sir Richard Neave, Bart, in the chair, unanimously and expressly agreed—"That the prompt determination of Lord Nelson to quit the Mediterranean, in search of the

French fleet; his sagacity in judging of, and ascertaining, their course; and his bold and unwearied pursuit of the combined French and Spanish squadrons to the West Indies, and back again to Europe; have been very instrumental to the safety of the West India islands in general, and well deserve the grateful acknowledgments of every individual connected with those colonies: and, that a deputation from the Committee of Merchants of London trading to the West Indies, be appointed to wait upon Vice-Admiral Lord Viscount Nelson, to express these their sentiments, and to offer him their unfeigned thanks."

The deputation, accordingly, having waited on Lord Nelson, at Gordon's Hotel, Albemarle Street, where his lordship had taken up his temporary town-residence, with a copy of the above resolutions, he immediately returned the following answer.

"London, August 28, 1805.

"SIR

"I beg leave to express, to you and the Committee of West India Merchants, the great satisfaction which I feel in their approbation of my conduct. It was, I conceived, perfectly clear, that the combined squadrons were gone to the West Indies, and therefore it became my duty to follow them. But, I assure you, from the state of defence in which our large islands are placed, with the number of regular troops, and numerous well-disciplined and zealous militia, I was confident, not any troops which their combined squadron could carry, would make an impression upon any of our large islands, before a very superior force would arrive, for their relief.

"I have the honour to remain, Sir, and Gentlemen, your most obliged and obedient servant,

"Nelson and Bronte.
"Sir Richard Neave, Bart. and the Committee of West India Merchants."

Lord Nelson had, at this period, no intention of again going speedily to sea.

All his stores had been brought up from the Victory; and he was, he said, resolved to enjoy a little leisure, with his family and friends, in the delightful shades of Merton. The Honourable Captain Blackwood, a few days afterward, brought intelligence that the combined fleets, reinforced by two more Spanish squadrons, and now amounting to thirty-four sail of the line, had left Ferrol, and got safely into Cadiz. All this, however, was nothing to him; "Let the man trudge it, who has lost his budget!" gaily repeated his lordship. But, amid all this *allegro* of the tongue, to his friends at Merton Place, Lady Hamilton observed that his countenance, from that moment, wore occasional marks of the *penseroso* in his bosom. In this state of mind, he was pacing one of the walks of Merton garden, which he always called the quarter-deck, when Lady Hamilton told him, that she perceived he was low and uneasy. He smiled, and said—"No! I am as happy as possible." Adding, that he saw himself surrounded by his family; that he found his health better since he had been at Merton; and, that he would not give a sixpence to call the king his uncle. Her ladyship replied, that she did not believe what he said; and, that she would tell him what was the matter with him. That he was longing to get at these French and Spanish fleets; that he considered them as his own property, and would be miserable if any other man but himself did the business; that he must have them, as the price and reward of his long watching, and two years uncomfortable situation in the Mediterranean: and finished, by saying—"Nelson, however we may lament your absence, and your so speedily leaving us, offer your services, immediately, to go off Cadiz; they will be accepted, and you will gain a quiet heart by it. You will have a glorious victory; and, then, you may come here, have your *otium cum dignitate*, and be happy." He looked at her ladyship for some moments; and, with tears in his eyes, exclaimed—"Brave Emma! good Emma! if there were more Emmas, there would be more Nelsons. You have penetrated my thoughts. I wish all you say, but was afraid to trust even myself with reflecting on the subject. However, I will go to town." He went, accordingly, next morning, accompanied by her ladyship and his sisters. They left him at the Admiralty, on the way to Lady Hamilton's house in Clarges Street; and, soon after, received a note, informing them that the Victory was telegraphed not to go into port, and begging they would prepare every thing for his departure. This is the true history of that affecting affair. Her ladyship feels, most severely, that she was the cause of his going; but, as she loved his glory, she could not resist giving him such advice. It is, however, the general opinion of those who best knew his lordship, that he would, in all probability, have fretted himself to death had he not undertaken this expedition. His lordship's services were "not only accepted at the Admiralty, but he was vested with powers less limited than had, perhaps, ever before been confided to any naval commander. He was to send home Sir Robert Calder, who had joined Admiral Collingwood in blocking up the enemy off Cadiz harbour with twenty-six sail of the line, and to take on himself the chief command of all his majesty's ships and vessels throughout the whole extent of the Mediterranean Sea; having full liberty to use his own discretion in following the enemy wherever he should think proper, without the slightest degree of censure or controul.

During the few days which he continued in England after being appointed to this important command, he so devoted the little leisure which his professional preparations allowed, to his beloved family and friends, that he refused all public visits, and dined only twice from Merton Place: once, with his Grace the Duke of Queensberry, who is a near relation of the late Sir William Hamilton; and once with his esteemed friend Abraham Goldsmid, Esq. and family, at Morden. On both these occasions, too, he was accompanied by Lady Hamilton and some of his own relations. The Duke of Clarence, previously to Lord Nelson's departure, took a dinner with him at Merton; when his lordship, pointing to his nephews, nieces, &c. who were seated at a separate table, observed: to his royal highness, that the sight of these young persons associated under his roof constituted the chief bliss of his life.

Among this amiable and interesting group, was Miss Horatia Nelson Thompson, Lord Nelson's adopted daughter, then an infant about five years of age. What real affinity, if any, that charming child may bear to his lordship, is a secret at present known by few; and, as it should seem, by none who feel at liberty to divulge it. She was, certainly, an object of his constant and most tender regard; and, though the family in general appear disinclined to believe her his daughter, it seems highly probable that she is so. Should this prove to be the fact, it cannot greatly affect his lordship's reputation; who, it is not to be dissembled, though by no means ever an unprincipled seducer of the wives and daughters of his friends, was always well known to entertain rather more partiality for the fair-sex than is quite consistent with the highest degree of Christian purity. Such improper indulgences, with some slight addiction to that other vicious habit of British seamen, the occasional use of a few thoughtlessly profane expletives in speech, form the only dark specks ever yet discovered in the bright blaze of his moral character. Truth must not be denied, nor vice advocated; but, surely, the candid admission of these disagreeable verities, can never induce a single virtuous mind unjustly to criminate the hero in any higher degree. Could the biographer believe, that Lord Nelson had ever indulged even an idea of dishonouring the wife of his bosom friend, which no one worthy and intelligent person intimately acquainted with all the parties ever yet did believe, he would that moment indignantly throw up his brief. With respect to the mysterious child, whose unfortunate mother may, most probably, now be no more, it is only certain that Lady Hamilton was induced to receive her, at a very tender age, as his lordship's adopted daughter. They had been godfather, and godmother, in the baptismal ceremony; and her ladyship, at Lord Nelsons request, kindly undertook the care of Miss Horatia's education: as she had already done, for some years, that of the present highly accomplished Lady Charlotte Nelson; and, since, of the amiable Miss Ann Bolton. Those who have had the pleasure of beholding with what incomparable skill, indefatigable zeal, and ardent affection, Lady Hamilton discharges the difficult and important duty of cultivating such comprehensive minds to the full extent of their faculties, will agree that Lord Nelson could not possibly have confided the guardianship of his adopted daughter to any person so well qualified, in all respects, for the due performance of such a task. When his lordship, on the 10th of May 1803, immediately after compleating his purchase of Mr. Axe's estate at Merton, executed his last will and testament, it does not appear that he made any sort of provision for this infant; nor is she mentioned in the first codicil thereto annexed, the 13th of the same month: yet, on this last day, it seems somewhat remarkable, the child was baptized in the parish of St. Marylebone, though then more than two years of age; and, a very few days after, his lordship first sailed to take the Mediterranean command. On the 6th day of the September following, however, Lord Nelson added a second and secret codicil to his will, in which he gives and bequeaths to his adopted daughter, Miss Horatia, the sum of four thousand pounds; appointing Lady Hamilton her sole guardian, until she shall have arrived at the age of eighteen years: the interest of the said four thousand pounds to be paid to Lady Hamilton for her education and maintenance. "This request of guardianship," his lordship expressly says, "I earnestly make of Lady Hamilton; knowing that she will educate my adopted child in the paths of religion and virtue, and give her those accomplishments which so touch adorn herself: and, I hope, make her a fit wife for my dear nephew, Horatio Nelson; who I wish to marry her, if he proves worthy, in Lady Hamilton's estimation, of such a treasure as I am sure she will be."

In another codicil, dated on board the Victory, at sea, the 19th of February 1804, his lordship gives and bequeaths to Lady Hamilton five hundred pounds a year, charged on the Bronte estate; and, the 7th of April following, leaves an annuity of one hundred pounds, payable quarterly, to poor blind Mrs. Nelson, the relict of his late brother Maurice: without noticing, in either of these codicils, his adopted daughter, Miss Horatia. On the 19th of December, however, in the same year, by a fifth codicil, executed on board the Victory, in the Gulph of Palma, Sardinia, his lordship confirms anew his legacy to Lady Hamilton, and to his adopted daughter: and farther gives to her ladyship two thousand pounds; to his secretary, John Scott, Esq. one hundred pounds, to buy a ring, or some token of his remembrance; and two hundred pounds to his friend, the Reverend Alexander Scott, then commonly called Dr. Scott, by way of distinction from John Scott, Esq. his lordship's secretary, and who has since taken his doctor's degree in the university of Cambridge. This distinguished legacy, and the still more distinguished words in which it is bequeathed—not my foreign secretary, chaplain, &c. but "my friend, the Reverend Alexander Scott,"—must ever bear ample testimony of a regard, even at that period, which does Dr. Scott so much substantial honour. The foundation of this amity, like all Lord Nelson's strongest attachments, was not merely private friendship, and personal regard, but esteem and affection arising from the ability and zeal of the party to assist the grand object ever uppermost in his mind, that of accomplishing, in every possible way, by artifice opposed to artifice, as well as arms to arms, the happiness and glory of his king and country. Dr. Scott's secret services, though very properly concealed from the public, are well known to, and liberally acknowledged by, several of the ablest and bravest commanders in the navy; and it was thus, still more than by his unaffected and agreeable manners in private life, that he endeared himself to our incomparable hero, who constantly possessed the most exalted degree of genuine patriotism combined with the truest and most unbounded loyalty. This sentiment must not be overlooked in the contemplation of Lord Nelson's character.

There cannot, perhaps, be a single proof adduced of the hero's violently strong attachment to any individual whatever, though he was a friend to the whole human race, and to every description of worth, if he did not, at the period of expressing his admiration and esteem, sincerely believe the person a valuable coadjutor in some way assisting the prosperity of his king and country. To this noble and virtuous source may be traced the origin of all the friendships which he greatly cherished out of his family; and even his family would have possessed less of his love, had any of them ever been found deficient in loyalty. This was the great bond of affectionate union which bound together so many brave hearts, and rendered the whole fleet one uniformly compact and invincible body. There was scarcely, perhaps, any single individual, among either officers or men, of a truly valorous and loyal spirit, who would not freely have yielded his own life, if necessary, to save that of the adored commander.

Few were the hours which this exalted man was permitted to enjoy the society of his beloved family and friends in his retreat at Merton. The improvement of his house and grounds, though the latter had been rendered delightful since the enlargement, were by no means even yet compleated; and his lordship, who was ever generous to the full extent of his ability, found it necessary, before he quitted England, to dispose of many jewels, and other valuable presents, which were purchased by Messrs. Rundell, Bridge, and Rundell, on Ludgate Hill, for the purpose of paying debts, and providing the various requisites of his present equipment. Even this was a state to which such a man should not have been subjected. His income had been rendered considerable, it is true: but the grandeur of his character had rendered him too great for his income; it ought, therefore, to have been sufficiently enlarged. The nation will never be ruined by rewarding such men! Numerous public services, it is well known, were in a great degree assisted by the influence of his own private purse; which was never closed against any claims of conceived duty, either professional or moral. Ever bountiful to indigent merit, his private benevolences were by no means small; and he was liberal and hospitable, both at sea and on shore, to a very unusual excess. After all, he had not been able conveniently to repay Mr. Matcham, his worthy and esteemed brother-in-law, four thousand pounds borrowed towards the purchase of Merton Place. Who, then, shall say, on a just consideration of these indisputable facts, that this great man was amply rewarded by his country? The truth is, that he could scarcely effect any thing which he wished, for the due support of that dignity and rank which he had himself acquired; or obtain, for his meritorious family and friends, the proportionate advancements which he was solicitous to see them possess. Mr. Matcham, it is true, was a man of fortune; but he had a very large family, with abilities which would not have discredited rank. Mr. Bolton, his other sister's husband, though a gentleman of great abilities also, and with a considerable family, had a very inadequate fortune; and his lordship was particularly desirous to have beheld him, at least, a Commissioner of the Excise or Customs. This, in fact, was what had been repeatedly promised; but his lordship experienced not the happiness of seeing it performed. The present Earl Nelson, indeed, his lordship's only surviving brother, had been presented to a prebendal stall at Canterbury; but, with this not over splendid exception, nothing had been given by government to his lordship's relatives, and very little to any of his chief friends. The claim of Lady Hamilton's pension, too, which he had so earnestly solicited, though it had been candidly acknowledged, remained still unnoticed: and, during the few days he continued in England, it does not appear to have been revived; probably, on account of the changes in administration which had taken place while his lordship was abroad, as well as the necessity of now confining himself to the requisite arrangements for undertaking his newly extended command.

As the day approached when Lord Nelson must take his departure from Merton Place, Lady Hamilton began severely to suffer for having advised the tender of his services. Her mind, no doubt, anticipated all the terrible consequences to be dreaded from his excess of valour, and his heroic disdain of death; nor is it at all improbable, that she now most sincerely regretted her enthusiastic zeal for the hero's glory. The consideration of that other impelling principle, the fearful apprehension of seeing him fall a prey to disappointment, should the desired victory be atchieved by any other hand, brought no solace to her bosom, for it scarcely entered her mind. Even the spirit and magnanimity of his lordship, were unable entirely to preserve his feeling breast from painful intrusions. Though commonly gay, he was sometimes thoughtful. He could not be insensible, that his post was that of danger; and, though he scorned all personal apprehension, he well knew what must ever be expected by a commander resolved never to yield. Before Lord Nelson quitted London, he called at Mr. Peddieson's, his upholsterer, in Brewer Street, where the coffin presented him by Captain Hallowell had been sent; and, with his usual gaiety and good-humour, desired him to get the attestation of it's identity engraved on the lid—"For," added his lordship, "I think it highly probable, that I may want it on my return."

That he wished to live, however, is as certain, as that he feared not to die. Of a social, tender, and affectionate heart, amid all the corporeal agonies he had suffered, and was doomed during life to suffer, in consequence of his various wounds, added to the still severer and more numerous inflictions on his mental tranquillity, he preserved a chearfulness of disposition which commonly diffused joy and gladness to all around him. If he saw, or suspected, any difficulty or distress, his mind was that moment occupied in endeavouring to afford some adequate remedy. "What will be of service! How shall I obtain it!" he would frequently exclaim to his friends, when he beheld any one unprovided for, of whom he had a good opinion, however slight the acquaintance: and these exclamations were generally followed up by naming some situation suitable for the party, and immediately using all his interest to obtain it. Innumerable are the persons whom he thus comfortably fixed, with their families, for life. Where he could not succeed, he felt more than the party disappointed; and, on such occasions only, lamented his limited powers. Never did man live less for himself. To his king and his country, his family and his friends, his life was entirely devoted; the promotion of their felicity and glory, was the chief source of his own. For himself, he had wealth more than sufficient; but he was too poor, satisfactorily to assist those who were most dear to him. Had his remunerations, and his honours, been as largely proportioned to those of the Great Duke of Marlborough, as his merits, and his services, he would not only have aggrandized his own family and friends, but proved a most munificent patron of genius, and a bountiful dispenser of relief to every species of human misery. Posterity will say, and it cannot be denied, that our first naval hero was rewarded with too parsimonious a hand. Should we ever see his equal, in all respects—which seems no more likely than that we shall behold another Shakspeare—it will probably be thought, that he is not unworthy of a dukedom. The King of Naples, as the ally of his British majesty, restored to his throne by Lord Nelson, deemed our hero entitled to the honour of a ducal coronet, with the princely revenue of a dutchy; and it can never be enough lamented, that any official etiquette, in his own country, should have prevented the gracious sovereign who so sincerely loved him, and who was so sincerely beloved by the hero, from bestowing on him, at least, an equal degree of dignity, with the correspondent domains and emoluments for it's due support. How many naval commanders have enriched themselves, by fortunate captures of unopposing treasure-ships, or on long preserved snug stations, without the smallest personal hazard, to a degree far beyond what his lordship ever acquired, who was continually engaged in scenes of the utmost fatigue and peril! All the prize-money he got, was by hard fighting; and it was, in general, only derived from the capture of those ships which his tremendous valour had frequently rendered wrecks of little value. Even then, but a small portion fell to his share; as he had, both at the Nile and Copenhagen, two of the greatest victories ever gained, a commander in chief who was regularly entitled to prodigiously more than himself. It is by no means pretended, that the captors of rich prizes, the possessors of advantageous stations, and commanders in chief, are not all of them justly and most honourably entitled to the vast wealth they have often the good fortune to acquire; it is only lamented, that our hero was, in these respects, constantly so peculiarly unfortunate. After the Earl of St. Vincent left the Mediterranean command, Lord Nelson was soon superceded by the arrival of Lord Keith; and, when Sir Hyde Parker returned home, after the battle of Copenhagen, his lordship almost immediately followed. On neither of these occasions, nor in the subsequent affair of Boulogne, so soon succeeded by peace, could he derive much advantage as a commander in chief: and, though he had now held the Mediterranean command more than two years, the terror of his name, by confining the enemy to their ports, prevented it's being very profitable; while the peculiar nature of his situation, with regard to the difficulties of obtaining intelligence, as well as requisite supplies and refreshments, occasioned private expences which considerably abridged his emoluments. It is true that, as far as related to himself, he might have contrived to live in retirement on his pension and half-pay; but he could by no means make any suitable provision for those whom he conceived to have claims on his protection. This expedition, he trusted, would enable him, at length, to accomplish the wish of his heart, by placing all who were most dear to him in situations of easy independence. If he should survive, the brilliance of the glorious victory which he anticipated, might probably qualify himself sufficiently to exalt them; if he should fall, he would not permit himself to doubt, that the generous nation which he loved, and in whose just cause his last blood would be so freely shed, could ever hesitate a moment amply to provide for every beloved object of his anxious regard, with this confident hope bequeathed to the benign protection of his king and country.

On Friday, the 13th of September, the Victory having been compleatly prepared, dropped down to St. Helen's, ready for the hero's reception. To his lordship and friends, this was a terrible day. Some of his relatives had previously left Merton, that they might escape the dreaded agonies of so painful a separation. Mr. and Mrs. Matcham continued to the last; and sustained, with their best fortitude, the severe shock of such a parting. His lordship, kindly affectionate to all, had repeatedly declared that, from the first prize-money which he should be fortunate enough to obtain, amounting to thirty thousand pounds, he would make a present of five thousand to his brother, and the same sum to each of his two sisters: and, on Mr. Matcham's expressing a wish that his lordship might retain Mrs. Matcham's share, he replied—"No; she has an equal claim with her other sister and my brother." So equally did they all participate in his fraternal regards.

Lord Nelson had not, yet, been quite a month in England, and much of even that short period was occupied in preparations for his departure; yet he had, now, lived longer in the society of Lady Hamilton and his friends, than at any time since the death of Sir William. The affection Lord Nelson and Lady Hamilton entertained for each other, is not to be doubted; but it was a pure and virtuous attachment, founded entirely on mental esteem. Their loves were mutually the result of a most enthusiastic admiration of each other's heroic and magnanimous qualities. Those know little of the human heart, who require to be told what this sentiment is capable of effecting; and how little it has to do with the more gross and less durable tie of mere sexual or personal regard. That they would have been united, if his lordship had survived Lady Nelson, is a fact sufficiently known. In the mean time, never did the most chivalrous knight of antiquity cherish in his heart a more extravagant degree of adoration for the peerless princess of his affections, than that which our hero manifested for this accomplished lady. It was with her image continually before him, that he combated the enemies of his country. Her portrait was always placed in his cabin, which he familiarly denominated his guardian genius; and he constantly wore a fine miniature representation of her ladyship's charming features, suspended in his bosom. In short, he always thought, and freely said, that there was not her equal in the universe. The agonies of this parting are not to be described. His lordship, about ten at night, after visiting the chamber of his adopted daughter, and praying over the sleeping innocent, tore himself from her agonized ladyship, surrounded by his remaining relatives, and entered the chaise which conveyed him, by six o'clock next morning, to Portsmouth.

As a proof of Lord Nelson's ceaselessly ardent desire for the advancement of his beloved relatives, when his esteemed brother-in-law, George Matcham, Esq. attended him to the chaise door, his lordship feelingly lamented that it was not yet in his power substantially to serve Mr. Matcham; who immediately said—"My dear lord, I have no other wish than to see you return home in safety; as for myself, I am not in want of any thing."—"With your large family, my dear Mr. Matcham," affectionately replied his lordship, "you certainly require a very considerable addition to your fortune!" Can any thing compensate, to his family, the loss of such a brother?

"Friday night," writes his lordship, "at half past ten, I drove from dear, dear Merton; where I left all which I hold dear in this world, to go to serve my king and country. May the great God whom I adore, enable me to fulfil the expectations of my country; and, if it is his good pleasure that I should return, my thanks will never cease being offered up to the throne of his mercy! If it is his good providence, to cut short my days upon earth, I bow with the greatest submission; relying, that he will protect those so dear to me, that I may leave behind! His will be done.

"Amen! Amen! Amen!"

In this, which is extracted from his lordship's own private journal, written at the moment, warm from the heart, as well as in almost every other action of his life, is manifested that exalted desire to promote the glory of his king and country, and that earnest wish to secure every comfort for his family and friends, which animated his heroic soul to perform any exploit, where there was a possibility of attaining either of those desirable objects.

Lord Nelson, on arriving at Portsmouth, immediately arranged all his business: and, having embarked at the bathing-machines, got on board the Victory, about two o'clock; accompanied by his esteemed friends, the Right Honourable, George

Rose, and the Right Honourable George Canning, who dined with the hero while he was preparing for sea.

The next morning, Sunday, September 15, at daylight, the Victory weighed, with light airs, and immediately sailed. Though five ships of the line, and a frigate, were then at Portsmouth, almost ready for sea, and under orders to join his lordship, he was resolved not to lose a moment in waiting for them. He had sailed, therefore, from St. Helen's, accompanied only by the Honourable Captain Blackwood in the Euryalus frigate: but, on the 17th, being off Plymouth, they were joined by the Ajax of seventy-four guns, Captain Brown; and the Thunderer of the same force, Captain Lechmere.

Lord Nelson, on the 26th of September, got round Cape St. Vincent; but it was late in the evening of the 28th, before he arrived off Cadiz, and joined Admiral Collingwood. His lordship was received, by the whole fleet, with every demonstration of the most enthusiastic joy. Being fully prepared to impart the particulars of the incomparable mode of attack which he had projected for the occasion, in all that force and vigour of genius which flashes irresistible conviction on the heart, and fills it, at once, with admiration, esteem, and astonishment, his lordship communicated, next morning, with the different commanders; whom he ordered on board the Victory, to be made acquainted with the particulars of his intended plan. "I believe," writes his lordship, "my arrival was most welcome; not only to the commanders of the fleet, but also to every individual in it; and, when I came to explain to them the *Nelson touch*, it was like an electric shock. Some shed tears, all approved. It was new, it was singular, it was simple; and, from admirals downwards, it was repeated—"It must succeed, if ever they will allow us to get at them! You are, my lord, surrounded by friends whom you inspire with confidence."—"Some," adds his lordship, "may be Judas's, but the majority are certainly much pleased with my commanding them." The letter from which this is extracted, was dated the 1st of October; on which morning, about four o'clock, our hero had been suddenly seized with a violent fit of those dreadful spasms which often so alarmingly afflicted him, "It is," says his lordship, "very odd! I was hardly ever better, than yesterday. Freemantle staid with me till eight o'clock; and I slept uncommonly well, but was awoke by this disorder. My opinion of it's effect, some one day, has never altered! However, it is entirely gone off, and I am only quite weak. The good people of

England will not believe, that rest of body and mind is necessary for me! But, perhaps, this spasm may not come again these six months. I had been writing seven hours yesterday; perhaps, that had some hand in bringing it upon me." Thus lightly does he speak of his own sufferings, thus good-humouredly notice the little consideration of the country for his individual ease.

The Euryalus had been immediately stationed close off the harbour of Cadiz, for the purpose of watching every motion of the enemy, and instantly communicating whatever intelligence might be obtained; a service for which, Lord Nelson was persuaded, there could not possibly be a better officer than his friend the Honourable Captain Blackwood. At a more remote distance, but still within sight of the port, a detachment of a few ships of the line was placed in constant readiness to act against any single ships, or small squadrons, which might attempt to push out for sea; between which, and the main body of the fleet, remaining off Cape St. Mary's, was posted a line of frigates, sufficiently close for the whole to communicate by signal: so that his lordship could always, in a few minutes, be informed of every movement of the enemy. There were now thirty-six sail of the line visible in Cadiz, and they bore every appearance of being nearly ready for sea.

The following excellent letter, developing the intended arrangements of his lordship; his full confidence of success; and the characteristic chearfulness of his friendly attachment to the Honourable Captain Black wood, originally founded on admiration of that active able officer's professional abilities in assisting the capture of Le Guillaume Tell at Malta; cannot fail to gratify every intelligent reader.

Victory, Oct. 4, 1805.

"MY DEAR SIR,

I have received, from Rear-Admiral Louis, your information
respecting the intended movements of the enemy. I am momentarily
expecting the Phoebe, Sirius, Naiad, and Niger, from Gibraltar;
two of them shall be with you, directly as I can get hold of them:
and, if you meet them, and there is any way of sending information,
and their dispatches from Gibraltar, keep Naiad and Phoebe. Juno is

a fixture between Capes Trafalgar and Spartel. Mars, Colossus, and Defence, will be stationed four leagues east from the fleet; and one of them advanced to the east, towards Cadiz, and as near as possible in the latitude. The fleet will be from sixteen to eighteen leagues west of Cadiz; therefore, if you throw a frigate west from you, most probably, in fine weather, we shall daily communicate. In fresh breezes easterly, I shall work up for Cadiz, never getting to the northward of it; and, in the event of hearing they are standing out of Cadiz, carry a press of sail to the southward, towards Cape Spartel and Arache. I am writing out regular instructions for the guidance of the frigates: but, I am confident, these gentry will not slip through our fingers; and, that we shall give a good account of them, although they may be superior in numbers. The Royal Sovereign and Defiance were to sail after the 24th. Belleisle is ordered here. I send you two papers, *I have stole them for you*. Ever, my dear Blackwood, most faithfully your's,

"Nelson and Bronte."

"The Honourable Captain Blackwood."

On the 8th, his lordship sent the Naiad to the Honourable Captain Blackwood; with a promise of the Phoebe and Weazle, as soon as he could lay hands on them: informing him, also, that the Defiance had joined, and the Royal Sovereign was then in sight. The next morning, at eight o'clock, his lordship, after thanking the honourable captain for intelligence respecting a livelihood of the enemy's sailing, and observing that he should wish never to be more than forty-eight hours without hearing from him, observes that—

"Agamemnon, Belleisle, and Superb, and very probably the London, are at this moment on their passage: therefore," he jocosely says, "if Mr. Decrees means to come forth, (if he would take my advice, which I dare say he will not) he had better come out directly. Those," he adds, "who know more of Cadiz than you or I do, say that, after these Levanters, come several days of fine weather; westerly winds for sea-breezes, and a land wind at night: and that, if the enemy are bound into the Mediterranean, they would come out in the night, which they have always done; placing lights on the Porpoises and the Diamond, and the shoal off Cadiz; run to the southward, and catch the sea breeze off the mouth of the Gut, and push through, whilst we might have little winds in the offing. In short, watch all points, and all winds and weathers. Remember me to Capel, Parker, Mundy, and Captain Prowse; and, be assured, I ever am your's most faithfully,

Nelson and Bronte.

The following short letter, written the following day, is too peculiarly characteristic, and impressive, to admit of any curtailment.

Oct. 10, 1805. Victory.

"MY DEAR BLACKWOOD,

Keep your five frigates, Weazle and Pickle, and let me know every movement. I rely, we cannot miss getting hold of them, and I will give them such a shaking as they never yet experienced; at least, I will lay down my life in the attempt! We are a very powerful fleet, and not to be held cheap. I have told Parker, and do you direct, that ships bringing information of their coming out, are to fire guns every three minutes by the watch; and, in the night, to fire rockets, if they have them, from the mast-head. I have nothing more to say; they will, I hope, sail to-night. Ever your's,
faithfully,
Nelson and Bronte.
Cadiz East Thirteen Leagues, 6 A.M.

"The Honourable Captain Blackwood."

It was on this day, that Lord Nelson issued his celebrated instructions for attacking the combined fleet, of which the following is a correct copy.

Victory, off Cadiz, Oct. 10, 1805.

Thinking it almost impossible to bring a fleet of forty sail of the line into battle, in variable winds, thick weather, and other circumstances which must occur, without such a loss of time that the opportunity would probably be lost of bringing the enemy to battle in such a manner as to make the business decisive; I have, therefore, made up my mind, to keep the fleet in that position of sailing, with the exception of the first and second in command, that the order of sailing is to be the order of the battle: placing the fleet in two lines, of sixteen ships each, with an advanced squadron of eight of the fastest sailing two-decked ships; which will always make, if wanted, a line of twenty-four sail on which ever line the commander in chief may direct. The second in command will, after my intentions are made known to him, have the entire direction of his line, to make the attack upon the enemy, and to follow up the blow, until they are captured or destroyed. If the enemy's fleet are seen to windward in line of battle, and that the two lines and advanced squadron could fetch them, they will probably be so extended that their van could not succour their rear. I should therefore, probably, make the second in command's signal to lead through about the twelfth ship from their rear; or wherever he could fetch, if not able to get so far advanced: my line would lead through about their centre, and the advanced squadron two, three, or four, ships a-head of their centre, so as to ensure getting at their commander in chief, whom every effort must be made to capture. The whole impression of the British fleet must be, to overpower from two or three ships a-head of their commander in chief, supposed to be their centre, to the rear of their fleet. I will suppose twenty sail of the line to be untouched; it must be some time before, they could perform a manoeuvre to bring their force compact to attack any part of the British fleet, or succour their own ships: which, indeed, would be impossible, without mixing with the ships engaged. The enemy's fleet is supposed to consist of forty-six sail of the line, British forty: if either is less, only a proportion of the enemy to be cut off. British to to be one-fourth superior to the enemy cut off. Something must be left to chance. Nothing is sure in a sea-fight, beyond all others; shots will carry away masts and yards of friends as well as foes. But I look with confidence to a victory, before the van of the enemy could succour the rear: and, then, that the British fleet would be ready to receive the twenty sail of the line; or to pursue them, should they endeavour to make off. If the van of the enemy tacks, the captured ships must run to leeward of the British fleet. If the enemy wear, the British fleet must place themselves between the enemy and the captured, and the disabled British ships; and, should the enemy close, I have no fear as to the result. The second in command will, in all possible things, direct the movements of his line, by keeping them as compact as the nature of the circumstances will admit. Captains are to look to their particular line as their rallying point; but, in case signals cannot be seen, or clearly understood, no captain can do wrong, if he places his ship alongside that of an enemy.

```
                      /Advanced Squadron  8\
British Divisions {    Weather Line ...    16 } 40.
                      \Lee Line ...         16/
```

Enemy ... 46.

The Divisions of the British fleet will be brought nearly within gunshot of the enemy's centre. The signal will, most probably, then be made for the lee line to bear up together; to set all their sails, even the steering sails, in order to get as quickly as possible to the enemy's line; and to cut through, begining at the twelfth ship from the enemy's rear. Some ships may not get through their expected place, but they will always be at hand to assist their friends. If any are thrown in the rear of the enemy, they will compleat the business of twelve sail of the enemy. Should the enemy wear together, or bear up and sail large, still the twelve ships composing in the first position the enemy's rear, are to be the object of attack of the lee line, unless otherwise directed by the commander in chief; which is scarcely to be expected, as the entire management of the lee line, after the intentions of the commander in chief are signified, is intended to be left to the admiral commanding that line. The remainder of the enemy's fleet, thirty-five, sail of the line, are to be left to the management of the commander in chief, who will endeavour to take care that the movements of the second in command are as little interrupted as possible.

"Nelson and Bronte."

About this period, the following admired extract of a letter to Alexander Davison, Esq. his lordship's most confidential friend, appears also to have been written; which, though published in most of the newspapers, and other periodical journals, cannot be too often reprinted.

"Day by day, my dear friend, I am expecting the fleet to put to sea; every day, hour, and moment: and you may rely that, if it is in the power of man to get at them, it shall be done; and, I am sure, that all my brethren look to that day, as the finish of our laborious cruise. The event, no man can say exactly; but I must think,--or render great injustice to those under me, that let the battle be when it may, it will never have been surpassed! My shattered frame, if I survive that day, will require rest, and that is all I shall ask for. If I fall on such a glorious occasion, it shall be my pride to take care that my friends shall not blush for me. These things are in the hands of a good and wise Providence; and, his will be done! I have got some trifle, thank God, to leave to those I hold most dear, and I have taken care not to neglect it. Do not think I am low-spirited on this account, or fancy any thing is to happen to me; quite the contrary: my mind is calm, and I have only to think of destroying our inveterate foe. I have two frigates gone for more information, and we all hope for a meeting with the enemy. Nothing can be finer than the fleet under my command. Whatever be the event, believe me ever, my dear Davison, your much obliged and sincere friend,

"Nelson and Bronte."

As, however, the combined fleet did not immediately come out, his lordship soon grew apprehensive that they were very little disposed speedily to venture from port; and, therefore, began to consider how he might annoy them even there.

"If they do not come forth soon," writes his lordship, on the 14th, to the Honourable Captain Blackwood, "I shall then rather incline to think they will detach squadrons: but, I hope, either in the whole, or in part, we shall get at them. I am confident in your look out upon them. I expect three stout fire-ships from England; then, with a good breeze, so that the gun-boats cannot move, and yet not so much but that a gig can with ease row out, I should hope that, at least, the gentry might be disturbed: and I should not be surprised if Mr. Francis and his catamarans were sent, and Colonel Congreve and his rockets. But, all this keep to yourself; for officers will talk, and there is no occasion to put the enemy upon their guard. When those things arrive, we will consult how to manage them, and I shall have the two bombs ready by that time."

On Lord Nelson's arrival in the Mediterranean, he had felt it his most difficult task to send home Sir Robert Calder. "I had never," said his lordship, speaking on this subject to his confidential friends, "but two enemies in the profession, that I know of, Sir Robert Calder, and Sir John Orde; nor do I feel conscious of having ever given either of them any just cause of offence. However," added this excellent and exalted man, "I will, at least, endeavour to make Sir Robert love me." Accordingly, on communicating his orders to this unfortunate commander, he earnestly advised him not to return home immediately; but to serve with himself on the expected glorious occasion, after which, there could be nothing to apprehend from any trivial enquiry respecting what might previously have happened. Sir Robert, however, though he could not but feel sensible of his lordship's kindness, was resolved by no means to protract his justification; and Lord Nelson, finding him determined to go home, as a last proof of tenderness and respectful consideration for a brother officer thus disagreeably situated, insisted that, instead of Sir Robert's departing in a frigate, as directed, he should at least have the honour of returning in his own ninety-gun ship, ill as it could at this eventful crisis be spared from that station. Thus did the hero willingly hazard a degree of censure from his country, through excess of feeling for Sir Robert Calder; nor is it altogether an extravagant impossibility that, to this generous action, he owed even his own death, which the addition of a ship of such force might perhaps have prevented. In writing to the Honourable Captain Blackwood a second letter, dated the, 14th, soon after Sir Robert Calder's departure, his lordship feelingly says—"Sir Robert is gone. Poor fellow! I hope he will get well over the enquiry." What a lesson is here of Christian virtue, left by our incomparable hero for the contemplation and admiration of mankind. It is asserted, on no light authority, that Sir. Robert Calder had formerly, rather rashly, advised a court-martial on our hero, for his departure from his commander in chief's orders on the memorable 14th of February; when the great Earl of St. Vincent, with a generous, noble, and dignified disdain, instantly replied—"You would, then, try a man for knowing better how to act than yourself."

Lord Nelson, in the foregoing letter to the Honourable Captain Blackwood, thanks him for some observations on the Salvages, which he will get inserted in the charts; and tells him, that the Defence and Agamemnon will be this day placed seven to ten leagues distant from Cadiz, and two or three ships between the fleet and them: "therefore," says his lordship, "you will be speedily supported, in case of an attempt to drive you off." Characteristically adding—"*I should like, most amazingly, to see them try it!"*

It has been said, that Lord Nelson, who was in hourly expectation of being reinforced by seven ships of the line from England, and impatient to encounter the enemy, purposely detached Rear-Admiral Louis, with that number of ships, in the most public manner, by way of encouraging them to risk an action with his apparently so diminished force; and, that this stratagem actually induced Admiral Villeneuve immediately to sail from Cadiz. That the expected reinforcement had arrived, and Admiral Louis had been thus detached to Tetuan, for fresh provisions and water, is most certain; and it is equally certain that the combined fleet, greatly to our hero's wish, however it might be to his expectation, he had the pleasure to learn, next morning; Sunday, October the 20th, on communicating with the Phoebe, Defence, and Colossus, were the evening before seen by them outside of Cadiz; but, the wind being southerly, the enemy, consisting of nearly forty sail, could not get to the mouth of the Straits. "We were," writes his lordship, for this is transcribed from his own private memorandum of that day, "between Trafalgar and Cape Spartel. The frigates made the signal, that they saw nine sail outside the harbour. I gave the frigates instructions for their guidance; and placed Defenced Colossus, and Mars, between me and the frigates. At noon, fresh gales, and heavy rain. Cadiz north-east nine leagues. In the afternoon, Captain Blackwood telegraphed, that the enemy seemed determined to go to the westward—*and that they shall not do, if in the power of Nelson and Bronte to prevent them*! At five, telegraphed Captain Blackwood, that I relied on his keeping sight of the enemy. At five o'clock, Naiad made the signal for thirty-one sail of the enemy north north-east. The frigates and look-out ships kept sight of the enemy most admirably, all night; and told me, by signals, which tack they were upon. At eight, we wore, and stood to the south-west; and, at four A.M. wore, and stood to the north-east."

To what an eventful period is the reader now conducted, by the hand of our immortal hero himself, in the forcible and unaffected language of his own manly and matchless heart; of that heart, which was, at this awful moment, glowing with all the heroism of patriotic ardour for his king and country, and anxiously waiting the first dawn of light by which he might be enabled to discover the enemy! It came; and, with it, brought the welcome sight of those whom his whole soul burned to behold. Few, and simple, are the words which immediately follow in his lordship's memorandum.

"Monday, October 21, 1805. At day-light, saw the enemy's combined fleet, from east to east south-east. Bore away; made the signal for order of sailing, and to prepare for battle: the enemy with their heads to the southward."

But now, at the very crisis when he is hastening into a battle for his king and country, which he feels confident must end in a glorious victory, though he might not himself survive it, with that potent patriotism and never-ceasing loyalty to his king and country, and that constantly tender regard for those who were nearest to his heart in the bonds of private affection, he thus piously invokes Heaven's protection for his king and country; and the protection of his king and country, should he fall in their service, for those most dear to his heart who would thus be deprived of his own. To add to the solemnity, though thus introduced in his lordship's private journal, it has the form, and in some respects the substance, of a codicil of his last will and testament; and is, accordingly, thereto annexed, having been duly proved in Doctors Commons.

"At seven," continues, and unfortunately concludes, his lordship—for these seem to have been the last words written by his own hand, which no man who deserves the name of a Briton will ever cease to remember and to regard—"the enemy wearing in succession—

> "May the great God whom I worship, grant to my country, and for
> the benefit of Europe in general, a great and glorious victory! and
> may no misconduct in any one tarnish it! and may humanity, after
> victory, be the predominant feature in the British fleet! For
> myself, individually, I Commend my life to Him who made me; and may
> his blessing light upon my endeavours for serving my country
> faithfully! To him I resign myself, and the just cause which is
> entrusted to me to defend.
>
> Amen! Amen! Amen!

"October the 21st, 1805, then in sight of the

combined Fleets of France and Spain, distant about ten miles.

"Whereas the eminent services of Emma Hamilton, widow of the Right Honourable Sir William Hamilton, have been of the very greatest service to our King and Country, to my knowledge, without her receiving any reward from either our King or Country--

"First, that she obtained the King of Spain's letter, in 1796, to his brother the King of Naples, acquainting him of his intention to declare war against England; from which letter the ministry sent out orders to the then Sir John Jervis, to strike a stroke, if opportunity offered, against either the arsenals of Spain or her fleets: that neither of these was done, is not the fault of Lady Hamilton; the opportunity might have been offered.

"Secondly, The British fleet under my command could never have returned the second time to Egypt, had not Lady Hamilton's influence with the Queen of Naples caused letters to be wrote to the Governor of Syracuse, that he was to encourage the fleet being supplied with every thing, should they put into any port in Sicily. We put into Syracuse, and received every supply; went to Egypt, and destroyed the French fleet.

"Could I have rewarded these services, I would not now call upon my country! But, as that has not been in my power, I leave Emma Hamilton, therefore, a legacy to my King and Country; that they will give her an ample provision, to maintain her rank in life.

"I also leave to the beneficence of my country, my adopted daughter, Horatia Nelson Thompson; and I desire she will use, in future, the name of Nelson only.

"These are the only favours I ask of my King and Country, at this moment, when I am going to fight their battle.

"May God bless my King and Country, and all those I hold dear! My relations it is needless to mention; they will, of course, be amply provided for.

"Nelson and Bronte."
"Witness,

Henry Blackwood,

T.M. Hardy."

This solemn call on his country can require no comment. Woe to the nation, which could dare to neglect such strong claims on it's justice and beneficence! The proverbial generosity of Britons will, no doubt, in due time, bountifully display it's accustomed munificence in favour of the parties.

The Honourable Captain Blackwood, who is a subscribing witness to the above codicil, after watching the enemy all night, had got on board the Victory about seven in the morning: and, with Captain, Capel, of the Phoebe; and Captain Prowse, of the Sirius; remained several hours in consultation with Lord Nelson. When his lordship became convinced, that the enemy could not possibly avoid an engagement, he displayed the highest degree of animation. Confident of victory, he said to Captain Hardy, and the other officers by whom he was surrounded—"They cannot now escape us! I think, we shall, at least, make sure of twenty of them. I may, probably, lose a leg; but that will be cheaply purchasing a victory." However, it is an undoubted fact, that when the Honourable Captain Blackwood, in taking leave of his lordship, previous to the action, observed that, he hoped they should, in a few hours, meet again; the hero replied, in a firm tone—"My dear Blackwood, I shall never again speak to you!" This was no sentiment of despondency, but a strong sense of the danger to be apprehended from so unequal a contest. The enemy's line consisting of thirty-three ships, eighteen of which were French, and fifteen

Spanish; and the British fleet only twenty-seven: and, by the advantage of size, as well as numbers, they had a superiority of about three hundred and fifty guns. Ten thousand of their choicest troops were also distributed throughout the fleet, to ensure success by boarding; and their ships were furnished with fire-balls and combustibles of every description, in the hope of setting our's on fire. The French were commanded, in chief, by Admiral Villeneuve; and not by Admiral Decrees, as Lord Nelson had lately supposed would be the case; with Rear-Admirals Dumanoir and Magon: The Spaniards, by Admiral Gravina, commander in chief; with Admirals Don Ignacio Morea D'Alva, Don Domingo Guadalharas, and Commodore Don Baltazar. The structure of the enemy's line was somewhat new, as well as the intended mode of attacking them. It formed a crescent, convexing to leeward: every alternate ship being about a cable's length to windward of it's second a-head and a-stern, so as to seem a kind of double-line; leaving between them, when on their beam, a very small interval, and this without crouding their ships. Admiral Villeneuve, in the Bucentaure, occupied the centre; and Admiral Gravina's flag was borne by the Prince of Asturias, in the rear: but the French and Spanish ships appear to have been mixed, without any regard to national arrangement.

The mode of attack having been long determined on by Lord Nelson, and recently communicated, as has been seen, on the 10th instant, to the flag officers and captains, few signals were necessary. On first discovering the combined fleet, his lordship had immediately made the signal to bear up in two columns, as formed in the order of sailing, to avoid the inconvenience and delay of forming a line of battle in the usual manner. Lord Nelson, as commander in chief, led the weather column, in the Victory; and Vice-Admiral Collingwood, as second in command, that of the lee, in the Royal Sovereign. The following are the respective ships of which the two British lines were composed—

BRITISH VAN, OR WEATHER COLUMN.

Ships.	Guns.	Commanders.
1. Victory	110	Admiral Lord Nelson, and Capt Hardy.

2.	Temeraire	98	Capt. Harvey.
3.	Neptune	98	Capt. Freemantle.
4.	Conqueror	74	Capt. Pellew.
5.	Leviathan	74	Capt. Bayntun.
6.	Ajax	74	Lieut. Pilfold.
7.	Orion	74	Capt. Codrington.
8.	Agamemnon	64	Capt. Sir Edward Berry.
9.	Minotaur	74	Capt. Mansfield.
10.	Spartiate	74	Capt. Sir Francis Laforey.
11.	Britannia	100	Rear-Admiral Northesk, and Capt. Bullen.
12.	Africa	64	Capt. Digby.

REAR, OR LEE COLUMN.

13.	Royal Sovereign	100	Admiral Collingwood, and Capt. Rotheran.
14.	Mars	74	Capt. Duff.
15.	Belleisle	74	Capt. Hargood.
16.	Tonnant	80	Capt. Tyler.
17.	Bellerophon	74	Capt. Cooke.
18.	Colossus	74	Capt. Morris.
19.	Achille	74	Capt. King.
20.	Polyphemus	64	Capt. Redmill.
21.	Revenge	74	Capt. Moorson.
22.	Swiftsure	74	Capt. Rutherford.
23.	Defence	74	Capt. Hope.
24.	Thunderer	74	Lieut. Stockham.
25.	Defiance	74	Capt. Durham.
26.	Prince	74	Capt. Grindall.
27.	Dreadnought	98	Capt. Conn.

Senior Lieutenants Pilfold and Stockham commanded for Captains Brown and Lechmere, who were called home to give evidence on the enquiry into the conduct of Sir Robert Calder.

FRIGATES, &c.

Ships.	Guns.	Commanders.
1. Euryalus	36	The Honourable Capt. Blackwood.
2. Sirius	36	Capt. Prowse.
3. Phoebe	36	Capt. Capel.
4. Naiad	36	Capt. Parker.
5. Pickle schooner	10	Lieut. Lapenotiere.
6. Entreprenante cutter	10	Lieut. Puyer.

While they were approaching the enemy's line, Lord Nelson repeatedly declared, that it was the happiest day of his life; and that, from the plan of his intended attack, he entertained not the smallest doubt that, before night, he should gain possession of at least twenty of their ships. The last signal which preceded the battle, was an emanation from his great mind which will long be remembered; this was a private signal to the fleet, communicating by telegraph the following most emphatic sentiment—

"England expects every man to do his duty."

This took place exactly at twelve o'clock, and the battle instantly commenced by the leading ships of the columns attempting to break through the enemy's line: Lord Nelson, in the Victory, about the tenth ship from the van; Vice-Admiral Collingwood, in the Royal Sovereign, about the twelfth from the rear. When Vice-Admiral Collingwood, at the head of the division under his orders, began the attack, and broke through the enemy's line, Lord Nelson, turning round to his officers, with the highest exultation, said—"Look at that noble fellow! Observe the stile in which he carries his ship into action!" The Victory, at four minutes past twelve, opened it's fire on the enemy's van, while passing down their line; in about a quarter of an hour after which, finding it impossible to penetrate through, the Victory fell on board the eleventh and twelfth ships. The Temeraire, Captain Harvey, by which the Victory was seconded, in consequence of the closeness of this part of the enemy's line, fell also on board one of them. These four ships were thus, for a considerable time, engaged together as in a single mass; so that the flash of almost every gun fired from the Victory set fire to the Redoutable, it's more immediate opponent. In this state, amidst the hottest fire of the enemy, was beheld a very singular spectacle; that of numerous British seamen employed, at intervals, in very coolly throwing buckets of water to extinguish the flames on board their enemy's ship, that both might not be involved in one common destruction. His lordship had been particularly desirous to have began the action, by passing a-head of the Bucentaure, Admiral Villeneuve's ship, that the Victory might be a-head of the French commander in chief, and a-stern of the Spanish Santissima Trinidada of a hundred and thirty-six guns, the largest ship in the world. The Bucentaure, however, shooting a-head, his lordship, who was thus obliged to go under that ship's stern, immediately raked it, and luffed up on the starboard side. The Bucentaure fired four broadsides at the Victory, before our hero ordered his ports to be opened; when the whole broadside, which was double shotted, being poured in, the discharge made such a tremendous crash, that the ship was instantly seen to heel. Lord Nelson now shot a-head to the Santissima Trinidada. In contending with this ship, on the celebrated 14th of February 1797, our hero had already acquired considerable renown. Having got alongside his tremendous opponent, which he familiarly called his old acquaintance, he ordered the ships to be lashed together. The battle was now raging with a fury not to be described; and the enemy's ships being full of men, and many of them engaged muzzle to muzzle of the guns with our's, the carnage was most horrible. The crash, too, of the falling masts, yards, &c. incessantly mowed down, by the respective shots on both sides, with the almost general blaze, and incessantly tremendous roar, had an aweful grandeur which no verbal or graphic description or delineation can ever faithfully convey to the eye and ear. Our hero, amidst this most terrific scene, appeared to be literally in his glory. He was quite enraptured with the bravery and skill of all under his command: he was not displeased to find, that the enemy, in general, fought like men worthy of being conquered; of being themselves conquerors, in a better cause. In a dress richly covered with the honours which he had acquired by his prowess in former battles, he stood a conspicuous object of emulative worth to all the heroic men who surrounded him in this. Never had his aspiring and enraptured heart beheld a victory more brilliantly glorious awaiting their noble exertions. Ineffable delight, blended with a divine benignity, beamed over the hero's countenance. He felt conscious of being engaged in contending for all that is dear to man; and, consequently, struggling in a cause which could by no means be displeasing to Heaven. He doubted little the success of his country, for he knew in what he confided; but he was not presumptuous, for he had early been instructed, that "the battle is not always to the strong." His own personal fate was ever humbly resigned to the will of the Great Disposer; live, or die, he was alone solicitous that he should live or die in glory. While victory, however, from all observation, appeared within his grasp, he could not but be conscious that individual danger every where hovered around. The Santissima Trinidada carried full sixteen hundred men; including a corps of troops, among whom were several sharp-shooters. Many other ships had, also, Tyrolese riflemen on board. Amidst the conflict of cannon, fired muzzle to muzzle, showers of bullets were directed on the quarter-deck; where the distinguished hero stood, fearlessly giving his orders, and chearfully abiding every peril. His heart was animated, and his spirits were gay. The stump of his right arm, which he always pleasantly denominated his fin, moved the shoulder of his sleeve up and down with the utmost rapidity, as was customary when he felt greatly pleased. Captain Hardy, apprehensive that Lord Nelson's peculiar attire pointed him out as too obvious a mark, advised the hero to change his dress, or cover himself with a great-coat; but he no otherwise regarded the precautionary advice, than by observing that he had not yet time to do so. It probably struck his great mind, that such an act might evince too much personal attention for a commander in chief to possess. In the mean while, the murderous desire of the enemy to single out the officers, continued growing more and more manifest. Of a hundred and ten marines stationed on the poop and quarter-deck, upwards of eighty were either killed or wounded. Mr. Pascoe, first-lieutenant of the Victory, received a very severe wound, while conversing with his lordship; and John Scott, Esq. his lordship's secretary, was shot through the head, by a musket-ball, at his side, Captain Adair of the marines, almost at the same instant, experienced a similar fate. This was about a quarter of an hour past one o'clock; and, a few minutes afterward, Captain Hardy, who was standing near his lordship, observed a marksman in the mizen-top of the Bucentaure, which then lay on the Victory's quarter, in the very act of taking a deliberate aim at his beloved commander. Scarcely had he time to exclaim—"Change your position, my lord! I see a rascal taking aim at you!" when the fatal bullet unhappily smote the hero; and, having entered near the top of his left shoulder, penetrated through his lungs, carrying with it part of the adhering epaulette, and lodged in the spinal marrow of his back. A shout of horrid joy, from the enemy, seemed to announce their sense of the cruel success. His lordship was prevented from falling, by Captain Hardy; to whom he said, with a smile—"They have done for me, at last!"

As the officers were conducting him below, his lordship deliberately remarked that the tiller-rope was too slack, and requested that Captain Hardy might be told to get it tightened. In the mean time, Mr. Pollard, a young midshipman of the Victory, not more than sixteen years of age, having levelled a musket at the man who shot his lordship, the fellow was seen instantly to fall. All the surgeons being busily engaged with the wounded, our hero, as usual, insisted on waiting till his turn. The surgeon who examined the wound soon clearly discovered what must be it's fatal effect. Lord Nelson had attentively regarded his countenance; and, on beholding him turn pale, calmly said—"It is, I perceive, mortal!"

The Reverend Dr. Scott, who was looking for his wounded friend, Lieutenant Pascoe, in the cockpit, to his utter astonishment and horror, discovered that his lordship had that moment been brought down. He immediately seated himself on the floor, and supported his pillow during the whole time of the surgeon's operations; indeed, except for a few moments, when he was sent to call Captain Hardy, he never left him. After enquiring about the state of the battle, which the dying hero far more regarded than that of his wound, his lordship, who was much agitated, and evidently suffering the most extreme agony, suddenly exclaimed, in a hurried manner—"Doctor, remember me to Lady Hamilton, remember me to Horatia! Remember me to Lady Hamilton, remember me to Horatia! Tell her, I have made a will, and left her a legacy to my country." This was afterward repeated, in a calmer tone, to Dr. Scott; with whom he conversed, at intervals, in a low voice, but perfectly collected. At times, the pain seizing him more violently, he suddenly and loudly expressed a wish to die. Then, again, he would grow calm and collected, and address himself to Dr. Scott; speaking in low, though broken and unconnected, sentences. At first, he expressed an eager desire for drink; saying—"Drink! drink! drink, doctor!" and continually had lemonade given him. After each time of drinking, he was a short time calm and collected, and spoke a few sentences to Dr. Scott; then, the pain again seizing him, he would hastily call out—"Drink! drink!" His lower extremities soon grew cold and insensible, and the copious effusion of blood from his lungs frequently threatened suffocation. His eyes, however, appeared to brighten, and his spirits to revive, on hearing the cheers given by the crew of the Victory as the different ships of the enemy surrendered. He frequently expressed much desire to have his face wiped; repeating, to Dr. Scott—"Wipe my face, doctor! Doctor, wipe my face!" This being done, for a considerable time, he seemed to receive some comfort; but soon grew prodigiously anxious to see Captain Hardy. His lordship had several times sent for him; and, not finding him come, began to imagine that he was no more. It was found difficult to efface this idea; and Dr. Scott felt it necessary himself to call Captain Hardy, who had been unwilling to quit his post at such an interesting period. About half past four, however, Captain Hardy attended on his lordship; who eagerly enquired, how many ships were captured. On being informed, by the captain, that twelve, which he could see, had certainly struck; and that, probably, more might have surrendered, as the victory seemed nearly compleat: the dying hero hastily exclaimed—"What, only twelve! there should have been, at least, fifteen or sixteen, by my calculation! However," added he, after, a short pause, "twelve are pretty well!" He requested that Captain Hardy would bear his kindest remembrances to Lady Hamilton, and to Horatia; and inform them that he had left them as a legacy to his king and country, in whose service he willingly yielded up his life. "Will you, my dear Hardy?" anxiously demanded his lordship. "Kiss me, then!" Captain Hardy immediately kneeling, respectfully kissed the wan cheek of his adored commander. The dying hero now desired that his affectionate regards might be presented to his brave officers and men: and said, that he could have wished once more to have beheld his beloved relatives and friends, or even to have survived till he had seen the fleet in safety; but, as neither was possible, he felt resigned, and thanked God for having enabled him to do his duty to his king and country. His lordship had, latterly, most vehemently directed Dr. Scott to rub his breast and pit of the stomach; where, it seems probable, he now felt the blood beginning more painfully to flow, in a state of commencing congelation—"Rub me, rub me, doctor!" he often and loudly repeated. This melancholy office was continued to be almost incessantly performed by Dr. Scott, till his lordship expired; and, indeed, for some time, afterward. The last words the immortal hero uttered, were—

"Thank God, I have done my duty!"

He had, before, pronounced them in a lower tone of voice: saying—"Doctor, I have not been a great sinner; and, thank God, I have done my duty!" Then, as if asking the question, he repeated—"Doctor, I have not been a great sinner?" Doctor Scott was too much affected immediately to answer. "Have I?" he again eagerly interrogated. A paroxysm of pain now suddenly seizing him, he exclaimed, in a loud and most solemnly impressive tone—"Thank God, I have done my duty! Thank God, I have done my duty!" After pronouncing these words, he had, apparently, suffered no pain; but gradually went off, as if asleep. Indeed, every person who surrounded him, except Dr. Scott, who had long felt the current of life sensibly chilling beneath his hand, actually thought, for some time, that he was only in a state of somnolency. It was, however, the sleep of death, the blood having entirely choaked up his incomparable heart.

Thus died the greatest naval hero, "take him for all in all," that ever lived. This will probably be said, as long as the world endures. It is not likely that he can ever be equalled, it is impossible that he should be surpassed.

The victory of this day, off Trafalgar, was one of the most compleatly glorious ever atchieved by Britons. About three o'clock, many of the enemy's ships having struck their colours, their line had every where given way, and as many as possible endeavoured to effect their escape. Eighteen men of war were taken; and three flag-officers, with a general, made prisoners of war. Among the ships captured, were the Santissima Trinidada of a hundred and thirty-six guns, the Santa Anna of a hundred and twenty, and the Bucentaure of seventy-four: the last having Admiral Villeneuve, the French commander in chief, on board; as well as General Contamin, who had four thousand select troops embarked under his command; and the two former, the Spanish Vice-Admiral Don Ignatio Morea D'Alva, who died of his wounds, with Rear-Admiral Don Baltazar Hidalgo de Cisneros. The Santissima Trinidada, soon after the action, sunk; and L'Achille, a French seventy-four, by some mismanagement of the crew, almost immediately on striking, took fire, and blew up. The number of killed, wounded, and taken prisoners, was most prodigious. The French Admiral Dumanoir, with three French ships, which had no share in the action, iniquitously fired, for some time, while making their ignominious retreat, on the Santissima Trinidada and other Spanish prizes which had struck their colours to our fleet; thus wantonly massacreing their defenceless friends and allies. Many of the ships taken or destroyed had upwards of four hundred men killed and wounded on board; and more than three thousand Spanish prisoners were liberally sent back to their own country, by the generous conquerors. The Bucentaure, it is said, had three hundred and sixty-five killed, and two hundred and nineteen wounded. Our loss, too, in killed and wounded, was far from inconsiderable; and many of our ships were materially damaged. The Royal Sovereign, in particular, was so cut up, that Vice-Admiral Collingwood, after the action, shifted his flag to the Euryalus, the Honourable Captain Blackwood, and towed his own ship out seaward. Besides Lord Nelson, two other brave and estimable commanders lost their lives on this most memorably fatal day: Captain Duff, of the Mars; and Captain Cooke, of the Bellerophon. Captain Duff had two sons on board his own ship; one only twelve years of age, the other about fifteen: early in the engagement, a shot carried away both legs of the youngest; the elder soon afterwards fell; and, finally, their unfortunate father. Not even these distressing circumstances were capable of exciting any great degree of generous commiseration for those worthy and gallant victims, so entirely was each heart occupied by agonizing reflections on the loss of him who had, in himself, ever been considered as alone a host. It was a victory the most compleatly brilliant, but never had a victory been gained which conveyed so little gladness to the hearts of the conquerors. Every bosom felt oppressed with sorrow, on a day of such triumph to their country; and not an eye closed, in the whole fleet, on the sad night by which it was succeeded, without pouring an affectionate tribute of manly tears to the memory of the godlike hero by whose merits it had been so certainly obtained, and by whose death it had been so dearly purchased. "He will never again lead us to conquest!" sobbed many a bursting heart. "Our commander, our master, our father, our friend, our companion, is no more, and when shall we behold his equal? Never, never, never!" Such was their love of the adored hero, that every virtuous individual in the fleet would gladly have lost his own life to have saved him. It is, indeed, stated as a positive fact, that a seaman of the Victory, who was, a little before the fatal catastrophe, suffering the amputation of an arm, actually said to the surgeon—"Well, this might, by some men, be considered as a sad misfortune; but I shall be proud of the accident, as it will make me the more resemble our brave commander in chief." Before the operation was finished, the sad tidings arrived below, that Lord Nelson was wounded. The seaman, who had never once shrunk, amidst all the pain he endured, now suddenly started from his seat; and vehemently exclaimed—"Good God! I would rather the shot had taken off my head, and spared his precious life!"

Vice-Admiral Collingwood, in his letter to the Admiralty, describing this great victory, says—"I have not only to lament, in common with the British navy, and the British nation, in the fall of the commander in chief, the loss of a hero, whose name will be immortal, and his memory ever dear to his country; but my heart is rent with the most poignant grief for the death of a friend, to whom, by many years intimacy, and a perfect knowledge of the virtues of his mind, which inspired ideas superior to the common race of men, I was bound by the strongest ties of affection: a grief, to which even the glorious occasion on which he fell, does not bring the consolation which, perhaps, it ought!"

When the dispatches, containing an account of the glorious victory off Cape Trafalgar, with the death of our chief hero, arrived in England, and were perused by his majesty, the king was greatly affected. Tears flowed from the royal eyes; and his majesty pathetically exclaimed—"We have lost more than we have gained!" They were read, at Windsor, by the queen, to the assembled princesses, and the whole royal group most affectionately wept the fall of the hero. His Royal Highness the Prince of Wales, with a dignified excess of grief, most acutely felt the loss of the heroic supporter of his father's house; and a private letter of condolence, which his royal highness wrote to Alexander Davison, Esq. on the death of their inestimable friend, is replete with sentiments which augur highly for the probably future sovereign's adding new lustre to the brilliant throne of his most renowned ancestors. The Duke of Clarence, too, long united in friendship to the hero, whom he venerated with an almost paternal regard, lamented him with little less than the truest filial sorrow. In short, from the entire royal family, through every subordinate degree of rank and virtue, to the humblest class of existence, wherever the tidings came, tears overflowed every eye, and grief took entire possession of every heart. The glorious victory, though one of the greatest ever obtained by mortal, and though the last, as well as the most splendid, of the hero so beloved; was scarcely considered, by the nation, as an object worthy of those public rejoicings with which very inferior triumphs are constantly attended. Cannon, indeed, as usual, announced the intelligence, but their sound conveyed a deep melancholy to the heart; the bells were rung, but their peals inspired no hilarity, and seemed little less than the mournful knells of death; nocturnal illuminations were displayed, but the transparencies which they discovered, amidst the gloom, presented only so many sad memorials of the universal loss, expressed by ingenious devices to the hero's memory, which the spectators beheld with sensations of augmented grief, and one general aspect of expressive but unutterable woe. If such was the state of the public feeling, what must have been that of the hero's dearest relatives and friends; of those who had to sustain all the superadded pangs of a loss so difficult to be supplied for the service of the country, so impossible for the felicities of themselves! Several months elapsed, before Lady Hamilton quitted her bed; and Mrs. Bolton and Mrs. Matcham, for a long time, suffered similar anguish and affliction. Indeed, even all the younger branches of this amiable and interesting family, as well as their respective parents, evinced the highest possible degree of sensibility and sorrow for their irretrievable calamity; a calamity which, to them, all the honours and emoluments a grateful nation may bestow, extending to his remotest kindred, at present as well as in future, can scarcely be considered as affording any adequate recompence.

The great council of the country failed not to express solemnly their strong sense of the irreparable loss, by unanimously voting all the grand ceremonials of a public interment beneath the centre of the dome in St. Paul's cathedral, and a monumental erection of commensurate grandeur to rise immediately above the hero's honoured remains.

His majesty, on the 9th of November, was also graciously pleased to elevate his lordship's brother and heir, the Reverend Dr. William Nelson, to the dignity of a Viscount and Earl of the United Kingdom of Great Britain and Ireland, by the names, stiles, and titles, of Viscount Merton and Earl Nelson, of Trafalgar, and of Merton in the county of Surrey; the same to descend to his heirs male; and, in their default, to the heirs male, successively, of Susannah, wife of Thomas Bolton, Esq., and Catharine, wife of George Matcham, Esq. sisters of the late Lord Viscount Nelson.

The city of London, the Committee of Merchants at Lloyd's Coffee-House, and the respective corporations of several cities and chief towns in different parts of the united kingdom, publicly expressed their sense of the national loss, by the death of it's principal hero; and proposed various plans for perpetuating the remembrance of his transcendent services, by monumental erections, &c.

The body of the hero, which had been preserved in spirits, was brought to England in the Victory; the crew having positively refused to part with the corpse of their adored commander, till it should be safely landed in their native country. They were resolved, they said, one and all, to accompany him, as it should please Heaven, either to the bottom of the ocean, or see his sacred remains deposited in the honoured tomb which would, doubtless, be proudly prepared for them by a grateful nation; and could not suffer the corpse to be sent home in any ship subject to capture by the enemy.

After laying in state, a few days, at Greenwich Hospital, the body was conveyed, with all possible aquatic grandeur and solemnity, to the Admiralty; from whence, the next day, Thursday, January 9, 1806, borne on a grand funeral car, and with a pomp of procession scarcely ever equalled the illustrious hero's hallowed remains were finally deposited beneath the dome of St. Paul's cathedral.

Never, perhaps, were the mournful obsequies of any hero so numerously and so respectably attended; never was any human being deposited in the earth more universally and sincerely wept by every eye which beheld any part of the solemn ceremony. The tears of millions, on that melancholy day, bore testimony to his matchless worth; to the truth of that sentiment which he had piously pronounced, in his last moments—"Thank God, I have been enabled to do my duty to my King and Country!"

May the same Almighty Power inspire the hearts of his King and Country, to fulfil, in their utmost extent, every wish and expectation of the Dying Hero! And may each virtuous individual, in whom the blood of the Nelsons shall flow, to the last drop which can be traced, for ever find friendly patronage among the rulers of a nation, which has certainly, at an eventful crisis, been powerfully exalted, and perhaps preserved, by the example and influence of the immortal hero, who so freely and fatally shed his own last drop in the faithful service of his King and Country!

THE END.

www.bookjungle.com *email: sales@bookjungle.com fax: 630-214-0564 mail: Book Jungle PO Box 2226 Champaign, IL 61825*

The Codes Of Hammurabi And Moses
W. W. Davies

QTY

The discovery of the Hammurabi Code is one of the greatest achievements of archaeology, and is of paramount interest, not only to the student of the Bible, but also to all those interested in ancient history...

Religion   ISBN: *1-59462-338-4*   Pages:132
MSRP *$12.95*

The Theory of Moral Sentiments
Adam Smith

QTY

This work from 1749. contains original theories of conscience amd moral judgment and it is the foundation for systemof morals.

Philosophy   ISBN: *1-59462-777-0*   Pages:536
MSRP *$19.95*

Jessica's First Prayer
Hesba Stretton

QTY

In a screened and secluded corner of one of the many railway-bridges which span the streets of London there could be seen a few years ago, from five o'clock every morning until half past eight, a tidily set-out coffee-stall, consisting of a trestle and board, upon which stood two large tin cans, with a small fire of charcoal burning under each so as to keep the coffee boiling during the early hours of the morning when the work-people were thronging into the city on their way to their daily toil...

Childrens   ISBN: *1-59462-373-2*   Pages:84
MSRP *$9.95*

My Life and Work
Henry Ford

QTY

Henry Ford revolutionized the world with his implementation of mass production for the Model T automobile. Gain valuable business insight into his life and work with his own auto-biography... "We have only started on our development of our country we have not as yet, with all our talk of wonderful progress, done more than scratch the surface. The progress has been wonderful enough but..."

Biographies/   ISBN: *1-59462-198-5*   Pages:300
MSRP *$21.95*

www.bookjungle.com email: sales@bookjungle.com fax: 630-214-0564 mail: Book Jungle PO Box 2226 Champaign, IL 61825

The Art of Cross-Examination
Francis Wellman

QTY

I presume it is the experience of every author, after his first book is published upon an important subject, to be almost overwhelmed with a wealth of ideas and illustrations which could readily have been included in his book, and which to his own mind, at least, seem to make a second edition inevitable. Such certainly was the case with me; and when the first edition had reached its sixth impression in five months, I rejoiced to learn that it seemed to my publishers that the book had met with a sufficiently favorable reception to justify a second and considerably enlarged edition. ...

Reference   ISBN: *1-59462-647-2*   Pages:412   MSRP *$19.95*

On the Duty of Civil Disobedience
Henry David Thoreau

QTY

Thoreau wrote his famous essay, On the Duty of Civil Disobedience, as a protest against an unjust but popular war and the immoral but popular institution of slave-owning. He did more than write—he declined to pay his taxes, and was hauled off to gaol in consequence. Who can say how much this refusal of his hastened the end of the war and of slavery?

Law   ISBN: *1-59462-747-9*   Pages:48   MSRP *$7.45*

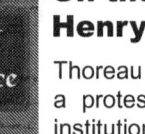

Dream Psychology Psychoanalysis for Beginners
Sigmund Freud

QTY

Sigmund Freud, born Sigismund Schlomo Freud (May 6, 1856 - September 23, 1939), was a Jewish-Austrian neurologist and psychiatrist who co-founded the psychoanalytic school of psychology. Freud is best known for his theories of the unconscious mind, especially involving the mechanism of repression; his redefinition of sexual desire as mobile and directed towards a wide variety of objects; and his therapeutic techniques, especially his understanding of transference in the therapeutic relationship and the presumed value of dreams as sources of insight into unconscious desires.

Psychology   ISBN: *1-59462-905-6*   Pages:196   MSRP *$15.45*

The Miracle of Right Thought
Orison Swett Marden

QTY

Believe with all of your heart that you will do what you were made to do. When the mind has once formed the habit of holding cheerful, happy, prosperous pictures, it will not be easy to form the opposite habit. It does not matter how improbable or how far away this realization may see, or how dark the prospects may be, if we visualize them as best we can, as vividly as possible, hold tenaciously to them and vigorously struggle to attain them, they will gradually become actualized, realized in the life. But a desire, a longing without endeavor, a yearning abandoned or held indifferently will vanish without realization.

Self Help   ISBN: *1-59462-644-8*   Pages:360   MSRP *$25.45*

www.bookjungle.com *email: sales@bookjungle.com fax: 630-214-0564 mail: Book Jungle PO Box 2226 Champaign, IL 61825*

QTY

	Title	ISBN	Price
☐	**The Rosicrucian Cosmo-Conception Mystic Christianity** *by Max Heindel* — The Rosicrucian Cosmo-conception is not dogmatic, neither does it appeal to any other authority than the reason of the student. It is not controversial, but is sent forth in the hope that it may help to clear... *New Age/Religion Pages 646*	1-59462-188-8	$38.95
☐	**Abandonment To Divine Providence** *by Jean-Pierre de Caussade* — "The Rev. Jean Pierre de Caussade was one of the most remarkable spiritual writers of the Society of Jesus in France in the 18th Century. His death took place at Toulouse in 1751. His works have gone through many editions and have been republished... *Inspirational/Religion Pages 400*	1-59462-228-0	$25.95
☐	**Mental Chemistry** *by Charles Haanel* — Mental Chemistry allows the change of material conditions by combining and appropriately utilizing the power of the mind. Much like applied chemistry creates something new and unique out of careful combinations of chemicals the mastery of mental chemistry... *New Age Pages 354*	1-59462-192-6	$23.95
☐	**The Letters of Robert Browning and Elizabeth Barret Barrett 1845-1846 vol II** *by Robert Browning and Elizabeth Barrett* — *Biographies Pages 596*	1-59462-193-4	$35.95
☐	**Gleanings In Genesis (volume I)** *by Arthur W. Pink* — Appropriately has Genesis been termed "the seed plot of the Bible" for in it we have, in germ form, almost all of the great doctrines which are afterwards fully developed in the books of Scripture which follow... *Religion/Inspirational Pages 420*	1-59462-130-6	$27.45
☐	**The Master Key** *by L. W. de Laurence* — In no branch of human knowledge has there been a more lively increase of the spirit of research during the past few years than in the study of Psychology, Concentration and Mental Discipline. The requests for authentic lessons in Thought Control, Mental Discipline and... *New Age/Business Pages 422*	1-59462-001-6	$30.95
☐	**The Lesser Key Of Solomon Goetia** *by L. W. de Laurence* — This translation of the first book of the "Lemegeton" which is now for the first time made accessible to students of Talismanic Magic was done, after careful collation and edition, from numerous Ancient Manuscripts in Hebrew, Latin, and French... *New Age/Occult Pages 92*	1-59462-092-X	$9.95
☐	**Rubaiyat Of Omar Khayyam** *by Edward Fitzgerald* — Edward Fitzgerald, whom the world has already learned, in spite of his own efforts to remain within the shadow of anonymity, to look upon as one of the rarest poets of the century, was born at Bredfield, in Suffolk, on the 31st of March, 1809. He was the third son of John Purcell... *Music Pages 172*	1-59462-332-5	$13.95
☐	**Ancient Law** *by Henry Maine* — The chief object of the following pages is to indicate some of the earliest ideas of mankind, as they are reflected in Ancient Law, and to point out the relation of those ideas to modern thought. *Religion/History Pages 452*	1-59462-128-4	$29.95
☐	**Far-Away Stories** *by William J. Locke* — "Good wine needs no bush, but a collection of mixed vintages does. And this book is just such a collection. Some of the stories I do not want to remain buried for ever in the museum files of dead magazine-numbers an author's not unpardonable vanity..." *Fiction Pages 272*	1-59462-129-2	$19.45
☐	**Life of David Crockett** *by David Crockett* — "Colonel David Crockett was one of the most remarkable men of the times in which he lived. Born in humble life, but gifted with a strong will, an indomitable courage, and unremitting perseverance... *Biographies/New Age Pages 424*	1-59462-250-7	$27.45
☐	**Lip-Reading** *by Edward Nitchie* — Edward B. Nitchie, founder of the New York School for the Hard of Hearing, now the Nitchie School of Lip-Reading, Inc, wrote "LIP-READING Principles and Practice". The development and perfecting of this meritorious work on lip-reading was an undertaking... *How-to Pages 400*	1-59462-206-X	$25.95
☐	**A Handbook of Suggestive Therapeutics, Applied Hypnotism, Psychic Science** *by Henry Munro* — *Health/New Age/Health/Self-help Pages 376*	1-59462-214-0	$24.95
☐	**A Doll's House: and Two Other Plays** *by Henrik Ibsen* — Henrik Ibsen created this classic when in revolutionary 1848 Rome. Introducing some striking concepts in playwriting for the realist genre, this play has been studied the world over. *Fiction/Classics/Plays 308*	1-59462-112-8	$19.95
☐	**The Light of Asia** *by sir Edwin Arnold* — In this poetic masterpiece, Edwin Arnold describes the life and teachings of Buddha. The man who was to become known as Buddha to the world was born as Prince Gautama of India but he rejected the worldly riches and abandoned the reigns of power when... *Religion/History/Biographies Pages 170*	1-59462-204-3	$13.95
☐	**The Complete Works of Guy de Maupassant** *by Guy de Maupassant* — "For days and days, nights and nights, I had dreamed of that first kiss which was to consecrate our engagement, and I knew not on what spot I should put my lips..." *Fiction/Classics Pages 240*	1-59462-157-8	$16.95
☐	**The Art of Cross-Examination** *by Francis L. Wellman* — Written by a renowned trial lawyer, Wellman imparts his experience and uses case studies to explain how to use psychology to extract desired information through questioning. *How-to/Science/Reference Pages 408*	1-59462-309-0	$26.95
☐	**Answered or Unanswered?** *by Louisa Vaughan* — Miracles of Faith in China *Religion Pages 112*	1-59462-248-5	$10.95
☐	**The Edinburgh Lectures on Mental Science (1909)** *by Thomas* — This book contains the substance of a course of lectures recently given by the writer in the Queen Street Hall, Edinburgh. Its purpose is to indicate the Natural Principles governing the relation between Mental Action and Material Conditions... *New Age/Psychology Pages 148*	1-59462-008-3	$11.95
☐	**Ayesha** *by H. Rider Haggard* — Verily and indeed it is the unexpected that happens! Probably if there was one person upon the earth from whom the Editor of this, and of a certain previous history, did not expect to hear again... *Classics Pages 380*	1-59462-301-5	$24.95
☐	**Ayala's Angel** *by Anthony Trollope* — The two girls were both pretty, but Lucy who was twenty-one who supposed to be simple and comparatively unattractive, whereas Ayala was credited, as her Bombwhat romantic name might show, with poetic charm and a taste for romance. Ayala when her father died was nineteen... *Fiction Pages 484*	1-59462-352-X	$29.95
☐	**The American Commonwealth** *by James Bryce* — An interpretation of American democratic political theory. It examines political mechanics and society from the perspective of Scotsman James Bryce *Politics Pages 572*	1-59462-286-8	$34.45
☐	**Stories of the Pilgrims** *by Margaret P. Pumphrey* — This book explores pilgrims religious oppression in England as well as their escape to Holland and eventual crossing to America on the Mayflower, and their early days in New England... *History Pages 268*	1-59462-116-0	$17.95

www.bookjungle.com email: sales@bookjungle.com fax: 630-214-0564 mail: Book Jungle PO Box 2226 Champaign, IL 61825

			QTY
The Fasting Cure by *Sinclair Upton*	ISBN: *1-59462-222-1*	**$13.95**	☐
In the Cosmopolitan Magazine for May, 1910, and in the Contemporary Review (London) for April, 1910, I published an article dealing with my experiences in fasting. I have written a great many magazine articles, but never one which attracted so much attention...		New Age/Self Help/Health Pages 164	
Hebrew Astrology by *Sepharial*	ISBN: *1-59462-308-2*	**$13.45**	☐
In these days of advanced thinking it is a matter of common observation that we have left many of the old landmarks behind and that we are now pressing forward to greater heights and to a wider horizon than that which represented the mind-content of our progenitors...		Astrology Pages 144	
Thought Vibration or The Law of Attraction in the Thought World	ISBN: *1-59462-127-6*	**$12.95**	☐
by *William Walker Atkinson*		Psychology/Religion Pages 144	
Optimism by *Helen Keller*	ISBN: *1-59462-108-X*	**$15.95**	☐
Helen Keller was blind, deaf, and mute since 19 months old, yet famously learned how to overcome these handicaps, communicate with the world, and spread her lectures promoting optimism. An inspiring read for everyone...		Biographies/Inspirational Pages 84	
Sara Crewe by *Frances Burnett*	ISBN: *1-59462-360-0*	**$9.45**	☐
In the first place, Miss Minchin lived in London. Her home was a large, dull, tall one, in a large, dull square, where all the houses were alike, and all the sparrows were alike, and where all the door-knockers made the same heavy sound...		Childrens/Classic Pages 88	
The Autobiography of Benjamin Franklin by *Benjamin Franklin*	ISBN: *1-59462-135-7*	**$24.95**	☐
The Autobiography of Benjamin Franklin has probably been more extensively read than any other American historical work, and no other book of its kind has had such ups and downs of fortune. Franklin lived for many years in England, where he was agent...		Biographies/History Pages 332	

Name	
Email	
Telephone	
Address	
City, State ZIP	

☐ Credit Card   ☐ Check / Money Order

Credit Card Number	
Expiration Date	
Signature	

Please Mail to: Book Jungle
PO Box 2226
Champaign, IL 61825
or Fax to: 630-214-0564

ORDERING INFORMATION

web: www.bookjungle.com
email: sales@bookjungle.com
fax: 630-214-0564
mail: Book Jungle PO Box 2226 Champaign, IL 61825
or PayPal to sales@bookjungle.com

Please contact us for bulk discounts

DIRECT-ORDER TERMS

**20% Discount if You Order
Two or More Books**
Free Domestic Shipping!
Accepted: Master Card, Visa,
Discover, American Express

www.ingramcontent.com/pod-product-compliance
Lightning Source LLC
Chambersburg PA
CBHW080447170426
43196CB00016B/2711